# GIACOMO MEYERBEER
# AND HIS FAMILY

## BETWEEN TWO WORLDS

# GIACOMO MEYERBEER AND HIS FAMILY

## BETWEEN TWO WORLDS

## Elaine Thornton

VALLENTINE MITCHELL

LONDON • CHICAGO

*First published in 2021 by Vallentine Mitchell*

Catalyst House,
720 Centennial Court,
Centennial Park, Elstree WD6 3SY, UK

814 N. Franklin Street,
Chicago, Illinois
60610 USA

**www.vmbooks.com**

Copyright © 2021 Elaine Thornton

British Library Cataloguing in Publication Data:
An entry can be found on request

ISBN 978 1 912676 75 0 (Paper)
ISBN 978 1 912676 76 7 (Ebook)

Library of Congress Cataloging in Publication Data:
An entry can be found on request

# Contents

# Acknowledgements

A biography such as this relies on the scholarship of others. I am deeply indebted to the work in Germany of Professor Heinz Becker, Dr Gudrun Becker and Professor Sabine Henze-Döhring, the principal editors of the eight-volume series of the correspondence and diaries of Giacomo Meyerbeer (*Giacomo Meyerbeer. Briefwechsel und Tagebücher*, Berlin: Walter de Gruyter, 1960-2006). I am equally indebted to Dr Robert Letellier's four-volume English translation and critical edition of Meyerbeer's diaries (*The Diaries of Giacomo Meyerbeer*, Madison, NJ: Fairleigh Dickinson University Press, 1999-2004). Without their work, this book would not have been possible.

My research into the Beer family developed from an interest in Giacomo Meyerbeer's operas, after I had seen a rare German-language production of *L'Africaine* at the Bielefeld Opera House in the early 1980s. I am deeply grateful to Robert Letellier for his encouragement of this interest, his sharing of his musical expertise, and his friendship.

I owe thanks to several people who read and commented on drafts. The interest and enthusiasm of my aunt, Alice Edwards, encouraged me to continue working on the project; Ruth Jenson offered insights that changed the shape of the book for the better at an early stage. The book's final form owes a great deal to the invaluable input of my brother Garry, who read and re-read versions over the years, putting his professional expertise in the English language at the Beers' service – any purple passages or clichés that remain are mine alone. I would also like to thank Magda Fletcher for facilitating contact with the Jagiellonian Library.

I am very grateful to Toby Harris, Lisa Hyde and all at Vallentine Mitchell for their work and perseverance in bringing a lengthy project to fruition.

Thanks are also due to the staff of the following institutions: Bavarian State Library, Munich; Berlin State Library – Prussian Cultural Heritage; Berlin-Brandenburg Academy of Sciences and Humanities; German Literature Archive, Marbach; Goethe and Schiller Archive, Weimar; Hessian State Archives, Darmstadt; Jagiellonian Library, Crakow; Klau

Library, Hebrew Union College, Cincinnati; Leo Baeck Institute Archives; Saxon State and University Library, Dresden; Schleswig-Holstein State Library; Stiftung Stadtmuseum, Berlin; Theatre Collection of the University of Cologne; University Library Johann Christian Senckenberg, Frankfurt am Main; University of Virginia Special Collections.

# Prologue

On 14 October 1801, in the Prussian capital of Berlin, 10-year-old Meyer Beer[1] gave his first public piano recital, playing Mozart's concerto in D minor with variations. The concerto had been premiered sixteen years previously in Vienna, with the composer himself at the keyboard. It had since become one of the most popular pieces in the piano repertoire, as well as one of the most demanding for the soloist. Meyer's performance received enthusiastic reviews in the German press: the influential Leipzig music journal, the *Allgemeine musikalische Zeitung*, reported that Meyer, described as 'a Jewish boy of 9 years old', had made the concert more interesting with his 'excellent piano-playing … accomplished mastery of the most difficult passages and other solo movements, and a delivery of rare sensitivity for his age'.[2]

Meyer's parents, the banker and sugar refiner Jacob Beer and his wife Amalia, were thrilled. To mark this success, they commissioned a life-sized portrait of their son from the fashionable court artist Friedrich Georg Weitsch. In Weitsch's painting, completed in 1802, Meyer, an elfin figure with artfully ruffled black hair and large, dark eyes, stands with an air of innocent, self-conscious pride beside his piano. He is dressed in the height of elegance, in a short, black jacket with a red collar, yellow trousers, and white stockings. In his right hand he holds a piece of sheet music; his left hand rests casually on the keys of the piano, on which a score by Mozart is visible. The underlying message is unmistakable: for Meyer's parents, their boy is a second Amadeus in the making.

The portrait was exhibited in the Prussian Academy of Arts, where it attracted a good deal of attention – not all of it favourable. No one had any fault to find with the artist's execution of the painting, but some of the visitors found its subject offensive. For these people, the Jews could have no place in respectable society, let alone in the hallowed halls of the Academy. Chief among the objectors was the lawyer Carl Grattenauer, an outspoken opponent of Jewish rights, and the author of popular tracts deriding the Jews' aspirations to European culture and to Prussian citizenship. In other parts of Europe, the Jews' situation had begun to change for the better; in France, they had been emancipated in 1791 in the first flush of revolutionary fervour. But in Prussia they were still officially treated as aliens: denied citizenship, subjected to demeaning regulations, and barred from almost all the professions.

According to Carl Grattenauer, the Christian population had much to fear from the granting of equal rights to the Jews, 'the most dangerous nation on earth', a plutocracy without morality or true religion.[3] His most vicious invective was reserved for those Jews who had integrated socially, and considered themselves cultured. He made a derisive reference to Meyer's portrait in one of his pamphlets. The Beer family are said to have withdrawn the painting from the Academy as a result of this public humiliation.[4]

Two centuries later, Weitsch's painting of Meyer is now in the Musical Instrument Museum in Berlin, where it is displayed as the earliest known portrait of Giacomo Meyerbeer, the most successful opera composer of his time. In the mid-nineteenth century, Meyerbeer's works dominated the international stages, creating and typifying the *grand opéra* style that characterised the era. His most popular work, *Les Huguenots* [The Huguenots], was performed over 1,000 times at the Paris Opéra from its premiere in 1836 up to the Second World War, and was staged all over the world, from Buenos Aires to St Petersburg, from Cairo to the Dutch East Indies. In his lifetime, Meyerbeer was a household name: monarchs showered honours on him, opera houses competed for his latest works, and ordinary people whistled and sang his airs in the streets. When he died in Paris in 1864, a special train was commissioned to carry his body to Berlin, where it was met at the Potsdam station by a huge crowd, headed by Prince George of Prussia.[5]

Meyer, or Giacomo as he later called himself, came from a more than ordinarily gifted family. The Beers played a central role in the German-Jewish renaissance and reformation which blossomed in the wake of the Enlightenment, as the Jews of Europe were emancipated from the ghetto in the upheavals of the French Revolution and the Napoleonic Wars. Giacomo's parents, Jacob and Amalia Beer, had married in 1788, two years after the death of Frederick the Great, who had ruled Prussia – and its Jews – with an iron hand for over forty years, and just a year before the storming of the Paris Bastille.

Change was in the air. The young couple were socially ambitious, and wealthy enough to be able to entertain on a grand scale. Amalia's generous nature made her a natural hostess, and in the early decades of the nineteenth century she established a glittering musical salon, where aristocrats and diplomats mingled with the stars of Europe's artistic world. The violinist Paganini, and the singers Henriette Sontag and Angelica Catalani, performed at her soirées, while the Prussian Chancellor dined regularly with the family.

Three of the Beers' four sons had hugely successful careers. Giacomo, the eldest and best-known, became the first Jewish composer to achieve world-wide fame. His brother Wilhelm was an amateur astronomer. Wilhelm built a state-of-the-art observatory in the family villa in Berlin's Tiergarten where, in the 1830s, he and his colleague, the scientist Johann Mädler, produced the first accurate maps of the surfaces of the moon and of Mars. Their work was not bettered until photography was invented later in the century, and it remains an important milestone in the history of astronomy. Wilhelm was active in a number of other fields: as a political and economic commentator, a railway director, and a member of the First Chamber of the newly-formed Prussian Parliament in the aftermath of the 1848 revolution.

The Beers' youngest son, Michael, who died at the early age of 33, was a dramatist and poet who became a favourite at the Bavarian court of King Ludwig I. His most successful play, *Der Paria* [The Pariah], which is set in India among the untouchable caste, was seen as a parable on the situation of the Jews in Germany. *Der Paria* was admired by Goethe, the greatest of German classical writers, who sponsored its production at the court theatre in Weimar.

The remaining son, Heinrich, the second eldest, was the black sheep of the family, although even he could claim the distinction of being a close friend of the philosopher Hegel.

Yet despite the Beers' wealth and their exceptional talents, as Jews seeking a place in German society they faced formidable barriers; discrimination and prejudice continued long after legal emancipation was granted in 1812. Throughout their lives, even at the height of their successes, they both anticipated and feared the sting of anti-Semitism, known to them by its Yiddish name of *Risches*, or *Richesse*. Giacomo, in particular, was keenly aware that in venturing into the arts and sciences, rather than working in the traditional Jewish fields of finance and trade, the Beer brothers were exposing themselves to public attack.

In 1818, he warned his youngest brother, Michael: 'Never forget, as I did when I chose [my profession], the iron word "Richesse". From individual to individual the word can be forgotten for a while (although not for ever), but by the collective public it never can, since it takes only one person to remember for all of them to recall it to consciousness.'[6]

The Beers also faced hostility from within the Jewish community. The Jews of the Diaspora were a people in exile, waiting for the return to the Promised Land. Their unique way of life, symbolised by their ancient laws, had been the glue that had held them together through the centuries of dispersal. The fear that cultural integration would inevitably lead to the dissolution of the Jewish nation had led them to endorse a strict separatism, and to oppose the slightest deviation from tradition.

By the early nineteenth century, many socially and professionally ambitious Jews felt caught between the two apparently incompatible worlds of traditional Judaism and German society. For some of these people, conversion to the majority religion of Christianity seemed a quick and simple way out of the impasse. The poet Heinrich Heine, who converted in 1825, famously called baptism 'the entrance ticket to European culture'.

Unlike many of their contemporaries, however, Jacob and Amalia Beer did not accept that their only options were either conversion to Christianity, or separatism: they were determined to find a way to live as both Jews and Germans.[7] In 1815 they became pioneers of Reform Judaism, when they established one of the first modernised synagogues in the world in their Berlin home. The services featured innovations such as choral music accompanied by an organ, and the use of the German language for some of the prayers and the Christian-style sermons.

Despite opposition from more traditionally-minded Jews, the new liturgy rapidly became popular. At its height, over 400 people were crowding into the Beer Temple, as it was known, on the Sabbath. The Temple had a relatively short history, lasting for only eight years before it was closed down and traditionalism reasserted itself, but the seeds of reform had been sown. Over the next century the movement spread throughout the world, and ultimately developed into the modern denomination of Reform Judaism.

At the heart of the Beer family's story is a search for identity in a changing world. Their refusal to be marginalised or designated 'other', and their determination to shape their own lives, played a significant role in the development of a new sense of what it meant to be both Jewish and German at a turning point in European history. As celebrated personalities in their society, they proved that it was possible to succeed in spheres not usually associated with the Jews, and to move in the highest circles – even to socialise with royalty – while remaining Jewish.

Yet they also attracted criticism and condemnation from all sides: from anti-Semitic Christians, from fellow Jews, and, occasionally, from those who had converted, and had subsequently found that the waters of baptism did not wash away popular prejudice. The Beers' story is inextricably bound up with the history of the Jews of Berlin, but it is in the struggle to escape being defined and limited by their context that their lives gain their wider significance.

## Notes

1.  Meyerbeer's original name is often given as Jakob Liebmann Beer. Although this name appears in early newspaper reports on the young Meyerbeer's musical performances, he was known to his family and friends exclusively as 'Meyer' in his youth, as evidenced by letters in the first volume of Meyerbeer's correspondence and diaries: see Giacomo Meyerbeer, *Briefwechsel und Tagebücher*, Heinz Becker, Gudrun Becker and Sabine Henze-Döhring (eds) (Berlin: Walter de Gruyter, 1960-2006), vol. 1, passim. Heinz Becker points out (pp. 40-1) that the birth register of the Jewish community of Berlin records the birth, on 5 September 1791, to Juda Herz Berr [sic], of a son named 'Meyer', and further adds that Meyerbeer himself never used the forenames 'Jakob Liebmann', although he occasionally signed letters 'J. Meyer Beer'. He began to sign letters with the combined version of his names, Meyerbeer, as early as 1811 and to use Giacomo, the Italianised version of Jacob, during his stay in Italy between 1816 and 1825. The historian and archivist Jacob Jacobson also records that Meyerbeer's original first name was Meyer, and that he received official permission from the Prussian authorities to use the name 'Meyerbeer' as a surname on 3 January 1822, and permission to use the first name 'Jacob' on 19 May 1826, after his father's death – see Jacob Jacobson (ed.), *Jüdische Trauungen in Berlin 1759 bis 1813* (Berlin: Walter de Gruyter, 1968), p.316 n 567. Meyerbeer himself only ever used 'Giacomo', or occasionally 'Jacques', however. I have followed the usage of the Beer family by calling him either 'Meyer' or 'Giacomo'. Similarly, as other family members changed their originally Jewish names to Germanised versions, to avoid confusion I have used the German versions throughout – e.g. 'Jacob' rather than 'Juda', 'Wilhelm' rather than 'Wolff', etc.
2.  *Allgemeine musikalische Zeitung*, 28 October 1801, cols. 77-8.
3.  Carl Grattenauer, *Erklärung an das Publikum über meine Schrift Wider die Juden* (Berlin: Johann Wilhelm Schmidt, 1803), p.36.
4.  Heinz Becker and Gudrun Becker (eds), *Giacomo Meyerbeer – Weltbürger der Musik* (Wiesbaden: Dr Ludwig Reichert Verlag, 1991), pp. 54-5; Deborah Hertz, *How Jews Became Germans. The History of Conversion and Assimilation in Berlin* (New Haven, CT & London: Yale University Press, 2007), p.59.
5.  Reiner Zimmermann, *Giacomo Meyerbeer. Eine Biographie nach Dokumenten* (Berlin: Henschel Verlag, 1991), p.410.
6.  Meyerbeer, *Briefwechsel und Tagebücher*, vol. 1, p.368.
7.  Atheism was not a real solution; those Christians who did not believe were nonetheless identified as part of Christian society, and non-believing or non-practising Jews would have continued to be identified as Jews.

# 1

## Ancestors: The Jews of Berlin

The Beers belonged to the upper echelons of Berlin's small Jewish community, a close-knit group of around 3,000 people living in the network of streets that clustered around the synagogue in the heart of the old city. Both Jacob's and Amalia's ancestors had arrived in Berlin in the late seventeenth century, when the city had been re-opened to the Jews after 100 years of exclusion. There had been Jews living in Berlin since the thirteenth century, but their existence had always been precarious. Between the thirteenth and the sixteenth centuries they had been expelled from Berlin four times. This was not an unusual history: mass expulsions were an inevitable part of European Jewish life. In 1492, the year that Columbus discovered America, the entire Jewish population of Spain had been forced either to convert to Christianity, or leave the country.

Jews had settled in the German lands by the fourth century CE, and for the next seven centuries they lived, for the most part, in peaceful co-existence with their Christian neighbours. But in the Middle Ages, the era of the Crusades and the Black Death, the Jews' situation worsened, and they became handy scapegoats for misfortunes of all kinds. They were commonly believed to poison wells, murder Christian children for their blood and steal communion wafers for use in satanic rituals. In 1510, around forty Jews were publicly executed in Berlin for the alleged theft and desecration of communion wafers. Most of the condemned were burnt at the stake, although those who agreed to convert to Christianity before their execution were granted the concession of being beheaded.

The last mass expulsion from Berlin, in 1571, was triggered when the Jews' leader, the master coiner Lippold, was accused of poisoning his patron, the Elector Joachim II, after the latter's sudden death. Lippold was imprisoned for two years while awaiting trial, and was eventually hung, drawn and quartered. The charges against him provided the excuse for the expulsion of the entire Jewish community 'for ever'.

In practice, 'for ever' usually meant just for a few years, or at least until any public unrest had died down and the authorities had begun to regret the loss of the Jews' financial expertise. After Lippold's death, however, the ban on Jews living in Berlin lasted for a century. The community was not re-established until 1671, when a small group of Jewish refugees from Vienna was granted admittance to the city. Amalia Beer's ancestors were among the leaders of these Austrian Jews, who had been driven out of Vienna by decree of the Holy Roman Emperor, Leopold I. The expulsion had been urged on the young Emperor by a group of local merchants, who disliked Jewish competition.

Leopold had hesitated initially, but had made up his mind following the death of his 3-month-old son, and a fire in the Imperial palace, both of which were attributed to the evil influence of the Jews. There could be no appeal against such a decision. All Jews were ordered to leave Vienna and Lower Austria by Corpus Christi Day 1671. Driven from their homes, their businesses seized or sold for a pittance, the Jews gathered together their valuables and fled, congregating on the borders of Austria, where they began to petition the rulers of nearby states for admittance.

Germany was not unified until 1871, and up until the nineteenth century the lands of the Holy Roman Empire consisted of a loose confederation of over 300 small kingdoms, electorates, dukedoms, archbishoprics and free cities. Jews had limited civil rights in these states, and local rulers could, and did, ban them altogether from living in cities or towns within their jurisdiction. Where the Jews were admitted, it was on the basis of a protection permit, or letter of toleration, which usually limited their right of residence to a certain number of years, and which could be rescinded arbitrarily.

The Jews had to pay the authorities an annual fee for the renewal of this permit, which contained detailed regulations as to where they could live, and what type of work they could do. The Christian Church disapproved of usury, so this forbidden yet necessary role was usually assigned to the Jewish communities. Almost everywhere, they were confined to money-lending and trading – and then vilified as leeches and swindlers. Jews entering and leaving cities commonly had to pay a 'body tax', which was otherwise levied only on animals.

Nonetheless, the situation in the German lands was in some ways more favourable for the Jews than it was in some larger, unified countries, such as Spain – or England, which had expelled its Jews in 1290, by decree of King Edward I. When the Jews were driven out from one German land, they could usually find refuge in another. The rulers of these small states were as anxious as any great monarch to display status and power, but they were often unable to finance the costs from their own resources.

Many of these petty princelings and dukes had found that they could not manage without the Jews, whose extensive cross-border family and trading networks had given them a rare expertise in international finance, and the ability to offer large-scale credit. The majority of the German courts in the seventeenth and eighteenth centuries came to rely on Jewish financiers for their supply of food, drink and luxury goods, as well as for the provision of weapons and ammunition for their armies, and silver for their mints. These particularly able men usually brought others with them: the rabbis, teachers, butchers, servants and other functionaries needed to establish a Jewish way of life.

A number of the Austrian refugees of 1671 were absorbed into the sizeable Jewish communities of neighbouring Silesia, Bohemia and Moravia. Amalia Beer's ancestors were part of a smaller group that travelled to the far north of the Empire, to found a new community in Brandenburg-Prussia at the invitation of its ruler, the Elector Frederick William. Prussia was not, at this time, the large and powerful state that it later became. Frederick William, known to history as the 'Great Elector', had come to the throne in 1640, towards the end of the Thirty Years' War. He had inherited a loose patchwork of lands: East Prussia was divided from the heartland of Brandenburg by hundreds of miles of Polish territory, and would not be unified with the rest of the country until the First Partition of Poland in 1772, while the tiny enclaves of Kleve and Mark lay in the distant west, closer to the Dutch Republic than to Berlin.

The Great Elector's lands, scattered across the sandy plains of northern Germany, had no natural defences, and thirty years of war had left his realm devastated and impoverished. Disease and famine had followed in the wake of the marauding armies. Much of the land had been laid waste, and over half of Brandenburg's inhabitants had died: Berlin's population had fallen from a pre-war total of around 10,000 to just 6,000.[1] The experience of inheriting a war-torn land had undoubtedly influenced Frederick William; he came to the throne determined to create a state that was administratively, militarily, and economically strong enough to defend itself against invasion.

As part of his efforts to repopulate the country and promote trade, Frederick William encouraged the immigration of groups of people with useful skills. When his envoy in Vienna informed him in 1670 that the Holy Roman Emperor was planning to expel the Jews of Austria, he calculated that the influx of a small number of these exiles, bringing with them their contacts and financial expertise, could prove highly advantageous. He was not, of course, prepared to accept poor Jews. He was an open-minded man for his time, but he was also an astute one – 'the shrewdest fox in the Empire' in the opinion of one French diplomat.[2] Tolerance, as always, came with a hefty dose of self-interest.

After lengthy negotiations, fifty of the wealthier refugee families made the arduous journey north to Brandenburg, although of these, only a small number were admitted to the capital city of Berlin; the remainder were settled in towns across the province. The terms that the Great Elector imposed on his new Jewish subjects were minimal by the standards of the time. The Jews would be permitted to buy houses; they could sell their goods openly in shops and at fairs; they would not have to pay the hated body tax on entering or leaving the city; and the inevitable special taxes – levied only on the Jews – were reasonable: the protection tax was set at eight thalers a year, with one gold gulden payable on marriage.

The Elector's terms, although relatively favourable, were limited to a period of twenty years, and included one major restriction: he refused to allow the Jews to build a public synagogue, as he felt that this might provoke hostility from the Christian population, although he did permit services to be held in private houses.[3] Despite this proviso, the conditions were certainly better than those existing in many areas of Europe, where the Jews were burdened by innumerable petty regulations and restrictions. In some cities, they were confined to ghettoes, often consisting of just one or two narrow streets, with gates that were locked from the outside on Sundays and Christian holy days.

The fact that there was no ghetto in Berlin did not, however, imply any real degree of integration. The newly arrived Austrian Jews were free to live side-by-side with Christians, but they naturally chose to live in close proximity to one another. Even where there were no physical barriers, the Jewish communities themselves fostered an exclusive way of life that reinforced separatism. This had its advantages. The strongly cohesive and self-contained nature of Jewish society preserved its autonomy, and offered security and a sense of solidarity to its members.

The community looked after its own, and provided a buffer between individuals and the often hostile outside world. The elected elders supervised a network of social services, overseeing voluntary groups that took responsibility for the care of the sick and the poor, and for the burial of the dead. The routine of daily life was subject to the requirements of the law, which had been passed down from antiquity, and expanded and explicated in the Talmud over the centuries of exile. Civil disputes and questions of religious law were settled by a rabbinic court, which could impose fines, or a sentence of excommunication, on offenders.

There was little social contact between Jews and Christians, who communicated almost solely for business purposes. Intermarriage between the two was legally forbidden: there was, of course, no such thing as civil marriage, and mixed couples could only marry after one of the partners had converted, almost always from Judaism to Christianity. The social separation was reinforced by a linguistic barrier. Within the Jewish communities, the common language was Yiddish, a hybrid mix of medieval German and Hebrew that was incomprehensible to outsiders.

Education was focused on the study of Torah and Talmud: in the community schools, Jewish boys were taught to recite prayers and read the sacred books in Hebrew. Secular subjects such as languages, European history, science and philosophy were banned, as they were considered unnecessary, even dangerous, by the rabbis. Given these circumstances, the newly-arrived Viennese refugees would live in Brandenburg-Prussia not as citizens, but as tolerated aliens who brought their own world-view, language and culture with them.

Amalia Beer (née Wulff) could claim descent from these refugees on both her father's and her mother's sides. Her father was a descendant of the Mirels-Fränkel family, while her mother was the great-great-granddaughter of Rabbi Model Ries. The Hamburg merchant's wife Glückel of Hameln, one of the few Jewish women of the seventeenth century to leave any record of her life, mentions that she met the Mirels and Ries families in Berlin several times in connection with family weddings. On one occasion, she had stayed at the home of Benjamin Mirels, where, she says, 'I cannot describe the honours heaped on me.'

Glückel developed a closer relationship with the Ries family when her sister Mata married the son of the 'rich and learned Rabbi Model Ries':

> Everyone knows what an excellent man the Rabbi Model was, and Pessele, his pious wife, had not her like for goodness in the wide world ... With it all, she was a mighty capable woman, she managed the business and amply provided for her husband and children, both in Vienna and when they later lived in Berlin. For Rabbi Ries was a bedridden man, not able to attend to overmuch business. Yet he was a man of such pre-eminent wisdom, the whole world rang with his fame. He was likewise greatly beloved of the Elector of Brandenburg, God heighten his name! who once said of him, 'If his legs were as good as his head, he would stand without rival.' Both of them died at Berlin, in riches and honour. Her last will and testament makes remarkable reading. I would rather not write about it, but whoever

wishes to see it can have it from her children, for they would surely not throw the like of it away.[4]

Glückel, a strong woman herself, clearly admired the equally robust Pessel. Unfortunately, Pessel's 'remarkable' will does not appear to have survived.

The Mirels and Ries families would have been well aware that, although they had reached a safe haven, their life in their new home would not be without its problems. They could expect hostility from their Christian neighbours, particularly from rival merchants and traders, although the Great Elector was not inclined to listen to baseless grievances. When some of the local merchants had complained about his decision to admit the Viennese refugees, he had responded laconically that, 'the Jews do no harm to the country, but rather appear to be useful'.[5]

Complaints were to be expected from Christians, but, more surprisingly, the strongest protest against the refugees' admittance into the city had come from a fellow Jew. Israel Aaron, a 'stern and cross-grained man',[6] had been one of the Elector's financial agents for several years, and he had viewed the re-establishment of a Jewish community in Berlin as a threat to his monopoly as sole Jewish supplier to the Brandenburg court and army. At first Aaron tried, unsuccessfully, to persuade the Great Elector to rescind his promise to admit the refugees. When this did not succeed, he demanded that the incoming families should agree not to compete with him in business, and that Frederick William should consult him over any further invitations to Jews. In reality, however, he had little or no hope of limiting the influx once the door had been opened.

Israel Aaron died in 1673, leaving, despite his apparent wealth, little but a pile of debts. His widow, Esther Schulhoff, remarried a few years later. Through this second marriage, to a jewel trader from Halberstadt called Jost Liebmann, Esther became Jacob Beer's great-great-grandmother. Like Amalia's ancestor Pessel Ries, Esther was a resourceful woman. After Israel Aaron's death, she had obtained a legal ruling releasing her from responsibility for any of his debts, and she had operated successfully as a merchant in Berlin in her own right.

Jost Liebmann, as Esther's second husband, was granted permission to settle in Berlin, and the couple rapidly established themselves as court jewellers, initially to the Great Elector, and then to his successor and son Frederick I, who crowned himself 'King in Prussia' in 1701. Frederick had elevated himself by inventing a new royal title, superior to that of 'Elector', which the ruler of Brandenburg had held since the fifteenth century as one of nine German Electors, all holding the right to vote in the election of the

Holy Roman Emperor. King Frederick's vanity and love of pomp put a great deal of business the Liebmanns' way: the jewels for the new royal crown, which were bought in Venice, cost 180,000 thalers alone.[7]

Jost died in 1702, but Esther did not decline into widowhood. She took over her late husband's business as 'Court Jewess' to the luxury-loving Frederick I, becoming one of the few women to have held such a position. She was said to have been beautiful, and a favourite of Frederick's, enjoying the unusual privilege of being allowed to enter the King's private apartments whenever she liked. Esther had a darker side to her character, however; she was certainly astute, with an eye to the main chance, but she was also a bully, and she dominated the fledgling Berlin Jewish community.

One of the most contentious disputes within the community was over the control of synagogue worship. In fact, Jacob Beer's ancestors fought a long-running battle with his wife Amalia's ancestors over this question, as Jost and Esther Liebmann competed with the Ries family, each side determined to establish their own home synagogue as the sole official place of worship. The dispute was not settled until the turn of the century, when the government authorised the building of a public synagogue, which was completed in 1714.

Esther's friendship with Frederick I seems to have extended her reach even beyond the Jewish community: the Solicitor General, who had been appointed by the King to oversee the community, is said to have begged the government to 'save him from the plots of a person as dangerous as this'.[8] Things changed abruptly for Esther, however, when Frederick I died, and his son, the rougher and tougher 'Soldier King' Frederick William I ascended the throne in 1713. Frederick William had no time for luxury or jewels, and no time for Esther Liebmann. She was put under house arrest, and a commission was appointed to investigate accusations of fraud against her. In the end, despite a spirited fight back, Esther was defeated. When she died, she asked to be buried with a gold chain that Frederick I had given her.

In 1699, Jost and Esther's daughter, Hindchen, had married Herz Aron Beer, a son of Aron Herz Beer Oppenheim, one of the wealthiest and most influential Jewish financiers in the Free Imperial City of Frankfurt am Main. Herz and Hindchen had settled in Berlin, although neither of them survived for long: Herz died in 1708, just nine years after their marriage, and Hindchen died five years after him.

In the early 1730s, their son Juda, who became Jacob Beer's grandfather, moved to the small city of Frankfurt an der Oder (not to be confused with the larger central German city of Frankfurt am Main). Juda's wife, Bela

Samuel, came from Frankfurt an der Oder, which was situated some fifty miles east of Berlin on the Prussian border with Poland. The move to his wife's home town would have given Juda the opportunity to develop business connections that extended eastwards into Poland and Russia. Frankfurt an der Oder had been an important commercial hub linking western and eastern Europe since the Middle Ages, and its three annual fairs attracted large numbers of Jewish merchants from as far away as Warsaw and Amsterdam. The Beer family were to remain in Frankfurt until Jacob Beer returned to Berlin on his marriage to Amalia Wulff, some fifty years later.

Amalia's ancestors remained in the capital city. The Jewish community in Berlin had increased rapidly in size since its foundation in 1671, as the relatively relaxed conditions there had attracted a flow of people from other Jewish settlements where life was not so pleasant. Some had obtained official permits, but a large number had entered the city clandestinely. By 1700, there were estimated to be around 1,000 Jews in Berlin.

This uncontrolled growth had alarmed the rulers of Brandenburg-Prussia, who had found that managing immigration was not an easy task. In the first decades of the new century, Frederick I and his son and successor, the Soldier King, had made three attempts to reduce the size of the Berlin Jewish community, by limiting the residence rights of the children of tolerated families, and expelling the poorer Jews. Nonetheless, despite the imposition of these restrictions, numbers continued to rise, and by 1740, when a new King came to the throne of Prussia, the community was nearing 2,000 people in a total population of around 100,000.

Frederick II, or Frederick the Great, as he is more usually known, was an enigmatic character, a man of contradictions and contrasts. Culturally a Francophile, and a champion of the Enlightenment with its ideals of rationality, tolerance and the equality of all men, he filled his court with philosophers, musicians and scholars, among them the philosopher Voltaire and the mathematician Maupertuis. Frederick actively promoted the arts, and was particularly interested in architecture: he turned the small and undistinguished northern town of Berlin into a capital city worthy of the name, building some of its finest edifices, including the imposing Opera House, the Royal Library and the rococo palace of Sans Souci.

The enlightened Frederick, who saw himself as a 'philosopher-king', gained a reputation for tolerance in religious matters. In reality, his apparently open-minded approach concealed a cynical attitude towards all faiths. He particularly disliked the Jews, whose loyalty to the State he felt to be suspect. In 1750, he issued a law which was aimed at excluding poorer

Jews from Prussia. His 'Revised Patent and Regulations for Jewry' would control all aspects of Jewish life in Prussia for the next sixty years. It rationalised and codified the laws, prohibitions and special taxes that his predecessors had gradually imposed on the Jews since the relatively free and easy days of the Great Elector. The new regulations divided the Jews into groups, defined by their material assets. The degree of toleration depended on the degree of wealth.

At the top of the pile, the 'Regular Protected Jews' would be allowed to extend their residency permit to just one child. On the next level down, 'Special Protected Jews' would be entitled to a permit for their own lifetime, but could not pass it on to any of their children. The status of those belonging to the lower groups, such as the servants of the protected families, depended entirely on their employment, as they were only allowed to live in Berlin for as long as they remained in their posts. The Charter's reach extended into the Jews' religious activities, their work and even their private lives – all marriages had to be authorised by the government, although those in the lower groups were forbidden to marry altogether.

The Charter listed the numerous and tight controls placed on the work that the Jews could engage in, and in particular which goods they could, and could not, trade in. Uniquely, the community as a whole was held accountable for the actions of its individual members. The elders had collected the special taxes imposed on the Jews since 1728, but in 1750 the community was also made responsible for the restitution of money that individuals had stolen or obtained through fraud, and for their unpaid debts.[9]

The radical French diplomat Count Honoré Mirabeau described Frederick's regulations as 'a law fit for cannibals'. Nonetheless, in the decades following the enactment of these draconian regulations, significant new business opportunities arose for Berlin's wealthier Jews, primarily as a result of Frederick's propensity for waging war on his neighbours. His driving ambition was to propel the relatively insignificant state of Prussia into the first rank of European powers. He had revealed his intentions almost as soon as he had acceded to the throne, by invading and annexing the rich Austrian province of Silesia in December 1740. This act of aggression had resulted in a five-year war with Austria, ending with the Empress Maria Theresa's cession of Silesia to Frederick in 1745.

The pivotal event of his reign was the Seven Years' War. By 1756, Maria Theresa had allied herself with the Empress Elizabeth of Russia and the French King Louis XV against Frederick. Prussia, supported only by Britain, appeared to have little chance of defeating this coalition of the three greatest

European continental powers. However, despite the overwhelming odds, Frederick emerged triumphant from the long and bitter struggle. By the end of the Seven Years' War, he had achieved his aim of making Prussia a force to be reckoned with in Europe. It had been a costly victory, however. Around 180,000 Prussian soldiers, and tens of thousands of civilians, had died in the conflict.

Frederick had needed large reserves of money to finance the war, and he had achieved this by devaluing the Prussian currency. Three Jewish men, Daniel Itzig, Veitel Heine Ephraim and Moses Isaac-Fliess, had been put in charge of the Prussian mint and tasked with adulterating the silver coins with less valuable metals. The scheme had succeeded in filling the war coffers – and in filling the pockets of Itzig, Ephraim and Isaac-Fliess – but it had, predictably, resulted in inflation, for which the Jewish mint masters, rather than the King, were held to blame by the public. The debased coins were known as 'Ephraimites', and in the streets of Berlin the children chanted a popular rhyme:

> *Outside silver, inside grime*
> *Outside Frederick, inside Ephraim.*[10]

After the war, Frederick turned his attention to developing a strong manufacturing base in Prussia, and he encouraged the wealthier Christian and Jewish merchants to invest in factories, particularly those producing luxury textiles such as silk, velvet and lace. These new opportunities to make money, combined with the spread of Enlightenment ideas of equality and tolerance, produced a class of acculturated nouveau riche Jews. They could be seen among the audiences at the theatres, applauding the latest play or opera, bowling along the fashionable avenue of Unter den Linden in their smart carriages, and strolling with their families in the Tiergarten. They learned to speak German instead of Yiddish, and many of the men shaved their beards, and began to wear fashionable clothes and powdered wigs.

By the 1780s, the upper-class Jews of Berlin had 'Germanised' themselves so well that a visitor to the city noted in surprise that, 'The Jewish community of Berlin is considerable … Their behaviour, especially if they have enjoyed a good education, is gentlemanly and courteous … Many wear their hair now just like Christians do, and they don't differentiate themselves from us in their clothing, either.'[11]

The wealthiest Jewish families built mansions in the most fashionable parts of the city. Veitel Ephraim's imposing rococo house on Poststrasse was known as the 'Ephraim Palace', and was a Berlin landmark for many years.

Daniel Itzig's mansion contained a synagogue with a retractable roof for celebrating the Feast of Tabernacles, and what was said to be the first private bathroom in Berlin. Another of his properties, a 'country seat' situated by the city walls, featured extensive gardens, with an open-air theatre set among orchards planted with thousands of fruit trees.

Critics of the new class of Jews were quick to suggest that they were developing pretensions to European culture. Both Itzig and Ephraim possessed significant art collections: Daniel Itzig owned a Rubens, and Ephraim works by Caravaggio, Poussin and Salvator Rosa.[12] For many of the aristocratic land-owning class, who had believed their monopoly on money and power to be an inalienable birthright, the rise of this emerging Jewish elite was a scandal. They complained that, 'The Jews have used the coinage to seize the wealth of the land and have now also gained permission to buy up noble property. In short, we are threatened with a complete overthrow of the existing order.'[13]

Itzig and Ephraim were undoubtedly the wealthiest, and the most conspicuous consumers, among the new Jews, but there were others, whose interests lay not in the making or spending of money, but in exploring the new world of Enlightenment knowledge. One of these intellectuals was to become arguably the most famous, and certainly the most well-respected, Jew of his time.

The philosopher Moses Mendelssohn had arrived in Berlin in 1743, as a poor student of the Talmud. In his early days as a Talmudic scholar, he had been determined to acquire an understanding of science and philosophy, and had studied German, English, Latin, mathematics and logic. In the years leading up to the Seven Years' War, he had begun publishing philosophical works in German. Mendelssohn's writings gained him the respect and admiration of his contemporaries in German intellectual circles, and he became a close friend of the playwright Gotthold Ephraim Lessing and the publisher Christoph Friedrich Nicolai, both leaders of the German Enlightenment. The main character of Lessing's 1779 play, *Nathan der Weise* [Nathan the Wise], a wise and virtuous Jew, was based on Mendelssohn.

Friendship like this, between Jew and Christians, was something quite unheard-of, and became the talk of the town. Mendelssohn was acknowledged as the leader of the Jewish Enlightenment movement, the *Haskala*, and he became well known in Berlin intellectual circles as the 'Jewish Socrates'. His house became a gathering place for visitors to the city, both Jews and Germans, who were interested in the philosophical questions of the day. However, even the famous Moses Mendelssohn had to endure snubs and rejection. The Academy of Sciences twice elected him as a member, but on both occasions Frederick the Great, despite his supposed tolerance, refused to confirm the nomination.

Mendelssohn, like all privileged Jews in Prussian society, was in a highly anomalous position. Despite the wealth and culture of this elite group, they were still subject to legal and social discrimination, and there was strong opposition to any demand for equality. There was also a growing backlash against modernisation in the Jewish community itself, with the more orthodox members fearing that it would end in the complete dissolution of Judaism.

In the closing decades of the eighteenth century, these divisions in the community began to force the Berlin Jews to confront the question of whether and how it might be possible to live as both Jews and Germans in the contemporary world. As a modern historian has pointed out, Jewish integration 'would involve problems not only of adjustment of the mutual perception of Gentile and Jew, but also the adjustment of Jews' perception of themselves'.[14] Jacob and Amalia Beer, growing up in this atmosphere of change, would be among the first in their generation to confront the challenges to the traditional way of life.

## Notes

1.   Derek McKay, *The Great Elector* (Harlow: Pearson Education Limited, 2001), p.49.
2.   Ibid., pp.197 and 229 n 1.
3.   Summarised from Jacob Rader Marcus (ed.), *The Jew in the Medieval World. A Source Book: 315-1791* (Cincinnati, OH: Hebrew Union College Press, revised edition, 1999), pp.86-90.
4.   Glückel of Hameln, *The Memoirs of Glückel of Hameln* (Marvin Lowenthal, trans.) (New York: Schocken Books, 1977), pp.160 and 123-4.
5.   McKay, *The Great Elector*, p.186.
6.   Selma Stern, *The Court Jew – A Contribution to the History of the Period of Absolutism in Central Europe* (Philadelphia, PA: The Jewish Publication Society of America, 1950), p.47.
7.   Vivian B. Mann and Richard I. Cohen (eds), *From Court Jews to the Rothschilds. Art, Patronage, Power 1600-1800* (Munich and New York: Prestel-Verlag, and The Jewish Museum, New York, under the auspices of the Jewish Theological Seminary of America, 1996), p.74.
8.   Stern, *The Court Jew*, p.53.
9.   See Marcus, *The Jew in the Medieval World*, pp.97-110; Steven M. Lowenstein, *The Berlin Jewish Community. Enlightenment, Family and Crisis, 1770-1830* (New York and Oxford: Oxford University Press, 1994), pp.12-13.
10.  Amos Elon, *The Pity of it All. A Portrait of Jews in Germany 1743-1933* (London: Penguin Books, 2004), p.17.

11.  Ruth Glatzer (ed.), *Berliner Leben 1648-1806* (Berlin: Rütten & Loening, 1956), p.227.
12.  Ruth Gay, *The Jews of Germany. A Historical Portrait* (New Haven, CT and London: Yale University Press, 1992), p.92.
13.  Glatzer, *Berliner Leben 1648-1806*, p.199.
14.  David Conway, *Jewry in Music. Entry to the Profession from the Enlightenment to Richard Wagner* (Cambridge: Cambridge University Press, 2012), p.38.

# 2

## The House on Spandauer Street

Amalia Beer's father, Liepmann Meyer Wulff, was born into the Berlin Jewish community in 1745, five years into the reign of Frederick the Great. A generation younger than the mint masters Itzig and Ephraim, he came from a family that was comfortably-off, rather than exceptionally wealthy. His father, Meyer Wulff Levy, a pawnbroker and dealer in clothing, had been classed as a 'Regular Protected Jew', the highest level in Frederick the Great's Revised Patent. Meyer was also a prominent member of the Berlin Jewish community, holding the posts of lay leader of the synagogue, and charity warden.

Meyer Wulff Levy died in 1759, leaving 14-year-old Liepmann as head of the family at perhaps the lowest point of the Seven Years' War. Prussia lost a series of battles that year, and Berlin was briefly occupied by both Russian and Austrian troops in October 1760. As the eldest child of his family, Liepmann inherited his father's protection permit on 16 September 1763,[1] allowing him to marry and set up home in Berlin the following January, less than a year after the Peace of Hubertusburg. His bride, Esther Bamberger, a great-great-granddaughter of Model and Pessel Ries, was a highly suitable match. Her family lived in the exclusive Königstrasse, in a large house which her father, the wool merchant Michael Bamberger, had bought in 1750.

Esther's father provided a healthy dowry of 4,800 thalers for his daughter, while Liepmann brought 3,000 thalers to the marriage.[2] It was not a vast fortune – the mint master Daniel Itzig was able to provide each of his daughters with a fabulous dowry of 70,000 thalers – but it allowed the young couple to begin married life on a secure financial footing. Their first child, a girl they called Malka – 'Queen' in Hebrew – and who would later call herself Amalia, was born three years after the marriage.

At the time of Amalia's birth, on 15 January 1767,[3] Berlin was a small city of just over 120,000 inhabitants. Compared to London, with a population of around three-quarters of a million, and to Paris with half a million, it had the air of a market town rather than a metropolis. As late as 1830, a visiting American described the city as 'a gigantic country village'.[4]

Market gardens and dairies flourished within the city walls, and small boys swam and fished in the River Spree, close by the palace.

In central Berlin, as in all cities of the time, great wealth and great poverty existed side by side: broad avenues lined with trees, palaces and baroque buildings gave way to narrow, dark alleyways with open sewers, where you had to pick your way through the dirt and dung, and hastily flatten yourself against a wall if a carriage rumbled past. The lively streets and bridges in the city centre were crammed with stalls and booths selling trinkets, ornaments, silks and lace. Those with little money to spare could dress themselves from head to foot from the second-hand stalls run by the Jews – some of whom, it was said, had the monopoly on clothing the local prostitutes in their cheap finery.

Amalia's parents, Liepmann and Esther Wulff, owned a large house on Spandauer Strasse, a broad and handsome street in the centre of the old city, which was popular both with the richer Jewish families, and with Christian merchants. No. 72 was spacious enough to serve them as both office and home: Liepmann could carry on his business from the ground floor, while Esther looked after the family on the upper floors. This was not an uncommon arrangement in a pre-industrial age, when many businesses were run from home.

Today, 72 Spandauer Strasse no longer exists. The area where it stood has been built over several times, and its remains most probably lie buried under Karl-Liebknecht-Strasse, a major route through the city, named after one of the founders of the Communist Party of Germany. But at the time of Amalia's birth, Spandauer Strasse was a respectable address for an upwardly mobile Jewish family, and No. 72 was in a particularly convenient location, just around the corner from the synagogue in the Heidereutergasse. One of the city's liveliest market squares, the Neue Markt, was just a few steps away, overlooked by the medieval Marienkirche, with its famous frescoes of the Dance of Death, painted in the aftermath of the plague of 1484. The city's town hall and the Royal Palace were both within easy walking distance.

Liepmann and Esther had three more daughters over the next twelve years: Hanka, Sara and Jitel. None of the Wulff girls were to retain their given names as they grew up. Hanka later changed her name to Johanna, Sara chose Seraphine, and the youngest, Jitel, became Henriette. As adults, Amalia and her sisters used the Germanised versions of their names within their family circles, as well as in wider society.[5] These changes of name did not imply, however, that the Wulff family was loosening its ties with Judaism. Amalia, unlike some of her contemporaries among the wealthier

Berlin families, was brought up in an atmosphere of orthodox piety. For the Wulffs, the practice of their faith was an integral part of their home life. They lived according to the traditional laws and customs, their lives punctuated by the Sabbath, and by the rhythm of the annual cycle of religious festivals.

Amalia's father, in common with all Jewish men, was required to pray three times a day. From around 1776,[6] when Amalia was 9 years old, he maintained his own home synagogue, where he employed a rabbi and a cantor. However, the mainly female make-up of the household meant that he had to look outside his family to make up the prayer quorum of ten men, the minimum number required by Jewish law for formal prayers.

As women, Amalia and her sisters had no public religious duties. They were not required to pray at set times, nor would they be expected to attend the synagogue until they were married. Even then, they were present as observers, rather than participants. The services were led by men, for men: women were physically segregated from the main body of the congregation. In some places, they were allowed to sit in a gallery, but they were often cut off altogether, hidden behind a screen, or in a separate annex, where one of the older women might be tasked with overseeing their prayers.

Unlike boys, girls did not study the Bible or the Talmud, so few understood Hebrew, the language used in the services. Many girls did learn to decipher the Hebrew alphabet, but mainly so that they could read Yiddish, which was often written in Hebrew characters. Religious instruction for girls was usually confined to books written especially for them in Yiddish, containing stories from the Bible, moral advice, and prayers pertaining to domestic concerns.

Amalia's traditional Jewish childhood influenced her later outlook on life. Despite her whole-hearted engagement with German culture and society, she retained a life-long attachment to Judaism, and a strong belief in the beneficial influence of religious faith, which she passed on to her own children, advising her eldest son, when he left home, that, 'it is essential, my dear Meyer, that there is something in the world that we hold holy, as there are times in our lives when religion is the only support that will keep us upright'.[7]

As Amalia and her sisters approached their teens, they would have been in no doubt that their destiny, and their duty, lay in becoming good wives and mothers. Some of their friends were married off at an early age: a close neighbour, Brendel Mendelssohn, who was a couple of years older than Amalia, was engaged by the time she was 14 years old to a man her father had chosen for her.

Brendel's father, the philosopher Moses Mendelssohn, may have been a pioneer of modern Jewish thought, but he would never have dreamt of allowing his daughters to choose their own husbands. Even for an enlightened philosopher, public life and domestic life were quite different matters. Marriages were not contracted solely for the happiness of husband and wife: they were family, and indeed, business, affairs. Girls were brought up to be obedient daughters, dutiful wives and good mothers; few parents would have wanted a daughter who was distinguished by her intellect rather than her beauty or domestic and social skills.

This does not imply, however, that either Brendel or Amalia grew up uncultured or ignorant. By the time of Amalia's childhood, the upbringing of girls belonging to the richer Jewish families, such as the Wulffs, was being modelled on that of aristocratic Christian families. Amalia's father was a devout Jew, but he was making good use of the opportunities for enrichment that were available in Frederick's Prussia. Liepmann was becoming a successful merchant and entrepreneur, and he was developing close working connections at the highest levels of Prussian society. His daughters were brought up with one foot in the world of Jewish tradition, and the other in the new and exciting world of European society and culture.

Since much of Liepmann's business would have been carried out at home, Esther and the girls would no doubt have been expected to help entertain visiting officials and members of the nobility. Amalia and her sisters would have been taught the polite accomplishments of music, dancing and languages, as well as the skills necessary for household management. The family would have spoken Yiddish at home, but in her later life Amalia spoke German, French and Italian, and was considered a cosmopolitan woman by her contemporaries.

Her letters, written in German, may lack polish – the spelling, grammar and punctuation are inconsistent – but they reveal a lively, forceful and expressive personality. In her more exuberant moments, her writing is peppered with Yiddish, Italian and French phrases, creating a multi-lingual patchwork: discussing a German-language production of one of Rossini's operas, she commented that, 'the public liked it a lot, I didn't so much perche sono Italiana e me ne vanto [because I am Italian and proud of it] but it isn't really too bad'.[8]

Previous generations of Jewish girls would have been literate in Yiddish, but learning German opened the door to a new world of literature for the Jewish women of Amalia's generation, giving them access to contemporary writers and dramatists such as Lessing, Goethe and Schiller. It was the golden age of German literature – and it was also a golden age for the reading public. The number of publishers, booksellers, lending libraries and reading clubs in Berlin had multiplied rapidly in the previous decades, making reading a popular leisure activity. Amalia was particularly fond of the lyric poetry of Friedrich Klopstock, a poet of the sentimental school, and of Schiller's plays.[9]

Not everyone was enthusiastic about the new opportunities for reading, however. Articles appeared regularly in the press warning of a 'reading mania' that was sweeping society. Too much reading was believed to be harmful to women's morals, and even to their health. A visitor to Berlin in the 1780s remarked on the Jews' new passion for European culture: 'They [the Jews] alternate aestheticism and poetry with reading the journals and going to the theatre. The rage for reading novels is extraordinarily popular among them – their women suffer particularly from this illness. The fair sex of the Israelites plays a large part in Berlin life. There are beauties in the real sense of the word among them.'[10]

Judging by her portrait, Amalia was one of these real beauties. The painting, which was completed in 1803 by the Prussian court artist Carl Kretschmar, and is now in the Berlin City Museum, depicts a young woman seated outdoors, framed against a background of a moody sky and distant woods. In her white, Empire-line dress, her dark hair knotted loosely on top of her head, Amalia could have stepped off the cover of a Jane Austen novel, but for a hint of the exotic about her sultry good looks that evokes the French music critic Henri Blaze de Bury's description of her: 'a strong woman, a Jewess of antique and superb stature!'[11]

Curls tumble from Amalia's piled hair, framing an oval face with large, almond eyes, a long, straight nose and full lips. Her clothes are in the height of fashion: her simple, white dress with its short, puffed sleeves and high waistline is cut revealingly low. The filmy material clings to her body, emphasising her curves. A deep blue shawl fringed in gold, and edged with a geometric pattern in red and green, falls over one shoulder to lie across her lap.

Amalia's style of dress had originated in France in the aftermath of the Revolution, in imitation of the supposed simplicity of ancient Greek clothing. This new look, which had been introduced into Prussia by Queen Louise, the young and beautiful wife of King Frederick William III, had swept away the older, more elaborate fashions of hooped skirts and high, powdered hair. Amalia's portrait – along with her choice of a fashionable court artist as painter – sends a clear message: this is a woman of culture and elegance, a privileged member of the European upper classes.

Portrait of Amalia Beer (Johann Karl Kretschmar c. 1803). Stiftung Stadtmuseum Berlin – Hans-und-Luise Richter Stiftung. Reproduction: Oliver Ziebe, Berlin

Amalia certainly had aspirations to culture, and she had a particular interest in music. As a young woman, she played the piano,[12] and had a soprano voice that was good enough for her to have taken lessons in singing and music theory from the Italian opera composer Vincenzo Righini. Righini, who was Kapellmeister [court music director] in Berlin from 1793, was a prolific composer, and his operas were hugely popular on the Berlin stage, although they have since disappeared from the repertoire. In his day, they were performed regularly at carnival time, and arias and excerpts from his works were a staple of every concert in the city.

In her old age, Amalia remembered her training with Righini with pride. Her great-nephew Felix Eberty describes in his memoirs a sumptuous dinner given for her 87th birthday. She sat between her friends the naturalist and explorer Alexander von Humboldt and the sculptor Christian Rauch, creator of the equestrian statue of Frederick the Great. A distinguished Privy Councillor gave a flattering birthday speech in honour of the hostess, describing her as 'the mother of the poor', but Amalia, rather deaf by then, was not listening. She leant across the table to regale Felix loudly, throughout the speech, with the story of how she had been musical in her youth, and had taken singing lessons from Righini.[13]

It is very unlikely however, that Amalia ever entertained any serious thought of going on the stage. Respectable women from her level of society did not perform in public: their talents were intended for a domestic setting, and exercised solely to give pleasure to an intimate circle of family and friends. In 1777 Joachim Campe, a respected Enlightenment educationalist and writer, gave his opinion that, 'The first virtuosos, the best singers, the most learned and perfected artists will be bad wives, bad housekeepers and bad mothers.'[14] In other words, women who performed in public automatically rendered themselves unfit for their real purpose in life. Amalia's own love of music would persist all her life, but would find its expression in her salon, and through the promotion of her son Giacomo's work.

Amalia did not, of course, have to worry about earning her living in any way. By the time she entered her teenage years, her father was becoming a wealthy man. Liepmann's first known business activity was in the traditional Jewish sphere of military logistics: he was a supplier of rye to the Prussian army in the Bavarian War of Succession of 1778-79. His partner in the business was a Captain von Unruh,[15] judging from his name, a member of a noble family. Liepmann was rumoured to have made a million thalers from the Bavarian War, although this is undoubtedly an exaggeration, especially in view of the short duration of the conflict.

Liepmann continued to deal in grain for a number of years, but the real turning point in his fortunes came in 1787, when he was offered a concession in the Prussian postal service. Unruh, his partner in the grain business, had recently died. A traveller passing through Berlin in 1779 had noted that a Captain von Unruh was in charge of the post and horses on various routes leaving the city.[16] If this was the same man, as seems probable, his death may have given Liepmann the opportunity to take on part of his late partner's business.

The concession involved the management of the route between Berlin and Potsdam. A twice-daily coach service, known as the *Journalière*, had been running for some decades on this important thirty-kilometre stretch of road, which linked the old Royal Palace with Sans Souci, Frederick the Great's rococo palace in Potsdam. James Boswell, Dr Johnson's biographer, who had used the service while on a visit to Berlin in July 1764, had not been impressed, describing the coach as 'a sad machine but cheap'.[17]

Liepmann would take over the responsibility for supplying the carriages and horses for the *Journalière*. He had taken up the concession at an auspicious moment: the King had decided to have the road between the palaces paved, and had commissioned the mint master Daniel Itzig's son Isaac to carry out the work. It would be the first paved road in Prussia, and this made the postal service concession a very attractive investment. The Prussian roads were notoriously bad: Brandenburg was known as the 'sandpit of the Empire', and it lived up to its name. In winter, carriages were bogged down in deep mud, and in summer they sank up to their axles in the soft sand. A new, paved highway on the popular route between Berlin and Potsdam would greatly improve the efficiency and comfort of the coach service.

Liepmann had the ready money and the entrepreneurial spirit to take on the job, and the business prospered under his management. An English visitor travelling from Potsdam to Berlin in 1792, five years into his management of the route, commented that:

> A public carriage, called the Journalière, was about to set off. We therefore paid our fare, which was extremely reasonable, and arrived here before the close of day. The road was admirable, and the last half of the stage superior to any I ever saw … The journalière, which I entered at Potzdam, is a sort of daily caravan: it affords a very useful accommodation to the cits of Berlin, who hold it among their highest luxuries to be rolled in a carriage to Potzdam upon days of festival or leisure.[18]

Liepmann's career had taken off. Most significantly, in the same year that he took over the concession in the postal business, he attained the highest recognition available to him as a Prussian Jew: he was granted a coveted 'General Privilege' on 14 February 1787.[19] Frederick the Great had created this new category in 1761, as a reward for exceptionally wealthy Jews who had contributed to the development of the Prussian economy. It gave recipients equal rights to Christians in business matters, and conferred residence permits on all their children.

Fifteen Prussian Jews were granted the Privilege between 1761 and Frederick's death in 1786; among the first candidates to receive this honour had naturally been the mint masters Itzig and Ephraim.[20] The award of the Privilege to Liepmann Meyer Wulff announced to the world of Berlin that Amalia's father had really arrived, and was regarded as an individual of some significance.

Liepmann had also become a leading figure in the Berlin Jewish community just as the struggle for equal rights began: he had been elected a charity warden in 1777, a treasurer in 1780, and an elder in 1783.[21] Two years before his election to the position of elder, a book had been published in Prussia that had drawn public attention to the question of Jewish rights. *On the Civil Betterment of the Jews* had been written by a high-ranking Prussian civil servant and political author, Christian Wilhelm von Dohm. He had produced the treatise at the request of his friend Moses Mendelssohn.

Dohm's book was a landmark, and it sparked a fierce controversy in Berlin. Dohm rejected the traditional view that the Jews were naturally dishonest and 'different', and therefore had to be strictly monitored and controlled. He agreed that the Jews' way of life was often undesirable, but asserted that their behaviour was not inherent, but was solely the result of the oppressive way in which they were treated by the State. If they were allowed to live under the same conditions as everyone else, they would become like any other German citizens:

> The Jew is even more man than Jew, and how would it be possible for him not to love a state where he could freely acquire property and freely enjoy it, where his taxes would not be heavier than those of the other citizens, where he could reach positions of honor and enjoy general esteem?…To make them [happier and better members of civil societies] it is FIRST necessary to give them equal rights with all other subjects.[22]

Dohm also disagreed with the prevailing view that the Jews' religious practices and beliefs were incompatible with citizenship. In his view, there was nothing in their religion to stop them becoming useful members of society.

Dohm's work had done a great deal to publicise the cause of Jewish citizenship, but little could be achieved while Frederick the Great still ruled over Prussia. It was only after Frederick's death in 1786, and the accession to the throne of his nephew, Frederick William II, that a glimmer of hope appeared. Frederick William was a very different sort of man to his highly disciplined and efficient uncle. Corpulent, self-indulgent and a serial philanderer, he bore a stronger resemblance to his distant relative Prinny, the dissolute heir to the throne of the United Kingdom, than he did to 'Old Fritz'.

The Jewish community elders petitioned Frederick William immediately on his accession. In response, the King established a commission, which was tasked with looking for ways to 'improve the condition of the Jews, and to make them more useful to the state'.[23] The elders themselves had framed their request in similar terms; these were no revolutionaries, but wealthy and established men, who had no desire to put themselves on a collision course with the Prussian authorities.

Liepmann Meyer Wulff was one of three senior members of the Jewish community appointed to negotiate with the government commission on behalf of the Jews of Prussia. The other two representatives, Isaac Daniel Itzig and David Friedländer, were strong advocates of radical modernisation and integration. Liepmann was the more traditional member of the group, and may have been chosen as a voice of moderation, given that the Jewish community was not solidly behind the campaign. Some of the more orthodox were hesitant, fearing that civil equality would be bought too hastily, and might result in a loss of Jewish identity.

Frederick William's initial response had been encouraging, but over the next few years the commission worked at a snail's pace, and little real progress was made towards the granting of civil rights. In 1789, the commission's report offered a few minor concessions, and demanded that the Jews accept civic duties, such as military service, without being granted citizenship. The report observed that Jewish regulations were still needed, to protect Christians from the immorality of the Jews, while the commissioners 'expressed the hope that Jews would be ready for complete equality within sixty or seventy years'.[24] It was a devastating blow. The community leaders responded with the comment that they were asking the King not merely to loosen, but to remove their chains, and that they would rather remain in their current position, however distressing it was, than accept such terms.

Although the slow progress of the negotiations for civil equality must have been disappointing for Liepmann, his personal affairs were not affected. As the holder of a General Privilege, he was one of the fortunate elite who already possessed extended legal rights as an individual. The Privilege had proved invaluable in business terms, as it gave Liepmann the right to own more than one property. He took advantage of this, buying mortgages on houses in central Berlin to build up a portfolio of property in some of the most expensive areas of the city. He also purchased a large house by the Potsdam canal, which he used as a post station for the *Journalière*.

The award of the Privilege had also come at a convenient time on a family level, as it would allow all four of his grown-up daughters to settle their own families in Berlin. The Wulff girls, as the daughters of a wealthy and prominent man who could guarantee his sons-in-law the prize of residence in Berlin, were undoubtedly excellent marriage prospects. By the 1780s, it was time to start thinking of marriages for the elder girls. Their husbands would need to be carefully chosen, both to ensure that the girls would be properly provided for, and to enhance the family's reputation and its prospects.

## Notes

1. Jacob Jacobson (ed.), *Jüdische Trauungen in Berlin 1759 bis 1813* (Berlin: Walter de Gruyter, 1968), p.127.
2. Hugo Rachel, Johannes Papritz and Paul Wallich, *Berliner Grosskaufleute und Kapitalisten* (Berlin: Walter de Gruyter, 1967), vol. 2, p.394.
3. Some sources give 1772 as Amalia Beer's year of birth, probably because the certificate dating from 1812 confirming the Beers' surnames (as required by the Prussian Edict of Emancipation) gives that year as her birth date. However, there is convincing evidence, mainly from comments in Meyerbeer's letters and diaries on his mother's age on several of her birthdays, that 1767 is correct. Possibly she simply chopped a few years off her age for the 1812 certificate. As the day and month of Amalia's birthdays vary slightly up to 1835, Heinz Becker believes that she celebrated her birthday up to around 1835 according to the Jewish calendar, and changed to the Christian calendar thereafter, settling on 10 February as her 'official' birthday. For a detailed discussion of Amalia Beer's birth date, see Giacomo Meyerbeer, *Briefwechsel und Tagebücher*, Heinz Becker, Gudrun Becker and Sabine Henze-Döhring (eds), (Berlin: Walter de Gruyter, 1960-2006), vol. 1, pp.34-5.
4. Redelia Brisbane, *Albert Brisbane. A Mental Biography with a Character Study* (Boston, MA: Arena Publishing Company, 1893), p.87.
5. Jewish names could be very confusing. Surnames were not widely used, and one person could be known by several, sometimes quite dissimilar names, which were also spelt in a variety of ways. Amalia's father was known variously as Lippman ben Meyer Levi; Liepmann Taussk or Tauss, and Uri Liepmann (or Lippmann or Liebmann) Meyer Wulff.

6. Rabbi Felix Singermann, *Die Lippmann-Tauss-Synagoge* (Berlin: self-published, 1920), p.10.
7. Meyerbeer, *Briefwechsel und Tagebücher*, vol. 1, p.62.
8. Ibid., p.380.
9. Adolph Kohut, 'Die Mutter Giacomo Meyerbeer's', *Illustrierte Frauen-Zeitung*, Year XVIII, issue 17, 1 September 1891, p.135.
10. Ruth Glatzer (ed.), *Berliner Leben 1648-1806* (Berlin: Rütten & Loening, 1956), p.227.
11. Henri Blaze de Bury, *Meyerbeer et son temps* (Paris: Michel Lévy Frères, 1865), p.14.
12. Veronica Beci, *Musikalische Salons. Blütezeit einer Frauenkultur* (Düsseldorf & Zürich: Artemis & Winkler, 2000), p.110.
13. Felix Eberty, *Jugenderinnerungen eines alten Berliners* (Berlin: Verlag für Kulturpolitik, 1925), p.104.
14. Quoted in Nancy B. Reich, 'Women as Musicians: A Question of Class', in Ruth Solie (ed.), *Musicology and Difference. Gender and Sexuality in Music Scholarship* (Berkeley, CA and London: University of California Press, 1993), p.133 n 21 [my translation].
15. Rachel, Papritz and Wallich, *Berliner Grosskaufleute*, vol. 2, p.394.
16. Anton Friedrich Büsching, *Beschreibung seiner Reise von Berlin nach Kyritz in der Prignitz* (Leipzig: Breitkopf, 1780), p.12.
17. Frederick A. Pottle (ed.), *Boswell on the Grand Tour: Germany and Switzerland, 1764* (London: William Heinemann Ltd., 1953), p.23.
18. John Owen, *Travels into different parts of Europe, in the years 1791 and 1792* (London: Caddell & Davies, 1796), vol. 2, pp.521-2.
19. Jacobson, *Jüdische Trauungen*, p.127.
20. Steven M. Lowenstein, *The Berlin Jewish Community. Enlightenment, Family and Crisis, 1770-1830* (New York and Oxford: Oxford University Press, 1994), p.30.
21. Sven Kuhrau and Kurt Winkler (eds), *Juden Bürger Berliner. Das Gedächtnis der Familie Beer–Meyerbeer–Richter* (Berlin: Henschel Verlag, 2004), pp.34-5.
22. Paul R. Mendes-Flohr and Jehuda Reinharz (eds), *The Jew in the Modern World. A Documentary History* (New York and Oxford: Oxford University Press, 1980), pp.28 and 30.
23. Kuhrau and Winkler, *Juden Bürger Berliner*, p.41.
24. Lowenstein, *The Berlin Jewish Community*, p.79.

# 3

## A Suitable Marriage

The bridegroom chosen for Amalia, the eldest of the four Wulff sisters, was Jost and Esther Liebmann's descendant, Jacob Herz Beer. Jacob was a member of the Jewish community of Frankfurt an der Oder, where his grandfather, Juda Herz Beer, had settled in the early decades of the eighteenth century. Juda had prospered in Frankfurt; by the end of the Seven Years' War his fortune had been assessed at around 10,000 thalers, making him one of the wealthiest Jewish merchants in the city.[1]

Juda must have been considered a significant figure in Frankfurt, as he was taken hostage by the Russians when they occupied the city in 1759, along with a city councillor, a Christian merchant and the Jewish chief elder. The four men were held in the Russian camp until a ransom was raised between the local merchants and the Jewish community.[2] Shortly after this unnerving experience, Juda bought a large house, for 5,000 thalers, on Frankfurt's Richtstrasse, which became the Beer family home.[3] Jacob, who was also originally named Juda, was born there on 10 June 1769.

The proposed marriage had distinct advantages for both sides. By the last decades of the eighteenth century, the importance of Frankfurt an der Oder as a commercial centre was waning. Marrying Amalia Wulff would open new doors for Jacob, guaranteeing him not only residence in Berlin, but also access to some of Prussia's most powerful people. From Liepmann's point of view, his new son-in-law would bring with him not only wealth, but a network of useful business contacts extending eastwards into Poland. The wedding took place on 4 September 1788. The couple lived in Frankfurt for the first year of their marriage, until Liepmann Meyer Wulff's General Privilege was officially extended to his son-in-law, on 24 November 1789.[4]

The marriage was certainly arranged – anything else would have been unheard-of. Jacob was the eldest son of his family, and it was his duty to make a good marriage at an early age – he was described in a letter written many years later by a relative, a son of one of his cousins, as having been married to Amalia at the age of eighteen 'according to the oriental custom'.[5] However, an arranged marriage was by no means synonymous with a forced marriage. Amalia's father was not a tyrant; she loved him deeply and was prostrated with grief when he died, more than twenty years after her marriage. With all her personal and social advantages, she was a highly eligible bride, and her parents had no reason to rush into accepting any offer that would be disagreeable to her.

Not all fathers understood their daughters well enough to choose a husband who suited them, however. Moses Mendelssohn chose a kindly, but uncultured Jewish businessman called Simon Veit for his daughter Brendel, a passionate and highly intellectual woman. Brendel was persuaded, rather than forced, into the marriage, but she found life with Veit dull, and became frustrated and unhappy. Her father believed to the end of his life that she was happy in her marriage, but after his death she renamed herself Dorothea, and left her husband to live with, and eventually marry, the Christian Romantic writer Friedrich Schlegel.

Dorothea Schlegel's spiritual life was as adventurous as her love life: she left Judaism and converted to Christianity, initially as a Protestant. Later on, she and her husband both converted to Catholicism, and Moses Mendelssohn's daughter ended her life as a fervent Roman Catholic who expended much time and energy in trying to convert both her Jewish and Protestant relatives.

Amalia was more fortunate in her marriage: the pious Liepmann Meyer Wulff might well have married his eldest daughter off to a respected rabbi with orthodox attitudes, but he chose a man whose character was sympathetic to her modern ideas. A pastel portrait painted around 1797 by Johann Heinrich Schröder, portraitist to the Duke of Brunswick and the Baden court, shows Jacob Beer nine years after the marriage. It depicts a handsome, confident, rather solid young man with powdered hair, dressed in contemporary German fashion, in a dark blue coat and white cravat. He is clean shaven, and hatless.

As with Amalia's portrait, there is nothing in the depiction of Jacob to show that he is a member of the Jewish community, although he would certainly have been brought up as a traditional Jew. His home town, Frankfurt an der Oder, was a centre of Jewish learning: it was famed in the Jewish world for its Hebrew printing press. In the middle years of the eighteenth century, Jacob's grandfather Juda had sponsored a new edition of the Pentateuch at the Frankfurt press.[6]

Fortunately, Jacob had not inherited the militant character of his notorious ancestor Esther Liebmann: he was a quiet man, described by all who knew him as kind, generous, and unfailingly good-natured. His bride had many of the traits of a Berliner, including a sharp wit, and on occasions

Jacob Herz Beer (Johann Heinrich Schröder c. 1797). Stiftung Stadtmuseum Berlin – Hans-und-Luise Richter Stiftung. Reproduction: Hans-Joachim Bartsch, Berlin

a sharp tongue, but those who knew her stressed her generosity of spirit. Amalia was described by her friend (and rival) Lea Mendelssohn, the mother of the musically talented siblings Fanny and Felix, as possessing 'a prevailing good nature, cheerfulness, liveliness, natural intelligence, unbounded philanthropy, great hospitality, and a soul, a disposition to do a great deal for her friends, and to be attached to them with a loyal heart'.[7]

Given the degree of compatibility with her husband, Amalia's preferences and her character must have been taken into consideration in the arrangement of her marriage. The young couple had much in common: they shared a deep attachment to Judaism, and an open attitude to modern German culture and society. Whether or not they had similar interests at the start of their marriage, they both became passionate theatre lovers, although Jacob's taste ran to comedies and farces rather than serious drama or opera. However, their greatest mutual interest was undoubtedly the future of their four sons, who they both idolised. Their first son, Meyer, later known as Giacomo, was born on 5 September 1791, three years after their marriage.

Giacomo's birth took place against a background of violent upheaval and change in Europe. In France, Louis XVI and Marie Antoinette were still nominally king and queen of the new constitutional monarchy, but their hold on power – and on life – was fragile, and they would go to the guillotine in 1793. One early decision of the new government of France would have far-reaching consequences for the Jewish communities of Europe: on 28 September 1791, just a few weeks after Amalia had given birth to her first son, the National Assembly voted to grant full rights of citizenship to the French Jews.

Against this stirring background, the future opera composer made a suitably dramatic entry into the world, arriving unexpectedly while his mother was travelling between Berlin and Frankfurt an der Oder. The coach was forced to stop at Tasdorf on the outskirts of Berlin, as Amalia began to experience labour pains. She was carried into the post station, busy with carriages and wagons travelling to and from the Prussian capital, where she gave birth safely, if not in the greatest comfort, to her first child. He was named Meyer, probably after his late grandfather, Meyer Wulff Levy.

Giacomo, or Meyer, was followed by Henoch (Heinrich) in 1794, Wolff (Wilhelm) in 1797, and finally Michael in 1800. The three older boys were given specifically Jewish names, indicating the family's attachment to their roots, but all of them took German (or in Giacomo's case, Italian) equivalent names as they grew up. The Beer children were born into privilege. By the time of Michael's birth in 1800, his grandfather, Liepmann Meyer Wulff, was rapidly overtaking the mint masters Itzig and Ephraim in wealth and influence. When the Itzig family had been naturalised as Prussian citizens in 1791, as a mark of extraordinary favour, their pre-eminence in the Jewish community had seemed unassailable. But only six years later, Daniel Itzig's son Isaac, who had been responsible for the paving of the Berlin–Potsdam road, was declared bankrupt after the French Republican government reneged on a deal worth 620,000 thalers.

The Ephraims, though not suffering such a rapid decline as the Itzigs, also suffered financial losses.[8] Their place at the top of the pile was taken by Liepmann, who, around the turn of the century, was described by a new arrival in the city as 'the richest and most pious of the Jews of Berlin'.[9] In 1799, Liepmann became chief elder of Berlin's Jews on the death of the previous post holder, Daniel Itzig. He had taken over leadership of the community at a time when hopes for emancipation were at a low ebb.

At least one of Liepmann's colleagues in the negotiations, Daniel Itzig's son-in-law David Friedländer, seems to have given up the struggle. That year, Friedländer wrote a startling letter to a prominent Christian clergyman, Dean Teller, suggesting that a number of leading Jewish families would be willing to undergo a form of baptism in return for citizenship, provided they did not have to accept the supernatural elements of the Christian faith. This proposal was naturally unacceptable to the Dean, but the fact that a respected leader of the Jewish community leadership could make such a suggestion reveals how hopeless the situation must have appeared.

Shortly after Liepmann took over the post of chief elder, the emancipation negotiations were temporarily revitalised. The government granted a few minor concessions, which included the abolition of the Jewish community's responsibility for compensating for the financial failures and misdemeanours of its individual members. There is an entry in the minute book of the Berlin Jewish community thanking Liepmann for his work in personally securing one of these measures, the removal of the community's responsibility for paying individuals' debts.[10] But again, after this temporary burst of activity, the negotiations for emancipation petered out.

The responsibility of the post of chief elder was a heavy one for Liepmann under the circumstances. The emancipation process had split the community: liberals like David Friedländer were frustrated by the lack of progress, while traditionalists were suspicious of, or even opposed to, the whole concept. The pressure of dealing with these tensions within the community was exacerbated for Liepmann by problems with his health, in particular his eyesight, which was so poor by this time that he had to have documents read aloud to him.[11] In February 1802 he tried to resign from the position of chief elder, but a community petition asking him not to give up the post persuaded him to remain.[12]

Despite the disappointments of his work for the Jewish community, however, Liepmann's business affairs were going from strength to strength.

His success was linked to his working relationships with two of the most prominent men in the government: Carl Friedrich von Beyme, who was Foreign Minister in 1806-07 (and again in 1817-19) and Justice Minister from 1808-10, and Count Friedrich von der Schulenburg-Kehnert, a Seven Years' War veteran, who at various times held the posts of Minister of War, Foreign Minister, and General Postmaster.

One of the most lucrative of Liepmann's ventures was his management of the Prussian national lottery. He took a lease on the lottery on 1 January 1795, having put down a security of 70,000 thalers. Over the next few years, he nearly doubled the number of tickets sold, bringing in an annual turnover of 1.5 million thalers. During the time this income was in Liepmann's hands, he invested it skilfully, and made considerable profits. In fact, he did so well out of the lottery that the politically liberal, but anti-Jewish government minister Count vom Stein complained that the state bank had clearly missed a trick in letting Wulff, who he described as an 'Old Testament banker', profit from the business.[13]

As Liepmann's wealth grew, he diversified into brokering foreign loans to the State, and supplying silver to the mint: in 1800 he delivered 2.5 million thalers' worth of silver, making a profit of around 100,000 thalers for himself.[14] He is said to have acquired the nickname of 'the Croesus of Berlin' around this time. However, despite his enormous wealth, Liepmann was never reported as indulging in the ostentation that had characterised the Itzig and Ephraim families. He is not known to have bought any artworks, nor to have built any private theatres or spectacular buildings, and there is not a single known portrait of him.

Following Amalia's marriage, Liepmann had expanded his business interests by making good use of his son-in-law's contacts in Frankfurt an der Oder. In 1793, the Commonwealth of Poland had been partitioned for a second time, with both Russia and Prussia taking over substantial portions of the dismembered state. Liepmann and Jacob had worked in partnership as suppliers to the Prussian army, which had been sent into eastern Poland to quell popular unrest. Their agent in Warsaw, a woman called Judyta Jacubowiczowa, was a business connection of Jacob's from Frankfurt an der Oder.

Judyta had been a member of the Buko family, wealthy and influential Jewish merchants in Frankfurt, before her marriage. At the time of the partition, she acted as negotiator for her husband, a Polish Jew; after his death, she became one of the most important army suppliers in Poland in the first years of the nineteenth century. She later established a banking business.[15] Jacob maintained business links with Judyta, and also personal interests in Frankfurt, for many years. On the death of his father in 1811, he inherited the family house at 50 Richtstrasse, which his grandfather Juda had bought in 1760, at the height of the Seven Years' War.

In 1800, Jacob moved into the industry that was to become the main source of his own wealth, purchasing a sugar refinery at No. 4 Heiligegeiststrasse in Berlin, on the northern bank of the River Spree, for just under 12,000 thalers. The importation and refining of cane sugar had operated as a monopoly under Frederick the Great, but after his death the industry had been opened up to competition. At the time Jacob bought his first refinery, imported cane sugar was the only type of raw sugar available. The Prussian chemist Franz Achard had recently succeeded in obtaining a small amount of sugar from European sugar beet, but it was still difficult to extract, and of relatively low quality.

Refined cane sugar had been imported into Germany from Venice since the fifteenth century, but it had been a rare luxury, available only to the richest families; the majority of people had used honey as a sweetener. By the middle of the eighteenth century, sugar refineries had been established in Germany itself, primarily in Hamburg, with a small number in Berlin. The raw sugar was imported mainly from the British and French colonies in the Caribbean, where it was extracted from the canes by slaves. It was refined in factories like Jacob's, to produce solid, cone-shaped blocks of sugar for household use.

Sugar remained a luxury product, offering high profits, not least because of the availability of cheap slave labour on the Caribbean sugar plantations. The need to constantly replenish this workforce was one of the main drivers of the slave trade. The Prussian sugar industry benefited from slave labour, although Prussia played no direct part in the trade itself, having a small navy and no colonial interests. Its military force was concentrated in its army, and its rulers tended to direct their acquisitive instincts towards Prussia's neighbouring states.

When Jacob had bought the factory in Heiligegeiststrasse, it had been the smallest of the four refineries operating in Berlin at the time. By 1804, however, the business was prospering, and his financial position was secure enough for him to buy the Spandauer Strasse house from his father-in-law. Liepmann and Esther had purchased a new home for themselves, in Königstrasse, for the considerable sum of 43,050 thalers.[16] An impressive three-storied building with a courtyard, stables and a garden, No. 33 Königstrasse had belonged to the founder of the first porcelain factory in Berlin, Wilhelm Caspar Wegely.

Liepmann and Esther's new house was situated in one of the most exclusive locations in Berlin, with a view onto the bridge that led to the old Royal Palace. The garden was particularly attractive. It was quiet and secluded despite its city centre location, and ran down to the riverbank, where a grove of mature trees shaded a summerhouse. Tradition has it that the Beers' youngest son, Michael, wrote his first play, *Klytemnestra*, in his grandparents' summerhouse.[17]

The Beers' move to the Spandauer Strasse house had several advantages. They had previously been living 'above the shop' at the refinery in Heiligegeiststrasse.[18] After the move, Jacob kept his offices at Heiligegeiststrasse, so that the Spandauer Strasse house could be used solely as a family home. It could easily accommodate the whole family, and in addition had a number of large reception rooms that could be used for formal entertaining. Amalia's portrait by Carl Kretschmar was painted around the time of the move, and may have been intended for one of the house's public rooms.

The Beers were ambitious for themselves, and for their young sons. They understood the value of education. Amalia and her sister Seraphine were financial supporters of the Berlin *Freischule* [Free School], founded in 1778 as the first Jewish school to offer poorer boys a broader and more modern curriculum.[19] Until then, the only real intellectual outlets for Jews had been rabbinical learning, or medicine for those training for the role of community doctor. Amalia and Jacob were determined to ensure that their own sons had the opportunity to benefit from a modern secular education, which would enable them to move freely in European society.

Giacomo was educated at home by private tutors – he never attended a school, unlike his younger brothers Wilhelm and Michael.[20] It seems probable that the second eldest, Heinrich, shared Giacomo's lessons. The boys' home curriculum was comprehensive for the time: Giacomo's schoolbooks show that he studied Latin, Greek, German, Italian and French, along with geography, history, philosophy and mathematics.

There was time for play as well as work, however. The Beer family were devoted theatregoers, and one of the boys' chief amusements at home was a puppet theatre, in which they staged plays for an audience consisting of their parents and family friends. When Giacomo left home in 1810, 13-year-old Wilhelm wrote to tell him that nothing much had changed since his departure, except that 'the puppet theatre has risen to an amazing level of perfection'.[21]

The next year, Giacomo bought some particularly fine puppets from Nuremberg as a fifteenth birthday present for Wilhelm, a thoughtful gift that gave Wilhelm a good deal of pleasure. The Beer children's miniature theatre became a treasured memory for Giacomo; years later, when he had daughters of his own, he bought them a puppet theatre, telling his wife that, 'I know from my own experience that it is the most enjoyable amusement for children.'[22]

Giacomo had proved a virtuoso piano player at a very young age, and at first it seemed likely that he would become a professional pianist. His talent was carefully fostered by his proud parents, who used every means at their disposal – and their means were by now considerable – to develop and encourage his interest in music. In 1798, when Giacomo was 7 years old, they engaged Franz Lauska, piano teacher to the Prussian court, as his music tutor. Lauska, a Moravian pianist and composer, had initially worked in Italy, then at the Bavarian court in Munich, and in Copenhagen, before moving to Berlin.

Giacomo also took lessons in composition with Carl Friedrich Zelter, a composer, conductor and teacher of music, who was the director of the Berlin Sing-Akademie, one of the most important musical institutions in the city. Carl Zelter was a friend of Goethe's and composed a number of settings for Goethe's poems. He was also, most unusually, a craftsman as well as a musician, a master mason who practised his trade for much of his life.

The Sing-Akademie had been founded in 1791 by Frederick the Great's harpsichordist Carl Fasch. It had begun as a small private group that met informally to sing choral music, focusing particularly on the works of Johann Sebastian Bach. By 1800, the Sing-Akademie choir had over 100 members. This choir was open to Jews – Amalia and three of her four sons were members at various times – and indeed, the Akademie's principal harpsichordist, Sara Levy, was Jewish, and a daughter of the mint master Daniel Itzig. As a young woman, Sara had studied music with Wilhelm Friedemann Bach, the eldest son of Johann Sebastian Bach.

It seems likely that Amalia, given her musical training, exercised an influence over the choice of Giacomo's tutors.[23] She certainly held strong opinions on the subject. In 1807, Giacomo left Carl Zelter, who was not an expert in dramatic composition, to study with the Kapellmeister Bernhard Anselm Weber, a prolific composer of operatic music and incidental music for plays. A few years later, Jacob reported Amalia's opinion of this change of teacher in a letter to Giacomo: 'Reichardt [the composer Johann Reichardt] was here yesterday and mother … talked a lot about Weber's music. Weber, he asked in astonishment, why Weber? Isn't he [Giacomo] with Zelter? No, said mother, it's a pity he spent two useless years with Zelter. Those two years are as good as lost.'[24] But whatever his mother's opinion of Zelter – whose manners and sense of humour could be earthy – Giacomo appeared to retain a fondness for his old tutor. While he was in Italy in 1826, he took the time and trouble to send Zelter a case of Madeira.

By the age of 12, Giacomo was a seasoned public performer. He had become a familiar figure in Berlin's musical circles, performing concertos and sonatas by Mozart, Beethoven and Cramer, sharing the stage with singers and musicians from the Royal Opera and visiting virtuosi. The *Allgemeine musikalische Zeitung*, the most influential German-language music periodical of the time, reported positively on his performances, almost always describing him as the promising young 'Jewish' virtuoso.

The journal's invariable designation of Giacomo as Jewish was not necessarily intended as denigrating, but for some Prussian citizens, who were already alarmed by the Jews' demands for equal rights, the sight of a Jewish boy claiming a place in public life was unacceptable. There was considerable resistance to the campaign for Jewish equality at the turn of the century, and between 1803 and 1805 a series of publications was issued by opponents of rights for the Jews.

One hostile commentator, a Prussian bureaucrat called Christian Paalzow, published a pamphlet in which he characterised the Jews as intent on world domination. He claimed that if any state gave the Jews citizenship, they would immediately seize control of trade and industry, and enslave the Christian population. His proposed solution to the 'Jewish question' was to eradicate Judaism altogether, and force the Jews into intermarriage and assimilation.

One of the most popular pamphlets was Carl Grattenauer's *Against the Jews*. This small and vitriolic tract, subtitled *A Word of Warning to all Christian Fellow Citizens*, had a huge print run of 13,000 copies.[25] The booklet presented old tales of child murder, poisoning and dishonesty as historical fact, and attempted to prove that Jews are devious and untrustworthy by nature. Grattenauer published several more pamphlets in answer to criticism of *Against the Jews*, in which he made it clear that his main targets were the more socially integrated Jews. He responded to the campaign for Jewish rights with a call to his fellow citizens to 'limit the Jews' power, destroy their arrogance, humble their pride, suppress their shamelessness and reject their importunity'.[26]

Grattenauer's attention was caught by Giacomo's public performances, and in particular the exhibition of his portrait in the Royal Academy, which he interpreted as insolent pretension:

Worse than all of this is having to put up with the arrogance with which they [the Jews] excitedly stop in the street anyone they think or know to have any understanding of art or science, clutch him by the collar, and extort from him an admission as to whether he has attended this or that concert, and whether he has heard the admirable little virtuoso Bär [Beer] whose life-size portrait has been hung in the Academy.[27]

In Grattenauer's opinion, the Jews' characteristics were racially determined, and so inalterable. Any attempts to change their way of life for the better by giving them equal rights, educating them into the Western way of life, or converting them to Christianity, were doomed to failure. The objects of his attacks were those Jews who dressed and behaved as Germans – underneath, he asserted, lay the grasping, corrupt nature of the eternal Jew, immutable and unacceptable. Moses Mendelssohn, in his opinion, had done no more than 'dress up rabbinic stupidity in the many-coloured coat of popular philosophy'.[28]

Carl Grattenauer especially despised – or feared – aspirational young Jewish women like Amalia Beer, describing them sarcastically as the 'learned, poetic, musical, beautiful daughters of Israel'. He warned his fellow Germans that the outward show of culture these women paraded was a façade: under the veneer of fashionable clothes and false sophistication lurked the repellent nature and the 'ineradicable stink' of the Jew. Grattenauer was obsessed with the idea that there was a smell by which Jews could be identified:

The toilettes of the Jewesses are very elegant, and I have often been unable to avoid thinking at the sight of the indescribable apparatus of smelling bottles, musk boxes, scent bottles, lavender bottles and vinaigrettes, that it might occur to a wicked person to assert that the lovely girls imagine that they really need all this equipment because their own smell is none too pleasant.[29]

In Grattenauer's opinion, Jewish women were constitutionally incapable of acquiring the refined sensibility of ladies of high society – 'no matter how many princes, dukes and gentlemen they associated with'.[30]

This last comment was a gibe at a small group of Jewish women who had come to public notice in Berlin in the 1780s and '90s, by opening their houses to both Christian and Jewish guests. This social mixing was a novelty in Prussian society, and the period has become known to historians as the era of the 'Berlin Jewish salons' – although the women themselves did not define their gatherings as 'salons', perhaps because the word retained a sense of the grandeur associated with the aristocratic houses of the French *ancien régime*.

The first of the Berlin 'salons' was initiated by Henriette Herz, the young wife of the Jewish community doctor Markus Herz. Around 1780 Markus, who had been a pupil of Immanuel Kant, had started to give philosophical and scientific lectures and demonstrations in their home in Spandauer Strasse. These talks became popular among Berlin's upper classes, and Henriette's gatherings developed naturally from them as the guests split into two separate groups: those who attended Markus's lectures in one room, and others, often younger men, who joined Henriette to discuss literature and art in another room.

Henriette's friend Rahel Levin, now the best-known of the early Berlin salonnières, is considered a minor literary figure on the strength of her copious letters to friends and family, and her promotion of the works of Goethe. Rahel was single when she began her gatherings. She was not considered a beautiful woman, unlike the lovely Henriette – she was small and plain, but she had a sparkling and original intelligence and great warmth. Her salon, held in her parents' house, attracted a wide range of guests, among them diplomats, writers, aristocrats, and even one of the younger members of the royal family, Prince Louis Ferdinand, who came with his mistress, Rahel's friend Pauline Wiesel.

We have few contemporaneous descriptions of these events. As the historian Barbara Hahn has pointed out, salons leave few traces.[31] Conversation and debate, unless recorded, are ephemeral by their nature. The Berlin salons have been depicted by some modern commentators as almost utopian places where Jews and Christians, commoners and aristocrats, men and women all met on equal ground. This does not appear to have been entirely the case, however. The Christian men who attended the salons frequently referred to their hostesses, in correspondence with their peers, in terms that suggested that they never quite forgot that they were socialising with Jews.[32]

There might have been some sympathy in Berlin for the ideals of equality disseminated by the French Revolution, but few Prussians really wanted to see the overthrow of their well-ordered system. However enthusiastically ideas of social change might be discussed in the safety of the drawing room, they were not, in general, translated into action. Those noblemen who were willing to enjoy the frisson of visiting Jewish homes did not issue return invitations to their own houses, and they continued to view their Jewish hostesses as outsiders, even as they enjoyed their hospitality.

Rahel Levin was painfully aware of the barriers she faced. She longed to be accepted into the highest circles of Christian society, and blamed her Jewish origins for any setback to her social ambitions. In a well-known passage in a letter to her friend David Veit, a young Jewish doctor, the 23-year-old Rahel exclaimed that as a Jewess, her whole life was 'a bleeding to death', and that she could ascribe 'every evil, every misery and every annoyance' to her Jewish descent.[33]

Rahel had several ultimately unhappy love affairs with aristocratic men, including Count Karl von Finckenstein, to whom she considered herself engaged for four years, and the Spanish diplomat Raphael d'Urquijo. Neither man, it seems, was prepared to marry her in the end. She was eventually baptised before marrying the diplomat and writer Karl Varnhagen in her forties. Varnhagen was not a nobleman; he came from a middle-class family, and held a diplomatic post in the Austrian civil service. He added the noble 'von Ense' to his name later in life.

Amalia Beer, who was occupied in bringing up a growing family in the 1790s, was on the sidelines of the 'salon society' led by Henriette Herz and Rahel Levin. The Berlin Jewish community was small, and Amalia knew both women, but she was never particularly close to them. Rahel and her family occasionally referred to Amalia rather disdainfully as '*L'Argentchen*' – 'little moneybags'.[34] Amalia and Rahel had been brought up very differently. Unlike Amalia, Rahel had experienced a difficult childhood, and, despite her great gifts, she lacked Amalia's security and easy confidence in herself. Rahel's tyrannical father had not been a practising Jew, and she had grown up alienated from Judaism, while Amalia's upbringing had inculcated in her a strong attachment to her faith.

Amalia certainly came from a wealthier background than Rahel, but she was just as eager to scale the social heights, although their motives and their approaches differed as sharply as their attitudes towards their faith. Rahel was both more intellectual and more unconventional than Amalia, whose ambitions were centred firmly on her sons – and it was thanks to Amalia's eldest son's musical talents that, around the turn of the century, she gained a foothold in the highest circles of Prussian society.

Giacomo's piano teacher, Franz Lauska, was court pianist to the King, Frederick William III, and music tutor to his sons, two of whom were to become monarchs, the elder boy as King Frederick William IV, and his younger brother as his successor William I, the first German Emperor. On at least one occasion, Giacomo was invited to play the piano privately for the young princes. Lauska's colleague, Friedrich Delbrück,[35] who was tutor to the royal children, made an entry in his diary on 9 May 1805, following a dancing lesson for the princes, that:

> I was on the whole pleased with their diligence during the dancing lesson at the palace, but their behaviour in other respects was too unruly, which struck me all the more as the lady-in-waiting Frau von Gaudi was present for a part of the lesson. Afterwards, Meier Beer gave us some admirable proofs of his skill on the forte piano.[36]

It was not unusual for virtuosi to be commanded to play at the palace for the entertainment of the royal family, but the Beer family's acquaintance with the young princes was more intimate. Over half a century later, on hearing of King Frederick William IV's death in January 1861, the 69-year-old Giacomo commented in his diary: 'During the night of 1 and 2 January the King died. I knew him personally since my childhood: we used to see each other as children, especially at Fräulein von Bischoffswerder's. He was always kind and graciously disposed towards me.'[37]

Amalia had begun making friends in very high places: Charlotte von Bischoffswerder was a prominent personality at court. She was the daughter of General Hans Rudolph von Bischoffswerder, one of the late King Frederick William II's most influential advisors. In 1786, Charlotte and her younger sister Marianne had been appointed ladies-in-waiting to Frederick William II's wife, Queen Friederike Louise.

Marianne had subsequently married a Polish Count, but Charlotte had stayed single, and had remained at court after the deaths of both Frederick William II and Friederike. She had a strong influence on the upbringing of their grandsons, the young princes of Giacomo's acquaintance. Charlotte remained particularly close to the eldest boy, the future King Frederick William IV, who valued her advice and friendship all his life. On her death in 1842, he described Charlotte as his 'second mother', who had 'nourished me and brought me up'.[38]

Amalia may have met Charlotte initially through Franz Lauska – as lady-in-waiting and piano tutor, both were members of the inner circle around the royal children. According to Friedrich Delbrück, the princes' dancing lessons often took place in Charlotte's rooms; it is possible that she and a fellow lady-in-waiting acted as dancing partners for the two little boys –and tempting to imagine that Meyer Beer might have been co-opted to provide the music on occasion.

Amalia and Charlotte went on to develop a close and warm friendship that was to be life-long. In general, Amalia retained an ingrained wariness in her relations with the majority of her non-Jewish acquaintances, believing that, 'in the end, the Gentiles will only pay you back with ingratitude'.[39] This was not the case with Charlotte, who must have been an unusual woman for her time: Amalia describes her as 'an exception to the rule, as she is completely free from Risches [anti-Semitism]'.[40]

Charlotte seemed equally at home in the royal palace and at her Jewish friend's house. She was fond of the Beer children, and joined in their amusements, providing an audience for the performances they staged in their puppet theatre. When Giacomo left home as a teenager to continue his musical education in Darmstadt, Charlotte wrote in his album: 'Remember in these lines a person who loved you as a child, and admired you as a youth.'[41]

Amalia's visits to the palace were, of course, by private invitation only, and did not imply acceptance at formal court occasions. These were strictly limited to the nobility, and governed by intricate rules of precedence. Up until the Napoleonic Wars, women of middle-class origin who were married to noblemen were banned from court, although their husbands were permitted to attend functions. Under these rules, the mother of Prince Otto von Bismarck was 'not received' at the Prussian court despite her high rank, because she had been born as the daughter of a government official who was a commoner.[42] The idea that the wife of a Jewish businessman might be 'presentable' at court would have been laughable.

Nonetheless, Amalia's access to the inner circles of the court, however private, was unique. When she died, many decades later, the scientist and explorer Alexander von Humboldt, who was close to both the royal family and the Beers, remarked that the 'greatness' of her character had made a strong impression on Frederick William IV in his childhood.[43] The royal children retained an affection for her into their adulthood; when Amalia's house came near to catching fire from a neighbouring building in 1851, both Prince William and Prince Carl visited her personally to enquire after her wellbeing.[44]

The uniqueness of Amalia's position within court society was also ...ned by Count Friedrich von Redern, a Prussian aristocrat, politician, ...ector of the royal theatres. Von Redern said of Amalia in his ...written in 1880, a quarter of a century after her death, that she ...d a place in the Berlin society of her time that no other woman ...d occupied before, or has ever since'. Von Redern knew the ... his own mother, Countess Wilhelmine von Redern, was a close friend of Amalia's. The Count remembered being taken to visit the Beers frequently as a child, and the Beer family paying return visits to the von Rederns in their grand house on Unter den Linden.[45]

In the opening years of the nineteenth century, as Amalia was beginning to develop these contacts at the highest levels of Prussian society, the heyday of the Berlin Jewish salons was coming to an end. The salons had opened up the possibility of social contact between Christians and Jews on an unprecedented level, and they occupy an important place in the history of German-Jewish relations. Consequently, and perhaps also because of the centrality of women in their history, the significance of the Berlin salons has often been interpreted in line with the social and political preoccupations of later periods.

The salonnières were condemned by German nationalist writers of the Nazi period, who saw the women as corrupters of German men. They were also criticised by some Jewish writers who considered them traitors to Judaism, given that the majority of them converted to Christianity and married Christian men. A later, more idealistic view of the salon era, as a successful, if brief, experiment in Jewish and German equality and integration, developed in the second half of the twentieth century. This has been seen by some more recent commentators as a nostalgic construct, perhaps reflecting a contemporary need to find some evidence of a time, prior to the horrors of the Holocaust, when Jews and Germans were able to live together in harmony.

The early Jewish salons were essentially a phenomenon of the last decades of the eighteenth century, a late flowering of the Enlightenment. In the opening years of the new century, they became minor casualties of a political and military crisis that shook Prussian society to its foundations. In October 1806, the Emperor of the French, Napoleon Bonaparte, inflicted a shattering defeat on the Prussian army at the battles of Jena and Auerstadt. By the end of that year, the royal family were in exile, and Berlin was a city under enemy occupation. It was a decisive turning point in Prussian history, and a catalyst for social and political change that was to profoundly affect the Jewish community of Berlin.

## Notes

1. Cornelia Aust, *The Jewish Economic Elite. Making Modern Europe* (Bloomington, IN: Indiana University Press, 2018), p.45.
2. Ibid., p.58.
3. Giacomo Meyerbeer, *Briefwechsel und Tagebücher*, Heinz Becker, Gudrun Becker and Sabine Henze-Döhring (eds) (Berlin: Walter de Gruyter, 1960-2006), vol. 1, p.30.

4.    Jacob Jacobson (ed.), *Jüdische Trauungen in Berlin 1759 bis 1813* (Berlin: Walter de Gruyter, 1968), p.316.

5.    Meyerbeer, *Briefwechsel und Tagebücher*, vol. 5, p.211.

6.    Jacobson, *Jüdische Trauungen in Berlin*, p.102.

7.    Lea Mendelssohn Bartholdy, *Ewig die deine. Briefe an Henriette von Pereira-Arnstein*, Wolfgang Dinglinger and Rudolf Elvers (eds) (Hannover: Wehrhahn Verlag, 2010), vol. 1, p.103.

8.    Steven M. Lowenstein, *The Berlin Jewish Community. Enlightenment, Family and Crisis, 1770-1830* (New York and Oxford: Oxford University Press, 1994), pp.92-3.

9.    Jacob Adam, *Zeit zur Abreise. Lebensbericht eines jüdischen Handlers aus der Emanzipationszeit*, Jörg H. Fehrs and Margret Heitmann (eds) (Hildesheim, Zürich, New York: Georg Olms Verlag, 1993), p.34.

10.   Lowenstein, *The Berlin Jewish Community*, p.225 n 22.

11.   Sven Kuhrau and Kurt Winkler (eds), *Juden Bürger Berliner. Das Gedächtnis der Familie Beer–Meyerbeer–Richter* (Berlin: Henschel Verlag, 2004), p.42.

12.   Rabbi Felix Singermann, *Die Lippmann-Tauss-Synagoge* (Berlin: self-published, 1920), p.9; see also Lowenstein, *The Berlin Jewish Community*, p.201 n 28.

13.   Hugo Rachel, Johannes Papritz and Paul Wallich, *Berliner Grosskaufleute und Kapitalisten* (Berlin: Walter de Gruyter, 1967), vol. 2, p.411.

14.   Ibid., p.415.

15.   Aust, *The Jewish Economic Elite*, pp.140-9.

16.   Jacobson, *Jüdische Trauungen*, p.127.

17.   Heinz Becker and Gudrun Becker (eds), *Giacomo Meyerbeer – Weltbürger der Musik* (Wiesbaden: Dr Ludwig Reichert Verlag, 1991), p.44.

18.   Berlin address book for 1801, at Zentral- und Landesbibliotek Berlin, http:/digital.zlb.de last accessed March 2015.

19.   Ingrid Lohmann (ed.), *Chevrat Chinuch Nearim. Die jüdische Freischule in Berlin (1778-1825) im Umfeld preußischer Bildungspolitik und jüdischer Kultusreform. Eine Quellensammlung* (Münster: Waxmann Verlag, 2001), vol. 1, p.1154.

20.   Sabine Henze-Döhring and Sieghart Döhring, *Giacomo Meyerbeer. Der Meister der Grand Opéra* (Munich: CH Beck, 2014), p.7.

21.   Meyerbeer, *Briefwechsel und Tagebücher*, vol. 1, p.86.

22.   Meyerbeer, *Briefwechsel und Tagebücher*, vol. 3, p.147.

23.   In an article on Amalia Beer in a popular women's journal in 1891 the writer and critic Adolph Kohut asserted that she 'kept a sharp eye' on her elder son's education, and he attributed the choice of his musical tutors to her. Kohut, 'Die Mutter Giacomo Meyerbeer's', *Illustrierte Frauen-Zeitung*, Year XVIII, issue 17, 1 September 1891, p.135.

24.   Meyerbeer, *Briefwechsel und Tagebücher*, vol. 1, p.57.

25.   Michael A. Meyer (ed.), *German-Jewish History in Modern Times* (New York: Columbia University Press, 1996-98), vol. 2, p.22.

26.   Carl Grattenauer, *Erklärung an das Publikum über meine Schrift Wider die Juden* (Berlin: Johann Wilhelm Schmidt, 1803), p.36.

27.   Carl Grattenauer, *Erster Nachtrag zu seiner Erklärung über seine Schrift Wider die Juden* (Berlin: Johann Wilhelm Schmidt, 1803), p.72.

28.   Grattenauer, *Erklärung an das Publikum*, p.14.

29.   Ibid., pp.10-11.

30.   Grattenauer, *Erster Nachtrag*, p.52.

31. Barbara Hahn, *The Jewess Pallas Athena. This Too a Theory of Modernity*, James McFarland (trans.) (Princeton, NJ and Oxford: Princeton University Press, 2005), p.43. Hahn comments (pp.50-2) that the studies of the Berlin salons are based on a small number of texts, relying in particular on the witness of a 'Count Salm' as given by Rahel's widower, Karl Varnhagen von Ense. It is suggested that Varnhagen von Ense was the author, or at least co-author, of the passage, and that it is a composite image, crowding a parade of 'famous people' and representative conversations into one evening.

32. For example, see Hahn, *The Jewess Pallas Athena*, p.53, for the Swedish diplomat Karl Gustav von Brinckmann's comments on Rahel Levin.

33. Rahel Levin Varnhagen, *Rahel Varnhagen im Umgang mit ihren Freunden (Briefe 1793-1833)* Friedhelm Kemp (ed.) (Munich: Kösel-Verlag, 1967), p.54.

34. Rahel Levin Varnhagen, *Familienbriefe*, Renata Barovero (ed.) (Munich: C. H. Beck, 2009), p.723.

35. Delbrück had become tutor to the Crown Prince, Frederick William, in 1800, before the Prince's fifth birthday, and tutor to the younger Prince William in 1802. The princes had been under the care of the royal nursery governess, a Madame Flesche, before Delbrück took over their education. Friedrich Delbrück, *Die Jugend des Königs Friedrich Wilhelm IV von Preussen and des Kaisers und Königs Wilhelm I* (Berlin: A. Hofmann & Comp., 1907), p.xxx.

36. Delbrück, *Die Jugend des Königs Friedrich Wilhelm IV*, p.259.

37. Giacomo Meyerbeer, *The Diaries of Giacomo Meyerbeer*, Robert Letellier (ed. and trans.) (Madison, NJ: Fairleigh Dickinson University Press, 1999-2004), vol. 4, p.191.

38. Theodor Fontane, *Wanderungen durch die Mark Brandenburg* (Berlin and Weimar: Aufbau-Verlag, 1994), vol. 3, p.302. Some internet sources, which are not necessarily reliable, refer to three sisters: Marianne (1767-89), Charlotte (1767-1812) and Caroline Erdmuthe (not known-1842). However, only two sisters are mentioned in contemporary sources: Marianne, and *either* Caroline or Charlotte, but not both. Charlotte's date of death as given in Wikipedia (1812) is incorrect, as 'Charlotte von Bischoffswerder' was a member of the Board of the Patriotic Women's Association from 1814 onwards, and was awarded the Order of Louise in 1827: see Dirk Alexander Reder, *Frauenbewegung und Nation. Patriotische Frauenvereine in Deutschland im frühen 19. Jahrhundert (1813-1830)* (Cologne: SH-Verlag, 1998), pp.58 and 64, and Louis Schneider, 'Der Luisen-Orden' in *Die Preussichen Orden, Ehrenzeichen und Auszeichnungen. Geschichtlich, bildlich, statistich* (Berlin: Hayn, 1867), p.23. She is mentioned in the Beer family documents up to March 1838, when Giacomo Meyerbeer notes a visit to her in his diary. As Charlotte was used as a diminutive for Caroline at the time, I believe 'Caroline' and 'Charlotte' to be the same woman, and the date of death of 1812 to be an error.

39. Meyerbeer, *Briefwechsel und Tagebücher*, vol. 1, p.79.

40. Unpublished, undated letter, Amalia Beer to Aaron Wolfssohn, Leopold Stein Collection; AR3263; Box 1; Folder 7; Leo Baeck Institute. Courtesy of Leo Baeck Institute.

41. Heinz Becker and Gudrun Becker (eds), *Giacomo Meyerbeer – Weltbürger der Musik* (Wiesbaden: Dr Ludwig Reichert Verlag, 1991), p.58.

42. Christa Diemel, *Adelige Frauen im bürgerlichem Jahrhundert. Hofdamen, Stiftsdamen, Salondamen 1800-1870* (Frankfurt am Main: Fischer Taschenbuch Verlag GmbH, 2014), pp.70-1.

43.  Meyerbeer, *Briefwechsel und Tagebücher*, vol. 6, p.334.
44.  Meyerbeer, *Briefwechsel und Tagebücher*, vol. 5, pp.336-7.
45.  Friedrich Wilhelm von Redern and Georg Horn, *Unter drei Königen. Lebenserinnerungen eines preussischen Oberkämmerers und Generalintendanten*, Sabine Giesbrecht (ed.) (Cologne, Weimar and Vienna: Böhlau Verlag, 2003), p.141.

# 4

## Napoleon: Crisis and Opportunity

The political situation in Europe had been deteriorating since December 1804, when Napoleon Bonaparte had crowned himself Emperor in Paris, and had begun an aggressive campaign to dominate the continent militarily, and to export the values and ethos of the Revolution to the rest of Europe. Austria, Russia and Britain had formed a coalition against the French, but the Prussian King, Frederick William III, a temperamentally indecisive man, had been reluctant to commit himself. Instead, he had stood by and watched as Europe unravelled in less than two years. Events moved quickly from late 1805, when Napoleon lost control of the sea to Admiral Horatio Nelson. Frustrated in his plans to invade Britain, he turned his attention to continental Europe, swiftly winning crushing victories over the Austrians and Russians at the battles of Ulm and Austerlitz.

On 12 July 1806, sixteen southern German states signed a treaty with France, forming the Confederation of the Rhine. Three weeks later, the states of the new pro-French Confederation seceded from the Holy Roman Empire. The Emperor Francis II was left with little choice: on 6 August, he declared the Holy Roman Empire of the German Nation dissolved. The French philosopher Voltaire had once remarked that the Holy Roman Empire was neither holy, nor Roman, nor even an empire, but however loose an organisation it was, it had somehow held together a patchwork of over 300 tiny kingdoms, dukedoms, electorates, free cities and archbishoprics for nearly a thousand years, before vanishing overnight in the face of Napoleon Bonaparte's belligerence.

Realising at last the seriousness of the threat, Frederick William III hastily concluded an alliance with Tsar Alexander of Russia, and declared war on France. Having abandoned his habitual caution, he then made the disastrous decision to move immediately onto the offensive, basing his plans on an over-optimistic assessment of his army's capabilities and state of readiness. The Prussian army's march south ended in catastrophe at the twin battles of Jena and Auerstedt on 14 October 1806, when it was routed before the Russians had time to come to its aid.

This major defeat came as a terrible shock to the Prussians, who had believed that their army was still the invincible military machine that Frederick the Great had created. In reality, its tactics were now rigid and outdated, and it was commanded by old men who had been promoted solely because of their noble birth. This creaking machine had little chance against Napoleon's more mobile *Grand Armée,* with its dynamic young Generals. The Prussian army was annihilated. Young Prince Louis Ferdinand was killed in action, and the royal family fled eastwards. So complete was the French victory, that when the Prussian Queen stopped a courier to ask him whether he knew if the King was still with the army, he was said to have replied, 'The army? It doesn't exist any more.'[1]

In the days after the defeat, uncertainty and confusion gripped the population of Berlin. Rumours that a major battle had taken place circulated in the city, and crowds gathered in front of the royal palace, anxiously waiting for an announcement. On 17 October, three days after the battles of Jena and Auerstedt, a placard appeared on the walls of all the main squares and street corners of Berlin, announcing that: 'The King has lost a battle. The first duty of citizens is now to remain calm. I call on all inhabitants of Berlin to do so. The King and his brothers live!' The notice was signed by the governor of Berlin, Liepmann Meyer Wulff's patron Count Schulenburg-Kehnert.

Shortly afterwards, Schulenburg-Kehnert fled Berlin, taking the remaining garrison troops with him. The city's inhabitants were left, defenceless and terrified, to await the arrival of Napoleon Bonaparte and his *Grand Armée.* No one knew whether to follow the court's example and flee, or to stay put and hope for the best. In the general panic, anything that had a Prussian eagle on it was torn down or concealed: even the post boys ripped the brass insignia from the arms of their uniforms.[2]

On 24 October, Bonaparte reached Potsdam, where he made a rather theatrical visit to Old Fritz's tomb. Standing with his hat in his hand, the Emperor is said to have told his companions, 'If this man were alive today, I would not be here.'[3] On the same day, the first French troops entered Berlin: around 200 cavalrymen, escorting a coach containing General Hulin, who had been appointed military commandant of the city.

On 25 October Marshal Davout, commander of the 3rd Corps, marched his troops through the city in a show of strength. The French foot soldiers, with their untidy, dark hair and torn and dirty clothes, were an extraordinary sight to the Prussians, used to well-disciplined troops with powdered hair, pigtails, and smart uniforms. One Berliner recorded his astonishment at seeing his first French soldier, a man in filthy clothes and with bare feet, leading a dog on a bit of string: 'Just imagine, a soldier with a dog on a lead, half a loaf of bread stuck on his bayonet, a goose hanging from his musket, and on his hat, instead of any insignia, a tin spoon ...'[4]

At three in the afternoon on 27 October 1806, a lovely, sunny autumn day, Napoleon Bonaparte entered Berlin through the Brandenburg Gate. Two divisions of cuirassiers provided a cordon: horses' hooves stamping, reins jingling, breastplates, helmets and sword blades flashing in the sun. Trumpets and drums announced the arrival of the Emperor, who was preceded by the astonishing sight of his Mameluke bodyguard, their faces fierce and dark beneath their turbans, their robes flying as their horses pranced along the wide boulevard of Unter den Linden. The Emperor himself, perhaps the least gorgeously clad of this swirling, glittering horde, a small, plump, ordinary-looking figure on a white Arab horse, accepted the keys of the city of Berlin.

Napoleon took over the royal apartments in the City Palace for himself and his entourage, while his guards bivouacked in the Lustgarten, in front of the palace. In the following days, the Berliners kept to their houses, few venturing outdoors. The streets were filled with foreign soldiers in strange uniforms, the sound of French voices and the rumble of baggage- and gunpowder-wagons. Some of Berlin's Lutheran churches were used as temporary stables for the army's horses, while mobile field blacksmiths set up their smithies in the streets. At night, the flames of campfires flickered in the Lustgarten and the city squares.

General Hulin's staff swiftly took control of the administration of the city, and began to quarter the French soldiers on the inhabitants. The General, a humane man, did his best to ensure that his troops remained well disciplined, and treated the citizens with respect. There were very few incidents of violence, although the sense of relief that they were not in any physical danger did not alleviate the humiliation of defeat for the Berliners, who found themselves no longer masters even in their own homes.

The attitude of restraint enjoined by General Hulin on the occupying army was not exercised by Napoleon himself, who enjoyed rummaging around the royal palaces choosing personal souvenirs, including Frederick the Great's belt and sword, to take away with him. He tasked his Director-General of Museums, the diplomat and archaeologist Baron Vivant Denon, to loot the city's art treasures, and have them transported to Paris, to be added to the collection at the Musèe Napoléon, as the Louvre had been re-named.

Most offensively to the Prussians, Napoleon ordered the removal of the sculptor Gottfried Schadow's 'Quadriga' – a chariot drawn by four horses and driven by the Roman goddess of war – from its position on top of the

Brandenburg Gate. It was taken to Paris, where it remained for the next seven years. The disappearance of the iconic Quadriga became a symbol of national humiliation for the Berliners, and earned the Emperor of the French the derisive nickname of 'the horse thief of Berlin'.

In mid-1807, Prussia suffered a final humiliation in the Treaty of Tilsit. Napoleon had stayed only a month in Berlin, moving eastwards in November 1806 to engage the Russian army, under Count Levin von Bennigsen, in Poland and East Prussia. After the French had decisively defeated the Russians at Friedland in June 1807, Tsar Alexander sued for peace. Napoleon and the Tsar met on a specially constructed raft in the middle of the river Niemen, near the town of Tilsit in East Prussia (now Sovetsk in Russia), to decide Europe's future. King Frederick William III was not invited to this ostentatious summit, and had to wait on the banks to learn his Kingdom's fate.

Napoleon appeared determined to humiliate him: under the terms of the Treaty, Prussia was reduced to a rump state, losing a number of territories in its eastern and western provinces amounting to a third of its lands and half of its population. The King of Saxony was given Prussia's former share of Poland, now re-named the Duchy of Warsaw. Frederick William did at least retain his sovereignty, although the departure of French troops from Prussian soil was made dependent on the payment of enormous war indemnities of 32 million Reichstaler. In the face of this impossible demand it looked as if the French would never leave, and the Berliners resigned themselves to the long haul.

Over the cold winter of 1806 to 1807 conditions in Berlin deteriorated rapidly. Napoleon had left a large number of troops quartered in the city, and the cost of housing and feeding some 15,000 French soldiers inevitably caused hardship. Even those whose houses were unsuitable for taking in men and horses had to pay billet money, calculated according to the size of their property. The price of necessities went up, and everyday food staples became scarce and highly expensive.

The economic problems were exacerbated by developments in Napoleon's strategy to undermine Britain. During his brief stay in Berlin, the Emperor had issued the Berlin Decree, establishing an economic blockade against Britain. His aim was destroy the British economy by isolating Britain from the continent, and crippling its export trade. The Decree forbade all trade with the British Isles and its colonies, and all commerce in British merchandise.

This was a worrying development for Jacob Beer. His main business interests depended on the import of cane sugar from the Caribbean, but he had also diversified into the import of other colonial luxury goods such as tobacco and coffee. All of these activities were now threatened. Additionally, aside from his personal concerns, Jacob had taken on a leading role in the regulation of Berlin's financial markets shortly before the occupation.

In 1805, the city's stock exchange had been reorganised. To house this important financial institution, the merchants of the city had paid for the construction of an impressive five-storied building, fronted by an enclosed colonnade, in the Lustgarten, near the cathedral and the palace. Jacob had been elected as one of four new 'directors for life' of the restructured Exchange.

Extraordinarily, two of these four directors – Jacob and Reuben Gumpertz – were Jewish. As the Jewish community formed only around 2 per cent of the total population of Berlin, these appointments were a reflection of the influential role played by the Jews in the Prussian economy. It was a great personal honour for both men to have been invited to fill the posts, and a public statement of confidence in their abilities. By 1807, however, leadership of the city's financial sector had become a heavy responsibility.

Berlin's economy was under enormous strain during the occupation. Taxes were constantly being raised to meet quartering charges and pay the war indemnities. An official in the Prussian administration reported that:

> The plight of private citizens was just as terrible [as that of the state]. The estate owners were drained by the contributions, delivery of supplies and billeting of troops. House owners suffered a similar fate, their properties also lost half their value ... The manufacturer was compelled, for lack of sales, to give notice to his workers. The merchant sold nothing, or did so only on credit.[5]

Both Jacob and his father-in-law, as two of the wealthiest men in Berlin, were significant personal creditors of the State during the occupation, making large loans (not all of them voluntary) of up to tens of thousands of thalers to the city and to the provincial authorities. Despite the depradations the wartime economy made on their private incomes, however, neither man made such major losses during the occupation that their fortunes were significantly dented: in 1809, Jacob was rated the fifth wealthiest Jewish taxpayer in the city. By 1814, he would be the second wealthiest.[6]

Other Berlin businessmen were not so fortunate, and some lost all of their money in the aftermath of the Prussian defeat. Among these was Joseph Mosson (or Moses), the husband of Amalia's sister Johanna, who was declared bankrupt in 1809. The Mossons' grandson, Felix Eberty, described Johanna in his memoirs as a proud woman, who was never able to forgive her husband for this failure.

The Mossons were not genuinely impoverished by Joseph's bankruptcy, as Johanna belonged to an extremely wealthy family who would ensure she did not suffer, but there were large numbers of less fortunate people who were left destitute by Prussia's defeat. The war and the continental blockade had caused mass unemployment in the textile industry, which in 1790 had employed around 40,000 workers in Berlin. In 1806 the industry failed, partly because both of its main markets – the army for woollen cloth, and the court for silks – had vanished overnight. The unemployed and their families, along with the remnants of the defeated army, and the widows and orphans of soldiers who had died in the battles of Jena and Auerstedt, were reduced to begging for food on Berlin's streets.

The collapse of the Prussian administration had also disrupted the city's welfare systems, and the existing charitable institutions – the poorhouses, orphanages and hospitals – could not cope with the growing numbers of the dispossessed. In the winter of 1806 the first Berlin soup kitchens, organised by the architect Louis Catel, provided more than 6,000 free meals a day to the hungry.[7]

In April 1807, Catel brought together a committee, which included several Christian clerics, to establish a new charity for the care of neglected or abandoned boys 'regardless of religion or class'.[8] This institute would offer shelter and food to some of the worst affected children, and would also give them a basic vocational education, to train them for a trade such as spinning, straw-weaving or carpentry. Jacob Beer was known to be interested in philanthropy – he had been a supporter of the respected Citizens' Rescue Institute before the war – and he was invited to join the committee at the beginning of June.

The institute had found a rent-free home in the spacious rectory of the Nikolaikirche, which had been unoccupied for some time, but large reserves of money were still needed to cover the running costs. The committee members were all asked to find sponsors, but Jacob was almost single-handedly responsible for raising the money needed to turn the ambitious plans into reality: by the beginning of August he had recruited eighty-nine donors, who had each pledged to give between one and ten thalers monthly. Most were prepared to support the institute for an initial two-year period, but some had committed themselves for their lifetimes.

With its future secured, the institute, which was named the Luisenstift, or Louise Institute, after the Prussian Queen, opened on 9 September 1807, with an intake of thirty-seven boys aged between 6 and 14. By the end of the first year the number of inmates had risen to sixty, with a waiting list of seventy. In 1811, the first group of boys to leave, eighteen in number, successfully took up jobs.

The Luisenstift, founded in the aftermath of defeat and occupation, became one of the most enduring and important charitable foundations for children in Berlin – and is still in existence today.[9] Jacob, a founding member, remained a director of the institute for the rest of his life, and took an active role in its management. He made weekly inspection visits, overseeing the general running of the home, and checking the standards of the meals and the treatment of sick boys. The charity's secretary, Theodor Heinsius, noted in his 1808 report that on 3 August that year, 'our esteemed member Herr Herz Beer' had entertained the children for the day at his country house in Templow, an area to the south of the city.[10] Somewhat ironically, Jacob was becoming a respected civic leader while, as a Jew, he was still ineligible for Prussian citizenship.

Support of the Luisenstift became a family affair. Wilhelm took over his father's directorship after the latter's death, and Amalia gave an annual party for the children for over forty years. When the composer Carl Maria von Weber, a family friend, paid a surprise visit to the Beers in August 1814, he found one of these parties in full swing, noting in a letter to his fiancée Caroline Brandt that 'The orphan children were being fed at the house of my friend Meyerbeer's parents today, and besides the big table there were eighty places set.'[11]

By the time that Jacob became a founding director of the Luisenstift, the Beers had owned the Spandauer Strasse house for three years. The house was large enough to host charitable events with ease, and it had also offered Amalia the ideal opportunity to begin to hold a 'salon' in her own style. The occupation had proved the final blow for the earlier Jewish salons, which were perceived as being French in style – and in the aftermath of the war, anything French was out of favour.

In 1808, Rahel told a friend that she sat alone at her tea table, and later commented, 'where are our days, when we were all together! They went under in the year '06. Went under like a ship: containing the loveliest goods of life, the loveliest pleasures.'[12] In the more nationalistic wartime atmosphere, the free-thinking Jewish literary and philosophical salons were replaced by patriotic political gatherings hosted by aristocratic Christian women, and by musical salons such as Amalia's.

Amalia's gatherings differed from those of Henriette and Rahel from the start in being more formal, and focused on artistic performance rather than on spontaneous conversation. By the time of the French occupation, the Beer house had become a meeting place for the stars of Berlin's theatrical world. Amalia's soirées were also designed to showcase her sons' talents. The violinist and composer Louis Spohr, who visited Berlin in 1804, attended a musical party at the Beers' house, where, he says, 'I heard for the first time, the now so celebrated Meyerbeer, play in his paternal house, then but a boy of thirteen years of age.'[13]

As a young mother, Amalia was keen to cultivate people she felt might be useful in furthering her sons' careers. Johann Reichardt, a frequent guest of the Beers, was a major opera composer and a respected music critic, and so, in Amalia's view, someone whose favourable opinion it was vital to obtain. She urged the teenaged Giacomo not to neglect him, 'because you want to be sure to keep people like these as your friends'.[14]

Perhaps the most important 'house friend' of the Beers at this time was August Iffland, who had been the first actor to play the lead role of Franz Moor in the 1782 premiere of Schiller's *Die Räuber* [The Robbers]. Iffland is now considered the most famous theatrical actor-manager in German history, and is still celebrated: the 'Iffland ring', a diamond-studded ring carrying his portrait, is held by the most important German-speaking actor of his day. Each holder chooses his successor, bequeathing the ring in his will.[15]

Iffland had been director of the National Theatre in Berlin since 1796. Amalia was very proud of her friendship with him, telling her eldest son that

> I could give you a thousand instances of his kindness to me—he's given an instruction that a box should be kept for me in the theatre up to 1 o' clock every day ... the Kapellmeister [Giacomo's tutor Bernhard Weber] says he doesn't know what it is I've done to I[ffland], he's never behaved like this towards a woman before.[16]

Amalia must have been referring to Iffland's homosexual leanings, which were an open secret, and which clearly made his preference for her company even more flattering. Her sons were not unaware of Amalia's reverence for Iffland – between themselves they referred to him by the nickname of 'the god'.

By the time of the occupation, Iffland had been a friend of the Beers for some time, and was one of the regular participants in the play readings that formed a part of their entertainments. Lessing's dramas were a popular choice for these evenings, and one guest remembered Iffland reading the roles of Nathan in *Nathan der Weise* [Nathan the Wise] and Marinelli in *Emilia Galotti*. Other parts were taken by members of the Beer family, including young Michael, who, at 7 years old, was said to have real acting ability.[17] In fact, all of the children were artistically gifted: Wilhelm was scientifically minded, but he also had the family musical talent, as did Heinrich. Both of them were members of the Berlin Sing-Akademie, and both sang regularly in amateur operatic productions at the Beer house and at the houses of other friends.

Amalia's salon was not overtly political, but the atmosphere was distinctly patriotic. Several of the Beers' 'house friends' fell foul of the French authorities. The young artist, writer and publisher Friedrich Gubitz[18], a known supporter of the Prussian cause, founded a nationalist journal called *The Fatherland* in 1807, which brought him to the attention of the French. He had a number of narrow escapes: at one point, he was put under house arrest for six weeks, as the French suspected, possibly correctly, given the content of some of the articles in *The Fatherland*, that he was in communication with the leaders of the Prussian Free Corps. He had also courted danger by allowing a patriotic poem that he had written to be recited at an open-air gathering in Field Marshall Möllendorf's garden, in front of a painting of Frederick William III.

Amalia, who had heard of Gubitz's activities and sympathised with him, decided to take the young man under her wing. In early 1808, she invited him to join her house circle. It says a good deal both for her character, and for her standing in Berlin society, that, although she had never met Gubitz, she did not hesitate to turn up unannounced at his house, and offer him her patronage. It also says a good deal for Gubitz that, as he noted in his memoirs, he was very glad to accept Amalia's invitation. He was struck by the 'lively, gracious social life' in the Beer house, where the atmosphere was one of 'intelligence, cheerfulness and gaiety', and he greatly valued his friendship with Amalia, remarking that for him, it was one of the few good things to have come out of the French invasion.[19]

August Iffland, like Gubitz, incurred the displeasure of the French authorities. The playhouse and the opera continued to stage productions throughout the occupation, although their managements did not have an entirely free hand. Napoleon had commanded that the birthdays of the Prussian royal family were not to be commemorated: instead, he ordered the city to be lit up in celebration of his own birthday, the peace of Tilsit, and the battles of Jena and Auerstedt – thus adding insult to injury. The birthdays of the Prussian royals had not, in fact, been widely celebrated before the occupation, but many Berliners now began to mark these forbidden dates with small festivities in their own homes, behind closed doors and shuttered windows.

A few prominent people, among them Iffland, defied the ban more openly. In 1808, he staged a ballet in honour of Queen Louise's birthday, which began and ended with shouts of 'Long live the Queen!' He was put under house arrest for two days—and, nine days later, was forced by the French authorities to repeat the performance on the name day of the French Empress, Josephine. The dancers, who had held up garlands of flowers to form the shape of the letter 'L' in the original performance, were instructed to do the same in the second, but to form the letter 'J' with the flowers instead.

Iffland's show of public support for the Prussian royal family made him a popular figure in Berlin, however. Shortly after the occupation came to an end, an anonymous document called 'The List of the Righteous' was circulated in the city. It contained the names of forty-two people, among them Iffland, who were considered to have shown particular courage and patriotism in the period of French rule.

Other friends of the Beers supported the absent royal family in less public ways. Charlotte von Bischoffswerder had remained behind in Berlin when the court had fled to East Prussia. The royal family had initially based themselves in Königsberg, but had subsequently moved further east, to Memel (now in Lithuania). Charlotte was in secret communication with the court in exile. In late 1807, she wrote to Memel warning the royal family that she had discovered from a trustworthy source that there were spies in their midst: 'Not a word is spoken by our unhappy and beloved princes that is not reported immediately to Paris. Everything that is said at court is known [there].'

Charlotte was aware that she was taking a huge risk in writing to the exiled court – unauthorised contact with the royal family was considered treasonous by the French authorities – and she assured her correspondents that, 'I live in the strictest seclusion, as is necessary in my position.' In common with many Berliners, Charlotte could see no end to the occupation, finishing her letter, 'I wish you good health; I dare not hope for more than that.'[20]

In fact, the end of the occupation would come sooner than she, or perhaps anyone else in Berlin, dared to hope or imagine. In 1808, circumstances forced Napoleon Bonaparte's hand. An uprising against France in Spain, combined with the news that Austria was re-arming, meant that he needed more troops further south, and the French garrison gradually began to withdraw from Berlin. In September, Frederick William

Berlin, c. 1808

signed a treaty with France in which he agreed to restrict the size of Prussia's army.

By December 1808, the last of the occupiers had left, and the first Prussian soldiers marched back into the city to a tumultuous welcome. King Frederick William and Queen Louise returned a year later, in late December 1809, to the cheers of their subjects. The economy was still suffering from the aftermath of the occupation and the effects of the continental blockade, but with the departure of the French troops from Prussian soil, and the return of their royal family, the Berliners began to hope that everyday life could return to normal.

## Notes

1. Frank Bauer, *Napoleon in Berlin. Preussens Hauptstadt unter Französischer Besatzung 1806-1808* (Berlin: Berlin Story Verlag, 2006), p.78.
2. Amalie von Romberg (ed.), *Vor hundert Jahren. Erinnerungen der Gräfin Sophie von Schwerin* (Berlin: Stargardt, 1909), p.175.
3. Bauer, *Napoleon in Berlin*, p.71.
4. George Cavan, *Erinnerungen eines Preussen aus der Napoleonischen Zeit 1805-1815* (Grimma: Druck und Verlag des Verlags-Comptoirs, 1840), pp.18-19.
5. Heinrich von Béguelin, as quoted in Karen Hagemann, *Revisiting Prussia's Wars against Napoleon. History, Culture and Memory* (Cambridge: Cambridge University Press, 2015), pp.43-4.

6.  Steven M. Lowenstein, *The Berlin Jewish Community. Enlightenment, Family and Crisis, 1770-1830* (New York and Oxford: Oxford University Press, 1994), p.229 n 6.
7.  Georg Holmsten, *Die Berlin-Chronik. Daten, Personen, Dokumente* (Düsseldorf: Droste Verlag, 1984), p.196.
8.  For the early history of the Luisenstift see Erik Lehnert and Marcel Piethe (eds), '*Lasset uns Gutes thun und nicht müde werden ...*' *200 Jahre Luisenstift Berlin* (Berlin: Lukas Verlag, 2007), pp.34-6, and Theodor Heinsius, *Geschichte des Luisenstifts bis zum Schlusse des Jahres 1808* (Berlin, 1809; reprinted Berlin: Archiv für Kunst und Geschichte, 1982).
9.  The Luisenstift has changed its location over the centuries, but still survives today, as a home and educational institute for young people.
10. Heinsius, *Geschichte des Luisenstifts*, p.51.
11. Letter, Carl Maria von Weber to Caroline Brandt, 5-6 August 1814, Carl-Maria-von-Weber-Gesamtausgabe. Digitale Edition, http://weber-gesamtausgabe.de/A040702 (Version 4.0.0 vom 20. January 2020).
12. Deborah Hertz, *Jewish High Society in Old Regime Berlin* (New York: Syracuse University Press, 2005), p.7.
13. *Louis Spohr's Autobiography* (London: Longman and Green, 1865), vol. 1, p.80.
14. Giacomo Meyerbeer, *Briefwechsel und Tagebücher*, Heinz Becker, Gudrun Becker and Sabine Henze-Döhring (eds) (Berlin: Walter de Gruyter, 1960-2006), vol. 1, p.77.
15. The actor Jens Harzer has held the ring since 2019.
16. Meyerbeer, *Briefwechsel und Tagebücher*, vol. 1, p.185.
17. Friedrich Wilhelm Gubitz, *Erlebnisse, nach Erinnerungen und Aufzeichnungen* (Berlin, 1868), vol. 1, pp.139-40.
18. Friedrich Wilhelm Gubitz (1786-1870) became a member of the Akademie der Künste in Berlin in 1805, and Professor in 1812. He published several periodicals, including *Der Gesellschafter* (1817-48), *Das Jahrbuch der deutschen Bühnenspiele* (1822-65) and the *Deutscher Volkskalender* (1835-69). He also wrote plays and poems and published various essays.
19. Gubitz, *Erlebnisse*, vol. 1, p.139.
20. Friedrich Delbrück, *Die Jugend des Königs Friedrich Wilhelm IV von Preussen und des Kaisers und Königs Wilhelm I* (Berlin: A. Hofmann & Comp., 1907), p.354.

# 5

## The Budding Genius

The Prussian people's joy at the return of their King and Queen did not last for long. The next year, in July 1810, the country was plunged into mourning following the premature death of Queen Louise from a chest infection, at the age of 34. The Queen had been an unusual woman, as well as a beautiful one. Behind the scenes, she had exercised a powerful influence on Prussian politics, demonstrating clearer sight and a great deal more resolution than her vacillating husband.

In the lead-up to the events of 1806, Louise had been the focal point of a 'war party', a group of senior politicians who had advocated early and pre-emptive action against Napoleon. Her circle had included some of the greatest statesmen – and reformers – of the day, such as Count Karl vom Stein and Prince Karl August von Hardenberg. In the Queen's opinion, Prussia had 'fallen asleep on the laurels of Frederick the Great', and needed to be woken up. In April 1806, six months before the battles of Jena and Auerstedt, she had written impatiently to her husband, 'The more people give in to him [Napoleon], the more he despises them for their stupidity. In my opinion the only thing to do is to use force against force: we have a good ally [the Russian Tsar], let us use him!'[1]

Napoleon, who disapproved of women interfering in politics, and believed them fit only for the kitchen and the bedroom, detested Louise. He referred to her derisively as 'the only man in Prussia', and 'my beautiful enemy', and ordered his newspapers to vilify her as a bloodthirsty and stupid harridan. In Prussia, the Queen's youth and beauty, combined with her patriotism, which culminated in an unsuccessful attempt to intercede personally with Napoleon during the 1807 summit in Tilsit, made her a national idol. She had been the first queen in Prussian history to become a public personality in her own right, and she was widely mourned. Amalia Beer remarked thoughtfully that the Queen's death was 'a great misfortune, and people are afraid that it will have damaging consequences'.[2]

For the Beers, the return of peace brought a family break-up that was no less painful for being inevitable. In April 1810, the two eldest boys, Giacomo and Heinrich, left home for Darmstadt, over 250 miles away from

Berlin, in the southern part of the Rhineland. Nineteen-year-old Giacomo had been accepted as a pupil by the Abbé Georg Joseph Vogler,[3] a well-known music theorist and composer. Although the Beers had initially envisaged a career as a pianist for their eldest son, he had been composing since 1803, and since 1807 had been making great strides in dramatic composition, under the tuition of the court music director Bernhard Anselm Weber.

Amalia and Jacob had taken a good deal of pride in the staging of a pastoral ballet, *Der Fischer und das Milchmädchen* [The Fisherman and the Milkmaid], created by the Berlin-based French choreographer Étienne Lauchery to music composed by their son. The ballet had been premiered at the National Theatre under the auspices of Bernhard Weber, just before Giacomo had left home, and had received good reviews in the local papers, although it had lasted no more than four performances.

Almost certainly, the Beers' social prominence and wealth had helped to obtain this commission for their inexperienced son, and Amalia was keen to pass on every crumb of praise to Giacomo, telling him that, 'Your ballet went very well and is very popular, even Zelter said to me that it seems that Meyer [Giacomo] has written a very good ballet – he hasn't seen it yet, as he has something on his foot, but he says, Meyer has taste … tell him in my name he should just work hard.'[4]

Bernhard Weber had himself been a pupil of the Abbé Vogler, and had strongly advised the Beers to send their son to him. Vogler was considered to be a bit of an eccentric. Ordained as a Catholic priest, he was a skilled organist and builder of organs, and also a highly original and inventive musician and theorist. He had travelled to areas considered at the time to be utterly remote, including Armenia, Africa, Asia, and even Greenland, collecting folk songs and national melodies, which he used in his compositions.

Vogler's experimental approach and colourful character had led some, including Mozart, to regard him as a charlatan, but he was a respected teacher, who inspired great affection in his pupils. Jacob and Amalia were already acquainted with the Abbé, as he had stayed with the Beer family while on a concert tour of Berlin in 1800, when he had been impressed by the musical talent of the 9-year-old Giacomo.

It had been Amalia's idea to send Heinrich (known as Hans in the family) to Darmstadt as a companion for his elder brother, as she felt it would do him good to spend some time away from home. Heinrich had already begun to show signs of the instability that would dog his later years. He was careless with money, and he had a tendency to erratic behaviour:

'Remind him', Jacob instructed Giacomo, 'that he is now 17 years old, and that it is high time that people should be able to rely on him.'[5] The boys would not be going to Darmstadt alone, however: they would, of course take at least one servant with them, but they would also be accompanied by their tutor, Aaron Wolfssohn.

Wolfssohn, who was Jacob's cousin,[6] had been hired in 1807 as house tutor to Giacomo and Heinrich. He was a prominent member of the Jewish Enlightenment movement (known as the *Haskala*), and from 1792 had been a teacher at a progressive Jewish school in Breslau, where he later became the headmaster. In 1804 he was given the honorary title of professor. He was also a founding member of the *Gesellschaft der Freunde* [The Society of Friends], an association of forward-thinking young Jewish men, which both Giacomo and Jacob were to join, almost certainly under Wolfssohn's influence.

Taking a post as a tutor in a wealthy family with an enlightened outlook was one of the few ways liberal young Jewish men like Wolfssohn could support themselves. It was difficult for them to make a living in the traditional Jewish community, where their modernising views were disapproved of, while as Jews they were barred from professional positions in the Christian community. The families who employed them also benefitted from the arrangement, as their children gained a broader education than they would from the community teachers, who were often Polish Jews with a very limited or, indeed, non-existent, knowledge of any subjects outside the traditional religious curriculum of Torah and Talmud.

It is not clear exactly which subjects Wolfssohn taught the boys, but it is likely that he would have supervised the religious side of their education, ensuring that they grew up with a thorough, but enlightened and modern, understanding of their faith. He was close to both of them, and became a mentor and friend to young Giacomo in particular. He was also, in effect, one of Giacomo's earliest librettists, as he wrote the text for two cantatas, the first dedicated to Amalia on her birthday in 1809, the second composed for Jacob's birthday in 1811. When Wolfssohn left the Beers, the family gave him an annual pension for the rest of his life.

Amalia placed a good deal of confidence in Wolfssohn's ability to manage the troublesome Heinrich, telling 'the professor', as she called him, that, 'I am completely convinced that [Heinrich's] going with you is for his own good. How could it be otherwise, since he is entrusted to your discretion and management? May God strengthen Hans's good will and your patience, and then everything will go well.'[7]

The two young men and their tutor set out on 1 April on the first leg of the journey, which would take them to Magdeburg. On 16 April, the local Darmstadt newspaper reported that the two Beer boys from Berlin had arrived, and were staying at the 'Bunch of Grapes' inn in the town. By the end of the month they had moved into their quarters at the Abbé Vogler's house at No. 4, Birngarten.[8]

The Beers were a close-knit family, and they felt the absence of the two elder boys keenly. Amalia began writing to them almost as soon as their carriage was out of sight. For the first few weeks following their departure, she lived in daily expectation of letters from Darmstadt, tormented by what she described as her 'well-known anxiety' when she had not heard from them for several days. The house felt empty without them, she told Giacomo and Heinrich, and her only comfort was in hearing all the details of their new life: 'Your letters are my only respite, I feel like someone abandoned, ten times a day I start to call for Meyer and Hans.'

Ten-year-old Michael was hardly less affected. After the carriage carrying his brothers away to Darmstadt had left, Michael was inconsolable: he cried so violently and for so long, that he became ill with a fever and headache. According to 13-year-old Wilhelm, even the family dog was in mourning following the boys' departure.[9]

After the first few weeks, Amalia became calmer. Letters from her sons, though never frequent enough for her liking, relieved her fears to some extent. Vogler, who had quickly become 'Papa' to the boys, had written to put her mind at rest and assure her that Giacomo – the 'budding genius' as he put it – was settling down well to his studies. Amalia's friends rallied round to try and provide some distraction. August Iffland, the composer Johann Reichardt, and Giacomo's former tutor Bernhard Weber all visited her in the first days after the boys' departure. Charlotte von Bischoffswerder came every day for several weeks, to ensure that her friend was not left alone to brood for too long, showing a thoughtfulness that earned Amalia's gratitude: 'I realise more and more every day what a true friend she is to me.'[10]

By mid-June 1810, around two months after the boys had left home, Amalia had recovered enough in health and spirits to travel to the seaside spa town of Bad Doberan for a rest cure. She took Michael with her, along with his tutor Eduard Kley, a former pupil of Wolfssohn's, whom the Beers had hired the previous year. Visiting spas, for both health and social reasons, was an important part of life in the eighteenth and nineteenth centuries. The causes of disease were not fully understood, and taking 'cures' was thought to help maintain the body's balance, and contribute to preventing, as well as treating, illness. In England, the waters of Bath and Harrogate were well known for their curative properties, while Europeans flocked to drink the waters of Carlsbad, Baden-Baden and Bad Pyrmont.

Sea-bathing was a new fashion. It had started in England, where resorts had sprung up to cater for an aristocratic clientele. King George III and the Prince of Wales (who was shortly to become Regent) both patronised the seaside, the King favouring Weymouth, while the Prince preferred the more louche attractions of Brighton. The Beer family were firm believers in the health benefits of spas. Amalia favoured sea-bathing; in later life, when she travelled further afield, she often patronised coastal resorts such as Genoa, Livorno and Boulogne, whereas Jacob preferred the inland Bohemian watering place of Carlsbad, where he went every summer in the hope of reducing his ever-increasing girth.

Bad Doberan, Germany's first seaside resort, was situated on the Baltic coast near Rostock, about 150 miles north-east of Berlin, a three-day journey by coach. Like all spa towns, it offered a lively social programme, centred on the pump room, the salon, and the pavilion buildings, which had been designed to house theatrical and musical performances, dancing and restaurants. However, Michael's tutor was unimpressed with the entertainment on offer at Bad Doberan that summer season. Kley described a ball he had attended as pitiful, adding that the performances at the theatre were so bad that he would probably not go again.[11]

If the social life at the spa was disappointing, its curative properties nevertheless had a beneficial effect on Amalia. She had been suffering from fainting fits and muscle spasms for some time, and bathing in the sea appeared to help relieve these symptoms. Nearly a year after the trip, in April 1811, she remarked to Aaron Wolfssohn that she had not had one of these attacks since the previous summer.[12] It is possible that the symptoms were caused by the stress of the war and the family break-up, but Amalia undoubtedly benefited from the exercise, sea air, and the break from the daily routine of city life in Berlin.

The Abbé Vogler's reassurances that the boys were settling down well in Darmstadt no doubt also contributed to Amalia's improvement in health. The Abbé's pupils were a very lively group. Several of them, including Giacomo and his friends Carl Maria von Weber and Johann Gänsbacher, formed a private musical society, the *Harmonischer Verein* [Harmonic Society], to help promote their careers. This promotion included writing favourable (and anonymous) reviews for newspapers and journals, praising each other's early productions. The letters between them are full of exuberance and youthful confidence.

Giacomo's letters reveal that he already had a good grasp of the importance of what today we would call public relations. This would stand him in good stead in his future career. He and his fellow students were living through an age of change. The old patronage system, in which musicians served the courts, the aristocracy and the Church, was gradually giving way to a professionalisation of music, as the demands of an emerging bourgeois audience allowed musicians to develop careers on a more commercial basis. Giacomo was learning more than just the technicalities of his art at Darmstadt.

Although Amalia might have been relieved that Giacomo had settled happily into his training, her hopes for Heinrich's new start were doomed to disappointment. He had not been in Darmstadt for long before he became embroiled in a love affair with Vogler's cook, a young woman called Eva. Heinrich had written indiscreet letters to Eva, possibly promising marriage, and the Beers were afraid that she was intending to use these compromising letters to blackmail them. The episode culminated in the successful retrieval of the letters and the dismissal of Eva from Vogler's service. The lovelorn Heinrich was removed from Darmstadt and sent to Bamberg, under Wolfssohn's supervision, to get over the affair.

Giacomo had taken some of the responsibility for dealing with Heinrich's indiscretion, consulting with his father and Wolfssohn on how to retrieve his brother's letters. Amalia had also begun to turn to her eldest son for support in difficult times. The Beers had more than enough to worry them in 1810. Napoleon's continental system, designed to isolate England from the rest of Europe, was beginning to seriously disrupt Prussian trade. The imposition in August that year of a significant increase in taxation on imported colonial goods, including sugar, had a damaging effect on Jacob's refinery business. Eduard Kley reported to Giacomo later that year that 'the talk in the house is mostly of sugar and the new tax'.[13]

In November 1810, Napoleon's Fontainebleu decree ordered the confiscation and burning of all stocks of prohibited goods. Amalia told Giacomo that 'we are living in a state of confusion and turmoil that is beyond anything; you can imagine how unpleasant it is for Grandfather, as he has a good deal of stock'. She asked for Giacomo's help in calming Jacob, as she was at her wit's end over the state he had worked himself into, and was afraid that his health would be seriously affected: 'Father's anxiety is beyond imagining, I don't know what to do with him anymore. If you write to him, try to comfort him, and tell him he mustn't take this business so much to heart, it's affecting the whole world, so all isn't lost, but he thinks sales are finished, and he has all his money in sugar'.[14]

Giacomo evidently did his best, as Jacob wrote to him in early December to say that he had followed his son's advice to 'put the continental system out of my mind'. He added, 'I can assure you that I have quite calmed down, you can't buy health for any amount of money ... My factory is open now, although there are no sales as the situation is too tense, but it will right itself in time, you go on studying as before and don't you think about it either.'[15]

Despite Jacob's reassurances to his son, wartime restrictions continued to hamper his businesses. In 1811, a cargo of sugar from his refinery was impounded in Saxony, and on another occasion a ship coming from America, which had coffee, tobacco and cotton belonging to Jacob on board, was seized in Copenhagen, and held until a loophole was found in the regulations that allowed it to be released.[16]

Of course, Amalia was right in saying that everyone was feeling the effects of the wars and the blockade. Moses Mendelssohn's sons, Abraham and Joseph, who had founded a bank in Hamburg, became involved in smuggling – like many others – in an effort to try and get round the problems. In January 1812, when a new French governor arrived in the city and their activities became known to him, these respectable bankers and their families, including Abraham's children Fanny and Felix, had to flee Hamburg in the middle of the night to escape arrest.

During the time that Giacomo was in Darmstadt, his relationship with his parents was naturally changing. He was 19 when he left home, a young man on the threshold of independence, and like all young men, he occasionally found his parents extremely embarrassing. Their eager desire to be involved in every detail of his life seemed to him at times like interference. Nothing in the world was more important to Amalia and Jacob than their sons. They hoped, dreamed, schemed and intrigued on their behalf. Certainly some of the Beers' 'house friends' were welcome primarily for their potential usefulness as promoters of the boys' careers – or to avert any possible harm to the boys' prospects.

In Amalia's letters to her son, she gives free rein to her distrust of, and on occasions contempt for, the people she cultivated and flattered for his sake. Writing to Giacomo shortly after he had left home, she told him that she had introduced 'that ass' Bernhard Weber to Countess von Voss, chief lady-in-waiting at the court of Berlin, a significant figure in royal and aristocratic circles, and that this favour had thrown Weber into transports of delight.[17]

In January 1811, Amalia warned Giacomo that Weber was upset at being treated negligently by him, and that he must be more careful. For her

part, she said, she simply could not stand Weber any more, and her door
would have been closed to him long ago if she had not kept it open for
Giacomo's sake. She advised him to follow her example, warning him that
Weber could do him a great deal of harm if he felt slighted. She did not
seem to think any more highly of Giacomo's old piano tutor, Lauska,
advising Giacomo, when reminding him of Lauska's birthday, that 'you must
treat him as you do all these dogs'.[18]

Giacomo had become a sensitive, introspective and intense young
man, a worrier who reacted strongly to slights, real or imagined. He had
grown up knowing that he was 'different'. As a young man visiting
Augsburg in 1812, he recorded in his diary a hurtful incident where he
was apparently subjected to hostility from complete strangers at an inn:
'Some lovely young women there wounded me to the depths of my soul,
and affected my spirits and cheerfulness for the entire day. When will I
finally learn to accept peacefully what is inevitable, as I have known for so
long?'[19] What Giacomo felt to be inevitable was that as a Jew he could
expect to experience rejection and slights, mockery and hatred, through
no fault of his own.

He was not good at keeping in touch with his family and friends, and
his mother was constantly reminding him to include messages in his letters
for people she felt he could not afford to offend. Amalia wavered between
treating him as an adult, relying on him for support and advice, and treating
him as if he were still a child, making arrangements for him without his
knowledge, consulting others on his welfare, and boasting of his triumphs
to her captive audience at her salon. It is undoubtedly the case that it was
his parents' wealth and influence which facilitated the production of
Giacomo's earliest works. On 8 May 1811 his oratorio *Gott und die Natur*
[God and Nature] was premiered at Berlin's Royal National Theatre under
Bernhard Weber's direction, and in the presence of Prince George of Hesse-
Darmstadt.

The oratorio had been previewed by a select, but influential, circle at
Amalia's salon a week or so before this production. Thirty guests – a 'small
gathering' according to Amalia – including the Director of the National
Theatre, August Iffland, had been present to hear the tenor Friedrich
Eunike and the Opera chorus sing excerpts. Amalia was anxious to reassure
her nerve-ridden and pessimistic son that he really was popular with the
Berliners:

> … as soon as I walk in any door I am immediately overwhelmed with
> questions as to what my dear son is doing, whether we can hope to

see him soon. So many people burst into such paeans of praise that I am quite embarrassed, your health is drunk at almost every table … on my word of honour, few people have the luck to be so admired by the public at your age.

According to Amalia, when the tenor Eunike had been congratulated on singing his aria like an angel, he had replied that if he had done so, it was because 'it had been written by a god'. [20] This anecdote clearly pleased Giacomo, as he repeated it to his friend Gottfried Weber in a letter later that month, only changing the ending to a slightly more modest version in which Eunike had replied that the music had come from heaven. [21]

Amalia's musical evenings were becoming larger and more formal, and despite Jacob's business worries, in the spring of 1811 he had the reception rooms in the Spandauer Strasse house extended and refurbished to accommodate them. Two rooms, at least, were knocked into one, creating a space large enough for an orchestra and a substantial audience. The work on the rooms was completed towards the end of May, and Amalia decided to inaugurate the new salon on 29 May with a surprise party for Jacob's 42nd birthday.

She kept the plans a secret from him, and encouraged him to go to the theatre with a friend for the evening, telling him that she was going to take tea with Charlotte Bischoffswerder. On his return later in the evening, Jacob was astonished to find the house lit up and filled with 100 guests, ready to hear a special performance of Giacomo's music, performed by a sixty-strong orchestra and singers conducted by the faithful Bernhard Weber. The soloists included Friedrich Eunike and the soprano Amalie Schmalz, both stars of the Royal Opera.

Jacob was delighted with the birthday surprise – and equally thrilled at the success of the new salon. He reported to Giacomo that all the musicians had told him that there was no other room in Berlin so suited to musical performances:

> Everything went splendidly, and I am now really pleased to have built this new salon, as the music sounds quite incomparable in it. I also think that the music is so clear and distinct because [the hall] is made of wood, and even better, of pine … it's also very high, and the whole is about 86 feet in length.

This successful surprise party went on until 3 o' clock in the morning, delighting the proud father: 'Your health was drunk again and again to the accompaniment of trumpets and drums, and I had only one wish left to me – to have my beloved son there with me.'[22]

Giacomo must have been flattered, but the circle of 'house friends' mobilised by Amalia in support of her son were at times a source of irritation to him. Her frequent requests for him to set poems written by her intimates to music were intended to enhance Giacomo's reputation in Berlin musical circles as well as to please her friends, but were not always appreciated by her son. Amalia's enthusiasm for her young friend Friedrich Gubitz's occasional poems was a particular annoyance. It was customary at the time for family and friends to compose amateur verses for birthdays and other celebrations, and Gubitz never appeared at any party without a *Festgedicht*, or festive poem, written for the occasion. The actress Karoline Bauer called him the 'most tireless' of occasional poets.

In the eyes of the youthful composer these effusions were worthless in artistic terms. Giacomo complained to his confidante, Professor Wolfssohn, that to please his mother he had wasted a great deal of time on 'ploughing the sterile field of [Gubitz's] poetry in the sweat of my brow'.[23] Although he was only at the beginning of his career, Giacomo already understood the serious nature of his calling, and was reluctant to fritter his talent away. It was a foretaste of the integrity and the unwillingness to compromise that would characterise his later career.

Giacomo was also upset by his mother's interference, however well-meaning, in plans for performances of his music. He was horrified to discover that Amalia had hatched a plot with Vogler, without his knowledge, for a concert of his works to be given in Darmstadt for the benefit of the poor. Vogler informed Giacomo that they had agreed that Amalia would pay for the concert, and that he, Vogler, would persuade the Grand Duke not only to give permission for it to take place, but also to bestow 'a little trinket' on Giacomo, that he could show off to people in Berlin.

Giacomo, incandescent with rage, wrote angrily to Aaron Wolfssohn:

> A thunderbolt could not have struck me any harder than these words. This (I really cannot call it anything else) deceitfulness of my mother, who could not entrust her wish to me personally, but conveyed it to Vogler ... so that I would be caught unawares by Vogler's authority, which has upset me all the more, as Mother ... must have known that I would carry out her wishes voluntarily, without having to be persuaded, provided they clashed only with my inclination, and were not harmful to my artistic integrity.[24]

He refused to agree to the concert, on the grounds that charitable concerts were not popular with the public in Darmstadt, and that the consequent low attendance and poor takings would neither add to his standing as a musician nor result in any real benefit for the poor.

However, despite his irritation, he understood that his mother was trying to do her best for him. He finished his letter to Wolfssohn in a resigned tone, saying that he knew what his mother's response would be: that no matter how the public behaved towards others, he was different; they would make an exception for him. '*L'amour*', he concluded, '*est toujours aveugle*' – love is always blind. He had written an angry twelve-page letter to Amalia, but had, perhaps wisely, torn it up, waited until he had calmed down, and then written another, more reasoned letter explaining his grounds for refusing the request.

Amalia's eagerness to promote Giacomo's interests also led her to involve herself in the negotiations for the staging of his first opera, with unfortunate consequences. In October 1811 Giacomo was finishing this work, *Jephtas Gelübde* [Jephtha's Vow], which was based on a Biblical story. The choice of location for the premiere would be crucial. Berlin, where Giacomo was already well known, was the obvious place, but Vogler was astonished and not at all pleased to discover that Amalia had already given the libretto, written by Aloys Schreiber, a minor author and professor at Heidelberg University, to her great friend Iffland to read, without Vogler's knowledge. As both Vogler and Amalia knew, this was a move that could make or break the fate of the opera in Berlin. Earlier that year, Iffland had been appointed general director of all the royal theatres, and as a result was now responsible for the Royal Opera as well as the National Theatre.

The libretto of *Jephta* had not been to Iffland's taste, however, and the Berlin door was now closed. 'But my dear, my best of friends!' wrote Vogler to Amalia, '…Have I recently lost your respect and your trust, that you hid from me the idea to let Iffland see it?' He added that the only path left open to them was to stage the opera in Munich – which would entail 'additional costs' to the Beers. These costs were presumably the expenses involved in arranging the debut of a young and inexperienced composer in a major city where he was not known.[25]

This comment did nothing to dispel the Beers' growing suspicion that Vogler's interest in continuing to supervise Giacomo's musical career might have been financially motivated. Jacob certainly seems to have been uneasy about Vogler's influence over Giacomo, telling his son that 'it appears that this Vogler has fooled you so much that you can't part from him at all. He is, and always will be, an arch-swindler.'[26]

Both Jacob and Amalia had a tendency to be jealous of people they perceived as rivals for their sons' affections, and their behaviour occasionally revealed a fear that the boys would reject their parents altogether as they grew older and more successful. The Beers had planned a trip to Darmstadt in May 1811 to visit their sons, but Giacomo's response had given his father the strong impression that he did not want his parents there.[27] In a later letter, Amalia told Giacomo that, 'If you gave poor Father the nod, he would come straight away, but he always thinks he embarrasses you.'[28]

By April 1812, Giacomo was in Munich with the Abbé Vogler, preparing for the premiere of *Jephtas Gelübde*, which had been delayed by a month, so that the libretto – and therefore some of the music – could be re-written on Iffland's advice. Giacomo had arrived in the Bavarian capital armed with an impressive array of letters of introduction to the court that his parents had procured for him. Count von Hatzfeld, the son-in-law of Liepmann Meyer Wulff's sponsor Count Schulenburg-Kehnert, had provided letters of recommendation to Grand Duchess Stéphanie of Baden, Napoleon's adopted daughter. Charlotte von Bischoffswerder had arranged access to the Bavarian King's adjutant general, and the Berlin court had authorised an introduction to the Prussian ambassador in Munich.

*Jephtas Gelübde* was finally premiered at the Munich Court Opera on 23 December 1812. Like many early works, it was not a great success, but it was a significant watershed in Giacomo's professional life, marking the end of his apprenticeship with the Abbé Vogler.

## Notes

1.  Frank Bauer, *Napoleon in Berlin. Preussens Hauptstadt unter Französischer Besatzung 1806-1808* (Berlin: Berlin Story Verlag, 2006), p.20.
2.  Giacomo Meyerbeer, *Briefwechsel und Tagebücher*, Heinz Becker, Gudrun Becker and Sabine Henze-Döhring (eds) (Berlin: Walter de Gruyter, 1960-2006), vol. 1, p.71.
3.  Georg Joseph Vogler, also known as the Abbé Vogler (1749-1814), was a German composer, organist, teacher and theorist, and also a Catholic priest. He invented a new system of fingering for the harpsichord, a new form of construction for the organ, and a new system of musical theory. He ran three schools, in Mannheim, Stockholm and lastly in Darmstadt.
4.  Meyerbeer, *Briefwechsel und Tagebücher*, vol. 1, p.62.
5.  Ibid., p.82.
6.  Jacob's mother, Jente, was Wolfssohn's father's sister. Noted in https://www.uni-potsdam.de/de/haskala/haskala-in-biographien/halle-wolfsohn.html (Potsdam University); see also Jutta Strauss, 'Aaron Halle-Wolfssohn, ein Leben in drei Sprachen' in Gerhard Anselm (ed.), *Musik und Ästhetik im Berlin Moses Mendelssohns* (Tübingen: Niemayer, 1999), p.62.

7. Unpublished letter, Amalia Beer to Aaron Wolfssohn, 08 May 1810; Leopold Stein Collection; AR3263; Box 1; Folder 7; Leo Baeck Insitute. Courtesy of Leo Baeck Institute.
8. Meyerbeer, *Briefwechsel und Tagebücher*, vol. 1, pp.53-4.
9. Ibid., pp.61, 64, 57, 58.
10. Ibid., p.59.
11. Ibid., pp.72-3.
12. Unpublished letter, Amalia Beer to Aaron Wolfssohn, 20 April 1811, University of Virginia, Albert and Shirley Small Special Collections Library, Miscellaneous papers (manuscripts), 1811, 1914.
13. Meyerbeer, *Briefwechsel und Tagebücher*, vol. 1, p.78.
14. Ibid., p.79.
15. Ibid., p.82.
16. Sven Kuhrau and Kurt Winkler (eds), *Juden Bürger Berliner. Das Gedächtnis der Familie Beer–Meyerbeer–Richter* (Berlin: Henschel Verlag, 2004), pp.68-70.
17. Meyerbeer, *Briefwechsel und Tagebücher*, vol. 1, p.67.
18. Ibid., p.85.
19. Ibid., pp.164-5.
20. Ibid., p.96.
21. Ibid., p.108.
22. Ibid., p.113.
23. Ibid., p.233.
24. Ibid., pp.125-6.
25. Ibid., p.130.
26. Ibid., p.87.
27. Ibid., p.105.
28. Ibid., p.384.

# 6

## Prussian Patriots

In the summer of 1812, Liepmann Meyer Wulff was taken seriously ill. He died on 16 August at the age of 66. Giacomo, who had been travelling in Austria during a break in the rehearsals for the premiere of *Jephta*, did not hear the news until his return to Munich on 29 August: 'I learnt the terrible news that my poor grandfather had died on 16 August after long suffering. God! My poor mother! I fear for her health.' Amalia had been helping her mother to nurse Liepmann, and was distraught at his death. Giacomo wrote to her begging her to look after herself:

> My dear, beloved mother, please bear in mind that the acute pain we all suffer could be intensified to the point of madness if your own health were to suffer under this grief. At least try to avoid vivid memories, and accept willingly any remedies that can dull the pangs; I beg you with tears in my eyes to do this.[1]

At the time of his death, Liepmann Meyer Wulff was still an extremely wealthy man, despite the economic difficulties of the occupation and its aftermath. Over the previous six years, he had been involved in arranging loans to state, provincial and city institutions hard pressed to find the money for the huge war indemnities demanded by Napoleon. He had also made private loans to social institutions such as the poorhouse, the hospital, and the new National Theatre.

In his will,[2] Liepmann had left his fortune to his grandchildren, with the proviso that his wife Esther and their four daughters would each receive an income from the interest on this money during their lifetimes. His four sons-in-law were entitled only to the relatively small sum of 15,000 thalers each, the amount of their wives' dowries. Liepmann's intention in leaving his fortune in this way was to protect his daughters from any reverses that their husbands might experience in their business affairs.

Esther Wulff retained the right to live in the grand house in Königstrasse, but after her death, it was to pass to Giacomo, on the condition that he kept the home synagogue open, and paid for the upkeep of six young Talmudic students. Giacomo agreed to these terms, and remarkably, the synagogue continued in existence up until the Second World War, although its location changed several times over the years. Liepmann had also been known in the Jewish community as 'Liepmann (or Lippman) Tauss' or sometimes 'Taussk', after the town in Bohemia where his family had originated. His synagogue became known as the 'Lippmann Tauss Synagogue'. Its last rabbi, Felix Singermann, who was murdered by the Nazis in 1942, left a short account of the synagogue's history, from its foundation around the year 1776, up to the 1920s.[3]

Liepmann was buried in the old Jewish cemetery in Grosser Hamburgerstrasse. His choice of burial place demonstrated the deep respect in which he held traditional learning, as he had paid a large sum to purchase a plot beside the tomb of Wolff Salomon, a Talmudic scholar and rabbi who he admired.[4] Today there is no trace of Liepmann's grave. The Hamburgerstrasse cemetery was completely destroyed by the Nazis in the Second World War, and all that remains is Rabbi Singermann's record, in his small history of the Lippmann Tauss synagogue, of the inscription on Liepmann's tombstone: 'Uri Lippmann ben Meir Halevi Taussk'[5] – Uri Lippmann, son of Meyer, descended from the tribe of the Levites, whose family originated from the town of Taus in Bohemia.

Liepmann's death had come just five months after the promulgation of the Edict of Emancipation of the Prussian Jews, which was announced in March 1812. The struggle for equal rights, which had dragged on for more than two decades since Frederick the Great's death in 1786, had been given renewed momentum by the shock of Prussia's defeat, and the subsequent collapse of the government. In the aftermath of the disaster, a group of liberal politicians, led by Count Karl vom Stein, had begun to implement a far-reaching programme of modernisation, aimed at replacing Prussia's antiquated feudal system with a society of citizens who were equal before the law. Achieving this ambitious goal would require, amongst other measures, liberating the peasants from serfdom, breaking the power of the guilds, which still controlled access to trades and crafts, and creating a free market in land, which, in theory at least, could only be owned by the nobility.

The question of the emancipation of the Jews became part of this broader programme of creating a more equal society. The first step towards the attainment of Jewish civil rights came from Minister vom Stein's reorganisation of Berlin's municipal government in 1808. Under Stein's new law, Berlin residents' rights to vote representatives onto the city council were to be determined by property and income, rather than by birth into a certain class.

As a consequence, a number of wealthier Jews were now qualified to vote in municipal elections, and, in order to do so, they were required to register as citizens. Jacob Beer and Liepmann Meyer Wulff had been among the first Jews to take the oath as citizens of Berlin in 1809. Liepmann was allowed to register in his own home, rather than in the city Rathaus, as was usual, because of his failing health.[6] Following the first elections under the new laws, David Friedländer, who for many years had been a leader in the campaign for equal rights, became the first Jew to be voted onto the Berlin city council. It was an enormous step forward.

Four years after Stein's law came into force, Baron Karl August von Hardenberg, who had been given the newly created post of Chancellor in 1810, formulated the Edict of Emancipation, which finally granted the Jews the right of citizenship of the Prussian State. On 11 March 1812, all Jews entitled to reside in Prussia were declared native inhabitants and citizens. The special taxes, marriage regulations and occupational restrictions were abolished, although the question of whether Jews would be allowed to occupy state posts was left unresolved, and discussion on the matter deferred to a later, unspecified date.

The Jews were made subject to military service, and were required to take surnames, if they had not done so already, and to keep all official records in German, rather than in Yiddish. The Edict was greeted with euphoria in the progressive circles of the Jewish community. The Jewish journal *Sulamith* reproduced the text in its entirety, commenting that: 'We can now rightly expect that the Israelites of the Kingdom of Prussia will always and everywhere show themselves worthy of the benevolence of our gracious King.'[7]

Liepmann had lived just long enough to see Jewish emancipation, but he did not survive to see Prussia finally freed from French domination. The Emancipation Edict had come at a time of growing tension in the European political situation. In 1810, Russia had begun trading with Britain in defiance of the continental system that Napoleon had imposed on mainland Europe. Napoleon had responded to this provocation by taking the ultimately disastrous decision to launch an invasion of Russia. The French army's route eastwards would lie through Prussia.

On 5 March 1812, a week before the promulgation of the Jewish Emancipation Edict, Frederick William III had signed the Treaty of Paris with Napoleon, which allowed the French army safe passage through Prussia, and guaranteed the provision of a Prussian corps of over 20,000 men in support of the invasion. A month later, the *Grand Armée* marched confidently through East Prussia, on its way to teach the Tsar of all the Russias a lesson.

However, as the French penetrated deeper into Russian territory, it became clear that Napoleon had overreached himself, and that the tide was beginning to turn against him. In late autumn, news began to filter back to Berlin of the burning of Moscow and the retreat of the French. By the time winter had set in, the retreat had become a rout, and the French troops and their allies, struggling through the frozen Russian terrain and harassed by partisan forces, were in a desperate situation.

The Berliners' hopes of freeing themselves from French domination rose, and popular support for an uprising began to spread. Frederick William was characteristically hesitant, but in the end his hand was forced by one of his own senior military officers, General Johann Ludwig Yorck von Wartenburg, commander of the Prussian forces under the French.

In December 1812, Prussia was still allied with France under the terms of the Treaty of Paris. General Yorck was tasked with covering the French retreat by holding off the advance of the Russian troops into East Prussia. But on 30 December, he detached his troops from the French army and signed a truce with the Russians, without a mandate from his King to do so, creating what amounted to an unauthorised change of alliance. It was an astonishing move for an otherwise loyal military man, and Yorck was taking a huge risk. Despite public acclaim of this initiative, he was accused of treason and threatened with court-martial.

The situation was tense, and Yorck's fate hung in the balance as a badly shaken Frederick William tried to negotiate with Napoleon, going so far as to propose a marriage between a Prussian prince and a member of the Bonaparte family. The tension grew as Yorck's action precipitated an uprising in East Prussia, which began arming itself for rebellion against the French. By February 1813, the situation was moving towards breaking point: Napoleon had failed to respond to Frederick William's increasingly desperate overtures; the Prussian people were clamouring for a declaration of war against the French; while the Russian 1st Army Corps, with Count Pyotr Wittgenstein at its head, was approaching the gates of Berlin.

The sense of crisis was heightened by the withdrawal of Frederick William, and almost the whole of the Prussian court, to Breslau in the province of Silesia. There had been reports circulating in Berlin that the French were plotting to take the Prussian King hostage, and, although these rumours remained unsubstantiated, the ever-cautious Frederick William had taken them seriously enough to remove himself and his headquarters to a safe distance from the capital.

On 20 February, a rumour swept Berlin that the Russians were about to enter the city. Lines of Russian troops could be seen moving through the outlying area of Pankow, threading their way past the Schönhauser windmills. The French soldiers still stationed in Berlin appeared to be making preparations for defence, dragging their cannons and gunpowder wagons into the Lustgarten, in front of the old Royal Palace. It began to look as if the city might become the scene of a major battle. Berlin was under siege; in the first few days, the city gates were closed to all traffic. They were not opened even to take the dead to the cemeteries outside the city limits, and coffins piled up by the walls.

The Berliners were by now awaiting the Russians as liberators. Some were so encouraged by the rumours of the imminent arrival of the Russian army that they decided to take direct action themselves, spiking the French cannons and dragging them away from their positions. Tensions ran dangerously high: a butcher's boy became a temporary folk hero by snatching a burning fuse from the hand of a French artilleryman and stamping it out in the gutter.[8] A few days later, however, the fear of a battle being fought out in the city streets receded as the French troops, under the command of Marshal Augereau, withdrew to the fortress of Spandau, at a safe distance of around ten miles from the city.

On 3 March 1813, the Russian army entered Berlin, to the relief and jubilation of its citizens. The first Russians to be seen on the streets of the city were a motley crew of Cossacks, trotting their horses down the Lindenallee. The city was illuminated in the liberators' honour, and the Russian army officers – among them a number of Prussians who had offered their services to the Tsar after the débâcle of 1806 – were entertained with balls and parades. The women of Berlin showed their appreciation by wearing tall turbans of white cloth edged with a red bandeau, called 'Chernyshyov bonnets' after young General Alexander Chernyshyov, commander of the first Russian troops to enter Berlin.

The King had still not issued any definite proclamation, but even he could dither no longer. Public confidence in him was wavering, and there was talk of an uprising in Berlin if he did not declare himself openly against the French. On 17 March 1813, Frederick William concluded a treaty with Russia, and issued his historic proclamation 'To my people', calling on the Prussians to rise up against the French. Prussia was now at war.

General Yorck was exonerated, and made a triumphal entry back into Berlin at the head of his troops that same day. When Yorck and Wittgenstein entered a box at the theatre together the next night, the performance was interrupted by prolonged cheering, and the orchestra spontaneously broke into trumpet fanfares and martial music. The King himself returned to a tumultuous welcome on 24 March.

Earlier that month, as the Russian army had advanced on Berlin, Giacomo had been travelling from Stuttgart to Vienna, following the premiere of his second opera, the comic *Wirth und Gast* [Host and Guest] in Stuttgart. Soon after this production, the Grand Duke of Hesse had appointed Giacomo 'court and chamber composer'. Giacomo had remarked in a letter to his friend Gottfried Weber that this was not a post that would make any heavy demands on him; apparently, the only duty it involved was that of sending a copy of any major work he wrote to the Grand Duke.

Giacomo spent a few days in the Bavarian city of Regensburg, from where he intended to take a boat down the Danube to Vienna. He had heard the news that Berlin was in a state of siege, and was extremely worried about the safety of his parents. He had received no letters from them for some time, as the German postal service had been severely disrupted by the crisis – the Leipzig music journal, the *Allgemeine musikalische Zeitung*, reported in its May 1813 issue that it had received no post at all over the preceding two months.

On 2 March, the day before the Russian entry into Berlin, Giacomo attended a masked ball in Regensburg, noting in his diary that he would have enjoyed it a great deal, 'had I not been tortured with unease about my parents in Berlin. Every day this thought haunts me before sleeping, in my dreams and on waking. If only I were already in Vienna, where I hope to find news.'

On the journey between Regensburg and Vienna the weather deteriorated, and he was confined to his cabin as blizzards pounded the ship. His anxiety mounted to such a degree that he dreamt about his parents. He superstitiously promised himself that if he found letters from home on his arrival 'the first needy person I meet will have 1 fl[orin]'. Landing at the small customs town of Aschach in Austria, he was held up for three days by the stormy weather, noting in his diary that, 'Added to the tedium is my fearful anticipation of news from my parents: this worried me all day.'[9]

The thoughts that he confided to his diary, with their constant concern for his family's welfare, and comments on the days spent alone with uncongenial travelling companions, contrast markedly with an account of the journey that he gave to his Darmstadt friend Gottfried Weber, to whom he boasted in a letter that 'we were assailed by a terrible storm, and had to spend 3 days – yes, *three*, at Aschach in Austria. Out of sheer boredom I seduced a merchant's daughter, a sergeant-major's widow, and an innkeeper's wife.'[10] Whether these three 'lovely creatures' had any existence outside Giacomo's fertile imagination must be debatable.

On arrival in Vienna, Giacomo found his brother Wilhelm waiting for him. Wilhelm, who was lodging at the Red Hedgehog inn, had procured rooms for Giacomo nearby, and was able to bring him up to date with family news. With his anxieties allayed, Giacomo put the war to the back of his mind, and plunged into Vienna's glamorous social life. On his first night, he went to an opera – Weigl's *Der Burgsturz*, now long forgotten – at the Kärntnertor theatre, noting in his diary that he was 'so excited and fascinated by the new house and public' that he could not trust himself to make objective notes about the experience. Indeed, after the first thrilling day in Vienna, he abandoned his diary for a fortnight, distracted by 'invitations, visits to famous composers, looking at the sights and attending the theatre'.[11]

One of the famous composers Giacomo met was Antonio Salieri, Mozart's erstwhile rival, who, at 61 years old, had retired from writing operas, and was occupied with teaching, and composing religious works for the Imperial chapel. Among Salieri's pupils in the later part of his life were Beethoven, Liszt and Schubert. Giacomo described the elderly composer as 'very small, with a fine, sharp face full of satirical wrinkles; his small, flashing eyes, full of movement, are his most striking feature'.[12]

Vienna was an intoxicating city for a young man embarking on a musical career, but beneath the surface of his carefree life, Giacomo knew that he was at a crossroads. As Prussian Jews were no longer excluded from military service, he had to decide how he would respond to the King's call to arms. Prussia's mobilisation on 17 March 1813, coming just a year after the Emancipation Edict of March 1812, had a powerful effect on the State's Jewish communities, whose members took their new responsibilities as citizens very seriously. Volunteers played a vital role in the Wars of Liberation, as the struggle against Napoleonic rule became known in Prussia, and young Jewish men flocked to prove themselves loyal subjects by offering their services to the Prussian army.

Rabbis held services of blessing for Jewish soldiers, and excused them from certain religious observations while on active service. In Berlin, Rabbi Simon Weyl held one of the earliest of these services on 23 March 1813, in which he urged his congregation to respond to their King's call in patriotic tones that could hardly have been bettered by a Christian preacher:

Our pious King does not put his trust in himself or in the strength of his army alone; no! His highest trust is in God, it is from God that he hopes for victory ... Already we can see that God is rewarding this childlike faith by filling the hearts of the tender young with love for their King and Fatherland, with the courage and strength to fear no danger, and to stand voluntarily under the flag of their King![13]

Rabbi Weyl also urged his congregation to support the war effort financially. The Prussian treasury had been catastrophically depleted by the heavy costs of the French occupation, and the State could not afford to equip and feed the thousands of militiamen and volunteers who came forward. People responded enthusiastically, rich and poor giving whatever they could.

The Jewish communities contributed willingly: the Berlin Jews gave 300 thalers from the communal fund, and the Jewish merchants of the city gave 700. The Society of Friends, the association of liberally minded young Jewish men which Giacomo's tutor, Aaron Wolfssohn, had helped to found, gave over 800 thalers. Jewish individuals also gave freely, among them Jacob Beer, who provided the funds to fully equip several cavalry volunteers.

The struggle for liberation against Napoleon was the first conflict to involve the whole Prussian nation. The introduction of conscription, and the call for those not liable for conscription to volunteer for military service, meant that almost every family had a father, brother or son in uniform. The women of Prussia also contributed publicly to a war effort for the first time. The impetus for women to involve themselves in war work had come from the royal princesses. On 23 March 1813, six days after the King had issued his mobilisation address, nine Prussian princesses, under the leadership of 27-year-old Princess Marianne, made their own proclamation: 'All [the men] are streaming to the colours, arming themselves for the bloody struggle for freedom and independence ... but we women must work too to help promote victory, we too must join with our men and boys to save the Fatherland.'[14]

The princesses' initial appeal was for donations of money and valuables to a fund they called the 'Women's Association for the Good of the Fatherland'. The money raised would primarily be used to help equip volunteers who were not able to pay for their own uniforms and weapons. Any money left over would be designated for the care of the wounded. The list of valuables that would be welcome included the sort of jewellery that ordinary people might be expected to own, in particular, gold wedding rings. In return for their wedding ring, donors would receive a specially made iron ring, engraved with the date 1813 and the inscription 'I gave gold for iron'. This proved a popular idea, and the Berliners wore their iron rings with pride. The Berlin newspapers made a regular feature of listing the 'patriotic sacrifices' of money and gold that had been donated that week.

Princess Marianne, the wife of the King's youngest brother, Prince William, had become the leading female member of the Prussian royal family after Queen Louise's death. She donated some of her own jewellery to the appeal, and also personally received many of the women bringing in money or goods, remarking in a letter to her husband, who had gone to join General Blücher's staff in Silesia, that at this rate she 'would soon be acquainted with half Berlin'.[15]

This was the first time that the royal princesses had aligned themselves with ordinary women in a common cause, and, in response, a large number of women's voluntary associations in aid of the soldiers and their families sprang up in Berlin and other cities. Initially, these societies were modelled on the Women's Association for the Good of the Fatherland, and raised money for uniforms and equipment. However, after the first battles had taken place, the priority shifted to the situation of the military hospitals.

As the uprising against Napoleon gained momentum in spring 1813, the Prussian and Russian allies were joined by Britain, Portugal, Sweden and Spain, forming the Sixth Coalition against France. Napoleon's own forces were bolstered by troops from French-held Italy and the Confederation of the Rhine. Once the fighting started in earnest, it quickly became apparent that the Prussian government had not given enough thought to the preparation of the military hospitals, which had been left in a filthy and disorganised state by the French, and which were now trying to cope with an overwhelming number of wounded soldiers flooding into Berlin. After the battle of Möckern in April, an early defeat for Napoleon, 2,000 wounded and sick men were crammed into a Berlin hospital with beds for 800, and virtually abandoned to their fate.[16]

Dr Johann Reil, a professor of medicine at Berlin University and a pioneer of psychiatry, visited one of the military hospitals and was shocked at the conditions he found. There were no doctors, no attendants, and no doorkeepers. There was no water for the patients, and the building had no lighting: thieves were robbing the wounded as they lay helpless in the dark. As Dr Reil quickly discovered, all of the Berlin military hospitals were understaffed, and had little in the way of equipment or medicines. Supplies were so low that moss was being used to pack wounds, bound with tow unpicked from hemp ropes. Reil turned to Princess Marianne – the only member of the royal family to have remained in Berlin – to rally support, and, with her encouragement, a number of voluntary women's associations were formed to offer aid, both financial and practical, to the hospitals.

Amalia Beer was one of the first women to volunteer to help with the organisation of hospitals and nursing for the wounded. In the spring of 1813, she joined the board of management of the earliest, and by far the most ambitious, of the Prussian women's voluntary hospital associations.[17] Rather than offering support to an existing hospital, this group of women proposed to establish, finance and run their own model military hospital. The association was led by two noblewomen, Frau von Podewils, the wife of a court chamberlain, and Frau von Sobbe, the wife of General von Sobbe. Princess Marianne herself agreed to act as President.

The board of management consisted of eighteen influential women; more than half of them were from the aristocracy, and three of them, including Amalia, were Jewish. The Jewish women were presumably included for their wealth, and their ability to access high finance through their husbands. On 6 April 1813, the association advertised in the Berlin newspapers for donors to support the establishment of the new hospital. Princess Marianne again led the way, giving an initial gift of 500 thalers, and pledging to donate 100 thalers a month for fourteen months.

The public response was immediate: within less than two weeks the women had raised enough money to rent and equip a large house at No. 101 Friedrichstrasse, in the centre of Berlin. The association was now formally named the 'Women's Association for the Private Hospital at 101 Friedrichstrasse'. Dr Reil, who had first approached Princess Marianne for help, agreed to act as the hospital's medical director. This was both an indication, and a guarantee, of the high standards that would be set. Reil was a forward-thinking man, and one of the most famous medical theorists and practitioners of his time. His best-known treatise on mental illness has been described as 'perhaps the most influential work in shaping German psychiatry before Freud'.[18]

The new hospital, which quickly became known to the Berliners as the 'Ladies' Military Hospital' [*Damen-Lazarett*], opened on 19 April 1813, initially taking in forty wounded and sick soldiers. Dr Reil was an inspirational doctor, but he proved to be something of an administrative maverick; he was not interested in bureaucracy or form-filling, and caused some difficulties by neglecting to send detailed reports of the Ladies' Hospital's activities to the director of the military hospitals in Berlin, Dr Graefe. Reil took no notice of Graefe's complaints, and likewise ignored a threat by the military governor of Berlin to send in an army doctor to take over the hospital. The government asked Princess Marianne to intervene; whether she did or not is unknown, but Dr Reil continued in his post.

Once the hospital was up and running, the number of beds was quickly increased to seventy, and it later expanded into a neighbouring house, bringing the total capacity to 100 beds. The women on the board of management personally supervised the standards of care and the provision of food, and set up a rota system to ensure that two of them were present in the hospital at all times. The services of two doctors were retained, and the board also employed a number of volunteer washerwomen and carers, and a cook.[19]

The patients in the Friedrichstrasse house were said to have been treated as tenderly as if they were sick children, and the hospital was meticulously run. As one of the hospital's supporters commented, the number of available beds might be 'a drop in the ocean' given the number of wounded and sick being brought into Berlin, but 'when you think what has been gained if only one of those suffering men has better air, food, and care, and a softer bed, it is a compensation for the impossibility of trying to help everyone'.[20]

At the time, military medicine was in its infancy: the majority of injured men could still expect to lie on the battlefield for days alongside the dying and the dead. Those who survived those first few days often died of their wounds in hospital. Many injuries, such as those to the head or stomach, were untreatable, as surgery was mostly confined to the amputation of limbs. Amputation did not by any means guarantee survival, however. As there was no anaesthetic available beyond a dose of strong alcohol, patients could die of shock during the operation.

Many of those who survived succumbed to infection and disease. Overcrowding in the hospitals, the absence of antibiotics, and poor standards of hygiene and sanitation created a breeding ground for infections. Typhus and dysentery were rife, and more soldiers were killed by disease than by wounds: in the Peninsular campaign, the British military lost nearly 25,000 men from disease compared to around 10,000 from injuries.

Nursing wounded and sick soldiers was not a job for the faint-hearted. Princess Marianne had to steel herself to visit the wards, but commented: 'I found all [of the wounded] so full of courage, so friendly and grateful, that it was really touching … the saddest was a man who had been shot through the chest, and would probably die. His wounded brother was lying opposite him, and had to watch him die.'[21] Amalia was equally dedicated to the work, according to her friend Friedrich Gubitz, who commented in a newspaper report many years later that, 'She was tireless in her work in the hospital, and a number of soldiers wounded in the service of the Fatherland died in her arms, in her motherly care to the last.'[22]

The board of management of the Ladies' Hospital was very successful in raising funds, bringing in an income of over 30,000 thalers from voluntary contributions during the hospital's two-year existence. Almost all of the money raised was used to pay for rent, food, heating, lighting and medical care. The board also paid funeral expenses when the families of those soldiers who had died in the hospital could not afford them.[23]

The patients' diet was carefully planned, and was far superior to that at the public hospitals, as it included 'coffee, good beer, meat broth, wine, meat and vegetables with good quality bread'. In addition to supplying the food for their own hospital, the Ladies' Military Hospital also paid for supplies to be delivered to two other hospitals caring for the wounded in Berlin.[24] In the first nineteen months of its existence, the Ladies' Hospital took in 865 wounded men, of whom sixty-four died.[25] Such was its reputation, that when one of the public military hospitals closed towards the end of the war, the few remaining Prussian soldiers in the wards requested to be transferred to the Ladies' Hospital.

In addition to her work with the Ladies' Hospital, Amalia made personal contributions to the war effort. She regularly sent provisions to the battlefield areas, and in autumn 1813, she took sole responsibility for supplying an encampment of 150 soldiers in the Tiergarten area with food and drink for several weeks.[26] As a founding member of the hospital's board of management, and as a private philanthropist, Amalia was playing a noteworthy role. She was also enhancing the Beer family's reputation both as patriots, and as significant benefactors of the city of Berlin at a time of national crisis.

## Notes

1. Giacomo Meyerbeer, *Briefwechsel und Tagebücher*, Heinz Becker, Gudrun Becker and Sabine Henze-Döhring (eds) (Berlin: Walter de Gruyter, 1960-2006), vol. 1, p.207.
2. See Sven Kuhrau and Kurt Winkler (eds), *Juden Bürger Berliner. Das Gedächtnis der Familie Beer–Meyerbeer–Richter* (Berlin: Henschel Verlag, 2004), p.46; and Hugo Rachel, Johannes Papritz and Paul Wallich, *Berliner Grosskaufleute und Kapitalisten* (Berlin: Walter de Gruyter, 1967), vol. 2, p.428.
3. Rabbi Felix Singermann, *Die Lippmann-Tauss-Synagoge* (Berlin: self-published, 1920).
4. Jacob Jacobson (ed.), *Jüdische Trauungen in Berlin 1759 bis 1813* (Berlin: Walter de Gruyter, 1968), p.xxxvi.
5. Singermann, *Die Lippmann-Tauss-Synagoge*, p.11.

6.   Jacob Jacobson (ed.), *Die Judenbürgerbücher der Stadt Berlin 1809-1851* (Berlin: Walter de Gruyter, 1962), p.92.

7.   *Sulamith*, vol. 4, issue 1 (1812), pp.55-6.

8.   Amalie von Romberg (ed.), *Vor hundert Jahren. Erinnerungen der Gräfin Sophie von Schwerin* (Berlin: Stargardt, 1909), p.345.

9.   Giacomo Meyerbeer, *The Diaries of Giacomo Meyerbeer*, Robert Letellier (ed. and trans.) (Madison, NJ: Fairleigh Dickinson University Press, 1999-2004), vol. 1, pp.313-14.

10.  Meyerbeer, *Briefwechsel und Tagebücher*, vol. 1, p.223.

11.  Meyerbeer, *Diaries*, vol. 1, pp.315-16.

12.  Ibid., p.318.

13.  Rabbi Meyer Simon Weyl, *Hoffnung und Vertrauen. Predigt wegen des Ausmarsches des vaterländisches Heeres gehalten am 28sten März 1813 in Gegenwart mehrere freiwilligen Jäger jüdischen Glaubens in der grossen Synagoge zu Berlin*, Isaac Levin Auerbach (trans.) (Berlin: August Wilhelm Schade, 1813), p.7.

14.  Wilhelm Baur, *Prinzessin Wilhelm von Preussen* (Hamburg: Agentur des Rauhen Hauses, 1886), p.154.

15.  Georg Schuster, 'Aus dem Briefwechsel der Prinzessin Marianne von Preussen', in Paul Clauswitz and Georg Voss (eds), *Erforschtes und Erlebtes aus dem alten Berlin. Festschrift zum 50jährigen Jubiläum des Vereins für die Geschichte Berlins* (Berlin: Verlag des Vereins für die Geschichte Berlins, 1917), p.389.

16.  Dirk Alexander Reder, *Frauenbewegung und Nation. Patriotische Frauenvereine in Deutschland im frühen 19. Jahrhundert (1813-1830)* (Cologne: SH-Verlag, 1998), p.69.

17.  Ibid., pp.58 n 91, and 71-2 n 169.

18.  Peter Watson, *The German Genius: Europe's Third Renaissance, the Second Scientific Revolution and the Twentieth Century* (London: Simon & Schuster, 2010), p.202.

19.  Reder, *Frauenbewegung und Nation*, pp.72-3.

20.  Romberg, *Vor Hundert Jahren*, p.378.

21.  Baur, *Prinzessin Wilhelm*, pp.156-7.

22.  *Königlich privilegirte Berlinische Zeitung von Staats- und gelehrten Sachen*, 20 October 1853.

23.  Ernst Gurlt, *Zur Geschichte der Internationalen und Freiwilligen Krankenpflege im Kriege* (Leipzig: F.C.W. Vogel, 1873), p.305.

24.  Ibid., p.304.

25.  Reder, *Frauenbewegung und Nation*, p.73.

26.  *Königlich privilegirte Berlinische Zeitung*, 20 October 1853.

# 7

## War and Peace

Amalia had become the first member of the Beer family to take part in the war effort when she joined the board of management of the Ladies' Hospital in spring 1813. In autumn that year, six months into the war, her third son, Wilhelm, made the decision to join the Prussian army as a volunteer. Of the three older Beer boys, it is perhaps not surprising that it was the boisterous Wilhelm who offered himself for military service at just 16 years old.[1]

He had been a lively youngster; his letters to his brothers are full of fun and in-jokes about family, friends and acquaintances. Unlike Giacomo and Heinrich, who had been educated at home, Wilhelm had attended an elite local school, the Joachimsthal Gymnasium, which was situated close to his father's sugar refinery in Heiligegeiststrasse. He volunteered for the Prussian cavalry just a few months after leaving school in summer 1813. On 12 October that year, a setting by Giacomo of Psalm 23, 'The Lord is my Shepherd', was performed in Berlin. According to some of Giacomo's early biographers, the piece was written for the occasion of Wilhelm's enlistment.

Soon after Wilhelm started his military training the war took a decisive turn, when the French army suffered a major defeat in the battle of Leipzig, one of the largest and bloodiest battles in European history. The fierce fighting lasted four days, from 16 to 19 October, with an estimated 100,000 men killed, wounded or missing. It also killed Dr Reil, the medical director of the Ladies' Military Hospital in Berlin, who had gone to Leipzig following the battle to help organize care for the casualties. He died of typhus, which he had contracted in one of the field hospitals. In the months following this crucial battle, the Allies advanced to Paris, where Napoleon was forced to abdicate on 11 April 1814. Two weeks later, the Bourbon King, Louis XVIII, landed at Calais, making his return to France after twenty-three years of exile.

In May 1814, as Louis took up the reins of government, and the ex-Emperor Napoleon departed France for the island of Elba, Wilhelm finished his six-month period of training. He was assigned to the 5th Brandenburg

Dragoon Regiment (Prince William's), known as the 'Blue Dragoons' because of their blue uniforms with black facings. The regiment, a part of the 3rd Corps under General Bülow, had taken part in the allied attack on Paris, and after Napoleon's defeat had been sent into Belgium, to occupy the area west of the River Meuse, where Wilhelm joined them. The war, it appeared, was over before he had seen combat, but he must have stood out, not just as a good soldier, but also as a leader of men, as he was promoted to officer rank, as a Second Lieutenant, three months later, on 16 August 1814, at the age of 17.

This was a defining moment for Wilhelm. Decades later, at a particularly happy time in his life, he told a friend that, 'I went around the whole day in a kind of happy intoxication. I was youthful again, and felt the same joy as I did when, in my eighteenth year, I became an officer in Prince William's Dragoons, which I had joined a year earlier as a common soldier.' He added that, 'You have to have been a soldier to understand the context, in which an officer is a completely different sort of man to a non-commissioned officer.'[2]

It was not just Wilhelm's youth that made his achievement so noteworthy. A list of the officers of the Regiment, compiled in February 1814, shows him as one of thirty-three second lieutenants, including both regular officers and volunteers. Twenty-seven of these young men were from noble families, including three who were Counts.[3] This was exalted company for a boy who was both a commoner and a Jew.

The Beer family's Prussian patriotism was now beyond question: Jacob had contributed funds, while both Wilhelm and Amalia had committed themselves personally to the war effort. Giacomo, however, had made the decision to remain in Vienna for the duration, and concentrate on his musical career. He told his tutor and confidante Aaron Wolfssohn, that 'When the Prussian government called on the entire youth of the country to volunteer for war service last year, I thought that from my point of view, and given my personality, it would be better for me if I could keep myself out of it.'[4]

He was certainly right in thinking he would be ill-suited to military life. He was sensitive and melancholic in character, and had already begun to experience the bouts of illness – some probably psychosomatic – that were to trouble him all his life. In a letter to Aaron Wolfssohn in early 1814, he described attacks of fever and biliousness, along with chest problems that resulted in him coughing up blood.

By the time of Napoleon's defeat and banishment to Elba, however, Giacomo was beginning to feel uneasy about his decision. His disquiet sprang, in part, from the fear that he would be condemned as a coward in Berlin. He had heard that there was strong feeling in the Prussian capital against young men who had not volunteered, and he did not want to return home under these circumstances. He was reluctant to admit his reasons for avoiding visiting Berlin to his parents, but a draft of a letter to Aaron Wolfssohn that has survived suggests that he confided his feelings to his old tutor.

In this letter, he told Wolfssohn that, in hindsight, he felt that he had betrayed the State by behaving selfishly at a time of national crisis, and that this failure to do his duty would damage his self-respect for the rest of his life. He added, rather dramatically, that, 'To return, under these conditions, seems so terrible to me that if, for example, the government issued a call for all émigrés to come back home, or my parents forcibly demanded my return, I would without any doubt rather put a bullet through my head if I found no other way to avoid the order.'[5]

Giacomo's self-recrimination was exacerbated by a feeling of guilt that he had not produced any serious work which might have served to justify his avoidance of military service. The one larger work that he had attempted had remained unperformed. In April 1814, his parents had procured a commission for him from August Iffland, for a small opera on the subject of the victorious return of King Frederick William III from the war. This work, to be called *Das Brandenburger Tor* [The Brandenburg Gate], was to be premiered in Berlin in the presence of the King on the day the Prussian troops marched back into the city. However, due to a series of misunderstandings about the timings of the event, Giacomo finished it too late for it to be performed.[6]

His relationship with his parents became strained for a while, particularly as they felt that they had let Iffland down. Aaron Wolfssohn, as was frequently the case, acted as a go-between. Giacomo complained to him that

> I have had a letter from Father about this business, which has really appalled me. He says in the letter that all the time I have been in Vienna I have told him nothing but a web of lies and fairy tales, yes, he even says quite openly that he believes I have deceived him over the money [for the librettist] ...[7]

Jacob was inordinately proud of his son, but as a businessman, expected to see some sort of return on the money he was investing in Giacomo's artistic career, a point of view that caused occasional bad feeling between them.

Giacomo's parents were hurt and puzzled by his reluctance to return home. They expected him to make his career in Berlin, and they felt that, now that the war was over, it was time for him to make a start. Coincidentally, in autumn 1814, a vacancy had arisen for a second musical director at the Berlin Opera, and Bernhard Weber, as senior musical director, had indicated that he would be happy to have Giacomo in the post.

Naturally, his parents thought this an ideal opportunity, but Giacomo disagreed. He suspected that Weber wanted a second-in-command he could dominate, and thought his old pupil would fit the bill. More importantly, Giacomo felt strongly that his musical education would not be complete until he had spent time studying in Paris and in Italy, the two great musical centres of the day. He wrote to Jacob in November 1814 pleading with him to be allowed to do this: 'I beg you to let me complete this final stage of my artistic education in peace and not embitter this one bright point in the focus of my life, the unhindered study and the practice of my art, with your constant dissatisfaction, which is so painful to me.'[8] Jacob and Amalia were reluctant, but eventually accepted his pleas to be allowed to complete his studies abroad, and in mid-November Giacomo left Vienna for Paris.

His stay in Vienna had been a time of transition. He had been considered a pianist as much as a composer when he had arrived in the city, and he had played frequently at the salon of Fanny Arnstein, which had become one of the most famous meeting places for the gilded society of the Vienna Congress. An acquaintance of Giacomo's, the young Bohemian piano virtuoso and composer Ignaz Moscheles, had commented that: 'His bravura playing is unparalleled – it cannot be surpassed.' Moscheles remembered Giacomo as one of a group of young musicians in Vienna who would often gather at a friend's country house outside the city, where they spent the long summer evenings going for walks, arranging tableaux, and composing and playing improvised pieces of music.[9]

Giacomo arrived in Paris at the end of December 1814, and was overwhelmed by his first experience of the city, telling his old Darmstadt friend Gottfried Weber that: 'The wonders of art and nature, and in particular the theatre, have taken possession of my whole being so powerfully, I have been gripped by such a spiritual hedonism, that I wander from museum to museum, from library to library, from theatre to theatre, etc., with a restlessness that would do credit to the Wandering Jew.'[10]

He was also busy meeting people who could introduce him into Parisian musical society. Jacob had marshalled his contacts to provide letters of introduction to some of the most prominent people in Paris, including the composers Spontini, Cherubini, and Nicolò, and the Princess Vaudemont, whose salon was one of the most exclusive meeting places in the French capital.

The cessation of hostilities in 1814, which had allowed Giacomo to go to Paris, had also prompted Wilhelm to consider his future. Jacob had made it clear that he expected Wilhelm to leave the military and join him in running the family business. He had known for some time that Wilhelm was the only one of the boys who was likely to become his successor. Giacomo and Michael were both artistic, clearly destined for lives dedicated to music and literature – Michael was still at school, but had already begun to write poetry – and Heinrich was continuing to prove unreliable, so Wilhelm was the obvious choice: stable, practical, and inclined towards the sciences. Later in his life, Wilhelm reminded Giacomo that he had been working in his father's business since his thirteenth year – presumably helping Jacob in his spare time while he was still at school.

Plans were made for Wilhelm to start work at one of Jacob's concerns in Hamburg. However, just as Wilhelm was preparing to take up the position, the news arrived that Napoleon had escaped from Elba. This dramatic act initiated the final phase of the Napoleonic Wars, the 'Hundred Days' campaign, a brief but fierce struggle climaxing in the Battle of Waterloo. On hearing the news that Napoleon was back in France rallying troops, Wilhelm immediately rejoined the colours.

This time, he was assigned to the 1st Silesian Hussars, exchanging the blue uniform of Prince William's Dragoons for the brown and gold of the Hussars. In 1815, the Silesian Hussars formed a part of the 1st Corps of the Prussian Army of the Lower Rhine, commanded by General Blücher. The 1st Corps would take part in the last battles of the Wars, fighting their way through Compiègne, Nanteuil, and Versailles to Paris.

After Paris had fallen, Carl Maria von Weber wrote to Giacomo in August 1815, to ask whether Wilhelm had survived: 'Relieve my mind over the fate of your brother. I don't have the courage to ask your parents about it, in case he has fallen a victim to the great world events, and I would not willingly re-open a wound.'[11] News was slow to filter back to family and friends from the battlefields. In some cases, weeks or even months after a battle, desperate families would put notices in the newspapers, asking if anyone could tell them the fate of their relative, 'last seen on the battlefield of —'. Fortunately, Wilhelm had survived the last battles of the Wars. He had entered Paris with the victorious allied armies in July 1815, shortly before Napoleon was exiled for a second time, this time for good, to the remote island of Saint Helena.

Giacomo had remained in Paris during the Hundred Days, and Wilhelm had stayed on there with his regiment after the end of the hostilities. Towards the end of the year, the brothers took a trip to England together, landing at Dover on Sunday 4 December. They headed for London, where they visited the tourist sites of St Paul's and Westminster Cathedrals, the British Museum and the Houses of Parliament.

Giacomo was eager to meet up with the numerous German musicians who were resident in London at the time, including the pianists Johann Cramer, Friedrich Kalkbrenner and Ferdinand Ries. The brothers spent almost every night in the capital's theatres, where they found a rich variety of performances to choose from, ranging from works by Shakespeare, Otway and Sheridan to more ephemeral musical comedies, farces and melodramas.

Giacomo noted in his diary that he saw Edmund Kean (then at the height of his fame as a tragedian) play Richard II, Iago, and the title role in Beaumont's *The Merchant of Bruges*, adding, rather mysteriously, after the third of these performances, that, 'I felt my opinion confirmed. He is a man of great talent, but a charlatan.'[12] Giacomo's command of English was not fluent by any means; he had been learning the language for just three months, and he admitted that, as the only book he had read so far in English was Goldsmith's 'The Vicar of Wackfield' (sic),[13] he was unable to follow plays in the London theatres without referring to the written text. Giacomo never did become as fluent in English as he did in French and Italian; he was still taking English lessons in his sixties.

By New Year's Day 1816, the brothers were back in France. Giacomo had no doubt what his next move should be: he was determined to go to Italy to continue his musical studies. Wilhelm, for his part, had made up his mind about his own future shortly before the trip to London. It had not been easy: he had been torn between becoming a career soldier, or leaving the army to join the family business.

Wilhelm was temperamentally suited to military life, and he had found much to admire in the Prussian army, which he felt exemplified to a high degree the qualities of courage, morale, discipline and loyalty. He was proud to be a member of the officer corps, describing his fellow officers as highly educated men, with a strong sense of honour. In late 1815, Wilhelm had written to his youngest brother Michael, asking what the family thought about the idea of him becoming a regular soldier.

Michael, then 15 years old, wrote back passionately to his brother to dissuade him:

You ask me what people here would think about you staying in the army? They think you are very wrong, and they are absolutely correct. The situation here in Berlin with regard to the Jews is terrible. Count Brühl [director of the royal theatres] has shown himself to be shameful, he has staged a play in which all Jews are horribly prostituted, and which expresses the Christians' hatred of the Jews in a dreadful way. When the King permits something like this against the Jews, what sort of promotion can you expect? You will truly regret it on your deathbed if you die a Second Lieutenant! … Do not remain a soldier!![14]

The play Michael was referring to was a particularly unpleasant anti-Semitic farce called *Unser Verkehr* [Our Crowd], written by a Silesian physician called Karl Borromäus Sessa, which viciously parodied the Jews. The point of the farce, echoing Carl Grattenauer's polemic of a decade earlier, was the impossibility of the Jews attaining any real culture. The play had been produced at the Berlin Opera House on 2 September 1815, and had been an instant success. The leading actor, the comedian Albert Wurm, was invited to the homes of wealthy and prominent Berliners to regale delighted gatherings with his imitation of Jewish stupidity, hypocrisy and cunning.

The play had originally been banned by von Hardenberg, the Prussian Chancellor, but he had been overruled. However, the outcry raised by the Berlin Jewish community was such that the play was eventually banned for a second time. In hindsight, though, Michael was right to be alarmed by the apparent resurgence of anti-Semitic feeling. In the post-war years, promises that had been made to the Jews before the war began to be retracted. When the King had called for volunteers in 1813, he had promised that all those who came forward and served their country in the military would be given preference for state posts after the war. However, it was later decided in retrospect that this promise did not apply to Jews. It also came to be considered unacceptable for Jews to command Christian soldiers, which effectively blocked promotion in the army.

Chancellor Hardenberg argued passionately against this trend, but his was a lone voice. The Justice Minister Friedrich von Kircheisen was probably expressing the opinion of the majority of his contemporaries when he maintained that the occasional display of courage by individuals in the service of the Fatherland did not cancel out the underlying low moral character of the Jews as a whole.

Opponents of emancipation had always insisted that the Jews would not be able to fulfil military duties. The laws regarding the Sabbath had frequently been evoked as an insuperable barrier to the Jews serving in the military, but there was also a widespread belief that Jews were by nature 'unmanly' – cowardly and unreliable. Their loyalty was also considered suspect. After the Wars of Liberation, these beliefs could only continue to be held by those who were ignorant of, or chose to ignore, the facts. Assessing the exact numbers of Jewish men who fought in the Wars is impossible. Many regimental rolls, where they still exist, do not record the religious faith of soldiers. Where they do record it, Jewish men were sometimes categorised as 'evangelical', a term used by the volunteers to disguise their real religious affiliation.

However, a list of Jewish individuals known to have participated in the Wars, drawn up from archival sources in 1906, lists around 500 young men, among them Wilhelm Beer, as volunteers.[15] Of these, twenty-seven were promoted to officer rank (including Wilhelm), twenty-four died on the battlefield or of their wounds, and sixty-five were awarded the Iron Cross. Five of the latter were Jewish doctors, who were awarded the Iron Cross on a white ribbon, for non-combatants. A Dr Assing of Hamburg, who became the regimental doctor of the 2nd Kurmark Cavalry Regiment, a distinction in itself for a Jew, had been noted for his fearlessness in the midst of the most ferocious fighting.

Chancellor Hardenberg, always well disposed towards the Jews, acknowledged their contribution to the Wars in a letter to Count August von Grote, the Prussian representative to the Hanseatic cities: 'Young men of the Jewish faith became comrades-in-arms of their Christian fellow-citizens, and among them we have seen examples of true heroism and the most laudable scorn for the dangers of war, with the rest of the Jewish population, especially the women, joining with them in self-sacrifice.'[16]

Hardenberg almost certainly had Amalia in mind when he made this remark about the Jewish women's contribution to the war effort. He knew the Beers well – Carl von Weber had been surprised when he had dropped in on Jacob and Amalia in August 1814, to find the Prussian Chancellor dining privately with them – and he took an interest in their activities.

For the Jews, the memory of the volunteers of 1813-15 became inextricably linked with that of the Emancipation, symbolising a high point in Prussian–Jewish history. The Jewish artist Moritz Oppenheimer's best-known painting, *The Return of a Jewish Volunteer from the Wars of Liberation*, painted in 1833-34, gained iconic status. It depicts a young man in military uniform, wearing the Iron Cross, surrounded by his orthodox family. The Jewish community had undoubtedly hoped and believed that the participation of their young men in the Wars would prove a huge step forward in combating prejudice.

Eduard Kley, Michael's tutor, had published a pamphlet in 1813, 'Address to the young men following the flags of the Fatherland', in which he had made this expectation explicit:

> There on the field of honour, where all hearts are animated by one spirit, where all work for a single goal: for their fatherland; there, where he is the best, who is most loyally devoted to his King – there we will see the barriers of prejudice come tumbling down. Hand in hand with your comrades in arms you will complete the great work; they will not deny you the name of brother, for you will have *earned* it.[17]

However, it appeared that now the crisis was over, the doors that had opened were closing, and the brother-in-arms was again becoming the pariah. In the reactionary atmosphere following the Wars of Liberation, appointments to the officer ranks reverted, in practice, to being the preserve of the nobility, and Jews were excluded.

The single, well-known exception was the Jewish artillery officer, Meno Burg. But even Burg, an honourable man who had the personal protection and friendship of Prince August of Prussia, was only allowed to remain an officer on condition that he was employed solely as a teacher in the artillery school, and would never be permitted to command Christian men. Further promotion was made dependent on his conversion to Christianity, which he refused to consider. Despite being an excellent instructor, a popular and talented officer, and the author of several highly regarded textbooks, Burg struggled against prejudice his entire career.

In the end, Wilhelm decided against remaining in the military. He resigned his commission in December 1815, and agreed to join the family business. It was almost certainly a wise move, although Wilhelm was to retain a passionate, nostalgiac love for the Prussian army for the rest of his life.

Nearly forty years later, in 1853, Amalia wrote to her friend, the influential scientist and explorer Alexander von Humboldt, asking him to intercede with the King to grant her favourite grandson, Wilhelm's son Georg, officer rank. Von Humboldt was one of the most famous men of his time. The late eighteenth century had been an age of scientific exploration, when naturalists had journeyed across the globe to explore new worlds, bringing back plants and animals previously unknown to Europeans. Von

Humboldt had travelled widely in South America at around the turn of the century, later publishing his journals and scientific findings. The American poet Ralph Waldo Emerson had called him a 'wonder of the world', likening him to Aristotle and Julius Caesar, while the Venezuelan General and politician Simon Bolívar described him as the 'true discoverer of South America', who had done more good for the continent than all its conquerors.[18]

Von Humboldt, who was close to the Prussian royal family, was a good friend to the Beers, and always promoted the family's interests where he could. However, in this instance he replied that, although there was no actual law banning Jews from officer rank, he could not interfere with the free choice of the military authorities: 'Your angel, dear lady, has won universal praise during his service here as a very cultured and charming young man, and given the noble and boundless self-sacrifice you made with the greatest patriotism in our time of need to the fatherland, and especially the army, then sympathy is tenfold increased for the naturally undeserved refusal of a just request!'

For all his fame and all his influence at the Prussian court, Alexander von Humboldt could not acquire a commission for Wilhelm's son, and was forced to admit to Amalia that 'so-called free choice also gives freedom to the old prejudices that are appearing again'.[19]

## Notes

1. Friedrich Gubitz, in a newspaper article in 1853, claimed that Heinrich Beer also volunteered: see *Königlich privilegirte Berlinische Zeitung*, 20 October 1853. There is an entry for a 'Hans Beer' in the list of Jewish volunteers in Martin Philippson, 'Der Anteil der jüdischen Freiwilligen an dem Befreiungskriege 1813 und 1814', *Monatsschrift für Geschichte und Wissenschaft des Judentums*, vol. 50 (1906), issue 1, pp.1-21, and issue 2, pp.220-46. However, there must be some doubt as to whether this was Heinrich Beer. The volunteer's name is given as 'Hans', rather than 'Heinrich' as might be expected in official documentation. He is also annotated as a *Handlungsdiener*, denoting an errand boy or shopkeeper's apprentice. This is not a word that would usually be used to describe a son of a wealthy and educated family. Wilhelm Beer is listed, but has no occupation against his name. If Heinrich did volunteer, nothing further is known of any service.
2. Unpublished letter, Wilhelm Beer to Heinrich Schumacher, 18 January 1841, Staatsbibliothek zu Berlin, Preussischer Kulturbesitz, Nachlass Heinrich Christian Schumacher.
3. Friedrich Paul von Probst, *Geschichte des Königlich-Preussischen Zweiter Dragoner-Regiments* (Schwedt, 1829), pp.103-4.
4. Giacomo Meyerbeer, *Briefwechsel und Tagebücher*, Heinz Becker, Gudrun Becker and Sabine Henze-Döhring (eds) (Berlin: Walter de Gruyter, 1960-2006), vol. 1, pp.244-5.

5. Meyerbeer, *Briefwechsel und Tagebücher*, vol. 1, p.245.

6. The opera remained unperformed for over a century and a half, until its premiere in 1991.

7. Meyerbeer, *Briefwechsel und Tagebücher*, vol. 1, p.237.

8. Ibid., p.249.

9. Charlotte Moscheles, *Life of Moscheles* (London: Hurst and Blackett, 1873), vol. 1, pp.13-17.

10. Meyerbeer, *Briefwechsel und Tagebücher*, vol. 1, p.267.

11. Carl Maria von Weber to Giacomo Meyerbeer, 26 August 1815, Carl-Maria-von-Weber-Gesamtausgabe. Digitale Edition, http://weber-gesamtausgabe.de/A040816 (Version 3.4.2 vom 8. Februar 2019). Friedrich Gubitz, in his 1853 newspaper article on Amalia Beer (see note 1) claimed that Wilhelm was 'almost blinded' while on active service, but later recovered. There is no reference in any other source to an injury in the months after the end of the Wars, when Wilhelm remained in Paris with Giacomo until he resigned his commission in December 1815, when he and Giacomo visited England together.

12. Giacomo Meyerbeer, *The Diaries of Giacomo Meyerbeer*, Robert Letellier (ed. and trans.) (Madison, NJ: Fairleigh Dickinson University Press, 1999-2004), vol. 1, p.332.

13. Meyerbeer, *Briefwechsel und Tagebücher*, vol. 1, p.298.

14. Ibid., p.648 n 295,1.

15. Philippson, 'Der Anteil der jüdischen Freiwilligen', vol. 50, issue 1, pp.1-21 and issue 2, pp.220-46.

16. Philippson, 'Der Anteil der jüdischen Freiwilligen', issue 2, p.6.

17. Eduard Kley and Carl Günsberg, *Zuruf an die Jünglinge, welche die Fahnen des Vaterlands folgen* (Berlin, 1813), p.10.

18. Quoted in Peter Watson, *The German Genius: Europe's Third Renaissance, the Second Scientific Revolution and the Twentieth Century* (London: Simon & Schuster, 2010), p.177.

19. Meyerbeer, *Briefwechsel und Tagebücher*, vol. 6, p.733 n 3.

# 8

## Dame of the Order of Louise

In the summer of 1814, with Napoleon apparently defeated and in exile on the Isle of Elba, King Frederick William III had decided to create a new award for service during the Wars of Liberation. The announcement generated enormous excitement, as the King made it clear that this was to be an order for women – the first in Prussia's history. It was intended to honour those women who had shown exceptional patriotism in volunteering for war work:

> When the men of our brave army were bleeding for the Fatherland, they found relief and healing in the nurturing care of the women … It is impossible to publicly honour all these acts of quiet service that graced their lives; but we find it only right to award an honour to those of them whose contributions are especially recognised.[1]

The new award was to be known as the Order of Louise, after the late Queen. Since Louise's death, a cult of celebrity had begun to develop around her, portraying the strong-willed Queen as a symbol of idealised Prussian womanhood: beautiful, gentle, and devoted to husband, family and fatherland. The order in her name was intended as a sister decoration to the Iron Cross, which the King had created in March 1813.

The Iron Cross was the only Prussian military award that was open to men of all ranks, a departure from tradition that was intended to symbolise the solidarity of all levels of society in the fight against Napoleon. Since this was, as the King remarked, a 'time of iron', the Cross itself was made from cast iron, and designed to be austere in form. It became an icon of the Wars of Liberation, and indeed of later German campaigns up to the end of the Second World War.

The equivalent women's award, the Order of Louise, was more delicate and feminine in design. It took the form of a black enamelled gold cross, with a central medallion in sky blue inscribed with a gold letter 'L' surrounded by seven stars. The dates 1813/1814 were engraved on the reverse of the medallion. The order was designed to be worn suspended from a large bow of white ribbon edged in black.

The King appointed a selection committee of four women, under the guidance of Princess Marianne, to consider the candidates for the new order. The committee was headed by Countess Antoinette von Arnim, the widow of a former War Minister. The other three members were women who had taken leading roles in the various voluntary associations. They met for the first time in Princess Marianne's apartments in the Royal Palace on 1 September 1814, to collate information on women who had been prominent in wartime activity. The Princess remarked in her diary that: 'Today the committee (of the Order of Louise) met, it was ridiculous at first, the ladies were quite embarrassed, and at first they were too overcome by the solemnity of the occasion to know what to say, but after a while it went well.'[2]

The Order was to be limited to 100 women – in the future, places would become available only through the death of existing members – and the King himself was to approve the final choice of candidates. Shortly after the statute founding the Order was made public, the committee started to receive nominations from wounded veterans, putting forward the names of women who had nursed them. Some of the women who had been involved in the associations even sent in their own names for consideration.

The committee quickly decided that the selection process would not be open to submissions from the public, but that they themselves would select suitable candidates from the lists of members of the associations. They also agreed that any woman who proposed herself as a candidate would automatically be debarred from being a recipient of the Order. Princess Marianne did not find the selection an easy task, as she admitted to her mother: 'You can well imagine, dear mother, how many interests there are to be considered, how I must understand what is fair, and how many enemies I could make, which is extraordinarily unpleasant for me.'[3]

By 15 September 1814, the committee had produced an initial list of nominees for the King's scrutiny. It contained thirty-five names, including that of Amalia Beer, placing her among the earliest candidates for the Order. Her nomination was annotated 'for independent activity', and was presumably based on her personal contributions as well as her work for the Ladies' Military Hospital Association, which had not only been the first of the hospital groups to be established, but was also the only one to have founded a major private hospital of its own. The majority of the other women on the list were members of groups attached to existing military hospitals.

The King replied briefly to the committee before leaving for Vienna, to take part in the Peace Congress that was assembling there. He approved only half of the names put forward. Those he accepted included the four members of the Order committee, along with a number of noblewomen. Amalia's name was among those rejected. The resulting list of seventeen awards was published on 20 December 1814. It is not clear whether Amalia knew of her failed nomination. If she did, the King's rebuff must have been painful, perhaps all the more so as, just weeks before the publication of this first list, Amalia had joined the board of a major new charity.

By the autumn of 1814, it had become apparent that the existing charitable institutions in Prussia would not have the resources to provide long-term care for the invalided veterans and the families of the war dead. Consequently, on 23 November, a new women's association had been founded to meet this need. This group, which was headed by Princess Marianne, later became known as the 'Patriotic Women's Association for the Care of Soldiers Wounded in the Years 1813, 1814 and 1815'. Countess Antoinette von Arnim and the statesman Karl von Kampf were appointed as directors, and there were seven female trustees, including Amalia and her friend Charlotte von Bischoffswerder. The charity became a Beer family affair: Jacob Beer was appointed treasurer, responsible for investing and managing the Association's considerable income.[4]

Six months after the founding of the Patriotic Women's Association, in May 1815, the Order of Louise committee produced a new list of eighty-three candidates. Amalia was again included among them. She was now actively involved in the leadership of two of the most significant women's charities of the war years. Both associations were headed by Princess Marianne, who knew Amalia personally. The King approved seventy-four of this second tranche of nominations before he left Berlin to resume the war against Napoleon, who had escaped from Elba and was back in France, gathering forces.

Amalia was again one of the candidates rejected by the King. The other seven were women of the lower classes (a baker's wife and a cobbler's daughter), young unmarried girls, and another Jewish woman, a Frau Hirsch of Königsberg, who had been a new candidate. The wife of a doctor, Frau Hirsch had organised an association in aid of soldiers' wives, widows and orphans in her home city. The Order of Louise, like the Iron Cross, was intended to be open to all ranks of society, but it had begun to look as if the King had reservations as to how far the principle of equality should extend where women were concerned.

The Wars of Liberation finally came to an end a few months after this second list of awards was made public. Napoleon, defeated at Waterloo, was exiled to Saint Helena – far away enough for there to be no opportunity for him to make a second surprise reappearance in Europe. Amalia's involvement with the Ladies' Military Hospital now ended, as the hospital closed its doors. The small sum of money left over from the venture was transferred to the Charité, the central teaching hospital for military surgeons in Prussia, to fund the continuing medical care of war invalids.[5]

Amalia's charity work was now solely focused on the Patriotic Women's Association. This would prove to be a long-term commitment – the support that the Association offered to impoverished veterans and their families would be needed for many decades to come. By November 1815, the Association was supporting seventy invalids, and the demands on its resources were growing rapidly. By 1817, it would have nearly 900 people in its care, including wounded and blind soldiers, military widows, and orphans. Amalia was an energetic fundraiser, organising concerts and events for the benefit of the Association.

One of her biggest projects had been the organisation of a major art exhibition in 1814, which she had managed in partnership with her old friend, Friedrich Gubitz. The Beers contributed several of their own artworks to the show, including a seventeenth-century Dutch painting listed as being by 'Southmann' (probably Pieter Soutman, 1593-1657), a mourning vase for the death of Frederick the Great, and a sculpture of a young Moor.[6] Jacob managed the finances of the exhibition, which was extremely successful.[7]

By the end of 1815, there were still a few vacancies left for members of the Order of Louise. On 2 January 1816, the committee put forward a final list of fifteen candidates. Amalia's name was included for a third time, and for a third time her nomination was struck off by the King. Frau Hirsch, the other Jewish candidate, was rejected for a second time. The committee's persistent inclusion of Amalia in all of their lists, despite the King's repeated rejections, was an indication of the strength of their support for her candidature. Princess Marianne was particularly determined not to let Amalia's nomination drop.

The Princess had shown a certain independence of spirit much earlier in the process. When the King had himself nominated a candidate from an aristocratic family, Marianne had informed him that, as the committee had no information on the wartime activity of the lady concerned, she could not be considered at that point. The King had been forced to accept this refusal, but he had outmanoeuvred her on the question of awarding the

Order to princesses of the royal family who had not contributed personally to the war effort, by simply informing her that he had already sent the Order to these ladies. Marianne and her committee had nonetheless insisted that these awards should not count towards the limit of 100 members, so as not to restrict the number of places available for women who had actively earned the Order.

The letter that the Princess had sent to the King with the final list of nominations made the committee's wholehearted endorsement of Amalia quite plain. Marianne had stressed in particular the more recent efforts that Amalia had made in fundraising for the Patriotic Women's Association, saying that she had 'dedicated her entire time over four or five months to the exhibition in aid of the wounded defenders of the Fatherland'.[8] The committee was not prepared to let the matter rest, and negotiations continued for several weeks. On 16 January 1816, sixteen months after Amalia's name had first been submitted to him, the King issued a special order to the selection committee:

> I have granted the two ladies of the Jewish religion in Königsberg and Berlin, who are greatly deserving for their care of the sick and wounded and have been put forward for the Order of Louise by HRH Princess William [Marianne], instead of this order, the cruciform shape of which might prove offensive to these ladies because of their religion, the golden medallion of the General Order of Merit First Class on the ribbon of the Order of Louise, white with a black border, and requested HRH Princess William to despatch the order to them.[9]

It was a compromise solution: the two Jewish women would be given a medallion rather than the cross of the Order, but they were to be included in the total of 100 Dames of the Order of Louise. There was a later attempt, in 1820, initiated by Count von Groeben, the Court Chamberlain, to remove them from the official number, in order to free up places for Christian women, but the King had the grace to reject the suggestion.

The award of the Order to Amalia was announced in the Jewish journal *Sulamith*, which reproduced in full the message that had accompanied the order:

> His Majesty has deigned, on the recommendation of Her Royal Highness Princess William of Prussia, and on the decision of the committee of the Order of Louise, who have unanimously chosen you to be a holder of the Order because of your universally

acknowledged services and endeavours, most graciously to determine that it is necessary, so as to avoid offending you with the form of the cross, for you to be given the decoration of the Order of Merit I. Class on the ribbon of the Order of Louise, which I am tasked with doing. I divest myself of this duty in the fullest conviction that you will not misinterpret the intention which clearly expresses the most delicate appreciation of your services.[10]

The King's explanation for the substitution of a medal for the cross was that he had been concerned that the offer of the Order in its usual form would be unacceptable to the two Jewish women. His solution to this problem would allow the women to accept the Order without offending their beliefs, and was therefore an act of consideration and respect on his part. However, the wording of the last sentence of the King's message suggests that he understood very well that there could be another, less flattering, interpretation of his decision, and indeed, the affair rapidly became the talk of Berlin society.

A story circulated in the city that Amalia had indicated to the King that she would refuse the Order if it was offered to her, because of its cruciform shape. This rumour evidently reached the ears of Rahel Levin Varnhagen, who was living in Prague, where she too had been involved in organising care for the wounded during the Wars. Rahel's brother, Marcus Robert (originally Mordecai Levin), wrote to her from Berlin on 4 February 1816, just a few weeks after the King had approved the award to Amalia, telling her that:

> You were quite wrong if you believed that Madame Beer had refused the cross. Quite the opposite – she and a large number of other people see the award of the medal as an affront. Princess William herself, as President of the Order of Louise committee, and the majority of the women on the committee, are of the same opinion. It's definitely true that the King disregarded the committee's recommendation of Madame Beer for the order several times, but finally, under pressure from everyone, came out with the remark that a Jewess could not wear the cross willingly, but only to please him, and he did not want that – and so he thought up this way out for himself.[11]

Robert added that Amalia only wore the Order when it was 'absolutely necessary' for her to do so. It is difficult to know the truth of this remark.

The Levin family certainly knew the Beers and moved in the same circles, but they were not particularly close.

The Levins were not the only observers to express scepticism about the official line. The Prussian minister and diplomat Friedrich Stägemann claimed that the re-design of the award was viewed by the Jewish community as an insult, rather than a mark of respect, and in fact, the Berlin Jews were said to refer to Amalia's order as the 'kosher cross'. Stägemann believed that the reason for the substitution was that it was the King himself who had found it unacceptable for a Jewish woman to wear an order in the shape of the cross. He asked ironically whether this meant that Jewish soldiers would be given a different version of the Iron Cross.[12]

Amalia may well have felt hurt by the substitution, as she certainly considered herself a loyal Prussian – and indeed, by 1815 she was a Prussian citizen in her own right. She and her sisters had each inherited a piece of land from their father, and in September 1814 they had taken the oath of citizenship, which was a prerequisite to taking up ownership of the land. The women had been allowed, as a concession, to take the oath in private, in their mother's residence, rather than having to go to the Rathaus, as was usual.[13]

Nonetheless, whatever the real reasons for the King's decision about the award of the Order to the Jewish women, or Amalia's own feelings about it, which her surviving letters do not reveal, it would have been ungracious and self-defeating for her to have done anything but accept the honour with apparent pleasure. The granting of the Order of Louise to Amalia was a remarkable recognition of the role she played in Berlin society, and, as the announcement in the journal *Sulamith* suggests, was treated as a significant event for the entire Jewish community of Berlin. It symbolised the Jews' perception of themselves, in the aftermath of the Emancipation Edict and the Wars of Liberation, as no longer an alien nation, but Prussians, who had fought alongside their fellow citizens in the great patriotic struggle against French hegemony.

During the decade of occupation and war, the Beer family's reputation for philanthropy had been firmly established, and their social prominence in Berlin's highest circles, well beyond the confines of the Jewish community, had been acknowledged. Princess Marianne, who had championed Amalia, and who may have felt that the modification of the Order was, at the least, insensitive, presented her with a plaster cast of Christian Rauch's statue of Queen Louise, as a special mark of honour.[14] Amalia's friendly relations with Marianne continued up until the Princess's death in 1846.

As a member of the Order of Louise, Amalia was permitted to send official New Year greetings to the Princess, but in fact the two women kept in touch more informally into their old age. There had been a further link between them during the Wars of Liberation, as the Princess's husband had been Wilhelm Beer's commanding officer in the Blue Dragoons. Wilhelm had greatly respected his commander, reminiscing later in his life that the mere sight of the Prince had been enough to turn common soldiers into heroes, despite the fact that he was known to be much more lenient than the other senior officers when meting out punishments – a very Prussian remark![15]

Amalia's private letters to Princess Marianne,[16] while observing the protocols appropriate for a commoner in communicating with royalty, are full of warmth and – as one matriarch to another – comments on the Princess's family affairs. Amalia's last letter to Marianne was written in March 1846, just a few weeks before the latter's death. The Patriotic Women's Association was still in existence at this time – in 1845 it was supporting over 150 individuals – but given Princess Marianne's close personal involvement, it probably came to an end after her death on 14 April 1846.

## Notes

1.  Louis Schneider, *Der Luisen-Orden* (Berlin: Hayn, 1867), appendix, 'Urkunde, Regeste und Verzeichnisse', p.3.
2.  Wilhelm Baur, *Prinzessin Wilhelm von Preussen* (Hamburg, Agentur des Rauhen Hauses, 1886), p.193.
3.  Ibid., p.194.
4.  Dirk Alexander Reder, *Frauenbewegung und Nation. Patriotische Frauenvereine in Deutschland im frühen 19. Jahrhundert (1813-1830)* (Cologne: SH-Verlag, 1998), pp.57-8 and 63.
5.  Ernst Gurlt, *Zur Geschichte der Internationalen und Freiwilligen Krankenpflege im Kriege* (Leipzig: F.C.W. Vogel, 1873), p.305.
6.  Sven Kuhrau and Kurt Winkler (eds), *Juden Bürger Berliner. Das Gedächtnis der Familie Beer–Meyerbeer–Richter* (Berlin: Henschel Verlag, 2004), p.66 n 63.
7.  Friedrich Wilhelm Gubitz, *Erlebnisse, nach Erinnerungen und Aufzeichnungen* (Berlin, 1868), vol. 2, pp.69-70.
8.  Cited in Reder, *Frauenbewegung und Nation*, p.58 n 91.
9.  Schneider, *Der Luisen-Orden*, appendix, p.6.
10. *Sulamith*, vol 4, issue 2 (1816), pp.287-8.
11. Rahel Levin Varnhagen, *Familienbriefe*, Renata Barovero (ed.) (Munich: C. H. Beck, 2009), p.646 ff.
12. Kuhrau and Winkler, *Juden Bürger Berliner*, p.63.
13. Jacob Jacobson (ed.), *Die Judenbürgerbücher der Stadt Berlin 1809-1851* (Berlin: Walter de Gruyter, 1962), p.109.

14. Felix Eberty, *Jugenderinnerungen eines alten Berliners* (Berlin: Verlag für Kulturpolitik, 1925), pp.102-3.
15. Wilhelm Beer, *Die Drei-Königs-Verfassung in ihrer Gefahr für Preussen* (Berlin: F. Schneider, 1849), p.8.
16. Hessischen Staatsarchiv Darmstadt, Nachlass Marianne, Prinzessin Wilhelm von Preussen, D22 Nr. 23/26.

# 9

## The Beer Temple: The First Phase

One of the longer-term consequences of the emancipation of the Jews, and their greater integration into German society, was the development of a movement for synagogue reform in the early decades of the nineteenth century. Jacob and Amalia Beer, with their devotion to Judaism and their modern outlook, were immediately attracted to these new ideas, and their wealth enabled them to play a leading role in the earliest days of the movement.

By the end of the Wars, in 1815, Jacob, along with many other younger men in the Berlin community, had become convinced that change in synagogue worship was both inevitable and necessary. A number of people in the Berlin Jewish community no longer understood Hebrew, the language of the liturgy, and some felt that the services had become irrelevant to their lives, which were no longer so closely bound up with traditional observance.

The philosopher Moses Mendelssohn had played a crucial role in the first stirrings of modernisation in the Berlin community. In 1783, he had produced a German translation of the Pentateuch, featuring the original Hebrew on one page, and a German version, in Hebrew lettering, on the facing page. This was considered revolutionary; previously, the only German versions of the Hebrew Bible had been translations by Christian scholars.

Mendelssohn's translation had been roundly condemned by traditionalist rabbis, but he had seen no reason to fear that secular education or scientific truth would harm religion. He had been a strong supporter of reform in Jewish schools: the year before his publication of the Pentateuch translation – and eight years before Giacomo's birth – he had lamented that 'We are still kept far removed from arts, sciences, useful trades, and the professions of mankind; every avenue to improvement is still blocked up to us …'[1]

Moses Mendelssohn had died in 1786. After his death, modernisation had accelerated in the last decades of the century. The Jewish *Freischule*, or Free School, founded by Mendelssohn's pupil, David Friedländer, and Isaac Daniel Itzig in Berlin in 1778, had been the first school to offer Jewish boys a chance to study subjects outside the traditional curriculum. At the same time, the power of the rabbis to compel obedience had been partially eroded by government measures that had forbidden the use of the 'ban', or excommunication, against those who broke the religious laws.

By the turn of the century, a significant number of Jews in Berlin had openly stopped observing the laws – a development that would have horrified Mendelssohn. Over the following decades, the number of conversions to Christianity rose. Some of the converts, particularly those men who found themselves still barred from certain careers, even after emancipation, simply saw no point in remaining Jewish. Women often converted before entering into a mixed marriage, but some, like Mendelssohn's daughter Dorothea Schlegel, also found in Christianity a religion that they felt was more attuned to religious emotion than Judaism, which, in their view, was obsessed solely with the outward forms of the law, and had lost its relevance for them.

For many of the more integrated Jews, the synagogue services had become a symbol of this perceived alienation of traditional Judaism from modern life. These people were disturbed by the negative view of Jewish worship held by their Christian neighbours, who often regarded synagogue services as 'oriental' at best, and 'barbaric' at worst. As the purpose of attending the synagogue was primarily to fulfil the duty of personal prayer, people often came and went during the services. Choirs and instrumental music were not allowed in rabbinic law, so there was little or no communal singing or praying; the cantor intoned the prayers while members of the congregation prayed individually, often aloud, sometimes shouting and swaying or stamping their feet. The atmosphere was frequently noisy and chaotic.

The English music historian Charles Burney visited an Amsterdam synagogue in 1772, and remarked that he found the cantor's chanting 'very farcical', adding, 'At the end of each strain, the whole congregation set up such a kind of cry, as a pack of hounds when a fox breaks cover. It was a confused clamour, and riotous noise, more than song or prayer ... It is impossible for me to divine what ideas the Jews themselves annex to this vociferation ...'[2]

Synagogue practice could appear alien not just to Christians, but also to Jews brought up in non-observant households. When Rahel Levin visited relatives in Breslau, she woke up on her first morning in her uncle's house to hear what she thought was the noise of men shouting loudly and quarrelling above the noise of the chickens, geese and ducks in the courtyard outside her bedroom window. She was horrified to discover that this uproar was the sound of morning prayer emanating from her uncle's home synagogue, and she was eager to disassociate herself from something she was afraid would appear primitive to her sophisticated Christian friends.

Many Christians who were sympathetic to Jewish aspirations believed that, once the Jews had integrated into European society, their religion would simply wither away and die naturally. They saw Judaism as a relic, kept artificially alive, and incompatible with the modern world. Partly in response to these negative views, a movement for the reform of Jewish religious practices developed in the early part of the nineteenth century. Perhaps surprisingly, the earliest steps towards this reformation did not take place in progressive Berlin, but in the Napoleonic Kingdom of Westphalia, where a Jewish layman called Israel Jacobson introduced a new style of worship in the years before the Wars of Liberation.

Napoleon Bonaparte had created the Kingdom of Westphalia in 1807 by merging a number of German territories, including Brunswick and Hesse. He had given this new French satellite state to his youngest brother, Jerome, who had reorganised the administration of its Jewish population along the lines of the system that Napoleon had already introduced in France. This involved the creation of 'consistories', or committees, composed of both rabbis and laypeople, to administer their local areas.

The central Jewish consistory in Westphalia was headed by a lay President, Israel Jacobson, a former court factor to the Duke of Brunswick, and a self-educated man with liberal ideas. His appointment gave him wide powers, enabling him to override the opposition of the more orthodox rabbis to change, and he seized the opportunity to introduce far-reaching reforms into religious life. Jacobson's aim, as he saw it, was to rid Judaism of the archaic customs and habits that had grown up over the centuries, and create a more 'enlightened' style of religious practice that would suit the modern age. His most ambitious project was the establishment of a synagogue in a completely new style, in the town of Seesen, on the northern edge of the Harz Mountains, in 1810.

The Sabbath services that Jacobson instituted in this new 'Temple', as it was called, had features modelled on the Protestant pattern of worship, including a sermon, and music provided by a choir accompanied by an organ. Both the sermon and some of the prayers were in the German language rather than Hebrew. The introduction of a regular sermon was in itself an innovation: the rabbi was primarily a legal expert, not a pastor, and his main function was to explain and apply the multiplicity of ceremonial laws that regulated everyday life. Jacobson's attempt to adapt Jewish synagogue worship to the contemporary, western world was given full backing by the Westphalian civil authorities. The opening ceremony was an impressive occasion, attended by Christian clergy and government officials.

Jacobson's reforms inspired the liberal Society of Friends, to which Jacob and Giacomo both belonged, to take up the question of synagogue worship in Berlin. The Emancipation Edict of 1812 had left questions of Jewish educational and religious reform in Prussia deliberately vague, stating only that these were to be left for consideration at a future, unspecified time. During the summer of 1814, the Society of Friends requested permission to hold a service in the Berlin community synagogue in the Heidereuthergasse, to mark the forthcoming peace celebrations. They indicated that they planned to introduce innovations along the Westphalian lines, such as a German sermon, and songs sung by a choir.

They also intended to make another radical break with tradition, by having men and women seated together. However, it quickly became evident that the Society's proposal had split the community leaders. The elders – including Jacob Beer – generally supported the proposal for a reformed service, while the rabbi, the synagogue wardens and the more orthodox members of the community were strongly opposed to any changes to traditional practice.

The Society's proposal had been approved by the elders, but Rabbi Weyl stipulated a number of conditions that would have to be met before he would permit the service to take place in the synagogue. Men and women would not be allowed to sit together, and women would not be allowed to sing. Most crucially, use of the German language for prayers was strictly forbidden. These restrictions made it impossible for the service to be held in the synagogue in the format that the Society wanted, and it eventually took place in their own building. It was now clear that any attempt to introduce change into services held in the official synagogue would be blocked by Rabbi Weyl and his supporters.

This was a setback, but the arrival of Israel Jacobson in Berlin the next year revived the enthusiasm of the reform-minded. Jacobson had left Seesen following the dissolution of the Kingdom of Westphalia after Napoleon's defeat. The French consistory system had been dismantled, and, as Jacobson's ideas had never been supported by the majority of Jews in Westphalia, continuation of his reforms there seemed unlikely. Berlin, with its nucleus of liberally-minded people, offered him fresh opportunities. In June 1815, Jacobson began to hold new-style services in the rooms he was renting in the old Itzig mansion on Burgstrasse in central Berlin.

Jacobson's Temple began to attract large numbers of people who had drifted away from Judaism, dissatisfied by the traditional liturgy, and unable to reconcile conservative Jewish practice with their lives. Rahel Levin Varnhagen's brother, Marcus Robert, attended one of the services, and reported to his sister that Jacobson had bought a small organ and gave the German sermon himself, 'dressed up like Luther and looking like him'.[3] Robert had noticed that some Christian clerics had been present, presumably to signal their support for this modernisation of Jewish practice.

Michael Beer's tutor, Eduard Kley, was also involved in the leadership of the new services: he was one of the lay preachers at the Temple. Leopold Zunz, a young reform-minded man who was to become the founder of Jewish studies as an academic discipline, described a service at Jacobson's Temple in October 1815: 'People who for twenty years had nothing in common with Jews spent the whole day there. Men who thought themselves above religious feeling shed tears of devotion ... [the preacher] Kley is lively and bold, his imagery arouses the imagination.'[4] Zunz was so impressed with the new-style sermons, that he went so far as to compare Kley with the prophet Ezekiel.

The number of people attending the services rapidly became too large for the space available in Jacobson's rooms in the Itzig mansion. According to Kley, the Temple was full every Saturday to the point of suffocation, and a large number of people had to be turned away. Jacob and Amalia were among those who had supported Jacobson's initiative: on 8 August 1815, Jacob had written to Giacomo asking him to compose a setting for a small poem to be sung as a Hallelujah Chorus in the new Jewish synagogue in Berlin.[5] Kley had remarked to Giacomo at the time that his parents were providing an excellent example in supporting the new movement – as they always did, he added, in any good cause.[6]

Certainly, by 1814, the Beers were not strict observers of the Law, as their name does not appear on a list of those paying the kosher meat tax that year.[7] Both Jacob and Amalia had been brought up in observant homes; Liepmann Meyer Wulff had been far more of a traditionalist in religious matters than his daughter and son-in-law. He had been a member of the prestigious Burial Society, which supported the practice of burying people on the day that they died, a long-standing custom within the Jewish community. Membership of this organisation was both an honour and a sign of religious orthodoxy.

The topic had become a deeply divisive one in the closing decades of the eighteenth century, however. Advances in medical knowledge had suggested that in adhering to this practice, the Jewish communities ran a very real risk of burying people alive. Nonetheless, any suggestion of change in this, as in any religious tradition, was unthinkable to the orthodox. The Society of Friends took a different view; its policy was to honour the wishes of any of its members who asked to remain unburied for three days after death. Jacob's own funeral would take place four days after his death, and both Amalia and Giacomo specified in their wills the interval that was to take place between their death and their burial.

For the Beers, non-observance of some of the precepts of the Law or of traditional customs did not imply abandonment of, or indifference to, Judaism. In common with many of their contemporaries, they no longer saw obedience to the multiplicity of laws governing everyday life as the essence of their religion, but they remained warmly attached to their faith, and brought their children up to respect their Jewish heritage. In 1811, writing to her eldest son in Darmstadt, Amalia had told him that she was delighted that the synagogue there had made such a solemn impression on him. She urged him to 'always treasure this holy feeling' in his heart, 'because, my dear ... only a strong faith in divine providence will keep us on the right path'.[8]

Giacomo had been deeply affected by Liepmann Meyer Wulff's death in 1812, and had spontaneously promised his mother in writing that he would always remain a Jew to honour his grandfather's memory: 'If poor Grandfather had even a glimmer of consciousness on his deathbed, it must have sweetened his last moments to know that his children will never leave the faith he was so warmly attached to. Therefore accept a solemn promise from me in his name that I too will *always* live in the religion in which he died'.[9] In fact, all of Jacob and Amalia's sons remained Jews, although none followed the strictly traditional way of life.

The Beers had wanted to be able to bring up their sons in a way that would allow them to remain Jews, yet feel at home in the modern, wider world. Jacobson's services, with their Europeanised format, appealed to them. In late 1815, given the inadequacy of the space in Jacobson's rooms in the Itzig mansion, Jacob and Amalia decided to offer their own house in Spandauer Strasse as a venue for the new services. The transformation of a section of the house into a semi-public building was a major undertaking, requiring a large-scale remodelling and refurbishing of some of the biggest rooms. The project was said to have cost Jacob 8,000 thalers.[10]

Three interconnected halls, with windows onto an inner courtyard, were turned into a single space for worship. The central hall, which contained an ark for the Torah scrolls, an altar, a marriage canopy and a pulpit, was richly decorated with gold columns and gold-embroidered silk

The Beer Temple: The First Phase 109

curtains. The wealthier members of the community sat closest to the central area, where the ark stood, with the remainder of the congregation filling the two outer halls. The men occupied one of these outer rooms, the women the opposite one, facing the men. Men and women had their own entrances.

This layout, with men and women separated, but on an equal footing, was more of a departure from tradition than the seating arrangements in Jacobson's Temple in Seesen had been. Jacobson had retained a more traditional balcony for women, keeping them out of the main body of the synagogue. It is possible that the arrangements for the seating of women in the Beer Temple (also known as the Beer-Jacobson Temple) reflected Amalia's influence; the historian of Reform Judaism, Michael A. Meyer, has commented that, 'Beer's wife, Amalia, was an educated, cultured woman deeply attached to her faith ... it is not unlikely that she was an important influence behind the establishment of the temple in her home in 1815.'[11]

The Temple's organ and a boys' choir were situated at the far end of the room where the men sat. Some of the music for the new liturgy was provided by Christian composers, notably Giacomo's old tutors, Carl Zelter and Bernhard Weber. The format of the services was taken from Jacobson's model. Although much of the Sabbath liturgy was still in Hebrew, it was pronounced in the Sephardic manner, which was considered to be more decorous than the Yiddish intonation. Some of the prayers were in German, and some, in particular the later ones arising from the Diaspora, had been removed altogether, as they contained references to persecution, with lamentations and prayers for the return to Jerusalem, which no longer seemed appropriate sentiments for loyal Prussian citizens.

There was also an edifying and uplifting sermon in German by one of the young lay preachers. Along with Eduard Kley, the preachers at the Beer Temple included many of the future leaders of the later reform movement, such as Isaac Auerbach, Carl Günsburg, and Leopold Zunz. The Temple rapidly attracted large numbers of worshippers, with over 400 people regularly crowding into it to attend the Sabbath services.

Not everyone was happy with the new Temple, however. The liturgy was not as radical as some, such as David Friedländer, might have liked. In 1812, Friedländer had put forward a proposal to change the day of worship to a Sunday like the Christian services, and remove Hebrew from the liturgy altogether, reducing it to the status of a dead language. Few would have gone as far as he did. The new leaders were walking a tightrope: on the one side, radicals like Friedländer despised them for their caution; on the other, the orthodox condemned them as traitors to Judaism.

The transition from being a separate people to being Germans of Jewish faith was a psychological leap that many could not, and did not wish to, make. The introduction of German into the synagogue had frightening implications for many Jews: the Hebrew language not only linked them to their past in Palestine, it also bound together all Jews living in the Diaspora, wherever they might be. The liturgy in Hebrew was common to all, and was a part of the glue that held the Jews together, while they waited in exile for the appearance of the true Messiah.

The more orthodox did not accept the proposition that tradition could be divisible into essential and non-essential elements: in their view, the whole of Judaism would be in danger of dissolution if the most minor of the laws and traditions were abrogated. This reasoning appeared outdated and anachronistic to the more integrated Jews, who were searching for a way of life that would retain what they felt was essential to Judaism, while allowing them to live in a contemporary fashion. Tensions were exacerbated by the attitudes of converts such as Marcus Robert, who remarked that the Beer Temple was 'an abomination to the bigoted Jewish Pharisees'.[12]

It was not, however, the traditionalists within the Jewish community who brought about the abrupt closure of the Beer Temple not very long after it had opened. In November 1815, the Prussian King happened to see a notice in one of the Berlin newspapers advertising the publication of a sermon by Isaac Auerbach, which was being sold in aid of a soldiers' charity. The sermon was described as having been given at a 'new private temple' in the city. The words 'private' and 'new' were quite enough to alarm Frederick William III.

A deeply conservative man who prized conformity, he was threatened by any challenge to the status quo, and particularly feared the formation of sects of any sort, believing that these would inevitably lead to chaos and anarchy. He was also keen on furthering the conversion of the Jews to Christianity, and was unlikely to look favourably on any development that might make Judaism more attractive to its adherents. Once he had heard of the new services, there was little chance of them being allowed to continue. On 9 December 1815 he issued an order banning all private synagogues.

On 11 January 1816, Jacob wrote to Chancellor Hardenberg, asking him for support in petitioning the King for permission to keep the Beer Temple open. He explained to Hardenberg that only the oldest people could still understand Hebrew, and that a German-language service was needed to cater for a large sector of the community. He stressed that the services, although partly in German, were 'strictly according to the Jewish rite'. The

Beer Temple was a 'place of refuge' where the religious needs of those people who could not understand the language of the traditional liturgy could be met. He added, 'The ban has deeply shocked me and a large number of my brothers in faith, as it has completely destroyed the comforting prospect of our being able to maintain an edifying public service for ourselves and for our descendants.'[13]

Frederick William replied to Hardenberg on 28 January, refusing Jacob's request. The King's view was that, if there was a problem with the language used in the services, the community should 'task their rabbis' with replacing the Hebrew with German. He confirmed the ban on holding services in any meeting place outside the main synagogue, adding: 'There is no intolerance in this, but merely the maintenance of order that is necessary to prevent the formation of sects that can arise from such secessions.'[14]

Frederick William cannot have had much understanding of the issues involved if he seriously believed that the rabbis would meekly acquiesce to a request to jettison Hebrew in favour of German. Nonetheless, the King's answer had to be accepted as final. It appeared that the Temple was closed down for good, and that religious reform in Berlin had been stifled at birth.

## Notes

1. Shmuel Feiner, *Moses Mendelssohn. Sage of Modernity*, Anthony Berris (trans.) (New Haven, CT and London: Yale University Press, 2010), p.142.
2. Charles Burney, *The Present State of Music in Germany, the Netherlands and United Provinces* (London, 1775), vol. 2, pp.301-2.
3. Rahel Levin Varnhagen, *Familienbriefe*, Renata Barovero (ed.) (Munich: C. H. Beck, 2009), p.655.
4. Unpublished letter, Leopold Zunz to M Ehrenberg, 16 October 1815, Leopold and Adelheid Zunz Collection; AR 3648; box 1; folder 75; Leo Baeck Institute. Courtesy of Leo Baeck Institute.
5. Giacomo Meyerbeer, *Briefwechsel und Tagebücher*, Heinz Becker, Gudrun Becker and Sabine Henze-Döhring (eds) (Berlin: Walter de Gruyter, 1960-2006), vol. 1, pp.280-1.
6. Meyerbeer, *Briefwechsel und Tagebücher*, vol. 1, p.295.
7. Steven M. Lowenstein, *The Berlin Jewish Community. Enlightenment, Family and Crisis, 1770-1830* (New York and Oxford: Oxford University Press, 1994), p.260 n 49.
8. Meyerbeer, *Briefwechsel und Tagebücher*, vol. 1, p.62.
9. Ibid., p.207.
10. Varnhagen, *Familienbriefe*, p.655.
11. Michael A. Meyer, *Response to Modernity. A History of the Reform Movement in Judaism* (Detroit, MI: Wayne State University Press, 1995), p.47.
12. Varnhagen, *Familienbriefe*, p.655.
13. Irene A. Diekmann (ed.), *Juden in Berlin. Bilder, Dokumente, Selbstzeugnisse* (Leipzig: Henschel Verlag, 2009), p.77.
14. Meyerbeer, *Briefwechsel und Tagebücher*, vol. 1, pp.32-3.

# 10

## The Villa in the Tiergarten

Jacob must have been disappointed by the closure of the Temple, which he had put so much money and effort into establishing. However, given that it was the King himself who had ended the initiative, there was nothing further to be done – at least, for the time being. There were other matters to claim Jacob's attention: fortunately, his business affairs were flourishing. His concerns over the future of the cane sugar industry had been dispelled once peacetime conditions had returned.

As soon as the continental blockade had been lifted, and the importation of raw sugar from the British colonies in the Caribbean had resumed, business had picked up. In the aftermath of the Wars, he closed down a dye factory in Hamburg, which had been losing money, and established a new pharmaceutical company. Jacob had also retained his old link with Judyta Jacubowiczowa, the Jewish army supplier and banker in Warsaw. In 1813, he was acting as her agent in Berlin, collecting a large sum on her behalf that she was owed by the Prussian state.[1] Both Jacob and Judyta came from Frankfurt an der Oder families, and no doubt she chose him as her agent because of this link – family connections still played an important role in Jewish business networks.

Although he never formally owned a banking house, Jacob's activities as a financier were extensive, and by the close of 1815 he was reckoned to be the richest individual in Berlin.[2] By the middle of the next year, while retaining the house in Spandauer Strasse, the Beers had bought a spacious and imposing villa in the fashionable environs of the Tiergarten, Berlin's great park. The date of the purchase is not known, but it is likely to have been linked with the continuing rise in the family's public status, in particular the award of the Order of Louise to Amalia, as well as with the establishment of the Temple in the Spandauer Strasse house.

The Tiergarten lay to the west of Berlin, between the city and the palace of Charlottenburg, bounded on the north by the River Spree. Its 500 acres of woodland, intersected by sandy paths and meandering streams, had originally been a royal hunting ground. Frederick the Great had turned it into a public park, creating picturesque vistas with water basins, grottos, plazas and classical statuary.

It was a hugely popular destination for outings: all of Berlin society was to be seen in the Tiergarten, strolling in the woods and groves, boating on the waterways and taking refreshments at the riverside beer stalls and coffee houses. In the late eighteenth century, wealthy Berliners had begun to build villas on the edges of the park. Amalia's father had owned a residence in the Tiergarten, and she and Jacob had spent their summers there in the early years of the century. August Iffland had been a frequent guest. He would arrive at seven in the morning, and stay until Jacob took him into town in the carriage, on his way to the office.

The large and impressive villa the Beers now owned had been built by Lieutenant General Karl von Goetze, the military commander of the Berlin garrison in the closing years of the preceding century.[3] The house and its extensive gardens were situated in the north-eastern part of the park, in an area known as the Zuckerbusch – the 'sugar bush' – an appropriate name for the site of the Beers' residence, given the source of their wealth. The plot sat between the Exerzierplatz, the old parade ground created by the 'Soldier King' Frederick William I, in 1730, and the riverside plaza known as In den Zelten – 'In the Tents'.

The plaza was popular for its numerous refreshment booths (originally tented, thus giving the area its name), and for the covered wooden boats known to the Berliners as 'gondolas', which ferried parties between In den Zelten's landing stage and the gardens of Bellevue, Prince August's palace further down the river.[4] The Zelten, fairly close to the city, and with attractive open views over the Spree and the park, was one of the busiest spots in the Tiergarten.

Initially, the Tiergarten villa was only habitable during the summer months, but the Beers had long-term plans for making it their main residence by winter-proofing and extending it. Over the years they would add a hothouse for exotic plants, an orangery, and a large hall for receptions and concerts, as well as stables and a coach-house. They also completely renovated the interior to provide a fitting setting for Amalia's soirées.

Her salon was rapidly becoming a focal point of Berlin's artistic and social life, attracting eminent musicians and artistes passing through the city in much the same way as, in the 1760s, Moses Mendelssohn's house had become a gathering place for philosophers and scholars. When the Viennese art dealer, Johann Artaria, visited Berlin looking for art works in 1818, Rahel Levin Varnhagen suggested that he should be introduced to

Amalia, both because of her knowledge of art, and because 'he will know the town, once he has been at a soirée of hers'.[5]

As the wife of the richest man in Berlin, and a Dame of the Order of Louise, Amalia held formal receptions and concerts of unrivalled magnificence in the Tiergarten villa. Her great-nephew Felix Eberty claimed in his memoirs that, in the first third of the century, no other house in Berlin could match the Beer villa for social brilliance. He recalled that as a child he was overcome by a sense of solemnity whenever he entered the imposing rooms where Amalia received her visitors. He also describes more intimate family rooms: a small, softly lit boudoir, with subdued light coming in through panes of coloured glass, a set of elegant bathrooms, and delicate interior garden rooms with domed glass roofs. Nothing like this was to be found in any other private house of the time.[6]

The villa was to become a well-known Berlin landmark. The Beers' friend, the dramatist Karl von Holtei, on hearing many years later that the house was to be turned into an institute for sea cadets, exclaimed:

> The Beer house in the Tiergarten! What a world of memories this thought conjures up! The house was thronged with all those who shone at court, who wielded power in the state, or taught from the professorial chair; all who were foremost in life, in learning, and in the arts, whether they were rich or poor, noble or humble, local or foreign.[7]

He would have been saddened to know that today there is no trace of the Beer villa. The city has grown up around the Tiergarten, and the German Chancellery now occupies the land where Amalia held her soirées.

But in 1816, even in its undeveloped state, the villa and its gardens offered a perfect venue for the receptions and concerts that Amalia enjoyed hosting. Some of the glamorous artistes who frequented the Beers' new residence were old friends. The Austrian soprano Anna Milder, who had been a pupil of Salieri in Vienna, and had created the title role in Beethoven's *Fidelio*, returned to Berlin in 1815. She had first visited the city four years previously, when she had enjoyed enormous success in Gluck's *Iphigénie en Tauride* and Mozart's *Zauberflöte*, and had become an intimate of the Beer family.

Milder had arrived in Berlin for this second visit in May 1815, and by March 1816 she had sung the role of Fidelio at the Berlin Opera sixteen times. Amalia had no doubt where the credit for the success of the opera lay:

However many good pieces there might be in this opera, in my opinion it was a great bit of luck for Beethoven that he wrote this role for Milder as it suits her voice so well, she sings it so beautifully, with so much love, and the real proof is that when anyone else now sings it in Vienna it is whistled off!

In May 1816, Milder performed at the Beer salon, singing so wonderfully that 'everyone present, men as well as women, were so moved that they had tears in their eyes'.[8]

A particularly welcome guest arrived in early June. Carl Maria von Weber, Giacomo's old fellow student at Darmstadt, was now director of the Prague Opera. He was in Berlin to oversee the production of a cantata he had composed the previous year to celebrate Wellington's victory over Napoleon at Waterloo. He had agreed to donate the proceeds of the concert to the Patriotic Women's Association, which made it a particularly important event for Amalia. Naturally, von Weber was invited to stay at the villa. Jacob and Amalia considered him a family friend: he had lodged at the Spandauer Strasse house previously when visiting Berlin on concert tours, and in 1812 had spent several months staying with the Beers while his opera *Sylvana* was being produced in Berlin.

The Beers had been instrumental in persuading August Iffland to accept *Sylvana*. Iffland had rejected the work after it had been abandoned at the rehearsal stage in 1811 by Righini, who had pronounced it unworkable. Jacob and Amalia had persuaded Iffland to try again, this time with Bernhard Weber as director instead of Righini, and the opera had been staged successfully on 12 July 1812. Not surprisingly, Carl von Weber was fond of Jacob and Amalia. He had given his Prague acquaintance Franz Bayer an introduction to the Beers the previous year, describing Amalia to Franz as 'a marvellous, good person, in whom everything distinguished is united', and Jacob as 'a splendid, dear man'.[9]

Von Weber arrived in Berlin on 9 June 1816, and wrote to the singer Caroline Brandt, his future wife, that he was received by the Beers with 'the sincerest love and care, a beautiful room, a piano, a wonderful view, comfort, everything ...'.[10] However, he soon found that there were disadvantages to living in the Tiergarten that summer. It rained almost incessantly in Berlin during his stay, and in fact, the weather was exceptionally cold right across Europe.

This poor summer was due to the after-effects of a massive volcanic eruption in Indonesia the previous year. On 10 April 1815, Mount Tambora had exploded with a force ten times that of Krakatoa, killing at least 70,000 people, and plunging an area 400 miles in radius into darkness for two days. The volcanic ash that had been thrown up twenty miles into the atmosphere by the eruption had gradually drifted across the world, causing bad weather and a widespread failure of crops. 1816 became known as the 'year without a summer'.

Von Weber frequently had to be in town in the evenings for rehearsals and social gatherings, returning to the villa late at night. The main road through the Tiergarten, leading from the Brandenburg Gate towards Charlottenburg, had been paved in 1799, but the smaller paths had no hard surface. In dry weather the soft sand was dusty, and in rainy weather it was muddy. Carriages were quickly bogged down in the wet summer weather, making travel to and from the Tiergarten houses uncomfortable. A lack of street lighting, even in the city, made the journey potentially dangerous as well as tiring. In wintertime, small oil lamps were hung on chains across the Berlin streets, giving out a flickering light, but in the summer even this partial illumination was unavailable, as the lamps were taken down between May and September.

Berlin's pavements and roads were notorious: paving, where it existed, was uneven or broken, full of holes and pits, and riven by deep gutters carrying effluent from the houses. The authorities issued regulations from time to time ordering householders to keep the pavements outside their houses clean, but few, it appeared, took any notice. It was not unknown for an unwary pedestrian to fall into one of the pits on a dark evening, and be found dead the next morning.

Carl von Weber had never been robust. He had been born with a congenital hip deformity that had left him with a limp, and his already frail constitution had been further undermined in 1806, when he had accidently drunk some engravers' acid that had been decanted into a wine bottle. More recently, he had been experiencing serious bouts of ill-health that stemmed from the tuberculosis that would kill him within a decade. He soon decided to stay over in town after late-night rehearsals or parties, telling Caroline that 'it's no fun, having to get back to the Tiergarten'.[11]

On his first afternoon in Berlin, von Weber met Anna Milder at the Beer villa, along with the Berlin opera singer Caroline Seidler, and the Austrian composer and virtuoso pianist Johann Nepomuk Hummel. Hummel had been a child prodigy, who had so impressed Mozart that he had taught the boy for free. Hummel was on a concert tour that summer, and had become friendly with the Beers during his stay in the Prussian capital, to the extent of calling Amalia his 'dear Mama'. But Amalia did not respond to him with equal warmth: her maternal pride had been injured by the Berlin public's enthusiastic reception of Hummel, and by the glowing press reports of his piano recitals. The *Allgemeine musikalische Zeitung* had claimed that in many respects he was 'better than any living pianist'.

To Amalia, this accolade was a direct insult to her son, despite the fact that by 1816 Giacomo had rejected performance in favour of composition. Hummel was not a handsome man, and Amalia made it clear to Giacomo that despite all the fuss in Berlin, she thought him neither as good-looking nor as talented as her dear son, adding for good measure that, in her opinion, Hummel's wife was clearly head over heels in love with Giacomo.[12]

Carl von Weber's presence in Berlin gave Amalia the opportunity to meet one of Giacomo's earliest collaborators, the Munich theatre director and actor Johann Gottfried Wohlbrück. Wohlbrück was the librettist of Carl's cantata, *Kampf und Sieg* [Battle and Victory], and had also written the text for Giacomo's second opera *Wirth und Gast* [Host and Guest]. Giacomo seemed to admire him, referring to him as 'good old Wohlbrück' and 'this outstanding artist' in his diary,[13] although critical opinion was divided about Wohlbrück's acting talents. Amalia did not take to him. She thought him insincere, a quality she particularly disliked, telling her son that 'He evinces so much sweetness that I really believe he must be the sole cause of the current fall in the price of sugar.'[14]

In spring 1816, both Giacomo and Wilhelm were in Rome. Wilhelm had been given permission by his parents to accompany his elder brother to Italy for a holiday, before entering the family business. In her letters to her sons, Amalia kept them up to date with theatre and family news, while Jacob added brief postscripts on practical and financial matters. On 30 March 1816, in a cryptic note, Jacob advised Giacomo that if he wanted to allude to anti-Semitism in his letters he should do so in a veiled manner, and should tell Wilhelm to do the same.[15]

Despite the Beers' success and social status, they were constantly alert to the possibility of rejection and prejudice. They were only too well aware that some of the people who were so anxious to attend their social events did not hesitate to abuse their hosts behind their backs for their Jewishness.

In 1814, Rahel Levin's niece Johanna had sent her aunt an account of one of the Beers' New Year's Eve balls, which she had attended. These balls were particularly popular, and invitations much sought-after. A young Prussian woman, who had not been invited, had nonetheless managed to gatecrash the party. Instead of remaining prudently inconspicuous, she had drawn attention to herself by barging into a quadrille, a dance with complicated set-piece movements, which had been practised beforehand by the participants. After spoiling this performance, the uninvited guest had then adjourned to the supper table, where she ate and drank avidly, and where she was overheard by Johanna asking her neighbour in a loud and contemptuous tone, 'So what am I supposed to do if a Jew asks me to dance?'

Johanna was outraged, asking her aunt: 'How do you like that for infamy? First she pushes herself in uninvited, eats as if she had never seen such lovely food before, then says something like that, and adds a lot more, serving as an excuse for how she came to get into such company. Shouldn't she be horsewhipped?'[16]

For some of the Beers' Jewish contemporaries, the continuing prejudice that the Edict of Emancipation had been unable to erase was reason enough for converting to Christianity. On 21 March 1816, Abraham and Lea Mendelssohn secretly had their four children, including 10-year-old Fanny and 7-year-old Felix, baptised into the Christian faith in the Jerusalemkirche in Berlin. Abraham and Lea themselves did not convert until 1822, and neither their, nor their children's baptisms were motivated by religious conviction.

Abraham Mendelssohn wrote to his daughter Fanny at the time of her confirmation, explaining that he had brought her up as a Christian purely because it was the majority faith in their society. He took the view, not uncommon in the age of Enlightenment, that all religions spring from a common ground, an innate ethical sense in human beings, and that the different forms they have taken are attributable purely to accidents of history and culture.[17]

It made no sense to Abraham Mendelssohn to subject his children to discrimination and hatred for the sake of a religion which he saw as incidental. The pragmatic course was to join the majority. Many nineteenth-century Jewish musicians and writers agreed: the composers Ignaz Moscheles, Jacques Offenbach, Anton Rubinstein and Ferdinand Hiller, and the writers Heinrich Heine and Ludwig Börne all converted. The Beers took a very different view: while thoroughly immersing themselves in German culture, they retained a strong self-identification as Jews.

Nonetheless, whatever their religious differences with the Mendelssohns, the Beer family remained on amicable terms with them. Amalia liked Lea in particular, describing her as 'a very intelligent woman, who knows a lot about music' – high praise, indeed.[18] Lea herself had a good deal to say about the Beers, towards whom she maintained a generally friendly, although detached stance. She was occasionally critical of the younger members of the family, although she was fond of young Michael, and she appreciated Amalia's qualities.

This friendliness between converts to Christianity and the Jewish community, like the social mixing of Jews with Gentiles, was a relatively new phenomenon. In previous centuries, converts had been excluded from Jewish society, and had led difficult lives: not fully accepted by Christian society, yet cut off from their families and friends. In one famous case, conversion had led to a legal dispute over a family inheritance.

Moses Isaac-Fliess, who had been associated with Daniel Itzig and Veitel Heine Ephraim in the mint business during the Seven Years' War, had stipulated in his will that, if any of his children converted, they would lose any right to their inheritance. When two of his daughters converted and married Christian men in 1780, shortly after Isaac-Fliess's death, their brothers refused to pay their dowries, and the case went to the civil courts. Eventually, King Frederick William II decided in favour of the brothers, on the grounds that their father had the right to leave his wealth as he chose.

Times were changing by 1816, when Amalia counted the convert Friederike Liman, formerly Fradchen Liepmann, as a friend. Friederike had been baptised in 1809, and had since separated from her husband. She had been thrilled to meet Anna Milder at one of Amalia's soirées, noting with pleasure Milder's warmth towards her when meeting her there, compared with her coolness on previous occasions. Friederike told her friend Rahel Levin that the Beer house was the only one she frequented, and that she preferred going there to anywhere else, because 'it's a place where you are received in such an easy and friendly way, where the highest degree of good-natured Jewish liberality reigns, where you see all classes of people, where there is singing, card games, readings'.[19]

As the successful summer season of 1816 progressed, Jacob and Amalia began planning a major project – a family reunion with Giacomo and Wilhelm in Italy. They had intended to leave Berlin on 16 June, but decided to put off their departure until after Carl von Weber's concert, which was due to take place two days later. The production of *Kampf und Sieg* in aid of the Patriotic Women's Association was a triumph, grossing 1,168 thalers.[20] The cantata, which was sung by Anna Milder along with Christian Fischer and Friedrich Eunike, bass and tenor respectively at the Berlin Opera, was described as imaginative and powerful by the influential *Allgemeine musikalische Zeitung*.

It was consequently scheduled for a second performance, this time as a benefit for the composer. Princess Marianne attended this performance, on 23 June, which, she said, enchanted the entire audience, adding that she much preferred von Weber's cantata to Beethoven's *Schlacht bei Vittoria*

[The Battle of Vittoria].[21] However, Carl von Weber did not make a great deal of money out of his benefit. As luck would have it, the date had clashed with the arrival of a new star in Berlin, the Italian soprano Angelica Catalani, one of the greatest operatic singers of the age.

Catalani, by then at the height of her powers at the age of 36, had enjoyed her greatest successes to date in England, where she had reigned supreme on the London operatic stage from 1806 to 1813. Her voice was astonishingly powerful and flexible, although her love of excessive ornamentation and her preference for Italian *bel canto* over German opera, especially that of Mozart, had convinced some critics that she was musically ignorant. She was now based in Paris, where Giacomo had already heard her sing, in January, in Simon Mayr's comic opera *Il Fanatico per la musica* at the Théâtre Favart. He had been decidedly impressed by her 'many-sided talent'.[22]

Amalia was eagerly awaiting Catalani's arrival. On 2 July, she told Giacomo triumphantly that, 'I am the object of envy of all Berlin, for she comes to no one but me. When she was here for the first time, an hour later there was so much excitement in the city, as if all the kings of the world were with me.' Catalani brought the Russian ambassador to take tea at the Tiergarten villa, where they remained for over two hours. Some 'gentlemen' who were also there, Amalia boasted to Giacomo, were so thrilled to see Catalani close up that they wouldn't have exchanged the experience for a thousand gold sovereigns.[23] A few days later, Amalia hosted a sumptuous dinner for Catalani, which began at five in the afternoon, and was still going strong at eight when the exhausted Carl von Weber quietly left the party and went to bed.

Angelica Catalani had arrived in Berlin with letters of credit and introduction to the Beers, with the result that Jacob was handling her finances while she was in the city. He was clearly impressed by the money she was able to earn, telling Giacomo that, after her first two concerts, she had given him proceeds of over 5,000 thalers to bank. He commented that Catalani must be a very rich woman indeed, adding that deputations from the opera houses in Frankfurt an der Oder and Stettin had arrived in Berlin to offer her huge sums of money to include their cities in her schedule.[24]

Catalani's six performances in Berlin all sold out, and the *Allgemeine musikalische Zeitung* reported that she had delighted the audiences, exceeding even the high expectations that her reputation had aroused. She had made enough money – 15,000 thalers according to Amalia[25] – to give her last two concerts for charity. The King himself graciously offered her the use of the Garrison Church for her final appearance.

Once Carl von Weber's and Angelica Catalani's concerts were over, the Beers' delayed plans for their trip to Italy for a reunion with their sons could be revived. It was a major undertaking. The 700-mile journey by coach would take them several weeks, with frequent stops for rest, and to change horses. They decided to travel at a leisurely pace, spending around a month en route, heading first for Leipzig, and then Prague. Carl von Weber was staging a production of Giacomo's comic opera *Wirth und Gast*, which had been re-named *Alimelek*, at the Prague Opera, and the Beers' journey was timed so that they could attend a performance.

*Alimelek* would be the first of Giacomo's operas that his family had seen on stage. It was set in Baghdad, with a plot derived from the *Thousand and One Nights*, in which a young man becomes 'caliph for a day' after being given a sleeping potion. It had failed at its premiere in Stuttgart two years previously; Giacomo had been horrified when he had arrived there shortly before the performance to find the cast almost totally unprepared, and two of the singers hoarse. However, von Weber had always admired the work, despite its lukewarm reception, telling Giacomo that, 'I have seldom had so much pleasure in a piece of music. It is an excellent work, dear brother, full of real dramatic features, truth, charm and novelty.'[26]

The performance took place on 13 August, and was met, according to von Weber, with enthusiastic applause. The Beers set off again the next day, travelling via Munich, Innsbruck and Milan to Genoa, where Amalia was intending to take a sea-bathing cure. Von Weber had asked Johann Gänsbacher, Giacomo's old Darmstadt friend who was now serving in the Austrian army, to look after the Beers when they arrived at Innsbruck after the tiring journey through the Tyrol. 'They are splendid, dear people,' von Weber told him, 'who truly overwhelmed me with love and attention in Berlin.'[27]

The mountainous route through the Tyrol was a spectacular one, but it could also be dangerous. George Gordon, Lord Byron, who was also travelling in northern Italy that autumn, reported in his letters home that a party of English carriages near Sesto in the Tyrolean Alps had been attacked by a band of robbers. They had 'ransacked some preceding travellers ... of cash and raiment, besides putting them in bodily fear, and lodging about twenty slugs in the retreating part of a courier'.[28]

Luckily, the Beers met with no such incidents, and had a safe passage over the mountains. Giacomo and Wilhelm travelled up from Sicily, where Giacomo had been collecting local folk songs, to Genoa, to meet up there with their parents and brothers. Jacob and Amalia had not seen their eldest son for five years,[29] but there is no record of this reunion; as the family were all together, there are no letters from the Italian journey, and Giacomo did not keep a diary over the period. However, Louis Spohr, the composer and violinist, now an old friend of Giacomo's, noted that he had the 'unexpected pleasure' of meeting Meyerbeer and his whole family in Venice on 20 October.

The family stayed in Venice for several weeks before Amalia and Giacomo moved on to Florence, while Heinrich, Wilhelm and Michael went directly to Rome, where they all intended to meet up again for Christmas. It appears likely that Jacob returned to Berlin in November when the rest of the family moved south from Venice. He had recently bought a newly patented English sugar refining system, which he was planning to install in the Heiligegeiststrasse factory in the New Year.[30] The new process would both shorten the time needed for refining, and increase the sugar yield, making the whole process more efficient. It was an important development, and Jacob may well have wanted to oversee the installation of the new machinery.

Louis Spohr's diary records that the three younger Beer brothers were in Rome in late November. This was not the most cheerful season to be in the Eternal City. During Advent the theatres were closed and public concerts prohibited, and in addition, the weather was extremely cold that year, with a chilly north wind blowing. However, they made the best of it, seeing the sights during the day, and entertaining themselves with card games in the evenings. Spohr records that

> I kept frequent company with the Beer family, and, as they had arrived later, I could now serve them as cicerone. Of an evening, when the light no longer permitted anything more to be seen (for the theatres were still closed during Advent), the three sons accompanied me sometimes to my lodgings, and we then shortened the long evenings with a game at whist. As it was at that time, however, very cold in Rome, and there was no means of heating my room, we used to set ourselves down in my enormous bed with our backs turned to the four cardinal points, with the leaf of a table between us, and in that manner played our rubber in comfortable warmth and in the best humour.[31]

Spohr was desperately short of funds, and admits in his memoirs that he was sorely tempted to ask for a loan from the wealthy Beer family. He was held back by the revulsion he felt at the idea of sponging off his friends, and could not pluck up the courage to ask them.

Giacomo and Amalia arrived in Rome from Florence, on 22 December. The theatres reopened after their Advent period of closure soon after their arrival, as Christmas ushered in the Carnival. On 27 December, Spohr records that he and Giacomo went to see a new opera buffa at the Valle Theatre, while Amalia went with Spohr's wife and children to hear Rossini's *Tancredi* at the Argentino. Gioacchino Rossini, just five months younger than Giacomo and Italy's preeminent composer, was leading a reform of Italian opera, replacing the stiff conventions of *opera seria* with a more natural dramatic characterisation.

His early works *Tancredi* and *L'italiana in Algeri* had been an instant success in 1813, only surpassed by the sensational *Il barbiere di Siviglia* in 1816. Giacomo was studying his works, with an eye to learning all he could from the maestro. It appears that he introduced the famous composer to his family during their stay in Rome, as in June the following year, Heinrich asked Giacomo in a letter, that, 'if you should chance to see Rossini, give him a thousand greetings from me'.[32]

The family's Italian holiday was over by early January 1817, when they returned to Berlin, apart from young Michael, who had been given permission to remain behind with his eldest brother. Giacomo accompanied his mother over the mountains as far as Munich, seeing her safely onto German soil before returning to Venice. It was not a happy journey. Amalia found the parting from Giacomo deeply painful, and began planning a return to Italy almost as soon as she arrived back in grey and wintry Berlin.

## Notes

1. Cornelia Aust, *The Jewish Economic Elite. Making Modern Europe* (Bloomington, IN: Indiana University Press, 2018), p.139.
2. Sven Kuhrau and Kurt Winkler (eds), *Juden Bürger Berliner. Das Gedächtnis der Familie Beer–Meyerbeer–Richter* (Berlin: Henschel Verlag, 2004), p.70.
3. Heinz Becker, 'Die Beer'sche Villa im Tiergarten' in Hans J. Reichhardt (ed.), *Berlin im Geschichte und Gegenwart. Jahrbuch des Landesarchivs Berlin* (Berlin: Siedler Verlag, 1990), p.61.
4. Bellevue was built in 1786 for Frederick the Great's younger brother Ferdinand, and is now the official residence of the German President.
5. Rahel Levin Varnhagen, *Familienbriefe*, Renata Barovero (ed.) (Munich: C. H. Beck, 2009), p.776.
6. Felix Eberty, *Jugenderinnerungen eines alten Berliners* (Berlin: Verlag für Kulturpolitik, 1925), p.103.
7. Karl von Holtei, *Charpie. Eine Sammlung Vermischter Aufsätze* (Breslau: Verlag von Eduard Trewendt, 1866), pp.171-2.
8. Giacomo Meyerbeer, *Briefwechsel und Tagebücher*, Heinz Becker, Gudrun Becker and Sabine Henze-Döhring (eds) (Berlin: Walter de Gruyter, 1960-2006), vol. 1, pp.310-11.

9.   Letter, Carl Maria von Weber to Franz Rudolph Bayer, 25 July 1815, Carl-Maria-von-Weber-Gesamtausgabe. Digitale Edition, http://weber-gesamtausgabe.de/A040799 (Version 3.4.2 vom 8. February 2019).

10.  Letter, Carl Maria von Weber to Caroline Brandt, 11 June 1816, Carl-Maria-von-Weber-Gesamtausgabe. Digitale Edition, http://weber-gesamtausgabe.de/A040908 (Version 3.4.2 vom 8. February 2019).

11.  Letter, Carl Maria von Weber to Caroline Brandt, 14 June 1816, Carl-Maria-von-Weber-Gesamtausgabe. Digitale Edition, http://weber-gesamtausgabe.de/A040909 (Version 3.4.2 vom 8. February 2019).

12.  Meyerbeer, *Briefwechsel und Tagebücher*, vol. 1, p.313-14.

13.  Giacomo Meyerbeer, *The Diaries of Giacomo Meyerbeer*, Robert Letellier (ed. and trans.) (Madison, NJ: Fairleigh Dickinson University Press, 1999-2004), vol. 1, pp.262, 265.

14.  Meyerbeer, *Briefwechsel und Tagebücher*, vol. 1, pp.311, 314.

15.  Ibid., p.311. Jacob uses the Yiddish term *Risches* [hatred or malice directed towards Jews].

16.  Varnhagen, *Familienbriefe*, p.366.

17.  Sebastian Hensel, *Die Familie Mendelssohn 1729-1847* (Berlin: B. Behr's Verlag, 1903), vol. 1, pp.94-5.

18.  Meyerbeer, *Briefwechsel und Tagebücher*, vol. 1, p.313.

19.  Birgit Bosold, *Friederike Liman. Briefwechsel mit Rahel Levin Varnhagen und Karl Gustav von Brinckmann sowie Aufzeichnungen von Rahel Levin Varnhagen und Karl August Varnhagen. Eine historisch-kritische Edition mit Nachwort*, Ph.D. diss., (University of Hamburg, 1996), p.79.

20.  Letter, Carl Maria von Weber to Count Brühl, 01 July 1816, Carl-Maria-von-Weber-Gesamtausgabe. Digitale Edition, http://weber-gesamtausgabe.de/A040915 (Version 3.4.2 vom 8. February 2019).

21.  Wilhelm Baur, *Prinzessin Wilhelm von Preussen* (Hamburg, Agentur des Rauhen Hauses, 1886), p.221.

22.  Meyerbeer, *Diaries,* vol. 1, p.338.

23.  Meyerbeer, *Briefwechsel und Tagebücher*, vol. 1, p.317.

24.  Ibid., p.318.

25.  Ibid., p.318.

26.  Letter, Carl Maria von Weber to Giacomo Meyerbeer, 11 October 1815, Carl-Maria-von-Weber-Gesamtausgabe. Digitale Edition, http://weber-gesamtausgabe.de/A040828 (Version 3.4.2 vom 8. February 2019)

27.  Letter, Carl Maria von Weber to Johann Gänsbacher, 04 August 1816, Carl-Maria-von-Weber-Gesamtausgabe. Digitale Edition, http://weber-gesamtausgabe.de/A040919 (Version 3.4.2 vom 8. February 2019).

28.  Lord Byron, *Letters and Journals* (Newcastle upon Tyne: Cambridge Scholars' Publishing, 2009), vol. III, p.235.

29.  Giacomo and his parents had made a trip down the Rhine together in August 1811.

30.  Kuhrau and Winkler, *Juden Bürger Berliner*, p.70.

31.  Louis Spohr, *Louis Spohr's Autobiography* (London: Longman and Green, 1865), pp.48-9.

32.  Meyerbeer, *Briefwechsel und Tagebücher*, vol. 1, p.329.

# *11*

# The Beer Temple: Revival and Closure

Over the course of 1816, Jacob had continued to fight for the re-establishment of the Temple. As there was clearly no point in pursuing the matter further with the King, he had decided to take a different approach, and began applying for 'responsa'. These were authoritative opinions given by rabbis in response to questions on interpretations of the Law, and they carried great weight in religious controversies. If Jacob could obtain positive rulings on some of the innovations that had been introduced into Berlin, he would be in a much stronger position to claim that the new services were a development of, and not a break with, tradition, and that they did not in any way undermine rabbinic authority.

Jacob chose to approach Italian, rather than German, rabbis, probably because he felt that it was more likely that he would obtain a positive response from them. The Italian Jews' synagogue services had been held up as a model of decorum to the more unruly German Jews by the journal *Sulamith*:

> Their devotions in their temples are orderly, quiet, solemn and edifying; most of their rabbis are truly learned men ... It is calm in their synagogues; they pray with true devotion and exaltation of the heart. The voices of the congregation are rhythmical; no one outshouts the others; their Hebrew language is pure and melodious and their mother tongue is unadulterated, without being a miserable jargon ...[1]

Jacob received mixed responses to his enquiries. However, several Italian rabbis confirmed that sermons in the Italian language were not uncommon in their synagogues, and two of them also agreed that it was permissible to have organ music accompanying services, provided that, on the Sabbath or festival days, when Jews were forbidden to play instruments, the organist was a Christian. These statements enabled Jacob to claim that he had the sanction of a number of learned rabbis for controversial elements of the new services.

There was a postscript to this correspondence several years later, however. It appears that when Jacob had made his enquiries in 1816, he had not told the rabbis concerned why he wanted their opinions. When the reform movement began to spread, and the Italian rabbis realised that there was a real possibility of schism in Germany, they hastened to explain that their original responses had referred purely to long-accepted local practice in their own regions, and had never been intended to support any innovation, in Berlin or elsewhere.[2]

In January 1817, however, as the Beers returned from their trip to Italy, an unexpected opportunity of re-establishing the Temple appeared. The King had given permission for the rebuilding and extension of the old synagogue in the Heidereuthergasse, which had been established in the early years of the previous century, and was now too small for the congregation. He had also agreed to a suggestion made by the elders that the design of this new building should include an annex for German-language services. The idea was that this would bring these services under the aegis of the main synagogue, and so prevent any appearance of division in the community.

As the building works would probably take a year or so to complete, services would need to be held in other locations while the work was underway. After some negotiation, the King agreed to the interim use of three private buildings, including the Spandauer Strasse house. This by implication allowed the resumption of the reformed services straight away. The Jacobson Temple was not reactivated, so the Beer Temple remained the sole reform synagogue in Berlin.

The Temple re-opened in the summer of 1817. In September that year, Eduard Kley conducted a Christian-style confirmation service at the Temple for two girls, a departure from tradition not only in its format, but also in that the bar mitzvah, the Jewish rite of passage to adulthood, had traditionally been confined to males. At the age of 13, Jewish boys became subject to the requirements of the Law – bar mitzvah translates as 'son of the commandment'. This transition was marked by the boy being allowed to read publicly from the Torah at synagogue services – which women, of course, were not eligible to do.

Israel Jacobson had already instigated a confirmation service for boys that differed from the bar mitzvah, in being based on a Christian-style catechism, which required the child being confirmed to understand and affirm the teachings of the Jewish faith. The first event in the Jacobson Temple in the old Itzig Palace had been the confirmation of Jacobson's own son, Naphthali, during the Festival of Weeks in 1815. Heinrich Beer had been among those present at the service.

Kley's confirmation service at the Beer Temple, however, was a radical innovation; it was the first time that girls had undergone a rite of passage before the Ark in the previously all-male sanctuary of the synagogue. The journal *Sulamith* reported the event:

> Shortly before his departure to Hamburg, where he has been appointed Director of the new Jewish Free School, Dr Kley blessed two girls of Jewish parents (Demoiselle Bernsdorf and Demoiselle Bevern) in the most solemn way in the magnificent Beer Temple [in Berlin]. A gathering of 400 people, as many as the Temple can hold, dissolved, so to speak, in tears ... The lighted candles, the two girls, the first to be confirmed in Israel, who passed their examination with the greatest praise; in short, everything combined to make this one of the most solemn and most beautiful of festivals.[3]

Unfortunately, the King found out about the girls' confirmation, in much the same way as he had originally discovered the existence of the Beer Temple. In late 1817, he saw a report in a St Petersburg newspaper about a 'new rite' which had been introduced in Berlin. This in itself was enough to frighten Frederick William, but he was especially outraged to read that, according to the newspaper's informant, he had approved this rite himself.

The King immediately ordered an investigation. There was a real danger that he would again summarily shut down the Temple. The elders argued that, as similar confirmation services for boys had already been held elsewhere, there was a precedent, so that the equivalent service for girls could not be called a 'new rite'. In December 1817, Frederick William reluctantly gave permission for the Temple to continue temporarily, but only until the next summer, when the community synagogue was scheduled to re-open.

A few weeks later the elders of the Berlin community – including Jacob – wrote a lengthy letter to the Minister of Education, in which they defended the use of German in synagogue services as a vital part of the education of Jewish youth. They made the point again that, as few of the younger people in the community could understand the Hebrew language, the traditional services were incomprehensible to them. They added that many of the rabbis did not speak good German – in fact, Rabbi Weyl employed an assistant to help him with the language – so their communication was poor: 'their preaching consists of Talmudic disputation ... [when] the Talmud is seldom studied now ... hardly any of the young people can understand the rabbis' jargon.'[4] The elders argued that it was not actually forbidden in Jewish law to pray in the local language; the use of Hebrew was rather a long-standing custom that some people had come to see as sacrosanct.

They also repeated the claim that the confirmation rite for girls was not an innovation, but despite these protestations, the service was in fact a challenge to the traditional marginalisation of women in Judaism, and reflected the beginnings of a change in the role of women in Jewish religious life. Traditional services had been male-oriented, but women were encouraged to attend the new, reformed services. Women benefited both from the introduction of the German language in place of Hebrew, and from a change in the focus of religious life, as scholarly knowledge of the Law gradually came to be supplanted by the cultivation of personal moral and spiritual ideals.

During the nineteenth century, women's role in the home as guardians of morality and educators of children took on a new importance. From 1812, the journal *Sulamith* ran a series of essays written especially for women by one of its editors, Gotthold Salomon, a well-known preacher. In 1816, Salomon produced a devotional book for women based on these articles, with the title *Selima's Hours of Devotion, a moral-religious work for educated women.* Salomon presented himself as the editor, rather than the author, of the book, which claimed to contain the pious reflections of the fictional Selima, a young Jewish woman, on morality, religion, nature and the human condition. *Selima's Hours* also contained sections on Jewish history, and meditations for Jewish holidays. It was the first German-language book of devotions written specifically for women.

Salomon knew the Beers, and had preached in their Temple. Amalia Beer perfectly fitted the pattern of the new ideal of highly cultured, yet devout, womanhood propagated in *Sulamith* and in Salomon's book. She was, at one and the same time, a sophisticated salonnière with links to the highest circles in Berlin society, a devoted mother to her sons, a pious Jew, and a leading light in religious reform. The historian Benjamin Maria Baader has described her as a 'counter model to the Jewish salon women'[5] in her commitment to Judaism.

Amalia's language on the few occasions when she wrote about her religious feelings reflected a mood of elevated emotions. In a letter to Giacomo in 1810 from the seaside resort of Bad Doberan, she had described her reaction as she watched a sunset over the sea:

> It's difficult for me to convey this to you, and I can't express it any better than to say that I have never felt such religious emotion as in

that moment. Seize such moments, my dear Meyer, in which you can worship God's mightiness, and I am convinced that your religious faith will be so strengthened that you will never go astray.[6]

The words might have come from the mouth of Selima – or the pen of Salomon, who must have recognised Amalia's similarity to his fictional heroine, as he dedicated the book to her 'with the most heartfelt respect', describing her in the inscription as 'the worthy promoter of so much that is good and useful'.[7] The work was published with the aid of subscriptions: Israel Jacobson ordered ten copies, and Amalia six.

While the community synagogue was being rebuilt, the Beer Temple flourished. It is estimated that, in 1818, around a quarter of the Jews in Berlin were attending the services. The Temple had its detractors, however. One of its sharpest critics was the 24-year-old teacher Isaak Marcus Jost, who later became a historian and author of linguistic textbooks. In 1817, Jost was headmaster of the liberal Bock School in Berlin. Israel Jacobson had invited Jost to become a preacher at his Temple in the Itzig Palace, but he had refused. Jost was not particularly interested in religion, as he believed that the reform of education was a more important priority in the process of modernisation.

He was a touchy young man, however, anxious that due regard should be paid to his status. He was particularly concerned that no preferential treatment should be given to the pupils of the Heinemann School, a rival institute to the Bock. The Heinemann School provided the choir for the Beer Temple, which Jost rather ungraciously described as 'clumsy' and 'shrieking'. He also complained bitterly about the prominent positions given in the Temple to the wealthier members of the community, who had seats reserved for them in the best places, closest to the Ark. He insisted that he and his pupils should be given equally good seats.

Jost won his point, but when he and four of his pupils turned up late for the Day of Atonement – a good half an hour after the service had started – the doorman turned them away, and there was a bad-tempered altercation, resulting in Jost threatening to 'take measures which would be unpleasant for everyone concerned'. Jost subsequently criticised the leaders of the new services for concentrating on 'mere externals' out of fear that the Jewish orthodox would accuse them of heresy, and the Christians of deism.[8]

There was a good deal of truth in this. The reform movement had its roots in social, rather than in theological, impulses for change. None of the early leaders were rabbis or theologians, and their reforms were aimed at strengthening the adaptation of Jewish life to mainstream bourgeois culture. Judaism had little theological dogma, in any case; at its heart was the claim of the Jews to be the chosen people. The battleground between the early reformers and the orthodox lay in the question of whether this required the Jews to keep themselves entirely separate from their surroundings, in readiness to return to the Promised Land, or whether, and to what extent, the Jews might integrate, and what this might mean for their status as chosen people.

At the time, almost all rabbis were vehemently opposed to change, preferring to adhere to the medieval worldview that had served to define Jewish life for centuries. They naturally wished to preserve their own power base, and the reforms aroused fierce opposition. Pioneer reformers like Jacob Beer trod carefully, concentrating on the 'externals' that served as expressions of their new status as both Jews and Germans. In doing this, however, they contributed to the early stages of the creation of a new German-Jewish identity. They also sowed the seeds of a much wider reform movement, which was developed from the 1830s, when men such as Rabbi Abraham Geiger took up the doctrinal challenges posed by modernisation, and began to hammer out a theoretical basis for a new understanding of Judaism.

For the Beer family, the most important events that took place at their Temple – at least, in personal terms – were undoubtedly Heinrich's and Wilhelm's weddings in late 1818. Heinrich's bride was Rebecka, or Betty, Meyer, a cousin of Felix Mendelssohn's. Betty, a lively girl with a talent for singing and amateur theatricals, had become engaged to Heinrich in the spring of that year.

Betty's mother Recha, one of Moses Mendelssohn's daughters, had married Mendel Meyer, the son of the court banker at the duchy of Mecklinburg-Strelitz, in an arranged marriage, which had ended in divorce in 1800, when Betty had been 7 years old. After the divorce, Recha supported herself and her daughter by running a boarding school for girls in Altona, near Hamburg. In 1812, Recha and Betty had moved to Berlin, to be close to Recha's brother and sister-in-law, Abraham and Lea Mendelssohn.

Recha was one of only two of Moses Mendelssohn's six children to remain Jewish; the other was the eldest son, Joseph. Betty Meyer had apparently been baptised when younger, but, unusually, reverted to Judaism in order to marry Heinrich.[9] Recha and Betty were both keen to be accepted into the cultural circles of their relations. Henriette Herz, the former salonnière, told her friend, the theologian August Twesten, that Betty held musical parties, and that she and her mother also had literary evenings, although Henriette thought that these were badly done.

Betty had hesitated for some time before accepting Heinrich's proposal. Rahel Levin Varnhagen's friend, Friederike Liman, had noticed Heinrich's interest in Betty as early as March 1816, two years before the couple became engaged. Friederike had remarked to Rahel that '[Recha's] daughter is a nice girl, who has learnt a lot, is very musical and so has made herself popular in the Beer household; also, one of the sons is paying court to her.'[10] According to Henriette Herz, Betty jilted a young man called Müller in order to marry Heinrich. Henriette reported to Twesten in July 1817 that 'Betty will probably get married, but not to Müller - keep quiet about this, as it is not yet announced', adding in a later letter that the unfortunate Müller could take comfort from telling himself that if Betty could leave him like this, then she had never really been his.

Henriette Herz thought that the engagement to Heinrich had been masterminded by Recha, who wanted her daughter to marry a wealthy man. Henriette commented that, '[Betty] will be very rich, but I think that's about it, as there is a huge difference in education and understanding between her and the young man ... He worships her, his parents will support them, she will be rich, and I don't think she can resist that', adding '[Recha] Meyer has been very clever - as she is enormously clever.'[11]

Betty herself appears to have taken a pragmatic view of her engagement. In a letter that she wrote to her friend Rosa Herz in spring 1818, she described her situation as 'all that a sensible person, who is prepared to supply what is missing in it, could wish for', adding that 'my future happiness depends on my ability to do so'. She went on to remark that, 'All the other members of my family live in the most peaceful, carefree way with each other. My outer circumstances will be similar to theirs, and my inner situation will be too, if I behave in the right way, as the young man has a quite incomprehensible love for me, and hangs - literally - on my every look.'[12]

Betty was 25 at the time of her marriage, and a rather unkind remark some years later by Giacomo, in a letter to his wife Minna, suggests that she was not physically attractive. In his letter of June 1838, Giacomo says to Minna that he fell in love with her charming face and figure, but now that he knows her spiritual qualities 'I would have married you even if you had looked like Betty.'[13] Whatever Giacomo's opinion of her looks, however, Betty was clearly able to inspire devotion in at least two young men.

Betty's aunt, Henriette Mendelssohn, who knew the girl well, remarked rather cynically about her engagement to Heinrich that, 'After all, the circumstances in which Betty is marrying are not of the type to justify any gloomy prognostications. The family is respected and happy, the young man so romantic and loving that one can fear Betty will be punished for her indecisiveness by falling in love with her husband after the marriage.'[14]

Wilhelm's engagement to 18-year-old Doris Schlesinger followed almost immediately on Heinrich and Betty's. Doris's family came from Hamburg. Her parents, Behrend and Jüttche Schlesinger, had been uncle and niece, with an age difference of twenty years between them. Doris was the third of their four children. There can be little doubt as to why the confident and ebullient Wilhelm was attracted to Doris: she was invariably described by all who mentioned her as a ravishing beauty. Amalia thought her 'as beautiful as Love itself'.[15]

Heinrich and Betty's wedding took place on 30 August, and Wilhelm and Doris's on 5 September 1818.[16] Jewish weddings had traditionally been held in the open air, but it was felt by the reformers that a wedding in the synagogue was more in line with the new order. Both weddings were held in the Temple, although a rabbinically qualified man had to be brought in to supervise the marriage ceremony, as the Temple's lay preachers were not qualified to do so.

The Beer weddings were naturally extremely smart affairs. Giacomo's former tutor Bernhard Weber composed songs for both occasions, to poems by the ubiquitous Friedrich Gubitz. Amalia's great-nephew Felix Eberty attended both weddings. He was a little boy of 6 years old, and was thoroughly overawed by the splendour of the occasions. In later life, he clearly remembered a raised platform with a baldachin in a huge hall filled with smart people. 'Old Frau Beer' (who was only just over 50!) stood majestically next to it in great state, impressing young Felix with her Turkish turban topped by an egret's feather. Dazzled by this vision of magnificence, he remembered little else beyond the crowds of guests, and the wonderful smell of coffee.

The weddings had been important enough to attract guests from outside the Jewish community: Jacob reported proudly to Giacomo (who had decided not to return from Italy for the occasions), that a whole host of diplomats had been present at Hans's wedding, including the British ambassador and his entire family. At around that time, Jane Austen's favourite brother, Henry, was chaplain to the Berlin embassy: he later published a series of lectures he had given on the Book of Genesis in the embassy chapel. It is tempting to imagine that he may have attended Heinrich Beer's wedding at the Spandauer Strasse Temple.

If the rebuilding of the official synagogue had gone according to plan, the Beer Temple should have been closed by the time of the weddings. However – as they always do – the building project took much longer than had been anticipated, and the Temple continued in existence for another five years. Nonetheless, when the main synagogue did eventually re-open, in 1823, it sounded the death knell for the Temple.

All private places of worship were closed down by royal command, and the King issued an order on 9 December 1823, decreeing that synagogue services had to be in accordance with the traditional ritual and without any innovations. There was no further talk of the annex for German-language services that had been envisaged by the elders. Jacob could not hope to salvage anything for his Temple from this complete ban. Moreover, he no longer had the crucial support at court of Chancellor Hardenberg, who had died the previous year. The King's order was a complete reinstatement of the old tradition, and a triumph for the orthodox.

Both the King and the Jewish traditionalists had wanted to see an end to Jewish reform, albeit for different reasons. This had created an unlikely alliance, as the orthodox Jews had seen the advantages of working with the government when it suited them. This cooperation did not imply any endorsement of Judaism by the King, however. He had made his intentions clear in 1822, when he had approved the establishment of a Berlin 'Society for the Propagation of Christianity among the Jews'. A year later, just as the Beer Temple was closing down, the Prussian government issued a declaration that the Jewish religion was merely tolerated, that rabbis were not religious teachers in same sense as Christian clergymen, and that they had no ecclesiastical standing.

After this second, and final, forced closure of the Beer Temple in 1823, the possibilities for religious reform in Berlin were clearly exhausted, and the men who had been preachers there moved to other parts of Germany to continue their work. Eduard Kley, who had left the Beers in 1817, became the director of the Jewish Free School in Hamburg, where he became the driving force behind a new reformed Temple. Isaac Auerbach moved to Leipzig to head a Temple there, and Leopold Zunz, who had become disillusioned with the synagogue reform movement, became a founder member of the short-lived but influential *Verein für Kultur und Wissenschaft der Juden* [Society for the Culture and Science of the Jews]. This society took a new, scholarly approach to Jewish history and thought, aiming to place it on a par with other fields of academic study. Heinrich Heine was a founding member of the Society, and Michael Beer is listed as a candidate.

The influence of the short-lived Seesen and Berlin experiments spread slowly throughout Germany, gaining a firmer theological basis in the following decades. Later in the century, the movement was taken across the Atlantic by immigrants into North America, where it put down roots, eventually developing into the modern denomination of Reform, or Liberal, Judaism. Reform was not to be revived in Berlin itself until 1845, when a 'Society for Reform in Judaism' was founded there, and began holding services in private homes. The Berlin Reform Temple was built in 1854, and in 1866 the New Synagogue was established on Oranienburgerstrasse. The services at these synagogues included an organ, a choir, and German-language sermon and prayers – very much like the services at the Beer Temple some thirty years previously.

## Notes

1.  *Sulamith*, vol. 1, issue 1 (1806-07), p.328.
2.  See Lois C. Dubin, 'The Rise and Fall of the Italian Jewish Model in Germany: From Haskalah to Reform, 1780-1820' in Elisheva Carlebach, John M. Efron and David N. Myers (eds), *Jewish History and Jewish Memory. Essays in Honor of Yosef Hayim Yerushalmi* (Hanover, NH: Brandeis University Press, 1998), pp.271-95.
3.  *Sulamith*, vol. 5, issue 1 (1817), p.279.
4.  Ingrid Lohmann (ed.), *Chevrat Chinuch Nearim. Die jüdische Freischule in Berlin (1778-1825) im Umfeld preußischer Bildungspolitik und jüdischer Kultusreform. Eine Quellensammlung* (Munster: Waxmann Verlag, 2001), vol. 1, pp.1153-4.
5.  Benjamin Maria Baader, *Gender, Judaism, and Bourgeois Culture* (Bloomington, IN: Indiana University Press, 2006), p.52.
6.  Giacomo Meyerbeer, *Briefwechsel und Tagebücher*, Heinz Becker, Gudrun Becker and Sabine Henze-Döhring (eds) (Berlin: Walter de Gruyter, 1960-2006), vol. 1, p.71.
7.  Gotthold Salomon, *Selima's Stunden der Weihe, eine moralisch-reliogioses Schrift für Gebildetes weiblichen Geschlechts* (Leipzig: Carl Gottlob Schmidt, 1816), dedication page.
8.  Nahum N. Glatzer, 'On an Unpublished Letter of Isaak Markus Jost' in *Leo Baeck Institute Yearbook* 22 (Oxford: Oxford University Press, 1977), p.132.
9.  R. Larry Todd, *Mendelssohn. A Life in Music* (Oxford: Oxford University Press, 2005), p.18.
10. Birgit Bosold, *Friederike Liman. Briefwechsel mit Rahel Levin Varnhagen und Karl Gustav von Brinckmann sowie Aufzeichnungen von Rahel Levin Varnhagen und Karl August Varnhagen. Eine historisch-kritische Edition mit Nachwort*, unpublished Ph.D. diss., (University of Hamburg, 1996), p.82.
11. Georg Heinrici (ed.), 'Briefe von Henriette Herz an August Twesten (1814-1827)', *Zeitschrift für Bücherfreunde*, Neue Folge 5 (1914), pp.301-16 and 333-47.
12. Felix Gilbert (ed.), *Bankiers, Künstler und Gelehrte. Unveröffentlichte Briefe der Familie Mendelssohn aus dem 19. Jahrhundert* (Tübingen: J.C.B. Mohr, 1975), pp.38-40.
13. Meyerbeer, *Briefwechsel und Tagebücher*, vol. 3, p.134.

14. Thomas Lackmann, *Das Glück der Mendelssohns* (Berlin: Aufbau Taschenbuch, 2007), p.77.

15. Meyerbeer, *Briefwechsel und Tagebücher*, vol. 1, p.381.

16. Heinz Becker gives a date of 13 September for Wilhelm's wedding; see Meyerbeer, *Briefwechsel und Tagebücher*, vol. 1, p.665 n 371, 1. Other sources give 5 September; see Sven Kuhrau and Kurt Winkler (eds), *Juden Bürger Berliner. Das Gedächtnis der Familie Beer–Meyerbeer–Richter* (Berlin: Henschel Verlag, 2004), p.98, and Jürgen Blunck (ed.), *Wilhelm Beer. Genius der Astronomie und Ökonomie 1797- 1850* (Berlin: Staatsbibliothek zu Berlin, Preussischer Kulturbesitz, 1997), p.11. In a letter of 11 August 1818 (Meyerbeer, *Briefwechsel und Tagebücher*, vol. 1, p.357), Amalia tells Giacomo that Wilhelm will be marrying 'in the first days of September', so I have taken 5 September to be the correct wedding date.

# 12

## A Musical Apprenticeship

By 1818, Giacomo had been away from home for eight years, and even the important family occasions of his brothers' weddings in the autumn of that year had not tempted him to return. He much preferred the atmosphere of Italy, where the fact that he was Jewish seemed to matter less than it did in Prussia, where the situation was worsening for the Jews. The political climate in the German states had changed in the years following the Wars of Liberation, moving away from the heady days of emancipation and liberation towards a more repressive regime. In Prussia, feelings ran high against anything French, and Jewish emancipation had come to be associated in many people's minds with the French occupation.

The years of struggle against Napoleonic rule had also promoted a growing sense of unity among the German lands. This had been strengthened by the decisions taken at the Congress of Vienna, which had reduced the old patchwork of the Holy Roman Empire to just thirty-five principalities and four free cities. These entities, while independent, formed a loose federation, in which the balance of power was held between the two largest, Austria and Prussia. In the peace settlement, Prussia had lost most of its Polish possessions, but its gains had included the Rhineland, which was later to become the industrial heartland of Germany.

The question of whether German society was essentially Christian, or whether it could include people of other faiths, primarily the Jews, was one of the major challenges that had emerged from the Enlightenment. The vision of German nationhood that gradually emerged from the consolidation of states after the Napoleonic Wars was often unsympathetic to Jewish aspirations. The constitution of the new German Confederation, which had been decided at the Congress, included a ruling on the question of Jewish emancipation. Despite protests from Prussia's Chancellor Hardenberg, the member states of the Confederation whose Jews had been granted equality under French rule were given the choice of reverting to the pre-Napoleonic situation in their territories. Many of them did so, some cities expelling their Jewish populations altogether. Prussia's Emancipation Edict was not revoked, but Frederick William III decided that it would not apply to the new territories gained at the Congress, thus creating an anomalous situation, in which some Prussian Jews were freer than others.

The struggle to establish a national identity involved, as it often does, self-identification through the exclusion of others. The Jews had traditionally been the 'outsiders' in European society, and little, it seemed, had changed. Many leading German writers and artists, adherents of the Romantic movement, had begun to look back to an idealised version of Germany's medieval past and its Christian culture as defining what it meant to be German. As early as 1811, the Romantic writer Achim von Arnim had founded a club called the Christlich-Deutsche Tischgesellschaft [Christian German Dining Society], which specifically excluded Jews – including baptised Jews – as well as women and 'philistines'.

Men who had frequented the salons of Henriette Herz and Rahel Levin in their youth began to turn with the tide. Even Henriette Herz's old friend Wilhelm von Humboldt, who had been a member of the Prussian delegation at the Congress of Vienna, and was publicly a great supporter of Jewish emancipation, told his wife Caroline in private that although he liked the Jews *en masse*, he avoided them as individuals. He added that the reason he wanted to see them fully emancipated, was so that he no longer needed to show his support for them by frequenting their houses. Caroline – who had been a friend of Henriette Herz and Rahel Levin Varnhagen – held stronger opinions, telling her husband that, 'In their degeneracy, their mercenary spirit, and the inborn lack of courage that stems from this spirit, the Jews are a stain on humanity.'[1]

A number of prominent academics publicly endorsed the concept of a German nationalism that specifically excluded the Jews. In 1816, Christian Rühs, professor of History and Scandinavian Studies in Berlin, published a pamphlet called *On the Jews' Claims to German Citizenship*, in which he defined the Jews as people of a different race, who could be tolerated only as a subject nation, unless they converted to Christianity. He called for medieval restrictions to be reintroduced, including the wearing of a distinguishing mark on clothing. Jacob Fries, a professor of philosophy at Jena University, went even further, as he did not agree with Rühs that converted Jews should be accepted as Germans.

Fries was one of the organisers of a patriotic festival, held at the Wartburg castle in the Thuringian hills in central Germany, on 18 October 1817. The event was a joint celebration of the 300th anniversary of the Reformation and the fourth anniversary of the Battle of Leipzig, a major turning point in the fight against Napoleon. Martin Luther had spent some time at the castle following his excommunication from the Church of Rome, and the choice of location for the festival was a conscious linking of the victory over Napoleon with German Protestantism.

Around 500 activists, mainly members of the nationalist student fraternities, the *Burschenschaften*, had taken part in a torchlight procession up the hill to the castle, where they sang patriotic songs, made speeches, and ceremonially burned the publications of authors they considered 'reactionary', along with symbols of Napoleon's rule. The swell of political and patriotic emotion fomented by the event culminated in the murder, in 1819, of the conservative dramatist August von Kotzebue by the student Karl Sand, who was a pupil of Jacob Fries. Sand was subsequently condemned to death and beheaded. In response to these events, the Austrian Chancellor, Clemens von Metternich, supported by Prussia, issued the Carlsbad Decrees, which introduced tougher censorship and surveillance laws.

The rise of a specifically Christian nationalism combined with political unrest and economic hardship resulted in an eruption of violence against the Jews. Unemployment had been rising since the end of the Wars of Liberation, when the lifting of the Napoleonic continental system had allowed an influx of cheap English goods into the German lands. There had also been a series of poor harvests over the years from 1816 to 1819, resulting in a steep rise in the price of basic foods, especially bread. The blame for the hard times fell, as it so often had in the past, on the Jews.

Rioting began in August 1819 in Würzburg, in northern Bavaria, following a dispute in the local press about Jewish civil rights, and spread quickly across much of Germany. The attacks were reminiscent of medieval pogroms: synagogues and Jewish shops were smashed and ransacked, and individual Jews abused and beaten in the streets to the rioters' cries of 'Hep Hep!'. The meaning of this battle cry against the Jews is unknown, although some associated it with the Crusaders. Whatever the origin of the phrase, it is clear that those who used it meant it as a rallying call to attack the Jewish inhabitants of the towns and cities of Germany.

Giacomo, hearing the reports of these disturbances, was very worried about the safety of his family, but his mother was able to reassure him that all was quiet in Berlin. The Prussian authorities had reacted quickly to the news of the spreading unrest, and had taken measures to ensure that any attempts to riot would be put down. Amalia firmly believed that it was the King himself who had given these orders out of concern for his Jewish subjects – although he had, in fact, already begun to limit their civil rights. She told Giacomo a story going the rounds in Berlin that Frederick William, on a visit to Frankfurt an der Oder, had asked the chief of police to assure him that there was no 'baiting' of the Jews going on in the city:

> ... and he answered, 'no, Your Majesty, there is nothing of that sort to be feared among us here', to which he [the King] replied, 'and so I would advise you, because I have given them civil rights, and they mean the same to me as my other citizens, and I expect them to be treated in the same way' ... so you [Giacomo] can be calm.[2]

Wilhelm Beer had also been confident that, in Prussia, the rule of law would prevail. He had downplayed the significance of the Wartburg festival and its consequences; in his opinion, the whole thing was a storm in a teacup, worked up by a few student hotheads led by a professor who would quickly find himself in trouble as a result.[3] He was partly right, and certainly the Prussian authorities acted quickly to quash the riots, but the reappearance of popular violence against the Jews was a frightening and bewildering turn of events for many who now thought of themselves as German patriots as well as Jews. It revealed that neither the legal equality the Jews had been granted by the state, nor their participation in the Wars of Liberation, had removed the old hatreds, and that true acceptance was still more of an aspiration than a reality.

Wilhelm had a more robust temperament than Giacomo and Michael, who both tended to anxiety. Giacomo was well aware that he and Michael were alike, telling him that, 'I see the speaking similarity between us in body and soul, in temperament and in inclinations ... and that you run even more quickly into the arms of melancholy and sickness.'[4] Both Giacomo and Michael were preoccupied with the question of *Risches* – prejudice against the Jews. In one of his letters, Michael reminded Giacomo that, 'like the good God, it always has been, it is, and it always will be; just now it may be masked, but who can say when the mask will be suddenly torn off?'[5]

Both of the brothers were keenly sensitive to slights, but internalised their hurt, confiding in each other while presenting a stoical, reserved face to the world. Giacomo saw clearly that he and Michael faced difficulties that Wilhelm did not, as they had both chosen careers that had not been traditionally associated with Jews. In a long letter to Michael in September 1818, he advised his younger brother to think carefully about his ambition to become a playwright:

> Never forget, as I did when I chose [my profession], the iron word 'Richesse' [*Risches*]. From individual to individual the word can be

forgotten for a while (although not for ever), but by the collective public it never can, since it takes only one person to remember for all of them to recall it to consciousness ... turn your back on the theatre as a profession. Write, as the nightingale sings, for yourself.[6]

Jacob found his eldest son's gloomy outlook difficult to deal with at times, writing to him impatiently: 'The good God certainly allots his gifts strangely. You, who have the kind of fortunate destiny that falls to hardly one person in a million, have embittered your life with sheer pessimism. Believe me, it is very depressing for me to get such miserable letters from you.' Jacob believed that Giacomo's pessimism was caused by his poor health, and was convinced that a visit to his favourite spa of Carlsbad would cure him in no time: 'I really think that this gloominess stems from your ill health, but you are to blame for that yourself. If only you had gone to Carlsbad ... [Privy Councillor Berends] went there last year in a very ill state and in four weeks it did wonders for him.'[7]

In the light of present-day understanding of the effects of the mind on the body, it may, of course, have been the other way around, and at least some of Giacomo's frequent illnesses and bodily dysfunctions may have been of psychosomatic origin. His comment to Michael, that his brother ran even more quickly than he did 'into the arms of melancholy and sickness' suggests a significant degree of self-knowledge on Giacomo's part.

Despite Jacob's occasional outbursts of irritation, he was immensely proud of his eldest son. He did not live to see Giacomo's greatest triumphs, but even so, Amalia's great-nephew Felix Eberty remarked that, in Jacob's eyes, Giacomo was the equal of, if not better than, Haydn, Mozart and Beethoven. Eberty added that Jacob had a habit of leafing through the daily newspapers each morning, then handing them to Amalia with the words 'there's nothing in them', meaning that they contained no reference to Giacomo Meyerbeer.[8]

The whole family had been thrilled when, in July 1817, Giacomo had experienced his first real taste of operatic success. *Romilda e Costanza* was a two-act opera with an Italian text by the prolific and experienced Veronese librettist Gaetano Rossi, who had provided the texts for several of Rossini's operas, and would later write for Donizetti and Mercadante. The story of *Romilda* was in the tradition of the 'rescue opera' that had become popular after the French Revolution, featuring star-crossed lovers, captivity, disguise, and a happy ending. The best-known work of this type was Beethoven's *Fidelio*, which Amalia's friend, the soprano Anna Milder, had done much to popularise in Berlin.

Giacomo Meyerbeer as a Young Man/J. Meyerbeer (lithograph, unknown artist). Stiftung Stadtmuseum Berlin

According to a report in the *Allgemeine musikalische Zeitung*, *Romilda e Costanza* had initially been intended for the San Benedetto theatre in Venice, but Giacomo had encountered difficulties in his negotiations with the theatre's director.[9] As a novice composer, he had agreed to forgo any payment, which was usual, but he had also paid Rossi himself for the libretto. In Italy, librettists were usually employed by the theatres, and the normal practice was for the theatre management to pay for a text. Giacomo was wealthy enough to be able to choose his own librettist and text, which gave him more control over the process of composition. However, when the director of the San Benedetto, scenting money, demanded a large additional sum from the composer, for the scenery and costumes, Giacomo withdrew the work, and offered it to the Paduan opera house instead.

The opera was premiered in the Nuovo Theatre in Padua on 19 July 1817, with Giacomo himself conducting the orchestra. The music was composed in the Rossinian style, with sparkling melodies and vocal pyrotechnics that made great demands on the singers. The part of the heroine, Romilda, was sung by the contralto Benedetta Rosamunda Pisaroni, who would create the male role of Malcolm in Rossini's *Donna del lago*, two years later. In Meyerbeer's opera, Romilda is disguised as a man for much of the time.

This would not have sounded strange to audiences in the early decades of the nineteenth century, when male roles still could be, and often were, sung by castrati, or by women in male costume. Some female singers with voices in the lower ranges, like Pisaroni, specialised in these 'breeches roles'. By the second third of the nineteenth century this tradition, along with the castrati themselves, would vanish, as the tenor voice came to dominate male heroic roles.

Giacomo, ever the perfectionist, had found the rehearsals for *Romilda e Costanza* stressful. The wilful behaviour of the leading ladies upset him to such a degree, that Amalia wrote advising him that, 'If the two prima donnas are making your life such a misery that it will ruin the opera, it would be best not to stage it at all.'[10] His anxiety increased to such an extent that the premiere had to be postponed because he had made himself ill with nerves.

He need not have worried. *Romilda e Costanza* was received with enthusiasm on the opening night, with the audience calling the composer onto the stage a number of times to receive applause. The reviews were flattering: the *Allgemeine musikalische Zeitung* described the premiere as a 'brilliant success', and had quoted from a Venetian newspaper which had claimed that: 'Padua can boast of being the first city to acclaim the high creative genius of Mr MB [Meyerbeer]' who was 'following in the footsteps of Mozart, Haydn, Cimarosa and Paisello'.

The Viennese newspaper *Der Sammler* reported that 'The great merit of this opera, which combines exceptional German mastery and instrumentation with the sweetest and loveliest Italian melody, is indisputable.'[11] Michael Beer, who was still in Italy, had been in the audience for the premiere of *Romilda e Costanza*, and his letter describing the opera's success arrived in Berlin two weeks later, on 5 August. The news delighted the family so much that they were, as Amalia put it, all drunk with joy, and she had cried so much with happiness that her head ached.

None of Giacomo's operas had yet been staged in Berlin, and his family were now eager to remedy this situation as quickly as possible. Count Carl von Brühl, who had been appointed Director of the Royal Theatres in 1815, following Iffland's death the previous year, approached Jacob soon after the Italian premiere of *Romilda e Costanza* to sound out the possibilities of acquiring the work for the Berlin Opera. The Beers were delighted, but it quickly became apparent that Giacomo did not share his family's sense of urgency. He was frustratingly slow in responding to Amalia's requests for the score of the opera, which was in the possession of the director of the theatre in Padua.

By October 1817, Amalia's patience was growing thin:

> I am asking you, dear Meyer, to send your opera Romilda here as soon as possible, I am in the greatest embarrassment, and don't know what to say to Brühl, who so often asks if I have an answer yet ... I know that B[rühl] has apparently been seriously and unfairly reproached by the court in writing for not asking for the opera ... buy it back from the infamous impresario, no matter what it costs, just get it here ...

Jacob was equally irritated, telling Giacomo that 'I can't believe that it's not possible to get anything from an Italian impresario for money.' Amalia urged Giacomo to send Michael to Padua as his emissary, to get the score back 'at all costs'. Michael could then bring it with him when he returned to Berlin in the New Year.[12]

By January 1818, Michael had been in Italy for more than a year. Like Giacomo, he felt at home in the atmosphere there, noting that, 'Art means everything here, and everything else seems to exist only to enhance it.'[13] Unlike his brother, however, Michael could not stay on indefinitely in Italy. He was still only 17, and he needed to return home to finish his formal education.

Giacomo sent him to Padua, as Amalia had suggested, where he appears to have accomplished his mission, as he arrived back in Berlin in the spring of 1818, bringing the precious score with him. Shortly afterwards, there was a private performance of one of the numbers from *Romilda e Costanza* at the Tiergarten villa, where Heinrich, Betty, and the Berlin Opera singer Christian Fischer, a close friend of the Beers, sang the trio from act 1 at a family party in May to celebrate Jacob's 49th birthday. Jacob and Amalia were both moved to tears.

The decision to allow even this very private performance had been a delicate matter. Count Brühl was still negotiating for the score of *Romilda* for the Berlin Opera, and any unauthorised public performance of the music in advance of the official premiere could have compromised this process. Michael wrote to Giacomo to assure him that he had only given permission for the piece to be sung at the house on the condition that Amalia swore that there would be no strangers present. 'Just think,' he added, 'Mother is so afraid of the two of us that she didn't dare even once to express the wish to have the trio sung again in the presence of a larger audience!'[14]

On his return to Berlin, Michael had moved in with his maternal grandmother, Esther Wulff, while he studied history, philology, philosophy and natural sciences at the new University of Berlin, which had been founded in 1810 by Wilhelm von Humboldt. Jacob, Amalia and Heinrich were living all the year round in the Tiergarten house, which had been weatherproofed against the harsh Prussian winters. The Spandauer Strasse house, which, once the Temple had been established, had become more of a public building than a home, was sold in 1819.[15]

In 1818, Wilhelm, like Michael, was living in the city. He had developed an interest in mathematics, and had started on a course of private study, which was to provide the foundation for his later work as an amateur astronomer. He told Giacomo in February that year that 'I am currently working on algebraic analysis, for my own enjoyment, and I have made rapid progress in this equally interesting and difficult area of mathematics.'[16]

Although Michael and Wilhelm no longer lived at the Tiergarten villa, they continued to be involved in the frequent social occasions there. Both Heinrich and Wilhelm were good singers, and took part in amateur operatic performances at the villa, often singing alongside professionals from the Opera. In February 1818, the family and their friends performed Mozart's *Cosi fan tutte* in elaborate costume, and a month later, there was a large gathering to hear a performance of the first act of Cimarosa's extremely popular *Matrimonio Segretto*, which was followed by dinner and dancing. Music was taken seriously at the villa, to the extent that Wilhelm felt guilty that, as he was working so hard at mathematics, he wasn't practising his singing as much as he should.

With Michael now back in Berlin, Giacomo was very anxious for their mother to return to Italy, telling Michael 'you know how important and how crucial this is for me.'[17] Amalia was equally eager to re-join her son. She was occupied over the summer of 1818 with the arrangements for Wilhelm's and Heinrich's weddings, but once these were over she was free to travel, and by the end of the year she was again in Venice. She was accompanied by a new addition to the family, a young woman of French extraction called Antoinette de Montalban, who had been hired as Amalia's companion. Antoinette became one of the family, and remained with Amalia until the latter's death. Her origin is unknown; she may have had her roots in Berlin's French Huguenot population.

In December 1818, Amalia and Antoinette were based in Venice, while Giacomo was in Turin, preparing for the premiere of his second Italian opera, *Semiramide*, which was scheduled for the following February. By this time, Amalia had learnt not to interfere directly in her son's career, although she continued to play a role as his intermediary. While Giacomo was in Turin, she passed on to him the suggestions that were put to her by local singers and theatre management in Venice, without, however, promising them anything on his behalf:

> Ariga said to me that there will be a big opera given at St Benedeto in the spring, all very magnificent, and, as she told me, she has suggested Meyerbeer as maestro, and people would be very willing if they thought he would accept. I kept very quiet at this, as I don't know your opinion, but if you like the idea, tell me, and I will make some sort of discreet answer without pledging your word.

Amalia was keen to join her son in Turin, but also very careful not to pressurise him:

> Your other worry, about my coming to Turin, is quite unnecessary, I won't come a moment earlier than your Highness orders.[18]

It seems likely that Amalia was at the premiere of *Semiramide*, in February 1819. The King and Queen of Piedmont-Sardinia were also present, to hear the prima donna Carolina Bassi sing the main role of Semiramis, the Queen of Babylon. Bassi had taken a great personal interest in the work, and had used her influence to persuade the Turin theatre to take it on. The performance was a success, and was reported to have created a 'furore'. However, despite this initial enthusiasm, the work was not destined to have a long life. The story was convoluted and confusing, and *Semiramide* had only a couple of revivals after the 1819 season.

Amalia was back in Berlin by the summer of 1819. There had still been no decision on which of Giacomo's operas would be the first to be staged by the Berlin Opera. *Semiramide* and its predecessors had now been eclipsed by the success of Giacomo's third Italian work, *Emma di Resburgo* [Emma of Roxburgh], which had been premiered in Venice in June 1819.

*Emma* was set in Scotland, which was becoming a popular setting for Romantic literature, mainly due to the huge success of Walter Scott's novels. The eighth novel in Scott's *Waverley* series, *The Bride of Lammermoor* (which Donizetti would set as *Lucia di Lammermoor*) appeared in the year that *Emma* was premiered.

*Emma* was not itself based on a work by Scott, but Giacomo and his librettist Rossi changed the location of the original story from Provence to Scotland, making it one of the first operas to have a Scottish setting. Rossini's *Donna del lago*, based on Scott's epic poem *The Lady of the Lake*, followed swiftly, having its premiere three months later in Naples.

*Emma* was the most successful to date of Giacomo's operas, and enjoyed huge popular acclaim. The Austrian music journal, the *Österreichischer allgemeine musikalische Zeitung*, reported that on the third evening, the composer, who was conducting the opera, was called six times onto the stage, showered with flowers and poems, and crowned with a garland of roses. The music pleased the reviewers as well as the audiences; the journal added that in the opinion of the cognoscenti, 'Herr Meyerbeer was someone with the ability to make an important contribution to the reformation of the Italian opera'.[19]

Most importantly for the Beers, the popular Berlin newspaper, the *Spenersche Zeitung*, reviewed the opera enthusiastically: 'In short, this is one of the most intelligent, popular, charming, distinctive and expressive operas created by any contemporary composer in Italy ... although the work, with the scent of its blooms, belongs to the South, it still clings to German soil with the finest tendrils'.[20]

It now looked certain that *Emma* would be the first of Giacomo's works to be performed in his home city. Amalia, who had been at the Venice premiere, had returned almost immediately to Berlin, where she had the score copied, as she assured Giacomo, 'in my house, behind closed doors, so that no one will see it'.[21] She was eager to obtain King Frederick William III's endorsement of the opera as soon as possible, and urged Giacomo to write to the King, but he, as ever, was slower in responding than she would have liked.

Amalia was thrown into a fever of anxiety when the Chancellor himself wrote to Jacob, congratulating him on his son's achievements in Italy, and adding that he hoped to see one of Giacomo's works staged in Berlin before long. 'You really are putting me in the most embarrassing situation,' she complained to Giacomo. Everywhere she went, she told him, people were asking her about *Emma*, and the stars of the Berlin Opera were vying to obtain copies of his arias.

Amalia's old friend, the famous soprano Angelica Catalani, had returned to the Prussian capital on a second visit in September 1819, at the height of the negotiations for *Emma*, and, according to Amalia, 'everyone is asking Catalani why she isn't singing something from Meyerbeer's wonderful opera, she is constantly plaguing me, asking when I will be able to give her something'.[22] Amalia told Giacomo that she and the children felt that his operas should be heard first in their entirety, rather than being issued piecemeal to the public.

At last, in November, to Amalia's great relief, the letter from Giacomo finally arrived, and the score was presented to the King, who wrote offering his congratulations. *Emma* was produced at the Berlin Opera, on 11 February 1820. As Giacomo had not been there to oversee the rehearsals (and given his growing perfectionism, attending every rehearsal had become almost an obsession with him), his brothers were entrusted with seeing that his wishes were carried out. Heinrich commented that:

> I saw the rehearsals of this music as being like a statue by Canova, emerging at first in crude outline, then becoming finer and finer until it gets so far that the great artist himself lays his own hand on it to perfect it … by the fourth rehearsal, which was the last in the Academy Hall, the whole thing had come together. This had such a powerful effect on me that I came out of the rehearsal as if half drunk.[23]

Wilhelm wrote to Giacomo to assure him that *Emma* had been a great success, to a degree that was almost unprecedented in Berlin. Amalia had spent the day following the premiere receiving congratulatory visits. But the most important accolade, as far as she was concerned, came after the third performance, in April. The King had been away from Berlin at the time of the premiere, but the whole royal family attended the third performance. Amalia's friend, Charlotte von Bischoffswerder, rushed around to her the next day to tell her how thrilled the entire royal family had been with the opera. She told the Beers that the Duke of Cumberland and his wife had also been present, and that the Duke had spoken to Caroline Seidler, who had sung the title role of Emma, to tell her how much pleasure the music and the performance had given him. Chancellor Hardenberg also wrote to Jacob with his congratulations.

Jacob added a note of caution to the Beers' initial euphoria, however, saying that, in his opinion, although the public had received the opera with applause, some German reviewers were likely to be hostile towards the

Italian style of the work. He advised Giacomo to take no notice of any adverse comments, given that he had written *Emma* for Italy, not Germany. Amalia hastened to reassure Giacomo that any attacks by critics were not to be taken seriously: 'I hope you will dismiss them lightly because they are real dogs who call everyone slipshod, they are tearing Spontini and Rossini down as if they were schoolboys, they can't even let Méhul rest in his grave. My request to you is to look on all reviews as the mere barking of dogs.'[24]

Jacob was proved right: the German reviewers were not as impressed as their Italian counterparts had been. An Austrian critic commented: 'What do we find? … Rossinian melodies, Rossinian characteristics, Rossinian effects, Rossinian abuse of all musical powers.'[25] These reviews reflected a rooted German dislike of the Italian reliance on melody and vocal acrobatics, together with a growing desire to challenge the long-standing supremacy of Italian composers by developing operas in a purely German style.

Lea Mendelssohn shared this view, remarking that Giacomo had 'Rossini'd himself', and that after listening to *Emma* she had felt as if she had gorged herself on cake, and needed a mouthful of schnapps to take away the taste.[26] Carl Maria von Weber, although he loyally staged *Emma* at the Dresden Opera, was similarly disappointed, believing that Giacomo's talent ought to be channelled into the development of a truly German operatic form. Von Weber was working on his own masterpiece of German Romanticism, *Der Freischütz*, which would have a hugely successful premiere in Berlin on 18 June 1821.

Although Count Brühl, the Director of the Prussian Royal Theatres, had politely pressed the Beers for the score of *Emma*, he was, like Carl Maria von Weber, keener to promote German opera than Italian. The King, however, had a decided preference for Italian music. In 1819, Frederick William had appointed the Italian composer Gaspare Spontini, whose work he had heard in Paris, to the position of General Music Director to the Prussian Court. Spontini had been resident in Paris for some time, where he had been the Empress Josephine's favourite opera composer, and had enjoyed a huge success with the neoclassical *La Vestale*, in 1807. Count Brühl had favoured Carl von Weber for the post, and – according to Jacob Beer – the King's appointment of Spontini had come as a complete surprise to him.

Spontini's compositions were known for their pomp and circumstance. Jacob saw his *Olympie* when it was performed in Berlin, starring Anna Milder, in 1821, and was impressed by the magnificence of the spectacle, and in particular, the expense of the staging. He calculated the costs at the enormous sum of 30,000 thalers. He reported to Giacomo that, 'there's a march in this opera which has 42 trumpeters – yes, that's forty-two trumpeters. Milder had to screech so much that her voice didn't sound good, but the opera was a success as you'll see from the paper'.[27] Lea Mendelssohn complained that Spontini's love of spectacle sometimes undermined the actual performance. On one occasion, he had brought in twenty horses for a scene, and the noise of them stamping behind the scenery had completely spoilt the music.

There had been no live animals on the stage at the Berlin premiere of *Olympie*, but it had featured a life-sized elephant made out of wood, with two men concealed inside the frame to move it around the stage. Jacob had estimated the cost of this contraption at 400 thalers, and Lea commented that, given Spontini's predilection for quadrupeds, it was fortunate for Berlin that it did not have a zoo to hand.[28]

The King, with his liking for Italianate works, must have been following Giacomo's career with some interest. Shortly before the premiere of *Emma*, Chancellor Hardenberg had approached the Beers with a commission from Frederick William, who had personally expressed a wish for Giacomo to come to Berlin to take up a post as a music director at court, presumably to work under Spontini. The offer was extremely flattering, but Giacomo was not anxious to return to Prussia –the fact that he did not bother to supervise the rehearsals for the Berlin premiere of *Emma* is witness to his lack of interest – and he turned it down tactfully.

By the end of 1820, Giacomo had four highly successful operas under his belt, all in the Italian style. His fourth work, *Margherita d'Anjou*, had been produced at the famous La Scala opera house in Milan in November that year – an accolade in itself for a foreign composer. He was not yet 30 years old, but he was fast becoming a significant force in the operatic world.

## Notes

1. Felix Gilbert (ed.), *Bankiers, Künstler und Gelehrte. Unveröffentlichte Briefe der Familie Mendelssohn aus dem 19. Jahrhundert* (Tübingen: J.C.B. Mohr, 1975), p.xxxvi.
2. Giacomo Meyerbeer, *Briefwechsel und Tagebücher*, Heinz Becker, Gudrun Becker and Sabine Henze-Döhring (eds) (Berlin: Walter de Gruyter, 1960-2006), vol. 1, p.383.
3. Meyerbeer, *Briefwechsel und Tagebücher*, vol. 1, p.351.
4. Ibid., pp.367-8.
5. Ibid., p. 355.
6. Ibid., p.368.
7. Ibid., p.371.
8. Felix Eberty, *Jugenderinnerungen eines alten Berliners* (Berlin: Verlag für Kulturpolitik, 1925), p.105.

9.   *Allgemeine musikalische Zeitung*, 23 July 1817, cols. 503-4.

10.  Meyerbeer, *Briefwechsel und Tagebücher*, vol. 1, p.326.

11.  Ibid., p.655 ff. n 333,1.

12.  Ibid., pp.338-9.

13.  Gustav Manz, *Michael Beer's Jugend und dichterische Entwicklung bis zum 'Paria'. Erster Teil einer Biographie des Dichters*, (unpublished dissertation, University of Freiburg, 1891), p.18.

14.  Meyerbeer, *Briefwechsel und Tagebücher*, vol. 1, p.354.

15.  Sven Kuhrau and Kurt Winkler (eds), *Juden Bürger Berliner. Das Gedächtnis der Familie Beer–Meyerbeer–Richter* (Berlin: Henschel Verlag, 2004), p.70.

16.  Meyerbeer, *Briefwechsel und Tagebücher*, vol. 1, p.349.

17.  Ibid., p.369.

18.  Ibid., pp.372-3.

19.  Ibid., p.668 n 375,2.

20.  Ibid., p.669 n 375,2.

21.  Ibid., p.379.

22.  Ibid., p.383.

23.  Ibid., p.414.

24.  Ibid., p.413.

25.  Ibid., p.674 n 410,3.

26.  Lea Mendelssohn Bartholdy, *Ewig die deine. Briefe an Henriette von Pereira-Arnstein*, Wolfgang Dinglinger and Rudolf Elvers (eds) (Hannover: Wehrhahn Verlag, 2010), vol. 1, p.26.

27.  Meyerbeer, *Briefwechsel und Tagebücher*, vol. 1, p.429.

28.  Lea Mendelssohn Bartholdy, *Ewig die deine*, vol. 1, pp.32 and 44.

# 13

## The Young Playwright

While Giacomo was building a reputation as a composer, Michael had embarked on a career as a dramatist. As the youngest of the four brothers, Michael had been brought up in his mother's salon, listening to the theatrical talk of the greatest German actors of the day. By the time he was 14, he was writing poetry, and reading his efforts to the Beers' celebrated – and indulgent – house guests.

The talented actress and singer Friederike Bethmann, who was as popular a performer in Lessing's and Shakespeare's plays as she was in Mozart's operas, was particularly fond of Michael, and in 1815 invited him to visit her at the spa of Bad Liebenstein in the Thuringian forest. The precocious 15-year-old entertained the middle-aged actress with scandalous gossip about the Berlin theatre, and she took him to a ball at the local court, where, as she wrote to her husband, she 'saddled him with a squinting lady-in-waiting' as a dancing partner.[1]

Michael's school education at Berlin's Werdersche Gymnasium had imbued him with a love of the classical world, and in particular the Greek tragedians. The year he had spent in Italy with Giacomo had been a turning point in his life: he had soaked up the atmosphere of the warm south, and witnessed his brother's operatic triumphs at first hand. Back in Berlin, he wrote to Giacomo in May 1818, telling him that,

> I live only for my studies at the moment … I am beginning to understand how fundamentally I have benefited from my stay in Italy. I enjoy working, my will is stronger than before, and my stamina much greater. Like you, I have set myself a lofty objective, and I only long to achieve it as gloriously as you have achieved yours.[2]

By 1818, Michael had already started work on his first play, a classical tragedy based on the Greek myth of the murder of Agamemnon by his wife Clytemnestra, in order to marry her lover Aegisthus. Clytemnestra is subsequently murdered by her own son, Orestes, to avenge his father's death. Michael's drama, modelled on Goethe's *Iphigenie auf Tauris*, was a free adaptation of this original myth. His Clytemnestra is more tragic than purely monstrous. She had never loved Agamemnon, and his sacrifice of their daughter Iphigenia had destroyed any possibility of affection.

Clytemnestra hopes for happiness with Aegisthus, but he rejects her after their marriage. She realises that he has all along been motivated by a lust for power, and has only pretended to love her. Tortured by this betrayal, and wracked with remorse over Agamemnon's murder, she persuades her son Orestes, who has returned in disguise, to murder Aegisthus. Orestes, determined to avenge his father's murder, kills first Aegisthus, and then his own mother.

Michael's *Klytemnestra* was premiered in 1819 at Berlin's National Theatre, with some of the most prominent actors of the German stage taking the leading roles. Pius Alexander Wolff and his wife Amalie played Orestes and Clytemnestra. Wolff, who had been a pupil of Goethe's at the Weimar Court Theatre, was admired throughout Germany for his performances in Shakespearean roles. Other well-known actors took the remaining roles: Auguste Crelinger played Elektra, and Friedrich Lemm, Aegisthus. No doubt, as with Giacomo's earliest productions, this startlingly impressive debut owed much to the Beer family's influence. The Wolffs, Crelinger and Lemm were all habitués of Amalia's salon. The play had been read in the Tiergarten villa two months before the premiere, with the Wolffs taking the leading roles, as they were to do on the stage.

With such a stellar cast, the play was certain to draw a good audience, even in the appallingly cold weather in Berlin that winter, which was so bitter that three sentries froze to death while on overnight guard. The premiere of *Klytemnestra*, on 8 December 1819, went off well: Chancellor Hardenberg asked for the manuscript, and Frederick William III, who generally disliked tragedies, sent a message to say that he had enjoyed the play. It was an encouraging start for the budding playwright, who received so many visits of congratulations that his head might easily have been turned. But Michael was a sensible young man, and he appreciated his good fortune, telling Giacomo that 'I experienced an easy and friendly cooperation from all sides, but especially from [Count] Brühl, that must come the way of few beginners.'[3]

Michael's family and friends were naturally delighted at this successful debut. Lea Mendelssohn, who had disliked Giacomo's *Emma*, was much more taken with *Klytemnestra*. Michael was Lea's favourite among the Beer children; she found Giacomo's more polished, metropolitan manner too formal and 'buttoned up' for her taste. Lea felt protective towards Michael, and was so annoyed by a review of *Klytemnestra* which accused him of plagiarising Count Vittorio Alfieri's 1783 tragedy, *Orestes*, that she took the trouble to read Alfieri's work in order to be able to refute the charge.[4]

Amalia was convinced that Michael's play would prove as popular as the Austrian dramatist Franz Grillparzer's *Sappho*, which was enjoying great success at the time. This was more than a little optimistic. *Klytemnestra* showed signs of real talent, but it was inevitably an immature work, clearly imitative of both Goethe and Schiller, and it had flaws. Michael's attempt to adapt classical themes to modern sensibilities was bold, but executed clumsily at times, and most commentators criticised a tendency to long, declamatory speeches.

Michael was said to have written *Klytemnestra* in his grandmother's garden, sitting in the summerhouse overlooking the River Spree. He completed his second play in a room with a truly romantic view: that of the Bay of Naples, with Vesuvius visible in the distance. Michael had returned to Italy in 1821, initially to accompany his mother to the seaside spa of Livorno, and had then travelled through Bologna, Florence and Rome down to Naples, where he arrived in the mid-summer heat of July. Michael was happy to be back in Italy, describing Naples as

> a paradise that is missing nothing but the angels! A magical garden of the present and the past! ... Rome is a grave of the ancient world, but in Naples it lives, and the undamaged streets of Pompeii, which I saw for the first time yesterday with an indescribable feeling of melancholy and delight, are eloquent of the history and the poetry of that colossal time.[5]

The play Michael was working on during his stay in Naples, *Die Bräute von Aragonien* [The Brides of Aragon], was set in Spain, with a plot that hinged on the love of two sisters for the same man, a triangle that ends in the tragic death of all three. The basic idea came from a ballad of Goethe's, *Die Braut von Korinth*, in which the ghost of a dead woman appears to her former lover, who is about to marry her sister.

By April 1823, Michael was back in Berlin, and in Amalia's absence (she was again in Venice with her eldest son), a select gathering was held at Wilhelm's house in Behrenstrasse to hear a reading of *Die Bräute von Aragonien*. Rahel Levin Varnhagen and her husband were present, as were the Mendelssohns, along with Friedrich Gubitz, the lawyer Georg Kunowsky, who was a friend of Wilhelm's, and the retired actor Heinrich Bethmann, the widower of Michael's now deceased old friend, Friederike. The Wolffs, and the actress Charlotte Pfeiffer, who was visiting Berlin from the Munich Court Theatre, read the main roles. Lea Mendelssohn wrote to Amalia to tell her that, 'Michael's piece surpassed my expectations by far … it had such a moving effect when read, how much more will it gain in performance!'[6] She asked her cousin, Henriette von Pereira-Arnstein, to use her influence in Vienna on Michael's behalf, if any opportunity arose.[7]

Despite this enthusiasm, *Die Bräute von Aragonien*, which had its premiere in Munich, rather than Berlin or Vienna, had only a moderate success. Michael had corrected some of the flaws of his earlier work, but it is possible that he was not familiar enough with the deeply Catholic culture of Spain to make the characters or setting convincing, and he admitted that it had taken a huge amount of work and effort to complete the play. He later described *Die Bräute* in a letter to a friend as 'the worst of my published sins'.[8]

*Klytemnestra* and *Die Bräute* were both published in 1823, and were reviewed in the literary journal that Goethe had founded in Jena, the *Jenaische allgemeine Literatur-Zeitung*. The article praised Michael's use of language as 'free of faults, noble, and in places, sublime', but criticised a degree of 'striving after tragic effects' in both plays – in making Clytemnestra a double murderess in his adaptation of the Greek myth, and in the 'heaping up of horrors' in the final act of *Die Bräute*. The article was over two pages long, and the reviewer commented that, 'it is appropriate to discuss in detail the work of a young man whose efforts arouse sympathetic interest, and whose talent, if he develops it with study and self-criticism, will undoubtedly produce work that is fine and worthy of respect'.[9] Michael must have been pleased by this lengthy and encouraging review in such a well-respected journal.

However, both of these first works, which had very short lives on the stage, were overshadowed by the much greater success of Michael's third play, the one-act tragedy *Der Paria* [The Pariah]. *Der Paria* was premiered at Berlin's National Theatre on 22 December 1823, with Pius Alexander Wolff and Auguste Crelinger taking the lead roles. It differed radically from his first two plays. The story is set in India, and relates the tragedy of the 'untouchable' Gadhi, a member of the pariah caste, who is treated as an outcast, a member of a lower order of humanity, yet longs for equality:

> They give affection to their dog and horse
> and shun us, as if our human form
> was given us by Nature just as a mask.
> Give me equality with you, then see if I am just like you![10]

Michael Beer

Gadhi's wife Maja is of noble caste. He had rescued her from *suttee* – being burnt alive on her husband's funeral pyre – and the couple now live hidden with their son in the depths of the woods. One day a wounded hunter is carried into their hut; he is a man of high caste and turns out to be Maja's brother. He decrees that Gadhi must die: as a pariah he has dishonoured Maja, a noblewoman, by marrying her. Maja decides to die with him. Her brother, moved by pity at their suicides and acknowledging the nobility of

Gadhi's character, decides to bring up their son as his own. The play ends on a note of hope amid the darkness.

*Der Paria* has traditionally been seen as a thinly disguised depiction of the situation of the Jews in Germany, presented in a way that was acceptable to the audiences of the post-Napoleonic era. In the previous century, at the height of the Enlightenment, Moses Mendelssohn's friend, the dramatist Gotthold Lessing, had staged two plays featuring high-minded Jewish protagonists. However, in the more hostile atmosphere of the years following the Wars of Liberation, the only plays that directly featured Jews were farces like *Unser Verkehr*, which held them up to ridicule. Michael appears to have sought a way of depicting the cruelty of social exclusion in a guise that distanced it from contemporary life.

Michael was not the only writer of the time interested in the Indian caste system, and its potential as a medium for exploring themes of religious and social divides. The mysterious east was fashionable with the Romantics: in Germany, interest in Indian culture had been aroused by Georg Forster's 1791 translation of the Sanskrit play *Sakuntala*, which derived its story from the ancient legends of the *Mahabharata*.

French authors were thinking along similar lines. The main characters of Bernadin de Saint-Pierre's short story of 1790, *La chaumière indienne* [The Indian Cottage] were a pariah and a woman condemned to suttee. Casimir Delavigne's 1821 tragedy, *Le Paria*, which Donizetti later used as the basis for an opera, featured a pariah who disguises himself as a person of higher caste. Most importantly for Michael, just at the time that his drama appeared in Berlin, Goethe was completing a trilogy of 'pariah' poems, which he had been working on for a number of years.

Few, if any, of the authors writing on the subject really understood eastern culture, however. Michael's characters in *Der Paria* are certainly more Prussian than Indian. His hero Gadhi's burning desire to fight for his fatherland has obvious roots in the Jewish experience of the Wars of Liberation:

> I have a fatherland; I will defend it.
> Grant me a life, and I will pay you back with interest.[11]

He tells his wife, who is frightened by the burning intensity of his desire to fight for his country,

> It is just a dream that frightens you – I am a pariah,
> I may not fight for my fatherland.[12]

Michael's most deeply held personal feelings are engaged in the *Paria*. At the heart of the play is the demand that individuals should be judged on their personal worth, and not by an accident of birth into any society, race or caste. This gives it a passion and energy that are not evident in his earlier works. He was understandably nervous about the play's reception, but to his delight and relief, it received an ovation on its first night.

He reported to Giacomo that, 'My *Paria* was given on the 22nd of this month, and received with an acclamation that exceeded all my expectations and my boldest hopes ... I will just say that no tragedy has appeared on any German stage in recent years that has met with such a decisive success on its first night.' He added that the usual malice, envy and *Risches*, or anti-Jewish feeling, that the brothers had so frequently detected in Berlin society, were nowhere to be seen and that, 'to my great astonishment, the public, with unusual intelligence, not only grasped the point of the play from the start, but also endorsed it with the loudest applause.'[13] The play had a lasting success in Berlin, and was performed thirty-eight times within the next decade.

In January 1824, a few weeks after the Berlin premiere of *Der Paria*, Michael was in Weimar. He had the honour of being received by Goethe, to whom he gave a copy of the manuscript of the play. Shortly after Michael's visit, Goethe commented in a letter to his daughter-in-law, Ottilie von Goethe, that he had read the play straight away, and had liked it very much, adding that he thought it would work well on the stage, and could be produced successfully at Weimar.[14]

Goethe had already decided to feature his own pariah poetry in the January 1824 issue of his literary journal, *Über Kunst und Altertum*, and had asked his friend, the author Johann Eckermann, to contribute an essay on the Indian social and cultural background. This article would now include comments on Michael's play, as well as on Casimir Delavigne's French tragedy, *Le Paria*. Eckermann's essay, which Goethe edited and augmented with his own comments before publication, praised Michael's construction of the drama. Eckermann had been particularly impressed by the way that Michael had managed to weave two of the more alien elements of Indian life, the pariah caste and *suttee*, into an effective tragedy. This was all the more notable, he added, given that Michael had achieved this in a play of just one act, set in one location, and with only three characters.

Goethe had retired from direct involvement in the Weimar court theatre, but he passed the manuscript of *Der Paria* to the Grand Duke, Karl August. The Duke was equally interested in the play, and gave his permission for it to be performed in Weimar. The Duke had reservations, however: he was not convinced that the general public would be able to understand the play without any background knowledge of Indian customs. He suggested that explanatory programme notes should be issued with the tickets for the performance.

He also felt that the character of the hero, Gadhi, was not entirely consistent: as a pariah, Gadhi was a member of the lowest order of society – the 'rabble', as Karl August put it – yet he spoke like a highly educated and cultured man. Goethe accepted this, but he saw the character of Gadhi as symbolic, representing all persecuted humans. Eckermann had expressed this view in his article: 'The pariah can justifiably serve as a symbol for all downtrodden, oppressed and despised peoples, and as a subject like this is generically human, it is also highly poetic.' Given the universal application of the character, he had judged that it was right 'to disregard improbability in order to attain a higher plane'.[15]

Not all critics agreed. For some, the appearance of a low-caste character on the stage as the hero of a drama was simply distasteful. The *Journal für Literatur, Kunst, Luxus und Mode* [Journal for Literature, Art, Luxury and Fashion], which had published several hostile reviews of Michael's plays (its paragraph on *Die Bräute* had the title 'Coarse Brides and Coarse Taste'), commented that:

> the appearance of a pariah on the stage is in itself preposterous. How can a creature, the very sight of whom is contaminating, be a principal character? But even accepting the unthinkable in itself – for the audience are not Hindus – how can we believe in such a pariah, who is as high-minded and noble as it is possible to be? How could it be possible that a prince's daughter would be able to overcome her revulsion for a pariah enough to give herself to him …[16]

These comments echo of some of the objections made in earlier decades to Lessing's plays featuring Jewish heroes, a parallel that Michael is unlikely to have missed.

Goethe took a personal interest in the Weimar production of *Der Paria*, writing the programme notes himself on the basis of Eckermann's article – which had, in any case, represented his views. He also contacted Count Brühl, to ask him for sketches of the scenery and costumes for the Berlin premiere. Brühl obliged, adding a detailed description of both. Michael kept in touch with Goethe during the run-up to the performance, and visited him for a second time in October, while passing through Weimar on his way to Bonn, where they had mutual acquaintances at the University. The play was given its Weimar premiere on 6 November 1824, and was well received; Goethe sent Michael a playbill as a souvenir.

Michael was delighted, both with the play's success, and with the kindness that Goethe had shown him. He described Goethe's attitude towards him as 'fatherly' in a letter to the older man: 'I am overjoyed that what appears to appeal most strongly to Your Excellency in my dramatic attempt is that which is most intimately connected with my very being … To receive this [endorsement] from such an exalted mouth is a balm that can heal all wounds.'[17]

Their mutual friend, the Professor of Natural History at Bonn, Christian Nees von Esenbeck, told Goethe that Michael had admitted to him that the play was not entirely objective, but contained elements of Michael's own situation and his personal feelings. Goethe kindly asked Nees to pass on the news that the second performance of *Der Paria* at Weimar had been received with real enthusiasm, and that the play was assured of a place in the theatre's repertory, adding 'Life is short, and we must try to do one another good turns.'[18]

The appearance of *Der Paria* marked a change in Michael's life. He had previously based himself in Berlin, chiefly at his parents' villa, but from 1824 onwards he had no permanent home. He spent some of that year in Paris, where he began moving in artistic circles, mingling with well-known personalities, such as the Romantic writer Victor Hugo, the painter Baron Gérard and the dramatist Casimir Delavigne.

He spent the latter half of the year in Bonn. He had by this time met another young German-Jewish writer, Heinrich Heine, who would become both a friend, and at times an enemy, of the Beers. It is most likely that Heine had originally met Michael in Berlin, where they had both been students. While in Berlin, Heine had joined the Society for the Culture and Science of Judaism that had been founded by Leopold Zunz, one of the preachers at the Beer Temple. Michael also had connections with the Society.

There must have been some degree of friendship between the two young men, as Michael had read the manuscript of *Der Paria* to Heine some months before its premiere. It may have been an inopportune moment, though, as at the time, Heine was smarting from an unpleasant experience with the premiere of his own play, *Almansor*, in Braunschweig. Heine's play, like the *Paria*, is a plea for tolerance. It is set in Spain during the sixteenth century, at the time of the persecution of the Moors and the Jews.

The story centres on the tragic consequences of the forced conversion to Christianity of a Moorish family. During the performance, a rumour had circulated around the audience that the play had been written by a local Jew, a money-changer, also coincidentally called Heine. The actors were drowned out by anti-Semitic shouting, and the production had to be halted. It was an absurd misunderstanding, but it had turned the premiere into a fiasco.[19]

When Heine heard about the success of Michael's *Paria* in Berlin, he remarked to their mutual friend, Moses Moser, that Michael Beer had a lot to thank him for, given that his *Almansor* had disproved the old axiom that any play written by a Jew must be bad.[20] Heine has been quoted by later commentators as describing *Der Paria* as a 'masterpiece'.[21] This is quite true, but the context of the remark reveals at least a degree of ambivalence, as it comes in a letter to Moser, in which he says 'Michael Beer's *Paria* is a masterpiece, I will willingly admit it, since he considers me a great poet.'[22]

Heine told Moser that he had, in fact, liked the play in general, but he bitterly condemned Michael for presenting a 'disguised Jew' on the stage - although his Moor, Almansor, has been taken to represent the Jewish, as well as the Moorish, experience in Spain. Heine took particular exception to the lines where the pariah, Gadhi, muses over how his people became cursed, speculating that perhaps it was because

> Once, long ago, in a gray time of legend
> A pariah refused to pay you homage,
> And scorned your god ...[23]

Heine read into these lines a covert and craven justification for the treatment of the Jews by the Christians:

> The very idea that the pariah supposes his ancestors to have deserved their sorry condition because of a bloody misdeed is totally stupid, damaging and blameworthy ... I wish Michael Beer would just get himself baptised, and speak out strongly, in a real 'Almansorish' way about Christianity, instead of anxiously walking on tip-toe around it, and even ... flirting with it.[24]

Heine's attitude towards Judaism was complex; his family background had not been observant, and he had been brought up much in the style of a middle-class German boy. He was nonetheless treated as a Jew by others, and he felt the sting of social exclusion deeply. A fierce hatred of prejudice and injustice runs through a number of his works: his unfinished prose story 'The Rabbi of Bacharach', begun in the early 1820s, features a rabbi who invites two strangers to the Passover meal, then finds that they have secretly hidden the body of a dead Christian child beneath the table, to incriminate him for child murder.

Heine's comments on Michael suggest that the figure of Almansor may reflect a part of Heine's personality, a desire to stand up openly against prejudice. In the end, Heine submitted to necessity and converted to Christianity. After his father was bankrupted, he became financially dependent on an uncle, and had to work for a living. He studied law with a view to making a career in the Prussian bureaucracy, an ambition that was scotched by the introduction of regulations barring Jews from state posts, precipitating his decision to convert in 1825.

Heine and Michael Beer were probably too dissimilar in their backgrounds and characters to develop a close friendship. All of the Beers were wealthy, but Heine was always short of money. It would hardly be surprising if Heine, who was in no doubt of his vocation as a poet, resented the fact that Michael had the financial security to devote himself to writing, while he had to struggle. Heine was much more political in temperament than Michael. A liberal who in later life became radical, he had a combative manner with a taste for biting satire. He could not understand Michael's stoicism in the face of anti-Semitic insults, which he took to be weakness, and remarked that Michael handled everything with kid gloves, adding sarcastically that he bore attacks with 'Christian' forbearance.[25]

Michael was probably unaware of the depth of Heine's ambivalence towards him, given that these remarks were made in private letters to other friends. If he had known, he would probably have avoided any confrontation. Michael, like Giacomo, disliked conflict. He had, in any case, much to be proud of. At 24 years old, he had written three plays that had been produced in major theatres, including one that had been promoted by Goethe himself at Weimar. By the end of 1824, Michael must have felt that he was well on the way to achieving the 'lofty objective' he had set for himself, of attaining the same level of fame with his plays, as his brother already enjoyed with his operas.

## Notes

1.  Gustav Manz, *Michael Beer's Jugend und dichterische Entwicklung bis zum 'Paria'. Erster Teil einer Biographie des Dichters* (unpublished dissertation, University of Freiburg, 1891), pp.16-17.

2.  Giacomo Meyerbeer, *Briefwechsel und Tagebücher*, Heinz Becker, Gudrun Becker and Sabine Henze-Döhring (eds) (Berlin: Walter de Gruyter, 1960-2006), vol. 1, p.354.
3.  Meyerbeer, *Briefwechsel und Tagebücher*, vol. 1, p.396.
4.  Lea Mendelssohn Bartholdy, *Ewig die deine. Briefe an Henriette von Pereira-Arnstein*, Wolfgang Dinglinger and Rudolf Elvers (eds) (Hannover: Wehrhahn Verlag, 2010), vol. 1, p.26
5.  Meyerbeer, *Briefwechsel und Tagebücher*, vol. 1, p.431.
6.  Ibid., p.467.
7.  Lea Mendelssohn Bartholdy, *Ewig die deine*, vol. 1, p.82.
8.  Michael Beer, *Briefwechsel*, Eduard von Schenk (ed.) (Leipzig: Brockhaus, 1837), p.96.
9.  *Jenaische allgemeine Literatur-Zeitung*, issue 91 (1824), Ergänzungsblätter, cols. 337-41.
10. Michael Beer, *Sämmtliche Werke* (Leipzig: Brockhaus, 1835), p.241.
    Sie schmeicheln ihrem Hund und ihrem Rosse,
    Und scheuen uns, als hätt' uns die Natur
    Zur Larve Menschenbildung nur gegeben.
    Stellt mich euch gleich und seht, ob ich euch gleiche!
11. Ibid., p.241:
    Ich hab' ein Vaterland, Ich will's beschützen.
    Gebt mir ein Leben und Ich zahl's mit Wucher
12. Ibid., p.242.
    Dich ängstet nur ein Traum - ein Paria bin Ich,
    Ich darf nicht streiten für mein Vaterland
13. Meyerbeer, *Briefwechsel und Tagebücher*, vol. 1, p.575.
14. Johann Wolfgang Goethe, *Sämtliche Werke, Briefe, Tagebücher und Gespräche* (Frankfurt am Main: Deutscher Klassiker Verlag,), vol. 37, p.142.
15. Goethe, *Sämtliche Werke*, vol. 22, p.59.
16. *Journal für Literatur, Kunst, Luxus und Mode*, issue 4 (January 1824), p.51 (review of *Die Braüte*); and issue 80 (October 1825), pp.645-6 (review of the published text of *Der Paria*).
17. Ludwig Geiger (ed.), *Goethe-Jahrbuch* (Frankfurt am Main: Rütten und Loening, 1907), vol. 28, pp.21-2.
18. Ibid., p.25.
19. Manz, *Michael Beer's Jugend*, p.52.
20. Heinrich Heine, *Säkularausgabe. Werke, Briefwechsel, Lebenszeugnisse* (Berlin and Paris: Akademie Verlag and Editions de CNRS, 1970-), vol. 20, p.134.
21. Susanne Balhar, *Das Schicksalsdrama in 19. Jahrhundert: Variationen eines romantischen Modells* (Munich: Martin Meidenbauer Verlagsbuchhandlung, 2004), p.123.
22. Heine, *Säkularausgabe*, vol. 20, p.122.
23. Michael Beer, *Sämmtliche Werke*, p.239:
    Weil einst, vielleicht in grauer Fabelzeit,
    Ein Paria die Huld'gung dir geweigert,
    Den Gott verhöhnt ...
24. Heine, *Säkularausgabe* vol. 20, p.137.
25. Ibid., p.385.

# 14

## Expanding Horizons

Jacob and Amalia were enormously proud of both their sons' artistic achievements. There was, however, one small fly in the ointment: Giacomo, at nearly 30 years old, was still a bachelor, and showed no signs of settling down. As two of his younger brothers were already happily married, his parents felt that it was high time he followed suit, and, with his growing international fame, they had begun to dream of a brilliant match for him.

In January 1821, Jacob had written to Amalia, who had travelled to Livorno with Michael for a sea-bathing cure, with an ambitious suggestion for a potential bride. The girl he had in mind was a member of one of the wealthiest and most illustrious Jewish families of Europe. Marianne von Eskeles was the daughter of the Viennese banker Bernhard von Eskeles, who, together with his brother-in-law Nathan Arnstein, had established the banking house of Arnstein and Eskeles. The bank had become extremely influential at the time of the Congress of Vienna, and Eskeles and his family had been at the heart of the glittering society of the Congress, socialising with men like Talleyrand, Wellington, Castlereagh, and Hardenberg.

In addition to the attractions of their material and social status, the von Eskeles family were musical; they were patrons of Mozart and the well-known pianist Ignaz Moscheles. Also, crucially for the Beers, they had remained staunchly Jewish. This potential match must have seemed made in heaven to Jacob and Amalia. The prospect of linking the Beers' fortune to that of the von Eskeles would ensure a glittering financial and social future for the family far beyond the confines of Berlin.

Jacob urged Amalia to go to Vienna to look Marianne over. He admitted frankly that he would like the match. However, as he told Amalia, ultimately the decision had to be Giacomo's alone. Frustratingly for Jacob, he had never been able to find out his son's real feelings about marriage, and could not predict how Giacomo would react to this proposal.

Giacomo's feelings about the proposed match remain unknown, but he was certainly in no hurry to visit Vienna, and he skilfully evaded his parents' attempts to pin him down to a meeting with Marianne von Eskeles. Despite his gloomy outlook, Giacomo, with his lean, dark face and polished manners, was attractive to women: when he left Vienna in 1814, he had been conducting an affair with the singer Catinka Buchwieser. Their mutual friend, the actor Carl Schwartz, remarked that Catinka had told him that she didn't believe he really loved her, as he had too many love affairs. Catinka herself had told Giacomo on parting that 'I don't need to wish you luck – the Parisian women will see to that.'[1]

By March 1821, Giacomo had not yet appeared in Vienna, despite his parents' urging, and Jacob attempted to recruit Michael's help in persuading the recalcitrant suitor to visit the Eskeles:

> I wrote to Meyerbeer on the last post day and begged him urgently to go to Vienna … They are expecting him, and as soon as he arrives there, we will go too. Eskeles has been made a baron. If he doesn't go, it will be very embarrassing for us … persuade him to go to Vienna with you, I won't be able to hold up my head again if he doesn't go to Vienna. I ask you urgently again to represent to him that he must not throw away this great piece of good luck, which will never be repeated.[2]

However, despite his family's enthusiasm for the proposed marriage, Giacomo continued to avoid any meeting with Marianne, and, eventually, the Beers had to accept that their son was not interested in this glittering match.

The scheme for an alliance with the Eskeles may have been prompted by a desire on Jacob's part to gain a foothold outside of Berlin, as the business there was going through a difficult period. In September 1821, six months after the Eskeles marriage plans had fallen through, Michael wrote to Giacomo suggesting that he returned to Berlin to hold a family conference, with the aim of finding a way of cutting the family's expenses without endangering their reputation. Michael even hinted that there was a possibility that the Berlin property might have to be sold. This may have been more an expression of the Beers' insecurity than a real threat, given the extent of their wealth, but there must have been some reverses, or at least some uncertainty, in their business affairs at the time.

Jacob had expanded the sugar business in 1818, when he had established a second refinery in Berlin. The new factory was located in a four-storey building in Friedrichsstrasse, close by the Weidendamm bridge over the river Spree, which made it convenient for unloading the raw sugar for processing, and loading the finished product for distribution. Jacob had paid 17,500 thalers for the building, which Wilhelm had considered a bargain at the time, as he calculated that if his father had built the new factory himself it would have cost him 40,000 thalers, given the high cost of building materials. However, by 1821, it looked as if the situation in Berlin was not good for Jacob. Michael, in his letter to Giacomo, commented that, 'You can see from father's letter how serious matters are for him, and how his losses there have given him a distaste for Berlin.'[3]

It is not clear how serious the family were about the idea of leaving Berlin, but it was around this time that Jacob founded a refinery in Gorizia, in Habsburg-ruled Italy. Given the family's existing links with Italy – Giacomo had been there for five years, and Jacob had had business dealings in Venice for many years – there may have been some plan for re-locating to Gorizia if the situation in Berlin became untenable. The anti-Jewish riots of 1819 may have provided an additional stimulus for the idea of a move away from Germany.

The location of the new refinery had financial advantages: the tax on raw sugar, which was imported through Trieste, was lower than in Germany. Jacob may have hoped that establishing a viable business in Gorizia would both offset any immediate losses in Berlin, and also provide a base outside Germany. He bought a large and luxurious villa in the vicinity of the factory, which suggests that he may have had plans for making this the family home.

The first mention of the refinery is in the autumn of 1822, when Jacob and Amalia travelled to Italy together. They both headed initially for Venice, to visit Giacomo. Amalia fell ill while in Venice, and remained there while Jacob went to Gorizia to oversee work at the refinery. By November, Amalia was seriously ill, and remained in a worrying condition throughout the winter.

Early in the New Year, just as she was beginning to recover, it became evident that Jacob was also ill, and that he was struggling to deal with problems at the refinery. These problems were so serious that Giacomo was forced to go Gorizia to assist his father, leaving Amalia in Venice, in the care of his Italian librettist, Gaetano Rossi. It was mid-February before Rossi was able to report to Giacomo that 'Mamma' had been able to go downstairs for the first time since the New Year, and had taken a short walk with him, leaning on his arm.[4]

Giacomo found Jacob in poor physical health. He had developed a serious bowel complaint, a fact that both he and Giacomo were keen to conceal from Amalia. Giacomo was relieved to hear that two experienced doctors in Gorizia had not thought an immediate operation necessary, however. It is possible that Jacob suffered from an inflammatory bowel disorder with a genetic basis, as in later life Giacomo frequently recorded similar symptoms, which were particularly troubling at stressful times, in his diary.

Although Giacomo was relieved as to Jacob's health, he was seriously worried about his father's management of the business. Jacob was dealing with a very difficult situation: the manager of the refinery had been demoted, but instead of removing him, Jacob had allowed him to remain in the factory, where he was now in a more junior position. Giacomo judged this to be an unwise decision, as there appeared to be a real danger that the demoted man would sabotage the refining process out of revenge, and he advised Jacob to get rid of him as soon as possible: 'I don't know if you, with your truly wretched indecisiveness, will have the strength to carry out such a drastic measure, but I do know that Mother ... is completely in agreement with me.'[5]

Giacomo was very frank with his father, making it clear that, in his opinion, Jacob was not taking a broad enough view of the European situation in his business decisions. At the time, France was mobilising, with the intention of invading Spain. In Giacomo's view, the threat of war between France and Spain required decisive action, and he strongly advised Jacob to buy up raw sugar in Hamburg.

Wilhelm had been left in charge of the business in Berlin while Jacob was in Gorizia, and Giacomo was also critical of Wilhelm's business acumen – while admitting that he himself had no practical knowledge of the business. He told Jacob:

> I know that, despite the fact that the biggest and by far the most important family businesses are in Berlin, your attention is always immersed solely in one favourite object, and at the moment this favourite object is the Gorizia factory. I am amazed that Wilhelm has not written to you to buy in Hamburg. It seems to me that he has a very narrow outlook and I believe (between us) that he will never raise himself to the true coup d'oeil of a real speculator.[6]

Giacomo may have had reason to be concerned about Jacob's ability to handle difficult business decisions given his poor health, but he was being less than fair to Wilhelm, who, as his future career would prove, was an excellent businessman and entrepreneur.

Giacomo's irritation with his father may have been fuelled by the timing of the episode. It was not the best time for him to be called away from his own concerns. His last opera, *L'esule di Granata*, had not enjoyed the same success as its predecessors. The librettist had been Felice Romani, who had also provided the text for the successful *Margherita d'Anjou*. Romani was the house librettist at La Scala, and extremely highly regarded. He was to provide the texts for some of the most famous Italian operas of the mid-nineteenth century, including Bellini's *Norma* and Donizetti's *L'elisir d'amore*.

There had been suggestions of intrigue against Giacomo at the premiere of *L'esule*. Romani's wife had commented that: 'The triumphs of the German composer had aroused in restless, jealous spirits … the wish that the new opera should fail, and they were ready to hiss it to express their disapproval.'[7] Whatever the reason for the coolness of the opera's reception, Giacomo was anxious not to repeat the experience.

In the autumn of 1822, he and Gaetano Rossi, who had been *Emma*'s librettist, had decided on a new opera, which would be set in Egypt in the early thirteenth century, at the time of the Sixth Crusade. The collaboration would involve over a year of intensive work, with Giacomo taking an active role in the development of the text as well as the music. He was working on the opera while he was in Gorizia, and must have found the distractions of dealing with his father's problems frustrating.

By the spring of 1823, however, the situation in the factory had been resolved, and both Amalia and Jacob were well enough to travel. Giacomo had made it clear to Jacob that he considered the family's real interests lay in Berlin, and he was anxious for his parents to return there as soon as possible. Jacob and Amalia left Italy in late spring, and arrived in Berlin on 7 July.

Wilhelm, Michael and Heinrich had travelled to Dresden from Belin to meet their parents, and to accompany them on the last leg of the journey home. Jacob and Amalia had been away for more than six months, and they must have been happy to see their much-loved Tiergarten villa again, in the full bloom of summer, after so many months of illness, difficulty and travel.

Once back in Berlin, Jacob's attention – which, as Giacomo had said, was 'always immersed solely in one favourite object' – switched from the Gorizia business to a new venture, which, he hoped, would allow him to achieve a cherished personal ambition. He had always been what the Germans called a *Theaternarr* – a fool for the theatre – and he had longed to play a role in Berlin's theatrical life. Just before he and Amalia had set out on their ill-fated journey to Italy in the previous autumn, he had seized the opportunity to join the board of directors of the first privately financed theatre to be established in the city, the Königstadt.

The idea for this 'people's theatre' had actually originated with King Frederick William III, who had visited the privately-owned Leopoldstadt Theatre in Vienna while on a state visit, and was keen to see a similar institution established in his own capital city. On 13 May 1822, to general astonishment, the concession for this theatre was awarded to a completely unknown individual, a converted Jew called Carl Friedrich Cerf (or Hirsch), who had settled in Berlin in 1816. Cerf's origins have remained elusive, although he is known to have run a horse-dealing business in Dessau, and it has been suggested that he had been employed by the Prussian government in secret negotiations with Russia at the time of the French Occupation.

He certainly appears to have had no connections of any kind with the theatre, or any other branch of the arts. Indeed, the young actress Karoline Bauer, one of the first stars of the Königstadt, claimed that he could neither read nor write, although this is unlikely. Cerf's intention, as it turned out, was not to manage the theatre himself, but to lease the business to a group of shareholders, who would between them pay him an initial lump sum of 120,000 thalers, and an annual rent of 3,000 thalers.

In September 1822, a board of directors, consisting of seven of these shareholders, led by Wilhelm Beer's friend, the lawyer Kunowsky, had been established to manage the new theatre. Jacob, who had a particular fondness for comedy, which would be a speciality of the Königstadt, had been delighted to accept an invitation to join the board. Its members also included Lea Mendelssohn's brother-in-law, Joseph Mendelssohn, and the retired actor Heinrich Bethmann. The new theatre building, created by the architect Carl Ottmer and situated in the Alexanderplatz, in the suburb of Königstadt, was impressive: it was about the same size as the Berlin National Theatre, with over 1,500 seats. Ottmer had done a good job; according to the *Allgemeine musikalische Zeitung*, the acoustics were better than they were in the National.

Not everyone was eager to see a popular theatre established, however. The Director of the Royal Theatres, Count Brühl, was strongly opposed to the idea. He could not stop the project going ahead, but he was anxious to ensure that the new theatre would not be able to compete directly with either the Opera House or the National Theatre. Consequently, it was ruled that no work could be produced at the Königstadt until a two-year period had elapsed since its last appearance on the stages of either the Opera or the National Theatre. Additionally, the Königstadt's repertoire was limited by law: it was only allowed to stage comedies, farces, operettas and melodramas. Tragedies, serious operas and ballets were to remain the sole preserve of the royal houses.

As a result, the actors and singers recruited for the Königstadt tended to be specialists in lighter or comic roles. They included the bass buffo Josef Spitzeder, who had made his name in Vienna, and the comedian Heinrich Schmelka. Their talents would not have been suited to the more serious repertoire of the royal theatres. As Brühl had intended, this situation ensured that the new theatre did not attempt to poach the stars of the royal theatres.

The grand opening night of the Königstadt was scheduled for 4 August 1824, in the presence of the King and the royal family. All of Jacob's children were there to witness his triumph: Michael was staying in Berlin while preparations for the production of *Der Paria* in Weimar were underway, and Giacomo had returned home from Italy for a visit, after an absence of fourteen years.[8]

The establishment of the Königstadt theatre had generated enormous excitement among the Berlin public, although the run-up to the first night was not without its anxieties for the Königstadt's troupe of actors. Bethmann, the one person with practical theatrical experience in the group, had left after a quarrel with Kunowsky, throwing the theatre into disarray. Sixteen-year-old Karoline Bauer, who had left a secure position in the Karlsruhe theatre to join the new company, described the anxiety she and her fellow actors felt as the day of the opening approached, with chaos reigning, and no one quite sure what was happening.

The Königstadt Theatre

But gradually the company pulled together, and it began to seem that all might go well. By the day of the opening, public expectation had reached fever-pitch. Large crowds poured into the Alexanderplatz to queue for four hours in the hot August sun until the ticket office opened. The crush was so great that the actors had to fight their way through to get into the theatre. By the time the curtain went up, the theatre was packed to the rafters. The Beer family, as 'management', were comfortably seated in a luxurious box. The premiere was in four parts: a Prologue, spoken by Karoline Bauer; Beethoven's overture *Die Weihe des Hauses* [The Consecration of the House]; a farce by the Viennese dramatist Adolf Bäuerle; and a *Singspiel*, or operetta, called 'The Ox Minuet', by a G. Hofmann.

The evening was a stupendous success. The Berliners were bowled over by the novel experience of having a theatre that belonged to them, rather than to the King, and were inordinately proud of their new institution, referring constantly to 'our theatre', and talking of the actors as 'our Spitzeder', and 'our Schmelka'. Everyone in Berlin, from the fishwives in the markets to the loungers on the street corners, now fancied themselves as theatre critics, and all of them simply had to have an opinion on every new performance.

Karoline Bauer, in later life, affectionately remembered Berlin at the time as still retaining a small-town air. It was a place, she said, where any novelty, such as a new opera or play, a controversial review by a newspaper critic, an original dress, a novel by Walter Scott, or an anonymous poem, could set the whole town buzzing, talking of nothing else for days. A few years previously, the Swedish poet Per Atterbom, writing to his brother in Stockholm while visiting Berlin, had told him that

> high culture has become really popular here; it has even penetrated down to the boot boys and maids. The waiters at the inns examine pieces of sculpture with an expert eye, barbers speak of the aesthetic sense and feeling for art, hairdressers talk of soul and refined taste. My waitress begged me not to miss a production of Schiller's *Jungfrau*: 'It is', she said, 'a dramatic poem that does honour to the German nation!'[9]

The Königstadt was all the rage in the late summer and autumn of 1824. The writer Willibald Alexis commented that the sense of ownership of the new theatre created a bond: 'It was our club, our meeting-place, a literary exchange … We grieved when the seats were empty, exchanged satisfied looks and handshakes when the house was full, as if at a family occasion.'[10]

The royal family continued to attend the theatre on occasions: when Princess Louise of Prussia married Prince Frederick of the Netherlands in May 1825, the couple attended a performance at the Königstadt before leaving Berlin. It was a gala occasion, and the theatre's librettist and secretary, Karl von Holtei, reported that the entrance to their box and the nearby rooms were filled with so many flowers that they looked like gardens.

However, once the novelty had worn off, the Königstadt soon found that it was at a serious disadvantage compared with the royal theatres. It was brand new and untried, while the National and the Opera were well established, and had ensembles of experienced singers and actors who had worked together for many years. In addition, both royal theatres had a complete freedom of choice in their repertoires, and both benefited from state financial backing. The Königstadt's limited access to new plays meant that it regularly staged older works, or hack pieces by its house writer.

One of the Königstadt's few real advantages was its superiority in comedy, and the theatre's directors soon recognised a golden opportunity in the growing popularity of comic opera, in particular the works of Rossini, Donizetti and Auber. The Opera House lacked singers suited to these lighter Italian and French operas, and had not been successful in staging them, so the field was open. The Königstadt was initially in a similar position, however, as it lacked a female singing star with the ability to take on the leading roles.

In 1825, an unexpected solution to this problem appeared, when the Italian Opera in Vienna had its financial backing withdrawn, and the whole troupe, including the young soprano Henriette Sontag, lost their jobs. Sontag had created a sensation in Vienna; her pure and technically perfect voice was admirably suited to the lighter operatic roles.

When the directors of the Königstadt heard the news that Henriette Sontag was on the market, they saw their chance to pull off a coup. Karl von Holtei, the theatre's secretary and director, tells an entertaining story about the acquisition of Sontag for the theatre. According to his memoirs, enquiries revealed that she had left Vienna for a temporary engagement in Prague, but that this had now ended, and she was on her way from Prague to Leipzig. A group of the Königstadt's directors, including Jacob, hired a carriage and fast post-horses, and galloped off to Leipzig. When they arrived, they were horrified to find representatives of other theatres there, also waiting for the diva, among them a delegate from the Berlin Opera. They promptly got back into their carriage and raced off in the direction of Prague, intercepting the prima donna on the road.

Their quick thinking paid off, and Henriette agreed to the generous terms of 7,000 thalers for a season at the Königstadt. Amalia gave a banquet to celebrate the occasion. Several of the failed competitors for Sontag's services were invited, although they were unaware that she had already signed a contract with the Königstadt until Holtei toasted her at the banquet as the theatre's new acquisition, enjoying the looks of astonishment and chagrin on the faces of the rival bidders.[11]

On 3 August 1825, almost a year to the day from the theatre's opening night, the 19-year-old Henriette debuted in Berlin, as Isabella in Rossini's *L'italiana in Algeri*, and 'Sontag fever' swept the city. The theatre and the street where Henriette lived were constantly besieged by adoring fans. The Opera and the National Theatre stood empty, and there was only one subject of conversation in all Berlin: Henriette Sontag was the toast of the city, and her praises were sung on every street corner and in every salon. Anyone who had not managed to get a ticket for *L'italiana in Algeri*, according to Holtei, hardly dared to show their face. Sontag had single-handedly saved the Königstadt.

The Beers basked in the reflected glory: von Holtei recalled attending a magnificent dinner at the Tiergarten villa, where the guests were a heady mixture of Berlin's intellectual and theatrical worlds, including the scientist Alexander von Humboldt, the philosopher Professor Georg Hegel, and the writer August von Schlegel, along with Henriette Sontag and Angelica Catalani, who was again visiting Berlin.[12]

There were, of course, a few people immune to the Sontag epidemic. Lea Mendelssohn was scathing about the whole affair:

> ... it's amusing to see the most sober, senior bankers like my husband's brother, Fränkel, Beer, etc. as directors, in suspense over the success of a farce, trembling at the debut of an actress, worrying about wigs, jackets and scenery, and making the whole thing the most important business of their lives and their only subject of conversation. I thank heaven that [her husband Abraham] Mendelssohn doesn't take the slightest interest in it.[13]

Jacob was indeed putting his heart and soul into the project. Karl von Holtei commented that the Königstadt was 'Father Beer's baby': anyone who worked for the theatre, or felt enthusiastic about it, was automatically a friend of Jacob's. He could scarcely bear to be away from it:

> When the hour struck for the theatre, the stout man could bear it no longer in the Tiergarten, no matter how delightful the evening, no

matter how choice the company. At the appointed hour coachman Lindner was at the entrance, and off they went into the dusty city. Lindner was a good coachman, but a smart fellow too, and understood how to flatter in his own way. Arriving in the Königstrasse, he contrived cleverly to bring the carriage into collision with others so he had to halt for a moment. The cry rang out 'What's happening, Lindner?' to which he regularly replied 'Oh Herr Beer, there's no making any headway, since the Königstadt's been open there's always such a crush here at theatre time!'

This flattery, said von Holtei, was sweeter to Jacob than any sugar from his refineries.[14]

The summer of 1824 had been a high point in the Beers' lives. Amalia had been delighted to have all her sons at home again, but it had been a short if happy time: by the November, Giacomo had left Berlin and returned to Italy. He was not intending to remain there indefinitely, however; he was now looking for an opportunity to stage his works in Paris, which he considered the centre of the operatic world. The previous year, he had written to the French bass singer Nicolas Prosper Levasseur, who had taken one of the leading roles in *Margherita d'Anjou* at La Scala, saying that 'it would be even more glorious for me to have the honour of writing for the French Opéra than for all the Italian stages'.[15]

The overwhelming success of Giacomo's most recent work, *Il Crociato in Egitto* [The Crusader in Egypt], would prove to be the key that unlocked the door to Paris. *Il Crociato* had been premiered at the Fenice theatre in Venice on 7 March 1824. The opera, set in thirteenth-century Egypt during the Sixth Crusade, appealed strongly to the prevailing fashion for the exotic, and the lead roles were created by three of the most famous singers of the time: the French soprano Henriette Méric-Lalande, the castrato Giovanni Battista Velluti (*Il Crociato* was the last opera to feature a major role for a castrato), and the tenor Gaetano Crivelli. The opera was an instant and overwhelming success, and was to win Giacomo European-wide fame.

The leading English musical periodical, *The Harmonicon* reviewed *Il Crociato* in its January 1825 issue. The periodical called the work 'one of those effusions of genius which appear rarely in an age … [Meyerbeer's] *Crociato* ranks him with the greatest composers of the day'.[16] Later that year, in June, the journal's Italian correspondent reported that after a performance at Trieste, 'the composer was met at the door of the house by a huge concourse of people, who came prepared with bands of music, and lighted torches, and accompanied him to his residence with tumultuous acclamations. He was then obliged to show himself at the balcony amidst the roar of a thousand *evvivas*.'

When visiting the casino, the article continued, he was 'crowned with laurel, in the midst of a tumult of applause, and a riot of acclamation, which only those who have witnessed it can form any adequate idea. The uproarious meeting did not disperse til four in the morning.'[17] The opera was produced in London and Paris in 1825, and was performed throughout Europe for decades, reaching St Petersburg in a Russian version in 1841. It was chosen as a festival opera to celebrate the coronation of the Austrian Emperor Ferdinand as King of Bohemia, in Prague in 1836.

When Giacomo was invited to bring *Il Crociato* to the Théâtre Italien in Paris in late summer 1824, he did not hesitate. By the New Year, he was established in the French capital, where Michael joined him. The last time Giacomo had arrived in Paris, in 1814, he had been an unknown young German musician, overwhelmed by the teeming life of the great metropolis. Now, as a successful and respected young composer, he was welcomed into the capital's musical circles as an equal.

Sixteen-year-old Felix Mendelssohn, visiting Paris with his father, Abraham, around that time, found himself in the next box to Giacomo at an opera. Felix enviously noted the exalted company Giacomo was in, which included Rossini himself, along with the pianists Hummel, Kalkbrenner, Pixis and Moscheles, and the violinists Rode and Kreuzer. Felix described the scene to his sister, telling her that his neighbours were constantly applauding and chattering knowledgeably among themselves, adding in a would-be contemptuous tone, 'I almost fell off my seat laughing.'[18] It was the first sign of a personal antipathy towards Giacomo that would become more intense, and more evident, as their respective careers progressed.

*Il Crociato in Egitto* had its first performance in Paris at the Théâtre Italien on 25 September 1825, with Rossini, then director of the theatre, conducting the orchestra himself. Nicolas Prosper Levasseur and the celebrated soprano Giuditta Pasta sang the leading roles. Pasta had taken over the part that Velluti had sung in Italy, since castrati were banned from the stage in France. Giacomo and Michael were both at the premiere, and wrote an ecstatic joint letter to their parents, to tell them the happy news of the opera's success. Michael reported that the theatre had been so packed for the opening night, that people who could not get a seat were renting stools in the corridors.

The Duchesse de Berry, daughter-in-law of King Charles X, had been present; she had sent her congratulations through the Comte de la

Rochefoucauld, and had said that she would like to meet the composer. The painter Baron Gérard had sent a note, and the great operatic composer Luigi Cherubini, director of the Paris Conservatoire and famed as a severe critic, had come to the brothers' lodgings to thank Giacomo for the pleasure he had given him.

Even better news for the family in Berlin was that Frederick William III, who was in Paris at the time, had attended the second night, and had been so impressed that he wanted Giacomo to write an opera for the Berlin Opera. 'Rejoice,' Michael finished his account, 'beloved mother, and you too, dear father Schmalz, with all your hearts.' (Schmalz was a family nickname for Jacob). Giacomo could not resist a world-weary tone: 'There is nothing in the world more tiring than a big success in Paris', he informed his mother.[19]

There was no sign that, a month later, the family's happiness would be shattered. Jacob had not been well for some time, but his death on 27 October 1825, from inflammation of the lower abdomen, was sudden and unexpected.[20] In June that year, Giacomo, who was temporarily in Padua overseeing a production of *Il Crociato*, had written to Michael saying that Wilhelm 'has given me the most excellent news of our dear parents, thanks be to heaven … who have never been so well, so cheerful and enjoying life so much as they are now. May God keep them so for a thousand years'.[21]

None of the family appeared to have any serious worries about Jacob's state of health in the weeks leading up to his death. It seems that Giacomo arrived in Berlin for a visit just a few days before Jacob died. His presence there was noted by Sir George Smart, the English conductor and composer who was himself visiting the city in the autumn of 1825. Smart recorded in his diary that Amalia had informed him on Saturday 22 October that Meyerbeer had arrived in Berlin that day.

Smart was keen to meet Giacomo; he had already dined at the Tiergarten villa, where he had met Henriette Sontag. Smart describes Jacob as 'a short, very corpulent man' – clearly the annual Carlsbad regime, that Jacob had so much faith in, had failed to keep his weight under control. On 24 October, three days before Jacob's death, Smart recorded another visit to the Tiergarten villa, 'where I saw Mr and Mrs Beer, and was introduced to Mr Meyerbeer, their son, who was polite and kind. We had a long chat about his plans … [I] was highly pleased with his reception of me. I gave him my London card.'[22] There is no mention of Jacob being ill.

Jacob's sudden death on 27 October was recorded in the English music journal *The Harmonicon*:

BERLIN - Jacob Hertz Beer, the great banker, died lately at this place. A more than common interest is now attached to his name, as being the father of the celebrated author of *Il Crociato in Egitto*. At the commencement of his illness, his son was in a distant part of Germany, but he hastened to watch at the death-bed of his father, and had the melancholy satisfaction of being able to hold him in his arms when he breathed his last. The charitable deeds of this worthy man are proverbial in this place, and no more honourable testimony can be rendered to his memory than to record that his earthly remains were attended to the grave by at least six thousand persons, all anxious to pay their last tribute of respect to worth and virtue.[23]

Other reports stated that over 3,000 people and 80 carriages accompanied the funeral procession, but whatever the exact number of mourners, it is clear that Jacob's burial was a major event in Berlin.[24]

Although the *Harmonicon* report claims that Giacomo was present when his father died, Heinz Becker, the editor of Meyerbeer's letters and diaries, says that Meyerbeer had intended to visit Berlin around this time, but did not actually do so. There are no extant letters or diary entries by Giacomo for this period, and Becker bases his comment on a description of a letter that has disappeared, but is described as having been written by Meyerbeer in Paris on 26 October, to Smart at his London address, promising him the score of *Emma*, if his father, who is ill, can find it for him.[25]

In contradiction to this, Sir George Smart's diary places Giacomo firmly in Berlin on 22 October 1825. Four days later, on 26 October, Smart, about to leave Berlin, mentions that he has received a letter from Meyerbeer, containing the scores of several pieces from *Emma*.[26] Additionally, Karl Varnhagen von Ense, who was also in Berlin, confirms Giacomo's presence there. In a diary entry for 31 October 1825, Varnhagen says, in connection with Jacob Beer's death, that, 'Meyerbeer, composer of the universally celebrated *Crociato* in Paris is here at the moment.'[27] All of this suggests that Meyerbeer was in Berlin from 22 to at least 31 October. It must be possible that the description of the missing letter gives the wrong place.

The Beers' friend Carl Maria von Weber arrived in Berlin in November to oversee the production of his latest opera, *Euryanthe*. He stayed with Heinrich and Betty, and visited Amalia, remarking in a letter to his wife that it had been a sad reunion. Weber proved a good friend to the bereaved family: he celebrated Wilhelm's birthday with them on 23 December, and spent Christmas Eve with Amalia. Lea Mendelssohn described Amalia as inconsolable, but outwardly composed: 'I have found her infinitely bowed down [with grief].'[28]

Some important decisions had to be taken. Jacob had not left a will, which attests to the unexpectedness of his death. Amalia refused the share of the inheritance that would have come to her, in favour of the children, and Jacob's fortune was divided between them. They made some charitable bequests in his memory, including one of fifty thalers to the poor of Frankfurt an der Oder. They also gave the large sum of 500 thalers to the *Bürger-Rettungs-Institut*, the Citizens' Rescue Institute, which had been founded in 1796 to assist working men who had fallen into poverty, and which Jacob had supported in his lifetime.[29]

Another of the organisations that Jacob had supported was the Jewish Free School, which reported his death in its 1826 report:

> Purely, and free from any suspicion of self-interest, the Institute is deeply saddened that Herr Herz Beer, that thoughtful and generous man of integrity, has had to leave this world prematurely. We will not miss the philanthropist – his noble widow will make sure of this – no, we will miss the man of good, honest sense, the man for whom to do good was a matter of heart and head, of feeling and duty at the same time.[30]

Jacob had been a generous donor to good causes. After his death numerous people applied to the family, claiming that Jacob had supported them. Wilhelm, who, as his father's heir to the business empire, was in charge of financial affairs, found it difficult to deal with the claimants, as the family had been unaware of the extent of Jacob's generosity.

It was agreed that Wilhelm and Doris would move into the Tiergarten house to live with Amalia. Although Giacomo was the eldest, Wilhelm was in many senses his father's heir, as he took over Jacob's role in the direction of the Luisenstift, as well as in the management of the family businesses. The Gorizia refinery had already been sold to Jacob's Venetian colleague Johann Hartmann, leaving Wilhelm – and Heinrich, who was still involved to some degree in the family's business affairs at this time – free to focus on the Berlin factories. Hartmann also now owned the magnificent villa that Jacob had bought in Gorizia, where Giacomo had spent time composing *Il Crociato in Egitto* during the difficult period of his parents' illnesses in 1823.[31]

Wilhelm also took over his father's position on the board of the Königstadt theatre, which he helped to manage until its bankruptcy following Henriette Sontag's departure in 1829. Sontag's decision to end her singing career to marry the Sardinian aristocrat, Count Carlo Rossi, was a serious blow for the Königstadt. Karl von Holtei had always believed that as long as Jacob was alive, the Königstadt was safe – due both to his enormous financial resources and his love for the theatre.

After Jacob's death, the management split into warring factions and channelled their energy into fighting with one another, and with the theatre's company and the stock holders. It would have broken Jacob's heart to have seen the Königstadt go into bankruptcy, although, against all expectation, this was not the end of the theatre. The mysterious Carl Cerf, the concession owner, reappeared at this point and took over, running the Königstadt until his death in 1845, staging mainly light, popular operas by Bellini, Auber, Adam and Mozart.

No one knew where Cerf had found the money to buy back the concession, but it is possible that he had royal backing. The idea of a private theatre had always been a favourite scheme of Frederick William III's. After the King's death in 1840, however, his successor Frederick William IV was unwilling to continue subsidising the theatre. It struggled on for a few years, and its later days are best remembered for an incident during the revolution of 1848, when a group of radicals holed up inside the theatre fired shots at government troops in the streets. The Königstadt was eventually closed in 1851, and the building, the repository of so many of Jacob's hopes and dreams, became a wool warehouse.

## Notes

1.  Giacomo Meyerbeer, *Briefwechsel und Tagebücher*, Heinz Becker, Gudrun Becker and Sabine Henze-Döhring (eds) (Berlin: Walter de Gruyter, 1960-2006), vol. 1, pp.256-7.
2.  Meyerbeer, *Briefwechsel und Tagebücher*, vol. 1, p.428.
3.  Ibid., pp.434-5.
4.  Ibid., p.458.
5.  Ibid., p.453.
6.  Ibid., p.449.
7.  Giacomo Meyerbeer, *The Operas of Giacomo Meyerbeer*, Robert Letellier (ed. and trans.) (Madison, NJ: Fairleigh Dickinson University Press, 1999-2004), p.82.
8.  Lea Mendelssohn Bartholdy, *Ewig die deine. Briefe an Henriette von Pereira-Arnstein*, Wolfgang Dinglinger and Rudolf Elvers (eds) (Hannover: Wehrhahn Verlag, 2010), vol. 1, p.113. Lea Mendelssohn's letter to her cousin of 26 July 1824 confirms that Meyerbeer was in Berlin in the summer of 1824. In the letter, Lea says that Amalia Beer is 'unbelievably happy right now', as Meyerbeer is with her, and Michael is on his way home.

9. Per Daniel Atterbom, *Reisebilder aus dem romantischen Deutschland* (Stuttgart: Steingrüben Verlag, 1970), p.65.

10. Willibald Alexis, *Erinnerungen* (Berlin: Concordia Deutsche Verlagsanstalt, H. Ehbock, 1900), p.374.

11. Karl von Holtei, *Vierzig Jahre* (Berlin, 1844), vol. 4, pp.192-3.

12. Holtei, *Vierzig Jahre*, vol. 5, pp.30-1.

13. Mendelssohn Bartholdy, *Ewig die deine*, vol. 1, p.120. The editors have misidentified Heinrich Beer as a director of the theatre, instead of Jacob.

14. Karl von Holtei, *Charpie. Eine Sammlung Vermischter Aufsätze* (Breslau: Verlag von Eduard Trewendt, 1866), pp.172-3.

15. Meyerbeer, *Briefwechsel und Tagebücher*, vol. 1, p.509.

16. *The Harmonicon*, January 1825, issue 25, pp.2-3.

17. *The Harmonicon*, July 1825, issue 30, pp.96-7.

18. Felix Mendelssohn Bartholdy, *Sämtliche Briefe*, Helmut Loos and Wilhelm Seidel (eds) (Kassel: Bärenreiter, 2008), vol. 1, p.160.

19. Meyerbeer, *Briefwechsel und Tagebücher*, vol. 2, pp.22-3.

20. See Lea Mendelssohn Bartholdy, *Ewig die deine*, p.157, where Lea Mendelssohn confirms that Jacob died after only a few days' illness.

21. Meyerbeer, *Briefwechsel und Tagebücher*, vol. 2, p.20.

22. Sir George Smart, *Leaves from the Journals of Sir George Smart*, Hugh Bertram Cox and Clara L.E. Cox (eds) (Cambridge: Cambridge University Press, 1907; digitally printed version, 2014), pp.168, 174, 179-80, 190, 193.

23. *The Harmonicon*, December 1825, issue 36, p.233.

24. Jacob Jacobson (ed.), *Jüdische Trauungen in Berlin 1759 bis 1813* (Berlin: Walter de Gruyter, 1968), p.316.

25. Meyerbeer, *Briefwechsel und Tagebücher*, vol. 2, p.25.

26. Sir George Smart, *Leaves from the Journals*, p.197.

27. Konrad Feilchenfeldt (ed.), *Karl Varnhagen von Ense: Tageblätter* (Frankfurt am Main: Deutscher Klassiker Verlag, 1994), p.125.

28. Lea Mendelssohn Bartholdy, *Ewig die deine*, vol. 1, p.157.

29. Sven Kuhrau and Kurt Winkler, (eds), *Juden, Bürger, Berliner. Das Gedächtnis der Familie Beer–Meyerbeer–Richter* (Berlin: Henschel-Verlag, 2004), p.81.

30. Ingrid Lohmann (ed.), *Chevrat Chinuch Nearim. Die jüdische Freischule in Berlin (1778-1825) im Umfeld preußischer Bildungspolitik und jüdischer Kultusreform. Eine Quellensammlung* (Munster: Waxmann Verlag, 2001), vol. 1, pp.1153-4.

31. Jürgen Blunck (ed.), *Wilhelm Beer. Genius der Astronomie und Ökonomie 1797-1850* (Berlin: Staatsbibliothek zu Berlin, Preussischer Kulturbesitz, 1997), p.11.

# 15

## 'Meyerbeer has made himself immortal'

Jacob's death brought immediate and major changes to Giacomo's life. As the Beers' eldest son, he was now head of the family, and was expected to marry as soon as possible. The grand plans for an Austrian alliance were gone, and the bride now chosen for Giacomo was his cousin Minna Mosson, the daughter of Amalia's sister, Johanna. Giacomo made a formal offer for Minna's hand on 28 November 1825, just four weeks after his father's death. He had made no attempts to evade the engagement this time; it seems likely that he accepted the necessity for marriage, and had no objection to marrying his pretty young cousin.

It was an old-fashioned, arranged marriage: at 34, Giacomo was thirteen years older than his bride, and, by his own account, did not know her very well before they became engaged. This is not so surprising, given that Minna had been just 6 years old when he had left Berlin for Darmstadt. Giacomo clearly found her attractive, however. Twelve years into their marriage, he told her that, 'When I first got to know you, I fell in love with your charming little face and lovely figure, and would have married you even if you had been a bad-tempered little fool', adding, 'but if I had known your noble spirit and divine character, I would have married you even if you had looked like Betty.'[1]

Giacomo's engagement surprised and pleased his friends, who had thought him a confirmed bachelor. Carl von Weber told his wife, Caroline, that, while visiting the bereaved Beer family over Christmas 1825, he had heard the news that Meyerbeer had 'been converted' and was going to be a bridegroom![2] The choice of Minna Mosson puzzled some people outside the family, however, who may have felt that Giacomo could have aimed higher for a bride. Lea Mendelssohn exercised her wit at Minna's expense: 'Everyone is surprised that this composer is marrying not a muse, but a Mosson, who isn't even a grace, from which the world will conclude that there are no muses or graces in the Mark [of Brandenburg].'[3]

The marriage took place in Berlin, on 25 May 1826. Giacomo and Minna were married according to the Jewish rites – Carl von Weber's comment that Giacomo had 'been converted' had been purely a joking reference to his inclination to bachelorhood. However, although the Beers had remained Jewish, a significant number of their relatives had taken the path of conversion to Christianity. As Lea Mendelssohn pointed out, the fact that the entire extended Beer-Mosson-Ebers clan could not put together a *minyan* or prayer quorum of ten men for the wedding ceremony was testimony to the inroads that Christianity had made in the Berlin Jewish community.

A few days before the wedding, Giacomo finalised the legal form of his name, registering himself as Jacob Meyerbeer.[4] However, as he was already widely known as a composer under the Italianised version of his first name,

Minna Meyerbeer

he continued to use 'Giacomo', rather than 'Jacob', in both public and private life – although he also signed some of his letters to his French correspondents as 'Jacques' Meyerbeer.

In June, Giacomo returned to Paris with his bride. He was entering a new phase of life and creativity, in a city where he felt at home both personally and professionally. He planned to compose an opera for the French stage, and, in preparation, began studying French culture and history, while attending as many theatre productions as possible. During his researches, he met the playwright and librettist Eugène Scribe, the man who was to become his most important collaborator.

Scribe, the most prolific French dramatist of his time, had produced a string of comedies and dramas for the theatres, and libretti both for the Opéra, and for the Opéra-Comique, which staged lighter works. He agreed to produce a French text for Giacomo and, after some initial hesitation, they settled on a three-act work for the Opéra-Comique, to be called *Robert le Diable* [Robert the Devil].

Life seemed full of promise for the Meyerbeers, but a series of personal tragedies would make the first few years of their marriage a testing time for the young couple. Just three months before their wedding, in February 1826, Giacomo's uncle, Martin Ebers, who was married to Amalia's sister Henriette, shot himself. Ebers may have had money problems – a few months after his suicide, Lea Mendelssohn had commented that since the New Year, there had been a 'chain of terrible bankruptcies, which have shattered the wellbeing, peace and health of so many families'.[5]

Of the four men Liepmann had chosen for his daughters, it appears that two failed in business – Joseph Mosson and Martin Ebers – and two succeeded. Victor Ebers, the husband of Sara or Seraphine, although not as wealthy as Jacob Beer, was a partner in the flourishing Ulrici tobacco company. His house on Unter den Linden was famous for a room decorated solely in white, something that was considered highly unusual and extravagant at the time, and for its beautiful rose garden.

Four months after Martin Ebers' suicide, when Giacomo and Minna arrived in Paris after their wedding, they heard the sad news of another death – that of Giacomo's old friend, Carl Maria von Weber, who had died in London, of tuberculosis. He had been 39 years old. He had been staying at Sir George Smart's house in Great Portland Street at the time of his death. It was Smart, in fact, who found his body:

> Carl von Weber was found dead in his bed about ten minutes to seven on the morning of June 5th, 1826. Lucy Hall [a servant] slept

in the room next to his, and he was asked to leave his door unlocked in case he required her help in the night, but this he refused to do. In the morning Lucy came down to inform me that the door was locked, and that she had knocked several times but received no answer ... We burst open the bedroom door, when we found Weber dead, lying tranquilly on his right side, his cheek in his hand.[6]

Weber was initially buried in London, at the Roman Catholic church of St Mary's, in Moorfields, but his body was taken back to Dresden for reburial eighteen years later. After his death, his widow, Caroline, asked Giacomo to finish an opera that her husband had been working on, called *Die Drei Pintos* [The Three Pintos]. Giacomo had agreed, but the project was to prove a burden for many years. He was never able to complete it, and he eventually paid Caroline the large sum of nearly 4,000 thalers in compensation. Gustav Mahler finished the opera in 1887, half a century after Carl von Weber's death, but it was never successful.

In May 1827, less than a year after their arrival in Paris, the Meyerbeers returned to Berlin. Minna was six months pregnant with their first child, and she wanted to be close to her mother for the birth. The couple did not, as might have been expected, go to the Tiergarten villa, but rented rooms in the city, on the second floor of a house on Unter den Linden. They may have felt that the atmosphere of the villa, where Wilhelm, Doris and their children now lived with Amalia, would be too hectic for Minna, while she was in an advanced stage of pregnancy.

The social life of the villa had recently revived: Angelica Catalani had returned to Berlin that spring, and Amalia had entertained her old friend with appropriate lavishness. Two months before Giacomo and Minna had arrived in Berlin, she had hosted a grand concert and ball, at which Catalani had sung to great applause. The guests had included the British, Russian and Danish ambassadors to Prussia, as well as Count Hatzfeldt, and several aristocratic ladies, among them the Swedish Countess Engström and the wife of the prominent General, Job von Witzleben. Karl Varnhagen von Ense, who had been present, and had seen the exalted guests mingling with the Beer family and their friends, had commented rather snobbishly that, 'Anyone seeing this would not imagine Berlin society to be aristocratic, and yet it is.'[7]

On 16 August 1827, Minna gave birth to a daughter, Eugènie. Giacomo noted joyfully in his diary that 'Today at seven o' clock in the morning God granted me a daughter.'[8] The couple's happiness was short-lived, however.

In December that year, Eugènie died, at just four months old. Giacomo wrote to a friend in Paris that 'I stayed at her bedside the entire week, day and night, and watched her suffer cruelly, to her last breath.'[9] His own health was affected by the baby's death; six months later, in June 1828, he told Count Brühl that 'I only got up a few days ago from my sickbed, where my grief at the loss of my only child had consigned me.'[10]

Minna quickly became pregnant again, and gave birth to a baby boy in October 1828. This second child, named Alfred, did not survive much longer than his sister. He died at six months old, on 13 April 1829. Giacomo and Minna were devastated. In the weeks following Alfred's death, they were left numbed. Abraham Mendelssohn commented that, 'it's no wonder that these people don't know where to turn or what to do; to be so cosseted by good luck, and then to be overwhelmed with such misfortunes would be enough to make anyone lose their reason.'[11]

Later that month, Giacomo and Minna left Berlin, after a stay of over two years, to spend the summer recuperating at spas, before returning to Paris. Giacomo accompanied Minna to Baden-Baden for a cure. They then travelled on to the Belgian watering place of Spa, where they spent the next two months, accompanied by Amalia. A site of healing cold springs in a wooded valley of the Ardennes, the small town of Spa was famous for its casino, built in 1763 by the Prince Bishop of Liège, and had become a highly fashionable resort. It was a favourite of the British, as well as the continental, aristocracy; its past illustrious guests had included Peter the Great of Russia, the Duke and Duchess of Orléans, and Georgiana, Duchess of Devonshire.

The practice of spending the summer at spas became habitual for the Meyerbeers in later years. Minna, weakened by pregnancies, and anxious to get away from Paris, where she never felt at home, developed a tendency to agonise over vague symptoms and infirmities, mirroring her husband's preoccupation with his own health. Their letters to one another, when apart, are filled with endless worries about their own, and each other's, health problems.

At the end of August 1829, the Meyerbeers returned to Paris, and moved into rooms in the Hôtel de l'Elysée in the Rue de Beaune, on the left bank of the Seine. Giacomo resumed work with Scribe on *Robert le Diable*, which they had now agreed to reshape as a five-act work for the Opéra, making it a much larger project than originally envisaged.

Amalia and her sister, Minna's mother Johanna Mosson, made a short visit to England together in the autumn of 1829. Felix Mendelssohn had been in London at the time of the sisters' stay there, and had reported, rather sarcastically, to his parents in Berlin that, 'Madame Beer and her sister, the Mosson, were here, and got to know London in four days.' He had also been irritated by Amalia airily referring to Rossini's new opera as 'Gioacchino's latest'.[12] Felix's dislike of the Beer family was becoming evident: he had been injured in a carriage accident while the sisters were in London, and had refused to allow Amalia to visit him in his sickroom, which had precipitated an argument with his parents, who felt that he had behaved rudely towards their old friend.

From this time onwards, Johanna Mosson is often mentioned as accompanying both Amalia and Minna on their various travels. Minna's father, the bankrupt Joseph Mosson, is never mentioned, although he was still alive – he died in 1834. According to their grandson, Felix Eberty, Minna's parents, while living in the same house in Berlin, were effectively estranged.

In July 1830, Minna gave birth to a third child, a baby girl, in Baden-Baden. Giacomo, who was in Paris working on *Robert*, fired off frantic letters to his mother-in-law and to the baby's nurse, demanding daily bulletins on the health of mother and child. When the baby, named Blanca, began coughing, her parents panicked, as both Eugènie and Alfred had died of a lung condition that had started with very similar symptoms.

Happily, the coughing was not a sign of anything serious; the little girl was fundamentally healthy, and thrived. Blanca would be the first of their children to live to adulthood. Minna returned to Paris with their daughter later in the year. The family lived in the Hôtel des Princes, in the rue de Richelieu, described by Paganini as 'the address where all the great put up'.[13] Although Giacomo was to spend much of his life in Paris, he never bought property there – perhaps because of Minna's dislike of the city – and the Hôtel des Princes became one of his favourite residences.

By January 1831, Amalia and her companion, Antoinette de Montalban, were also in Paris, living in the Hôtel Wagram in the rue de la Paix. There is a rare description of Antoinette from around this time, by the Austrian dramatist Franz Grillparzer, who noted in his diary that he had visited Giacomo in his apartments in Paris, but had found only Amalia there, along with her companion, who was 'not good-looking, but obviously sweet-natured, and therefore pleasing to me'.[14] Antoinette had become a part of the family; after Amalia's death, she acted as a companion to Giacomo's daughters, and was left a pension in his will.

Amalia led a busy social life in Paris, with evenings filled with trips to concerts, theatres and fashionable salons. Gaspare Spontini, the General Music Director at the Berlin court, was also visiting Paris and occasionally dined with Amalia at her hotel, as did the political writer Ludwig Börne. Börne, who had been born in the Frankfurt ghetto as Loeb Baruch, had converted to Christianity in 1818 after being forced to resign from his post as a police actuary because of his Jewish background. Börne and Heinrich Heine were both now based in Paris, and their work as foreign correspondents for German newspapers had inspired a new, politically active literary movement, 'Young Germany', whose adherents supported liberal causes such as democracy and the emancipation of both women and Jews.

Börne had met the Beers in Berlin in 1828, and had been invited to lunch at the Tiergarten villa. He had described Giacomo, in a letter to a friend, as 'a small, dark, ugly little Jew', and Amalia as 'an old Jewess with a nasal twang'.[15] This contemptuous attitude reflects that of a number of converts towards the Beers, and may have derived from a need to disassociate themselves from their own Jewish origins, which still pursued and hampered them, even after baptism. Attacks on both Börne and Heine by German conservative commentators almost always alluded unfavourably to them as Jewish.

Börne clearly had no objection to enjoying the hospitality of the old Jewess and her ugly little son in Paris, where they were well known in high society. Giacomo's diary of the time is filled with the names of Parisian socialites: Madame Récamier, Viscount de Chateaubriand, Princess Vaudmont, Countess de Saint-Aulaire, Countess Merlin, Countess Apponyi, and the Rothschilds all appear alongside the greatest musicians, artists and writers of the time.

While Amalia was in Paris, Giacomo developed a habit of spending some of his free evenings working on his compositions in his mother's rooms at her hotel. It appears that Minna found Amalia's presence in their marriage more than a little overwhelming. Giacomo recorded his irritation on one occasion, when he had intended to spend the evening with his mother, but had been prevented from doing so, by what he described as 'a little obstinacy of Minna's':

> I wanted to work at my mother's, so as not to leave her alone, and Minna had agreed (although not very enthusiastically) to spend the evening there as well. I therefore had the box containing my work taken there. However, Minna went to sleep after dinner, which she never usually does, and stayed lying on the sofa a long time without a word about our going out. This hurt me inwardly, although I said nothing.[16]

Giacomo always avoided confrontation – even with those closest to him. Nonetheless, Minna would have to get used to the difficult fact that Amalia would always occupy a central place in Giacomo's affections.

She would also have to learn to share him with the many people involved in the creation of his operas. His work involved him in constant meetings and social events. He spent a good deal of time and energy cultivating those whose goodwill might be crucial to his future success, and was especially careful not to neglect journalists and critics. He had learnt this lesson early in life, watching his mother cultivating 'useful' people for his sake, and hearing her constant admonitions not to neglect anyone who might be helpful to him in his career.

Giacomo had settled in Paris at a time of major change in France's political and cultural life. In July 1830, the last of the Bourbon kings, the autocratic and reactionary Charles X, was forced to abdicate, after he had tried to tighten censorship, dissolve the newly elected parliament, and restrict the right to vote. After three days of rioting in the streets of Paris, known as the 'July Revolution', Charles X was replaced by Louis-Philippe, Duke of Orléans, who was proclaimed King of the French on 9 August 1830.

Louis-Philippe, known as the 'Citizen-King', was more bourgeois than aristocratic in his habits and tastes. His father had remained in France during the Revolution, abandoning his title, and calling himself 'Philippe Egalité'. Philippe had voted for the execution of Louis XVI, but he had himself been guillotined during the Reign of Terror. His son had fled France, and had lived in exile for twenty-one years, returning in 1815. Under Louis-Philippe's rule a growing middle class, mainly composed of bankers and financiers, was to displace the aristocracy as the most powerful force in French society.

The management of the Opéra – more properly titled the Académie Royale de Musique – was fundamentally affected by this change in regime. Prior to the July Revolution, it had been a state institution, under the direct control of the royal household. It had received huge annual subsidies from the interior ministry, from the King, and from the secondary theatres of Paris, which were forced to pay a 'contribution' to the Opéra. It had nevertheless never made a profit.

Under Louis-Philippe, the Opéra was privatised and offered out to tender, although it still retained a degree of state subsidy and oversight. The man who took on the management and leasehold of the Opéra in 1831 had no prior experience of running a theatre, but he was an excellent businessman. Dr Louis-Désiré Véron had made a fortune selling a patented chest medicine, and in 1829 he had founded the *Revue de Paris*, a successful literary magazine.

Véron saw an opportunity to make money from the Opéra by democratising it, and adapting its productions to the taste of the bourgeois audience. He envisaged the Opéra as 'the Versailles of the middle classes', their chief place of amusement, where they would go to see, and to be seen, just as the old aristocracy had.[17] This new audience, accustomed to the comedies and melodramas of the boulevard theatres, demanded operas with exciting plots and accessible music that entertained them, and made a direct appeal to their emotions. The genre of *grand opéra*, which was developed during Véron's four-year tenure at the Opéra, would offer them the spectacle they wanted.

Operas in this style had a number of defining characteristics: the story typically focused on a personal dilemma set against a background of sweeping historical events, often featuring doomed relationships that crossed religious or social divides. The staging demanded massed crowd scenes, a large orchestra, and spectacular stage effects. Great attention was paid to accuracy in evoking the period and place of the operas' settings, not just through costumes and scenery, but also through the introduction of music with 'local colour'.

Véron summed up his concept of grand opera in his memoirs:

> An opera in five acts cannot exist without a highly dramatic plot, involving the greatest passions of the human heart and powerful historical interests; that dramatic action must nevertheless be designed for the eyes like a ballet; the chorus must play a vital role and be, so to speak, one of the interesting characters of the piece. Every act should provide a contrast in scenery, costumes, and above all, skilfully created situations.

Véron believed that, as director of the Paris Opéra, with an orchestra of over eighty musicians, a chorus of the same size, and a corps of technicians numbering sixty men at his command, 'the public expects and demands great things of you'.[18]

One of the first examples of *grand opéra* had been Daniel-Esprit Auber's *La Muette de Portici* [The Dumb Girl of Portici], premiered in Paris in 1828. The opera was set in Naples, at the time of the 1647 uprising against Spanish rule, and ended with a thrilling scene, in which the dumb heroine (danced by a ballerina) threw herself into the crater of Mount Vesuvius, as it erupted onstage.

Auber's opera famously played a role in the Belgian revolution of 1830 against Dutch rule. A performance of *La Muette de Portici* was scheduled to be given at the Théâtre de la Monnaie in Brussels, on 25 August that year, as part of the celebrations for the fifteenth anniversary of the Dutch King William's reign. The rebels secretly chose a stirring duet in the second act, 'Sacred Love of the Fatherland', as the signal for the outbreak of revolt. At the point in the performance when the singers began the duet, the audience rioted, and poured out into the streets to join a workers' demonstration, sparking the uprising which led to the secession of the Belgian provinces from the United Kingdom of the Netherlands.

Giacomo Meyerbeer would become *grand opéra*'s greatest exponent. His talents and character were admirably suited to Véron's vision of the Opéra. His last Italian opera, *Il Crociato in Egitto*, had a number of features that foreshadowed the later genre: the story is centred on a love affair across a religious divide, between a Christian knight and a Moslem woman at the time of the Crusades. The large chorus in *Il Crociato*, as in *grand opéra*, plays an integral part in the action, rather than being confined to commentary on the sidelines. An Italian reviewer had commented that, 'The dances introduced in to the various choruses, the numerous and beautiful sets ... the changes of a very rich wardrobe, two bands, two hundred participants ... all presented a spectacle that surprised and interested.'[19]

Each of Giacomo's Italian operas had been bigger and more spectacular, both musically and in terms of stagecraft, than the preceding one. In the finale of the first act of *Il Crociato*, the opposing armies were led by two on-stage military bands. Rossini is reputed to have said, with a smile, when someone asked him about Meyerbeer's operas, 'Oh, you mean the BIG Rossini operas!'

Giacomo's Italian operas were not copies of Rossini's works, however. According to Giacomo's German biographer, Reiner Zimmermann, 'He scoured his musical environment for its most successful elements, analysed their effects, and reviewed their usefulness for his own work.'[20] Giacomo had expressed his own thoughts on this process as early as 1820, when he had remarked to his friend, the Austrian music critic Franz Kandler, that he would only write for Germany again if he could find a librettist with whom he could work on the amalgamation of Italian form and German individuality and strength.[21]

By the time he arrived in Paris, he had already begun to establish a style of his own, that combined melody with imaginative and expressive orchestration, and that paid great attention to the dramatic demands of the libretto. It was a style that would be perfectly suited to the form of opera that developed in Paris in the 1830s. His partnership with his librettist, Scribe, was to prove crucial. Scribe, the son of a silk merchant, understood the aspirations and tastes of the newly powerful middle classes – he was, after all, one of them. The story of *Robert le Diable* tapped into the mood of the time. The old heroic mythological and classical themes and the rigid musical conventions that had pleased court audiences were a thing of the past.

*Robert* was set in the Middle Ages, and appealed to the Romantic taste for the Gothic past and the supernatural. In Scribe's libretto, the hero, Robert, is faced with a Faustian choice between good and evil (and in fact, Goethe considered Giacomo to be the composer most suited to setting his *Faust* to music). Robert's father Bertram, who is a devil in disguise, represents the forces of evil, and tries to entice his son into wrongdoing. Robert's foster-sister, Alice, represents the forces of good, and speaks on behalf of Robert's late, saintly mother.

Robert is no heroic figure, however. He is an indecisive man, and in the end, his choice is made for him, when the clock strikes midnight, and Bertram is dragged down into hell. Scribe's depiction of Robert as vacillating, unable to choose between Bertram and Alice, has been criticised as a weakness in the plot, but it has also been perceived as a reflection of the individual's dilemma in contending with the impulses to good and to evil that co-exist in the human psyche. Robert can be compared with Sir Walter Scott's 'passive' heroes in the Waverley novels: ordinary men torn by conflicting demands acting on them.

Giacomo was closely involved in the development of the libretto, making suggestions, re-shaping the story and characters, and constantly demanding revisions. This was something that his Italian librettist, Gaetano Rossi, had begun to find irritating in his last years of working with Giacomo. Eugène Scribe often worked in collaboration with other writers – he and Germain Delavigne had created the text for Auber's *Muette de Portici* between them – but even he, at times, found Giacomo's constant re-workings of the text exasperating.

It was usual for composers to consider their work finished when they handed the score over to the theatre, but Giacomo paid close attention to every aspect of *Robert*'s production. He attended every rehearsal, constantly fine-tuning the music, and overseeing the details of the scenery and the costumes. He was fortunate: at the time that he arrived in Paris, the Opéra's set designer, Pierre-Luc-Charles Ciceri, and its stage manager, Henri Duponchel, were two of the greatest exponents of their respective arts. The stage setting for the 'Ballet of the Nuns' in act 3 of *Robert*, in which the ghosts of long-dead, debauched nuns rise from their graves at Bertram's call, to tempt Robert into wrongdoing, was sensational.

The audience at the premiere gasped as the curtain lifted, revealing a scene of ruined cloisters and tombs bathed in moonlight. The creation of this moonlit scene was achieved by the use of a new type of dimmable gas lamp. The role of the ghostly abbess was danced by a young ballerina who had recently taken Paris by storm. Marie Taglioni revolutionised ballet, her dancing *en pointe* giving her an ethereal lightness and grace that made the earlier athletic, more muscular, style of dancing, look ungainly.

The Nuns' Ballet in *Robert le Diable* was a perfect vehicle for her style of dancing. Taglioni floated across the stage in her white tulle dress, accompanied by eerie, haunting music that gave the seductive beauty of the scene an unsettling undertow of dangerous sexuality and corruption. The ballet's function was as revolutionary as its form, as this was the first time that a ballet had been presented as an intrinsic part of the action of an opera, rather than as a divertissement. The Nuns' Ballet shaped the future of the Romantic ballet, influencing seminal works such as *Giselle* and *Swan Lake*.

Giacomo's close supervision of every detail of the production of his operas bordered on the obsessive. During the preparations for *Robert le Diable*, he often expressed fears that others were conspiring against him, or trying to cheat him. He agonised in his diary over the possibility that the composer Ferdinand Hérold, who was chorus master at the Opéra, and therefore had access to Giacomo's work, would appropriate his ideas. He even asked Scribe to try and ensure that Hérold's *Zampa* was not premiered before *Robert*, in case it stole his thunder.

At the same time, he worried that Scribe would give the composer Daniel-Esprit Auber preferential treatment: 'What if Scribe tells Auber … about our contract, and Auber takes a fancy to the subject himself, and asks Scribe to reserve it for him, and Scribe agrees? Or again, what if Scribe betrays our deep secret about my position with regard to Hérold in the matter?'[22]

In the event, Giacomo's fears proved groundless, and *Robert le Diable* was premiered at the Paris Opéra on 21 November 1831. Meyerbeer's new opera had been anticipated as a major musical event. The seats at the premiere were filled with celebrities: Chopin, George Sand, Berlioz, Balzac, Cherubini and Dumas were all present.

The long-awaited premiere was marked by a number of extraordinary on-stage accidents. Stage machinery was fairly unsophisticated, and could be difficult to handle, so that accidents were not unknown – but to have three major incidents in one evening was unusual. As Véron described the evening in his memoirs, the problems began in act 3, when a heavy support holding twelve lighted lamps crashed to the stage, narrowly missing the soprano Julie Dorus, who was singing the role of Alice. In the same act, during the Nuns' Ballet, a piece of scenery representing a cloud broke loose from its moorings, and plunged down towards the dancer Marie Taglioni, who was lying on a tomb, waiting to come to life at Bertram's call. She had to spring off the tomb to avoid being hit.

The most spectacular accident took place in the final act, when Robert's evil father Bertram, sung by the French bass Nicolas Prosper Levasseur, disappeared down the trapdoor to hell as midnight struck. The tenor Adolph Nourrit, playing the role of Robert, should have remained on stage. Nourrit, however, either threw himself, or fell, down the trapdoor after Levasseur in his excitement. The other singers were halted in their tracks, and a cry of 'Nourrit is dead!' went around the theatre. Luckily, however, the mattresses placed to soften Levasseur's fall were still in place, and the rather portly Nourrit bounced off them, to be asked by an astonished Levasseur, 'What the devil are *you* doing here? Have they changed the ending?'

After a brief interval, Nourrit reappeared on the stage, where the cast were milling around in shock, assuming that he had been injured or killed. He resumed his role as if nothing had happened.[23] In its review of *Robert's* premiere, the newspaper *La Gazette de France* felt it necessary to reassure its readers that 'no one was killed or wounded'.[24]

Giacomo seems to have taken the accidents in his stride, without suspecting any anti-Jewish plot or intrigue, which he surely would have done, had they happened in a Berlin production. The incidents did not, in any case, affect the outcome of the premiere, which was an instant and brilliant success. The audience, the critics, and Giacomo's fellow musicians were all united in their praise.

The respected critic François Joseph Fétis wrote in the *Revue musicale* that 'the score of *Robert le Diable* is not only M. Meyerbeer's masterpiece, it is a remarkable production in the history of art … it has placed M. Meyerbeer incontestably at the head of the modern German school'.[25] Italian opera had often been criticised for its concentration on vocal melody, and on the singers at the expense of the orchestra. Giacomo's use of the orchestra to convey atmosphere and emotion was a revelation.

The influential composer François Le Sueur predicted that, 'Your colossal reputation has already travelled around Europe. From now on, it will spread across the whole inhabited world.'[26] Frédéric Chopin described *Robert* as 'a masterpiece of the new school', adding that, 'Meyerbeer has made himself immortal.'[27]

This was an unusual show of enthusiasm from the quiet and reserved Chopin, especially as Giacomo's music was so different to his own intimate, delicate piano compositions. The two men met frequently in Parisian society, but were not close friends – Chopin was nearly twenty years younger than Giacomo, and their personalities were as different as their attitudes to music. However, when Chopin died in 1849, at the tragically early age of 39, Giacomo was chosen to be a pallbearer at his funeral, along with the great painter Eugène Delacroix.

The Beers' friend, the scientist and explorer Alexander von Humboldt, had been in the audience for the premiere of *Robert le Diable*, and could not go to sleep that night before writing to Giacomo offering his congratulations. He kindly passed on a scrap of conversation he had overheard as he left the theatre, that he knew would give Giacomo pleasure, telling him that 'the crowd left rejoicing, and, what made the strongest impression on me, was that I heard a voice behind me, saying, "If it's true that his mother was present, how happy she must be tonight!"'.[28]

François Le Sueur had been right in his prediction that *Robert* would take Giacomo's name around the globe. The opera was a world-wide success, and continued to be immensely popular for the rest of the century. By 1850, it had been produced in places as diverse as Calcutta, New Orleans, Rio de Janeiro, Mauritius and Moscow. At one point, *Robert* was playing simultaneously in three theatres in Vienna. By the end of the nineteenth century, it had been produced over 750 times at the Paris Opéra.

*Robert le Diable* became a cultural icon, with a number of well-known artists producing paintings of scenes from the opera. When Edgar Degas wanted to paint the orchestra of the Paris Opéra in 1871, he chose to depict them playing during the Nuns' Ballet. In England, *Robert* became so popular that the Staffordshire potteries produced a figurine of the Swedish soprano Jenny Lind in the role of Alice, in a famous pose from act 3 of the opera, clinging to a large cross.

The music of *Robert* was popularised by arrangements of airs from the opera. People who could not attend the opera itself became familiar with the music through piano, voice and band arrangements, which allowed the arias to be played and sung in people's homes, in concerts, and at dance halls. Chopin and Liszt both helped to popularise the music from *Robert*. Liszt wrote piano arrangements of music from all of Giacomo's French operas, and his *Réminiscences de Robert le Diable* – which sold out on the day of publication – remained one of his own favourite concert pieces for decades.

# Notes

1. Giacomo Meyerbeer, *Briefwechsel und Tagebücher*, Heinz Becker, Gudrun Becker and Sabine Henze-Döhring (eds) (Berlin: Walter de Gruyter, 1960-2006), vol. 3, p.134.
2. Letter, Carl Maria von Weber to Caroline von Weber, 19 December 1825, Carl-Maria-von-Weber-Gesamtausgabe. Digitale Edition, http://weber-gesamtausgabe.de/ A042536 (Version 3.4.2 vom 8. February 2019).
3. Lea Mendelssohn Bartholdy, *Ewig die deine. Briefe an Henriette von Pereira-Arnstein*, Wolfgang Dinglinger and Rudolf Elvers (eds) (Hannover: Wehrhahn Verlag, 2010), vol. 1, p.182.
4. Jacob Jacobson (ed.), *Jüdische Trauungen in Berlin 1759 bis 1813* (Berlin: Walter de Gruyter, 1968), p.316. Jacobson says that Meyerbeer's original first name was Meyer, that he received official permission to use the name 'Meyerbeer' on 3 January 1822, and permission to use the first name 'Jacob' on 19 May 1826.
5. Lea Mendelssohn Bartholdy, *Ewig die deine*, vol. 1, pp.190-1.
6. Smart, Sir George, *Leaves from the Journals of Sir George Smart*, Hugh Bertram Cox and Clara L.E. Cox (eds) (Cambridge: Cambridge University Press, 1907; digitally printed version, 2014), pp.248-9.
7. Konrad Feilchenfeldt (ed.), *Karl Varnhagen von Ense: Tageblätter* (Frankfurt am Main: Deutscher Klassiker Verlag, 1994), p.144.
8. Giacomo Meyerbeer, *The Diaries of Giacomo Meyerbeer*, Robert Letellier (ed. and trans.) (Madison, NJ: Fairleigh Dickinson University Press, 1999-2004), vol. 1, p.386.
9. Meyerbeer, *Briefwechsel und Tagebücher*, vol. 2, p.66.
10. Ibid., p.68.
11. Felix Mendelssohn Bartholdy, *Sämtliche Briefe*, Helmut Loos and Wilhelm Seidel (eds) (Kassel: Bärenreiter, 2008), vol. 1, p.265.
12. Felix Mendelssohn Bartholdy, *Sämtliche Briefe*, vol. 1, p.421.
13. Meyerbeer, *Diaries*, vol. 1, p.426 n 48.
14. Meyerbeer, *Briefwechsel und Tagebücher*, vol. 2, p.682 n 517, 3.
15. Ludwig Börne, *Über das Schmollen der Weiber* (Cologne: c.w. leske verlag, 1987), pp.237-8.
16. Meyerbeer, *Briefwechsel und Tagebücher*, vol. 2, p.131.
17. Louis Désiré Véron, *Mémoires d'un bourgeois de Paris* (Paris: Librairie Nouvelle, 1857), vol. 3, pp.104-5.
18. Ibid., pp.181-2.
19. Robert Letellier, *The Operas of Giacomo Meyerbeer* (Madison, NJ: Farleigh Dickinson University Press, 2006), p.95.
20. Reiner Zimmermann, *Giacomo Meyerbeer* (Berlin: Henschel Verlag, 1991), p.118.
21. Meyerbeer, *Briefwechsel und Tagebücher*, vol. 1, p.420.
22. Meyerbeer, *Briefwechsel und Tagebücher*, vol. 2, p.127.
23. Véron, *Mémoires*, vol. 3, pp.164-6.

24. Patrick Barbier, *Opera in Paris 1800-1850. A Lively History*, Robert Luoma (trans.) (Portland, Oregon: Amadeus Press, 1995), p.48.
25. Meyerbeer, *Briefwechsel und Tagebücher*, vol. 2, p.618 n 153,1.
26. Ibid., p.156.
27. Robert Letellier, *Meyerbeer's Robert le Diable* (Newcastle: Cambridge Scholars Publishing, 2012), p.1.
28. Meyerbeer, *Briefwechsel und Tagebücher*, vol. 2, pp.153-4.

# 16

## At the Court of King Ludwig

Michael had been living in Paris during 1829 and 1830, while Giacomo was working on *Robert le Diable*, and he was there again at the end of 1831 to support his brother at the opera's premiere. Michael enjoyed life in Paris – and the company of his favourite brother – but he did not intend to make the city his permanent home. He was something of a social butterfly, and found it difficult to buckle down to writing serious drama there; as he admitted, he was far too easily distracted from his work by what he described as the 'social maelstrom' of such a cosmopolitan city.

Since his success with *Der Paria* in 1823, Michael had led a nomadic existence, moving mainly between Paris, Bonn, and the Bavarian capital of Munich. Although he had no settled home, he had, however, begun to collect a circle of like-minded friends, mostly other German authors, with whom he kept in touch, mainly by letter. One of the most important people in this group was the Bavarian poet and politician, Eduard von Schenk.

Michael had first met Schenk in the summer of 1826, when he and Amalia had passed through Munich on their way south to Italy. Amalia had been ordered by her doctor to take a sea-bathing cure in Genoa and Livorno, to recover her health after the shock of Jacob's death the previous autumn. Michael was accompanying his mother on her travels, as he often did.

At the time of the Beers' stay in Munich, von Schenk, who was twelve years older than Michael, was becoming an important figure in the Bavarian government, where he held a senior post in the Ministry of the Interior. He would become Minister for Home Affairs in 1828. He had also achieved his first significant success as a dramatist a few months before the Beers' arrival, when his tragedy, *Belisar*, had been premiered at the Munich Court Theatre. Michael, who admired the play, was eager to meet its author, and arranged an introduction through a mutual friend.

Michael and von Schenk took to one another immediately, and quickly became close friends. Michael looked up to the older man, asking him in a letter of 1827 to 'answer me soon, telling me that you miss me, and that I am still worthy of you'.[1] The admiration was mutual, though: when Michael arrived back in Munich from his travels one evening, Schenk, unable to wait until the following morning to see his friend again, rushed around to his lodgings at 11 o' clock that night. By the spring of 1827, they were discussing starting a literary journal together, although this scheme did not come to fruition.

Schenk was close to the new ruler of Bavaria, King Ludwig I, who had come to the throne in 1825. Ludwig was considered a liberal on his accession – one of his first acts had been to abolish censorship. He was also a poet (although a bad one), and an enthusiastic patron of the arts: he admired the culture of ancient Greece and the Italian Renaissance, and built a number of neo-classical buildings in Munich, which, during his reign, became the artistic centre of Germany. After the July Revolution in France in 1830, however, Ludwig's reign became more repressive. He reinstated a strict censorship, and began to rescind the civil rights of Protestants in Catholic Bavaria. His indiscreet affair with the dancer and notorious adventuress Lola Montez in the 1840s added to his unpopularity, and was a factor in his abdication in 1848 in favour of his son, Maximilian.

Ludwig admired Eduard von Schenk's writing, and treated him as a literary mentor, asking Schenk for his opinions on his poems – which Schenk gave with the greatest of tact. When Michael returned to Munich after his trip to Italy with his mother, von Schenk introduced him to the Bavarian court, later commenting that 'The King received our poet with favour, and he was greeted with warm good will and the greatest friendliness in all social circles.'[2] Michael himself commented that the King behaved towards him in 'an exceptionally friendly' way.[3]

Michael was quickly drawn into the social life of the court. In the carnival season of 1827, he took part in a pageant where aristocrats, dressed in the costumes of Greek, Italian and Bavarian peasants, presented the King and Queen with poems in their honour, composed for the occasion. Michael had written two of the poems: Ludwig was an active supporter of Greek independence in the war between Greece and the Ottoman Empire, and Michael's 'Greek' poem contained the lines: 'After the bloody struggle, we want to be free – as free as the King of Bavaria and the Bavarian people, for who on this earth is more free?'[4]

Michael had not produced a play since *Der Paria* had appeared four years previously, but his friendship with von Schenk and the atmosphere of the Bavarian court revived his creativity. By 1827, he was again working on a serious drama. *Struensee*, a five-act tragedy, was based on the life of the eighteenth-century German doctor, Johann Struensee, who became court physician to the Danish King, Christian VII. Christian, who came to the throne as a 16-year-old in 1766, suffered from a mental illness, which was characterised by hallucinations and paranoia. It is possible that he suffered from schizophrenia.

As Christian's personal physician, Struensee held a position of trust and authority. By the beginning of the 1770s, his influence over the King had become so strong that he was able to rule Denmark in Christian's name, as *de facto* regent. He did so conscientiously, attempting to introduce liberal reforms, including the abolition of torture, censorship, and the slave trade. These reforms were supported by Christian's wife, Queen Caroline Matilda, but were strenuously opposed by conservative factions at the court. In the end, it was Struensee's love affair with the unhappy Danish Queen – which resulted in a daughter, Princess Louise – that gave his enemies the pretext for his downfall and execution in 1772.

Michael encountered difficulties in staging *Struensee* in Germany, however, as these events were considered too recent to be depicted on the stage – so recent, in fact, that close relatives of some of the royal characters portrayed in it were still alive. Queen Caroline Matilda had been the youngest daughter of Crown Prince Frederick, the son of George II of England and Hannover, and so was closely related to a number of German royal families. One of the mainsprings of the plot of Michael's *Struensee* was the Queen's adultery with the royal physician, which was historically true, but not a fact that her relatives wished to see portrayed on the public stage.

As a result, the play was banned from many of the German court theatres, including that of Berlin. King Ludwig was willing to give his permission for it to be staged in Munich, however, and he allowed Michael to dedicate *Struensee* to him. It appears that Ludwig had taken a liking to Michael. There must have been some suggestion at court, when in 1828 Eduard von Schenk was promoted from Undersecretary to Minister of Home Affairs, that in his new position it would be better if the Minister saw less of his young Jewish friend. In a letter to Schenk in September of that year, Ludwig made it clear that he approved of the friendship: 'If, as Minister, you were to have less contact than you have had as Undersecretary with the Israelite Michael Beer, who has distinguished himself through his talent and his behaviour, it would make an unpleasant impression on me.'[5] 'Israelite' was the polite term at the time, as the word 'Jew' was considered to have perjorative connotations. In using 'Israelite', Ludwig was displaying courtesy towards Michael in his choice of words.

*Struensee* was produced at the Bavarian court theatre on 27 March 1828, and was well received. There were reviews in both of Munich's daily newspapers. Eduard von Schenk, perhaps not surprisingly, wrote an enthusiastic article for the evening paper. The review in the morning paper, however, was written by Heinrich Heine, who was in Munich at the time. Heine's article was lengthy, and his comments on *Struensee* were flattering: he described Michael's language as 'pure and clear', and remarked that, 'We admire his understanding of drama and knowledge of stagecraft. He has not only thought out, prepared and executed each individual scene, but each scene is an organically necessary development, both in and for itself, and in relation to the main theme of the play.'[6] Commenting on the character of the Danish Queen, he praised Michael's writing as showing an ability that 'is more than what we usually call talent, and that we could almost call genius'.[7]

In private, however, Heine's attitude to Michael was more ambiguous. He commented sarcastically to Moses Moser that 'our national poet Michael Beer is here and his play is being staged'.[8] A couple of weeks later, he wrote to another friend that '... the two great lights of the day, the Dioscuri [Heavenly Twins] in the starry sky of poetry are here, Michael Beer and Eduard Schenk. I have given a report of the former's tragedy in the *Morgenblatt*, and shown the world how little I envy him, and how little his fame hurts me.'[9]

Despite Heine's protestations, there was more behind his friendly review than a desire to demonstrate his indifference to Michael's success. He had written to a third friend shortly after the review had appeared, saying 'Forgive me for the article, I had to write it. You don't know how worried I am.'[10] Heine was always in need of money, and at the time of *Struensee*'s premiere, he was anxious to obtain a professorship at the new Munich University. He wanted Michael to introduce him to von Schenk, in the hope that the Minister would exert influence on his behalf.

Heine had taken care to compliment the King in his review of *Struensee*, saying that 'Here in Bavaria we have a free people, and, what is more unusual, a free King.'[11] The review had the desired effect, insofar as Michael did introduce Heine to Eduard von Schenk, although Heine did not obtain the professorship – for which, in any case, he was not qualified. Heine turned against the Bavarian regime in later years; in the 1840s he published a short series of poems ironically titled 'Songs in Praise of King Ludwig', in which he viciously satirised Ludwig and his poetic pretensions.[12]

Heine was not the only person to approach Michael for favours with the Bavarian court; Michael's own, much more famous, brother also used him as a conduit to approach the King. In August 1829, Giacomo asked

Michael, who was in Spa with him at the time, to contact von Schenk, with a view to obtaining the King's consent to his setting one of Ludwig's poems to music. The King agreed, and later wrote formally to von Schenk, granting Giacomo permission to dedicate the work – the *Bayerische Schützenmarsch* – to him.

Ludwig clearly regretted Michael's absence from his court; he finished his letter to von Schenk with the words, 'Many friendly greetings to his brother [Michael], who I wish to see settled in Bavaria.'[13] Ludwig's wish was tantamount to a command, but Michael was in no hurry to settle anywhere. He spent most of 1829 and 1830 in Paris, with a break to tour the Netherlands in the summer of 1829 with the German Romantic artist Friedrich Schadow, to study Dutch paintings – Michael was very interested in art. His brother's fame had opened the doors of Parisian society to him, and Michael had quickly made his own friends there, among them the politician and writer Count Louis de Saint-Aulaire. The Count, who had translated Goethe's *Faust* into French, admired *Struensee*, and translated some scenes from it for the *Revue encyclopédique*.

However, although Michael enjoyed the social life of Paris, he did not feel entirely comfortable there in the political climate of the late 1820s. He described the atmosphere of the city in the last years of the rule of the reactionary Charles X as 'grey and foggy, with an autumnal chill'. Michael was a liberal, and he welcomed the July Revolution. He believed that the change of regime heralded 'an epoch of light and freedom', which would restore the rule of law.

He had no republican leanings, however. In early August 1830, he commented that 'the people have acted with praiseworthy moderation, as well as courageously, up to now, and it is hoped that the crown will be offered to the Duke of Orleans under strict guarantee, saving France from the demon of anarchy.'[14] He considered constitutional monarchy to be the ideal form of state, as he believed that 'a state that has a constitution should allow all of its subjects, regardless of their religion, to enjoy the same <u>civil</u> rights.'[15]

Michael did not produce any serious dramatic works while in Paris; he commented to a friend that the life he led there inclined him more towards comedy than tragedy. Unlike Heine, he did not need to work in order to earn money: in the two years he spent in Paris, his output consisted of two negligible comedies, and some poetry. One of his poems of this period, 'Der fromme Rabbi' [The Pious Rabbi], gives rare expression to his views on religion, a subject that Michael seldom discussed outside the safety of the family circle.

In the poem, the rabbi of the title, who lives in an isolated town without a Jewish community, longs to fulfil three important religious laws: offering hospitality to strangers; caring for the sick; and looking after the dead. He has had no opportunity to do so, however. When a lone Jewish traveller appears one day in the town, the rabbi welcomes him joyfully to his home, but then unexpectedly attacks him in the night. The next day, he carefully binds up the man's injuries, and begs him to stay another night. That night, he attempts to murder the man. When questioned, the rabbi explains that he has had to commit these acts, in order to fulfil all three religious laws.

Michael's ending of the poem is characteristic: the rabbi dies suddenly, but instead of being condemned or castigated for his pedantic stupidity, as the reader might expect, his soul is carried to heaven by an angel, who kisses him tenderly, and tells him: 'Alas! Did not the Lord inscribe his holy laws on the clear tablet of your heart, yet you tried to decipher them laboriously from sombre books, peering with dim eyes at a feeble will o' the wisp, while the sun stood high in the sky!'[16]

Michael had been brought up in a reform-minded family, and was not an observant Jew – as 'Der fromme Rabbi' makes clear – but, like all of Amalia's children, he remained loyal to Judaism, despite the pain his Jewish identity undoubtedly caused him. He was a sensitive young man, but he tended to keep silent when wounded. When he did speak, he maintained a dignity and restraint – Heine's 'kid gloves'. Michael rarely became involved in Jewish affairs, and only once broke this self-imposed rule, in order to assist Aaron Wolfssohn, Giacomo's former tutor.

Wolfssohn had settled in the Bavarian town of Fürth, which had a large Jewish population. In late 1830, the reform-minded rabbi Isaac Löwi had been chosen to take up the post of rabbi at Fürth, but, despite the government's confirmation of the appointment, the orthodox among the community had protested. The controversy had become so fierce that the appointment required a special decree of installation from the King to enforce it. Wolfssohn asked Michael to appeal to von Schenk, to ensure that the King issued the necessary order.

Although Michael was averse to taking any public stance on Jewish questions, he was fond of Wolfssohn, as were all the Beer family, and he agreed to take up the issue. He reported back to Wolfssohn that:

> The Minister [von Schenk] has a most favourable opinion of Dr Löwi, as indeed he does of all who want to promote the spiritual reform of Judaism in a legally responsible way. I myself have the

greatest respect for men of this persuasion, although I fear – and only too much experience has taught me to fear – that their aims will never succeed. Therefore I have resolved never to use my friendly relations with highly-placed officials here to work for the reform of the Jewish church … However, your letter, esteemed Professor Wolfssohn, has persuaded me to be untrue to my principle for the first time.[17]

Subsequent to Michael's conversation with Schenk, King Ludwig issued the decree authorizing Löwi's installation as rabbi of Fürth in March 1831. Löwi's tenure was successful, despite continuing orthodox resistance, and he remained in the post for forty-two years, until his death in 1873.

Although Michael was not generally prepared to speak publicly on behalf of his fellow Jews, in private he avoided contact with people who held or promoted anti-Semitic views. He had wanted to meet the Baden-based historian and politician Karl von Rotteck for some time. In 1831, when he arrived in Baden's capital, Karlsruhe, with an introduction to von Rotteck, he found that the Duchy's chamber of deputies was discussing whether or not to give full emancipation to the local Jewish population. When he discovered that von Rotteck had spoken against the proposal, Michael wrote to his publisher, Cotta, who had given him the letter of introduction, saying that, 'Herr von Rotteck has, by his vote on the citizenship which the government wished to grant to the Israelites, taken away from me all desire to make his personal acquaintance.'[18]

Michael found German hostility towards the Jews particularly distressing, because he felt himself to be German. As he admitted, 'For all the cosmopolitanism of my outlook, thoughts and poems, I would not, for all the world, want the ground of my soul to be anything other than German.'[19] When one of the minor uprisings in Germany that were sparked by the July Revolution took the form of an anti-Jewish riot, Michael commented bitterly that '… the cane of German freedom is once again dancing on the broad backs of the oft-beaten Jews.'[20]

Michael was particularly sensitive to slights against his own family. This touchiness almost ended a promising friendship with a fellow author, Karl Immermann. It came to Michael's ears that one of Immermann's comedies contained a mocking reference to Jacob Beer. Michael immediately wrote to Immermann, demanding that he remove the offending verse: 'You cannot think that I could accept my father's name being used as a signal for a German audience to erupt into laughter … I would not be worthy to be his son if I allowed his name to be mentioned in such a tone on the stage.'[21]

In response, Immermann sent Michael the script of the play, to prove that it contained no reference whatsoever to Jacob, or, indeed, to any of the Beer family. It turned out that one of the actors in a production of the comedy in Hamburg had ad libbed the offending comment without the author's knowledge. Immermann became one of Michael's closest friends, although, as he lived in Düsseldorf, their friendship was mostly carried on via correspondence, with only occasional meetings.

Immermann wrote a series of historical tragedies between 1827 and 1832, and he and Michael frequently exchanged drafts of their work for each other to comment on. This occasionally led to ruffled feathers: according to Eduard von Schenk, Michael was incurably honest, and always strictly impartial in his judgement of the work of other writers – even those who were among his closest friends. Immermann certainly found Michael's opinions a little too frank at times. Michael wrote to him in November 1830, commenting on a draft of Immermann's latest play, *Die Bojaren* [The Boyars] with such freedom of expression that a six-month silence ensued.

When Michael eventually contacted his friend, to ask whether he had offended him in any way, Immermann replied that, 'Yes, I was angry with you. When someone says of a work, that the poet has made the secondary characters into main ones, that maybe a five-act play could be condensed to three acts, and that a whole act, the fourth, is superfluous, it amounts to an accusation of a complete lack of planning, and immaturity.'[22] He went on to say that he could only think that Michael had read the play while travelling in his coach between Paris and Munich. Michael took the view, however, that when criticising others' works, he did not think about whether the author was a friend or foe, but was motivated solely by the desire to make the work itself as perfect as possible.[23]

Their friendship was strong enough to overcome such upsets, however, and by the next month they were again exchanging drafts of their work for each other's comments. Immermann had a portrait of Michael on the wall of his study, which, he once told Michael, only smiled silently when he asked it the questions he wanted to discuss with his friend: 'I wish you were sitting here under your portrait and we were arguing so as to make the walls shake!'[24]

On one occasion, however, Michael was drawn into a more unpleasant literary controversy through his friendship with Immermann. In 1827, Heinrich Heine had published the second volume of his travel writings, *Reisebilder*. The book had included some verses by Immermann which mocked the poetry of the aristocratic writer Count August von Platen. Von

Platen had retaliated by writing a comedy satirising Immermann's dramas, but had also brought the debate down to a personal level by including some anti-Semitic remarks about Heine.

Heine had responded with a novella, *Die Bäder von Lucca*, published in 1829, in which he attacked von Platen not only as a writer, but as an aristocrat, and as a homosexual. The invective was explicit and crude, as well as personally offensive. This attempt to crush his opponent rebounded on Heine, however. The book caused widespread revulsion, as he had intended – but it was directed towards the author, rather than his victim.

Immermann mentioned to Michael in April 1830 that Heine had written to him several times, 'and seems to have your wellbeing very much at heart, he mentions you in almost every letter'.[25] Heine's intentions soon became clear. Two years after he had first approached Michael for help in obtaining a professorship at Munich, he was still clinging on to the hope that von Schenk might find him a position at the University. He was afraid that the story of the 'von Platen affair', as it had become known, might spoil his chances, and he wanted Michael to persuade von Schenk to present his side of the affair to the Bavarian King.

Immermann admitted to Michael that he thought that it would be difficult to defend Heine's behaviour towards von Platen. In his reply, Michael came as close as he ever did to discourtesy:

> I will gladly be Heine's advocate, in writing or in person, as far as honesty allows. If Heine asks you again if you have had an answer from me, and what I said about him, tell him that he should remember how often he has said to me that I handle most things with kid gloves. I put those gloves on to read his book, and found that I was, as ever, too weak to stomach such crude fare as his satire without indigestion. In a word, it made me rather sick. Nonetheless, tell him that I send my heartiest greetings to him, and my personal regard for him is the same as ever.[26]

Heine does not seem to have taken offence at this plain speaking; rather surprisingly, he invited Michael to accompany him on a holiday to Boulogne that summer. Whatever their differences, the two men must have had some fellow feeling as Jews, despite Heine's conversion to Christianity some five years previously. In his reply to Heine's invitation, Michael was unusually frank in his expression of his feelings about his position as a Jew:

There [in Boulogne], there is soft silver sand, here there are stones. I avoid the latter as much as possible! As someone who, as you once so rightly said, has been burdened by heaven before my birth with the three worst misfortunes, namely to be a Jew, a German, and a poet, I find enough offensive stones in life. If only I could wash off at least one of these plagues in the sea. Vana spes! [Vain hope!] No sea baptises so radically that it can get rid of the old, hated Adam, that is so antipathetic to our dear German compatriots ...[27]

The reference to baptism does not necessarily imply that Michael seriously considered conversion to Christianity, despite the unhappiness his Jewish identity caused him. He disliked dogma in any form: von Schenk remarked that Michael perceived God in nature, and in the evolution of world history, rather than in any organized religion. There was also the question of Beer family loyalty: according to von Schenk, who was a fervent Catholic and may have attempted to influence his younger friend, Michael had told him that he would not consider conversion under any circumstances, as it would upset his mother too much.[28]

Schenk's Catholicism – and his political conservatism – did not prejudice him against forming a real and close friendship with the more liberally minded young Jewish man. Indeed, after they had known each other for several years, Schenk asked Michael to use the familiar *du* [thou] when addressing him, instead of the more formal *Sie* [you]. Michael was delighted. This invitation marked a momentous change in their relationship; only family members and the very closest of friends would use *du* to one another. In asking Michael to do so, Schenk was inviting him into his family circle on brotherly terms.[29]

Towards the end of 1830, Michael began a new drama, *Schwert und Hand* [Sword and Hand], a tragic love story set in the recent Napoleonic period. He completed the work in spring 1831, but spent much of the second half of that year helping his brother with the premiere of *Robert le Diable* in Paris. Michael admitted that the 'enormous' amount of work he had put into the preparations for *Robert* had prevented him from making any further progress with his own work. It was not until the beginning of 1832 that he was able to turn his thoughts back to *Schwert und Hand*. The play was due to be premiered at the end of April, in Berlin. Coincidentally, the Berlin premiere of *Robert le Diable* was scheduled to take place just a few weeks afterwards. Michael went to Berlin in the early spring to oversee the preparations for his own production, but, to his growing concern, found himself also taking on a great deal of the responsibility for the staging of his brother's opera.

Giacomo had gone to England, to oversee rehearsals for the premiere of *Robert* at the Haymarket Theatre in London, which would take place at around the same time as the Berlin production. Giacomo's habit of not answering letters (and the fact that it could take ten days or more for letters to travel between Berlin and London) increased the tension. Michael was forced to combine overseeing the rehearsals for his own play with keeping an eye on *Robert*, and he complained to Amalia that he had written an eight-page letter to Giacomo about the production of *Robert*, but had received no reply. Just days before the première of his own play, Michael was still involved in heated discussions with the management of the Berlin Opera over the allocation of roles for *Robert*.

*Schwert und Hand* was premiered on 30 April 1832, to a mixed reception. Many critics felt that the quality of the writing was uneven, and that the first three acts were much more effective than the last two. Its admirers included Rahel Levin Varnhagen, who had described Michael to the French writer Astolphe de Custine in 1824 as 'one of our most promising young poets'. She wrote to Michael after the premiere of *Schwert und Hand*, saying 'I am for the piece … at the end I wept bitterly at what the General said. And the fifth act is not superfluous, but a really necessary component of the play … I find it a really fine work.'[30]

In May, Michael wrote to Giacomo to tell him that *Robert* had been postponed, but only until 15 June. The family were anxious for Giacomo to come to Berlin as soon as possible. They had been horrified by a hostile newspaper report in the *Allgemeine musikalische Zeitung*, which had accused him of insulting the Prussian King by delaying sending him the score of *Robert*. The anonymous author of the report also attacked the libretto of the opera as immoral and sacrilegious.

The article went on to claim that Heinrich Beer had approached the Berlin critic Ludwig Rellstab, and asked him to take on the translation of the opera into German, with the aim of diverting the expected blame for Scribe's shocking text onto Rellstab. The writer hoped that the Opera's management would not fall for such a 'clumsy trick'. It was highly unusual for an article in the *Allgemeine musikalische Zeitung* to criticise a work before its premiere, and in such a personal tone. The report was clearly designed to influence the reception of the work in Berlin, and to damage Giacomo's reputation.[31]

To the family's relief, Giacomo decided to return to Berlin to oversee the last stages of the production of *Robert*, and the performance finally took place on 20 June. The Berlin newspapers were generally positive, except for the *Vossische Zeitung*, which carried a hostile article by Ludwig Rellstab, who was a supporter of German opera, and generally opposed foreign works.

It had been a fraught spring, and both Giacomo and Michael must have looked forward to the summer, with its round of spa visits. Michael's Boulogne trip with Heine was not repeated, however. The rapprochement of the previous year seemed to have dissolved, and Michael appeared to have become more wary of Heine. He was not at all happy that Giacomo had recommended Heine to a French newspaper as a correspondent for contemporary German literature, and, in particular, that he had told Heine to mention Michael's name to the paper. Michael warned Giacomo to be careful in his dealings with Heine, who he described as 'perfidious', adding 'Heine's friendship is more dangerous than his enmity.'[32]

Michael returned to Munich in late 1832 to resume his life there. A revival of *Struensee* was planned, and he made several new acquaintants, including Count August von Platen, who was back in Germany after a six-year stay in Italy. By the end of the year, however, Michael was occupied with new and exciting plans. He had been invited to go to Greece by King Ludwig's second son, 17-year-old Prince Otto, who had been crowned King of Greece earlier that year.

Following the end of the Greek War of Independence in 1829, Otto had been chosen by the Great Powers at the Convention of London to be the country's first modern king. The Bavarian royal family could claim Greek ancestry, and Otto's father, Ludwig, had been a supporter of Greek independence, loaning one and a half million florins of his own money to the cause.

Michael had always loved classical Greek culture, and was thrilled at the prospect of experiencing in reality the land he had known for so long in his imagination. He also had ambitious expectations of the change in his life that the move to Greece would bring. Otto was a minor, and it had been decided that a Regent should be appointed to rule in his stead until he came of age. This powerful role had been assigned to Count Josef von Armansperg, the Bavarian Foreign Affairs and Finance Minister.

Armansperg, who would eventually become Prime Minister of Greece, had promised Michael a job in the Greek administration, specifically in the department of Foreign Affairs. Michael saw himself on the threshold of a new career, imagining that he might well return to Paris in the not too distant future as a secretary in the Greek Legation. He applied himself industriously to learning the modern Greek language in preparation for the move.

Michael wrote to his brother Wilhelm in December 1832, confiding not only his hopes for a diplomatic career, but also a rather startling plan for contracting a suitable marriage before his move to Greece. He had no particular lady in mind; this was to be a marriage of convenience, and he told Wilhelm that he was approaching the project without any romantic sentiments.

He foresaw one problem, however. As he had no intention of converting to Christianity, his wife would have to be Jewish. Given the small number of available young Jewish women in his social circle, he felt that he could not be sure of finding just the right person. He had therefore hatched a plan to go to England, to look for a suitable bride from a wealthy Anglo-Jewish family. He asked Wilhelm to make discreet enquiries as to whether he would stand much chance of success, in particular whether the size of his personal fortune would carry any weight with a potential father-in-law in England.[33]

This was not quite as eccentric an idea as it appears: after the Napoleonic Wars, England had become something of a mecca for impoverished German noblemen seeking wealthy brides. Six years previously, in 1826, Count Hermann von Pückler-Muskau had devised a truly extraordinary scheme to restore his finances and save his beloved family estate at Muskau in Saxony.

The Count was, in fact, happily married – his wife Lucie was the only daughter of the Prussian Chancellor, Hardenberg – but neither he nor Lucie saw their marriage as a hindrance to his plans for finding a wealthy wife in England. The couple decided to divorce, in order to allow Pückler-Muskau to travel to England and find a bride, with whom he would return to Germany. After a discreet interval, Lucie would join the couple at Muskau, forming a cosy *ménage-à-trois*. We will never know how this ingenious plan would have worked out, however, as, perhaps fortunately for the putative bride, the Count's courtship tour of England was ultimately unsuccessful.[34]

We will also never know whether Michael would have had more success than Pückler-Muskau in England, or how his plans for a new life in Greece might have worked out. In March 1833, Michael was taken ill. He frequently suffered from chest problems and colds, and the attack did not seem serious at first, so he ignored it. However, this apparently minor indisposition turned into a violent fever, which progressed quickly,[35] and within days his doctor became so alarmed by Michael's deterioration that messages were sent to the Beer family in Berlin, and to Giacomo in Paris. Wilhelm and Heinrich rushed down to Munich, but found that Michael had died before their arrival. He had been unconscious for several days, and had died on 22 March.

Giacomo arrived in Munich three days after Michael's death. He practised a strange deception on his wife: he wrote to Minna twice from Munich, on 25 and 26 March, saying that Michael was very ill, and unconscious. It was not until 28 March, when he had left Munich and had travelled on to Stuttgart, that he told Minna that he had found Michael dead on his arrival. He explained that he had not wanted to give her the bad news without preparing her, and so had written the two previous letters pretending his brother was still alive.

Giacomo was deeply distressed by Michael's death. He told his friend, the violinist and composer Wilhelm Speyer, that '[Michael] was, from our youth, the confidant of my most private thoughts and feelings, and the void that his loss has created in my life cannot be filled.'[36]

Michael was buried in the Jewish cemetery outside Munich, in accordance with his wishes. A year after his death, a marble monument was erected on his grave, in the form of a miniature Greek temple, with the titles of his best-known plays engraved on its sides. In his will, apart from bequests to family and friends, he left a large sum of money to establish the Michael Beer Foundation for artists. The annual income from this Foundation would be used to pay for two young Jewish artists to spend a year studying art in Italy, eight months of which had to be spent in Rome.

Michael had loved Italy, and he had been deeply interested in art during his lifetime. He had been a patron of young artists, recommending them to his friend, the artist Friedrich Schadow. The Michael Beer Foundation continued to help Jewish artists for many years after Michael's death. The bursary assisted the Orientalist Salomon Munk to go to Italy in 1828, and in 1873 the American sculptor Moses Jacob Ezekiel became the first non-German Jew to win the Michael Beer prize.[37]

Michael's best plays are now considered to be *Der Paria* and *Struensee*, and it is impossible to know whether he would have surpassed these works in his more mature years. However, despite his early successes, and the praise of men such as Goethe and the influential scholar and critic August Schlegel, Michael had doubts about his own powers, which he had expressed freely to Heinrich Heine in his reply to Heine's invitation to join him in Boulogne in 1830: '... as far as poetry is concerned, I fear heaven has given me just enough not to be able to live without it, and not enough to achieve anything through it than will stamp me as a tamed Jewish bear [*Bär* / Beer]'. Michael had ended this passage with a comment that perhaps sums up his feelings about his life as a Jewish poet in German society: 'I am, in reality, a fish that is condemned to flap on dry land.'[38]

# Notes

1. Michael Beer, *Briefwechsel*, Eduard von Schenk (ed.) (Leipzig: Brockhaus, 1837), p.6.
2. Michael Beer, *Sämmtliche Werke* (Leipzig: Brockhaus, 1835), p.xviii.
3. Beer, *Briefwechsel*, p.28.
4. Beer, *Sämmtliche Werke*, p.884.
5. Max Spindler (ed.), *Briefwechsel zwischen Ludwig I von Bayern und Eduard von Schenk* (Munich: Parcus & Co., 1930), p.60.
6. Heinrich Heine, *Säkularausgabe. Werke, Briefwechsel, Lebenszeugnisse* (Berlin and Paris: Akademie Verlag and Editions de CNRS, 1970-), vol. 4, pp.227-8.
7. Ibid., p.233.
8. Heine, *Säkularausgabe*, vol. 20, p.329.
9. Ibid., p.331.
10. Ibid., p.327.
11. Heine, *Säkularausgabe*, vol. 4, p.225.
12. Heine, *Säkularausgabe*, vol. 2, pp.131-3.
13. Spindler, *Briefwechsel*, p.103.
14. Beer, *Briefwechsel*, pp.81 and 205.
15. Unpublished letter, Michael Beer to Aaron Wolfssohn, 19 January 1831, Leopold Stein Collection; AR3263; Box 1; Folder 7; Leo Baeck Institute. Courtesy of Leo Baeck Institute.
16. Beer, *Sämmtliche Werke*, pp.860-5.
17. Unpublished letter, Michael Beer to Aaron Wolfssohn, 19 January 1831, Leopold Stein Collection; AR3263; Box 1; Folder 7; Leo Baeck Institute. Courtesy of Leo Baeck Institute.
18. Gustav Manz, *Michael Beer's Jugend und dichterische Entwicklung bis zum 'Paria'. Erster Teil einer Biographie des Dichters* (unpublished dissertation, University of Freiburg, 1891), p.55.
19. Beer, *Briefwechsel*, pp.107-8.
20. Ibid., p.211.
21. Manz, *Michael Beers Jugend*, p.56.
22. Beer, *Briefwechsel*, p.260.
23. Ibid., p.242.
24. Ibid., p.88.
25. Ibid., p.176.
26. Ibid., p.182.
27. Heine, *Säkularausgabe*, vol. 24, pp.86-7.
28. Manz, *Michael Beers Jugend*, p.54.
29. Unpublished, undated letter, Michael Beer to Eduard von Schenk, Bavarian State Library Munich, Schenkiana II.12. Beer, Michael.
30. Barbara Hahn (ed.), *Rahel. Ein Buch des Andenkens* (Göttingen: Wallstein Verlag, 2011), vol. 4, p.453 and vol. 5, pp.508-9.
31. *Allgemeine musikalische Zeitung*, 4 April 1832, cols 228-232; see also Giacomo Meyerbeer, *Briefwechsel und Tagebücher*, Heinz Becker, Gudrun Becker and Sabine Henze-Döhring (eds) (Berlin: Walter de Gruyter, 1960-2006), vol. 2, pp.180 and 626 n 180,1.
32. Meyerbeer, *Briefwechsel und Tagebücher*, vol. 2, p.276.

33. Michael's career and marriage plans appear in an unpublished letter to Wilhelm of 13 December 1832, Goethe- und Schiller-Archiv, Klassik Stiftung Weimar, GSA 96/132.

34. See Peter James Bowman's *The Fortune Hunter. A German Prince in Regency England* (Oxford: Signal Books, 2010), for an entertaining account of Pückler-Muskau's ultimately unsuccessful foray.

35. The progress of Michael's illness is documented in a series of daily notes sent to von Schenk by Doctor von Walther, who was attending Michael. They have been preserved with Michael's letters to Schenk in the Bavarian State Library, Munich, Schenkiana II.12. Beer, Michael.

36. Meyerbeer, *Briefwechsel und Tagebücher*, vol. 2, p.298.

37. American Jewish Archives, Manuscript Collection No. 44, at http://collections. americanjewisharchives.org/ms/ms0044/ms0044.html (accessed 16 April 2016).

38. Heine, *Säkularausgabe*, vol. 24, pp.86-7.

# 17

## The Black Sheep

Michael's death in March 1833 hit his mother particularly hard. He and Amalia had become close companions in recent years, perhaps because he was the only one of her sons who had not married. In his memoir of Michael, Eduard von Schenk remarked that, in all the time that he had known him, Michael had never had a relationship with a woman. Schenk was almost certainly unaware of Michael's plan for an English marriage, as Michael had sworn Wilhelm to secrecy, and had not wanted even his mother or Giacomo to know of his intentions.

Michael had made it clear that this marriage was to be a business arrangement with no sentimental ties, but he had been capable of forming close relationships with women. Von Schenk had certainly known that Michael had been strongly attracted to his sister-in-law, Charlotte, or Lotte, von Neumayr. In the early days of Michael's friendship with von Schenk, he had told Schenk, in a letter from Bonn, that he had left Munich 'intoxicated' by Lotte's charm, and that the 'arrows darted from her beautiful eyes' had remained deeply embedded in his heart. Lotte herself must have been aware of Michael's attraction to her, as he added, 'ask Fraulein Lotte, if she will allow me to carry her dear image with me, in my heart, over hill and through dale'.[1] These passages were cut out of the relevant letter in the volume of Michael's correspondence that Schenk edited after Michael's death.

It is impossible to know whether this was a light-hearted flirtation or a more serious attraction, but Lotte, the sister of von Schenk's wife Therese von Neumayr, was the daughter of a Bavarian Catholic politician, and would certainly not have been allowed to marry a Jew. Michael and Lotte remained good friends, however; in what must have been his last letter to von Schenk, in February 1833, Michael mentions a 'charming' letter he has had from Lotte which he describes as 'a model of the most delicate feminine grace and mischievousness'.[2] Lotte, who lived until 1877, never married.

Michael was also capable of deep and lasting friendships with men. His relationships with Immermann and von Schenk, which were based on a shared interest in literary work, were intense and sincere. According to von

Schenk, however, 'the highest love of which [Michael] was capable was directed to his worthy mother; he never thought of her without the greatest tenderness and longing'.[3]

Michael's death was a dreadful blow to Amalia. For the first few weeks after the news had reached her, she had kept an iron grip on her feelings, maintaining an outward show of calmness. Lea Mendelssohn commented that she had seldom seen anyone display such 'composure and self-possession' in such tragic circumstances, adding that her affection and respect for Amalia had increased hugely as a result.[4] Those closest to her, however, were worried that she was suppressing her grief, making it difficult for them to help her. Wilhelm wrote to Giacomo, who was visiting Minna in Baden-Baden, asking him to come to Berlin. He felt that Giacomo was the only member of the family who might be able to give their mother some comfort.

Giacomo described the reunion with Amalia as 'shattering'. She was able to open up her grief to him, however, which he felt was a good sign. He saw no one outside the family circle for eight days, feeling that he could not leave her alone for a moment: 'Sadly, she looks terrible and is daily losing the calmness she had forced herself to show at first.'[5] On 1 May he told Minna, who had remained in Baden, that Amalia seemed to be deteriorating, as 'her mood grows more inconsolable every day, her appearance is pitiable, and her health badly affected'.[6] He could not think of leaving her; she still felt unable to receive condolence visits without his support.

This state of affairs continued for another month, and it was not until early June that Giacomo felt able to leave Berlin, and re-join Minna. Later that summer, Amalia felt strong enough to travel to Belgium for her annual visit to Spa, and from there to Genoa for a sea bathing cure. Michael, as the unmarried brother with no business or family ties, had been her usual companion on these trips. He had often been required to subordinate his own plans to hers: in 1828, he had postponed a trip to Düsseldorf to visit Immermann, which both men had been looking forward to, as Amalia had changed the date of her departure for Belgium. Michael had told his friend that '[my mother] will not even allow me enough time to visit you in dear old Düsseldorf before her cure in Spa', and that he would have to accompany her there first, and return to Germany later on, once she had settled in.[7]

Amalia's travelling companions on her trip to Italy after Michael's death in 1833 were her second son, Heinrich, and his wife, Betty. Heinrich had more time to devote to his mother than his two remaining brothers did, as he had no real career, beyond a minimal involvement in the Beer family businesses, which were, in reality, managed by Wilhelm. There may well have been another reason for Heinrich and Betty's decision to travel abroad that summer, however. They may have hoped that a stay in Italy would be beneficial for them, as well as for Amalia, as at the time, they were still recovering from a shattering loss of their own: just eighteen months before Michael's death, they had lost their only child, Ludwig, at 10 years old.

In the summer of 1831, Heinrich, Betty and Ludwig had been staying in the Bohemian spa of Teplitz (now Teplice in the Czech Republic). Towards the end of their visit, they had heard the terrifying news that there had been an outbreak of cholera in Berlin. An epidemic disease, cholera had been common in India for centuries, but had spread to Western Europe for the first time in 1830. There was no known cure, and death could occur within a few hours of the onset of the violent diarrhoea that characterised the disease.

Twenty thousand people died in Paris alone in the epidemic. No one felt safe; as Giacomo commented to Minna, 'The cholera in France has a very liberal nature, as it takes the noblest, the richest, the most solid, and the healthiest people.'[8] Nearly twenty years later, cholera was still rife, and in 1849 was to claim Amalia's old friend, Angelica Catalani, as a victim. Catalani, who had retired from the stage, died of the disease in Paris.

We now know that cholera is spread by contaminated water, and can easily be treated, but in the 1830s, doctors believed it was spread by 'miasma' or bad air. News of the arrival of the disease in areas that had previously been free of cholera created panic. People fled to unaffected places that they believed had 'healthy' air – often taking the deadly disease with them in their intestines. Heinrich and Betty decided to remain in Bohemia rather than take the risk of travelling back to Berlin. This was, on the face of it, a sensible decision, but by sheer bad luck their extended stay at the spa ended in tragedy, when Ludwig was suddenly taken ill, and died of a brain inflammation at Teplitz on 26 September.

There had been no warning: Ludwig had been a lively, healthy, good-looking boy – the salonnière Henriette Herz had described him at the age of two as 'a *heavenly* child'.[9] Fanny Mendelssohn's husband, the artist Wilhelm Hensel, had painted Ludwig's portrait the year before his death, and the painting had been much admired. The boy had been, as Lea Mendelssohn commented, idolised by his parents.[10] They had already had one terrifying experience when Ludwig was 4 years old. In December 1825, Carl Maria von Weber, who was staying with Heinrich and Betty, had reported to his wife that a whole pan of boiling lye had fallen onto the boy, badly scalding his back and arm. Weber had commented that if the caustic liquid had hit his face, he would have been blinded.[11]

Betty was especially badly affected by Ludwig's death; her mother, Recha, had died five months previously, and she seemed unable to rally from this second, shocking blow. The American author and socialist, Albert Brisbane, who was studying philosophy in Berlin in 1831, met Heinrich and Betty later that year, and noted in his diary that she had been completely crushed by her son's death: 'It seemed to me to have torn out her existence and left her never-the-less alive.'[12]

In his autobiography, written in his old age, Brisbane said that, during his stay in Berlin, he formed a strong friendship with Betty, who came to rely on him for comfort – he described her as 'a woman of fine sentiment and broad aspiration'. He felt that she treated him almost as a surrogate son, and that she found some relief from her intense grief in her interest in him. Brisbane does not seem to have been impressed by Heinrich, who he described as 'a heavy man, claiming no resemblance to his brother on the artistic side, and but little given to speculations, other than those of a tangible character at the Bourse [stock exchange]'.[13]

Sadly, Heinrich and Betty were unable to comfort each other in their loss. They had grown apart by the time of Ludwig's death, to the extent that their love for their son had been the only common ground in their otherwise separate lives.[14] Their marriage had seemed to be happy initially, despite Betty's hesitation in accepting Heinrich's proposal. The couple had shared a degree of artistic talent, and an enjoyment of amateur dramatics and singing. Betty was a good actress and dancer, as well as a talented singer. Heinrich was also a talented performer, with a fine tenor voice, good enough to sing with professionals at private performances.

Betty's relatives, the Mendelssohns, had welcomed Heinrich into their family, and had included him in their entertainments. On Felix's twelfth birthday in 1821, his parents had staged a sumptuous production of one of his early works, a *Singspiel*, or comic operetta, *Die Soldatenliebschaft* [Soldiers' Love Affairs], in their home at 7 Neue Promenade. Abraham and Lea had gone to a good deal of trouble and expense to showcase this youthful work, hiring the players of the orchestra of the Royal Chapel, and soloists from the Opera. Heinrich had taken a major role, singing alongside the Berlin Opera tenor Johann Stümer.

Heinrich and Betty were very sociable, and, in the Beer family tradition, they invited well-known musicians to perform for their guests at their house in Behrenstrasse. In May 1829, Fanny Hensel and her husband attended an evening party given by Heinrich and Betty for the virtuoso violinist Paganini, who was visiting Berlin. Fanny wrote to her brother describing how 'the great Heinrich triumphantly led in his minister, Paganini', who entertained the company 'divinely' by playing a sonata, followed by his 'Glöckchen Rondo', and an air from one of Paisello's operas.[15] Paganini appears to have been a regular guest performer at the couple's home: Rahel Levin Varnhagen had heard him playing there three months previously.[16]

Fanny's rather sarcastic comment on Heinrich's manner when bringing in Paganini to meet his guests reflects a growing estrangement between the younger generations of the Beer and Mendelssohn families. Fanny was pleased enough to accept an invitation to meet the famous Paganini at Heinrich's house, but she described other evenings there as 'boring', and she also noted that Felix was often irritated by Heinrich, and did not trouble to hide his feelings.

In February 1830, Felix remarked in a letter to his friend, the diplomat Karl Klingemann, that, 'My birthday went well ... Heinrich Beer, whom I treat in a shamefully rude manner, gave me the score of Beethoven's C Major Trio and an almost touching letter of Mozart's in which he applies to the Vienna city authorities for an unpaid post.'[17] Heinrich, who owned a valuable musical manuscript collection, which included a number of Beethoven scores, seems to have been very generous towards his cousin by marriage, who was also a keen collector of musical memorabilia. After Heinrich's death, his entire collection was acquired by the Mendelssohns, and was eventually presented to the Berlin Royal Library.

Heinrich's manuscripts were part of a wider preoccupation, however. In the absence of any real career, he had developed a passion for collecting, and spent a good deal of money on the various objects that caught his interest. Heinrich Heine, who had no time for Heinrich, characterised him as a near idiot, who, 'instead of using his great wealth to make a name for himself in art or science, squandered it on foolish trivia; and, for instance, spent six thousand thalers in one day on walking sticks'.[18]

Lea Mendelssohn also remarked on Heinrich's collecting mania. In the late 1820s, he began to take an interest in the public lectures on scientific subjects that had become popular in Berlin at the time. Lea noticed that he enjoyed associating with distinguished men, commenting that: 'Heinrich Beer is now collecting learned men in the same way he once collected theatre programmes and pipes; the last time we were there we dined with Stägemann, Lichtenstein, Ritter, Hegel and Humboldt.'[19]

Most of the guests mentioned by Lea were acquaintances of the wider Beer family, but the philosopher Georg Wilhelm Friedrich Hegel was a close personal friend of Heinrich's. Hegel had come to Berlin in 1818 – the year of Heinrich and Betty's marriage – to take up the Chair of Philosophy at Berlin University. He later became Rector of the University in 1829. Many people in Berlin were puzzled by the apparently close relationship between, as Albert Brisbane put it, 'the most abstract of philosophers' and 'this most positive and concrete of Jewish bankers'.[20]

Hegel, unlike a number of his academic colleagues, was not anti-Jewish; he did not think much of Judaism as a religion, but he insisted that the Jews, as individuals, should have the same rights as people of other faiths. Felix Mendelssohn surmised that Hegel had somehow been fooled into thinking Heinrich more intelligent than he really was: Felix's *bon mot*, that it was Hegel who could not understand Heinrich Beer, and not vice versa, was quoted by his family and friends as an example of his brilliant wit. Felix remarked on the surprising fact that Hegel regularly took Heinrich with him into the university professors' conference hall, commenting that, 'what would make another person lose his wits, will perhaps make [Heinrich] lose his stupidity and become clever'.[21]

Heine noted in his memoirs that Heinrich Beer 'enjoyed the closest association with Hegel, was the intimate of the philosopher ... and accompanied him everywhere like a shadow'. Heine thought, like Felix, that he had discovered the reason for this unlikely association. In his opinion, Hegel knew that Heinrich Beer was not intelligent enough to understand a word of what he said to him, and so felt free to express himself without restraint in Heinrich's presence in a way he could not do with other, quicker-witted people. According to Heine, Hegel had once said something derogatory to him about religion, and had then been alarmed, as he thought someone else might have overheard. Hegel had 'looked anxiously about, but was quickly reassured when he saw that it was only Heinrich Beer, coming to invite him to a game of whist'.[22]

Hegel's own letters, however, give a very different, and much warmer, picture of his relationship with Heinrich. In 1827, Hegel wrote to his wife from an inn in the town of Kassel, where he had stopped on the way to Paris, to tell her of a chance meeting with the Beers: 'I was just wondering yesterday evening – it was 10 o' clock – whether to start a letter to you, when who do you think but Heinrich Beer and his wife came into my room! You can imagine our joy over this unexpected meeting.'[23] In another letter to his wife a few days later, Hegel remarks on the pleasant day he spent with the Beers in Kassel.

Albert Brisbane had noted that Hegel and Heinrich invariably spent their evenings together playing whist.[24] This was Hegel's favourite form of relaxation – Giacomo's former music teacher, Carl Zelter, was his most frequent partner in the game. However, it seems that, in addition to playing card games with Hegel, Heinrich did attempt to take an interest in his friend's philosophical ideas. Hegel's response suggests a sympathetic attitude, and a desire to help Heinrich to develop himself intellectually. In August 1831, shortly before Ludwig's death, Hegel wrote to Heinrich telling him that

> You express the interest that certain sections of my last lectures have aroused in you. This proves to me both that I have hit upon the truth in these points, and how strongly sensitive you are to this deeper truth … Do continue, however, to enrich the most valuable gift for which I am indebted to you: the conviction that the insights to which I have contributed may gain ever more solid footing in your mind and character, and bear abundant fruit.[25]

Just a few weeks later, Hegel received the terrible news that Ludwig had died. He wrote to Heinrich immediately:

> This is a moment in your life, in the hard experience of life, in which your good-naturedness and human kindness, as valuable as they are in the normal course of life, must draw an inner strength from a still deeper source, so that the power of the spirit can prove itself able to endure even such grief as this. I press your hand in the most heartfelt pain, born of friendship.[26]

Two months later, on 14 November, Hegel died suddenly, reportedly of cholera. In quick succession, Heinrich had lost his only child, and the man who was not just a close friend, but perhaps also the only person who took him seriously, and encouraged his aspirations.

Heinrich was not by any means a stupid man, but he lacked the self-discipline to apply himself seriously to any area of life. He was not, however, jealous of others' successes, and he supported his friends and family loyally. One of his closer friends was the composer Carl Maria von Weber, who had remained on friendly terms with Heinrich since their days at the Abbé Vogler's school in Darmstadt. Weber often stayed with Heinrich and Betty during his later trips to Berlin. In December 1825, not long after Jacob Beer's death, he had lodged at their house while overseeing the rehearsals for his opera *Euryanthe* – this was the occasion when Ludwig had been scalded by an overturned pan of lye. Giacomo had come home from Paris to make a formal offer for Minna's hand, and this was probably the last time that the brothers saw Weber before his death.

It appears that after Weber's death, Heinrich, together with the natural scientist Hinrich Lichtenstein, had been given the legal right to represent the Weber family in Berlin. In 1828, two years after Weber's death, his opera *Oberon* had still not been produced in Berlin, and many people believed that the court musical director, Gaspare Spontini, was deliberately prolonging the negotiations with Weber's widow to avoid having to stage the work. Heinrich and Lichtenstein responded to these rumours by publishing an article, in which they described themselves both as the late composer's oldest friends in Berlin, and the legally appointed guardians of the Weber family's interests there. They set out the reasons for the delay, which revolved around a dispute over whether the Königstadt theatre had the right to stage the opera or not.[27]

Heinrich's staunch support for his friends and family could occasionally manifest itself in embarrassing ways, however. In January 1833, he decided to take a hand in the casting for a repeat performance of *Robert le Diable* in Berlin. The Opera's management was looking for a replacement ballerina to dance the role of the abbess, since Marie Taglioni was not available. Giacomo had heard that the Elssler sisters, Therese and Fanny, both well-known ballerinas, were in Berlin, and he had told Amalia that he would like one of them to take the part. Heinrich and Wilhelm were overseeing the rehearsals on their brother's behalf, and Heinrich had decided unilaterally that Fanny Elssler – one of the greatest ballerinas of the time – was not a suitable candidate, and had refused to accept her.

Heinrich wrote quickly to Giacomo, to try to get his story in ahead of Wilhelm, who was furious with him. He justified himself by saying that he could not 'in all conscience' agree to Fanny's engagement to dance the role, as 'this scene can cause offence if it isn't performed decently, and Fanny would have done it like an archwhore, and the whole of the beautiful third act would have gone to the devil'. He added that, 'I did it for your honour and that of the opera.' Giacomo can hardly have found Heinrich's parting words reassuring: 'I have to be at the rehearsal tomorrow and the day after to make sure all goes according to your wishes, you can rely on me that nothing will escape my notice.'[28]

Perhaps despite, rather than because of Heinrich's attentions, the performance went well, and he reported on it to Giacomo in glowing terms: 'Triumph! Triumph! Triumph! The annals of the Berlin theatre will mark yesterday with three stars. No one here has ever heard a performance like it ... it really was as if God himself had had a hand in it yesterday ... words are inadequate to describe the truly universal enthusiasm for your opera.'[29]

Heinrich bathed in the reflected glory of his brother's successes, and was keen to see Giacomo rewarded and honoured in the eyes of the world. In early 1833, Giacomo was aware that he had been nominated for the Prussian Academy. He had already been made a member of the French Academy, and a Chevalier of the *Légion d'Honneur*, but this latest nomination had stirred up his deep-seated anxiety about his standing in his home city. There was always a good deal of secrecy surrounding the list of nominees for the Prussian Academy, as the King had to approve them before they could be made public, but there were rumours that Frederick William was not going to confirm this year's list at all, as his favourite, Spontini, was not on it. Heinrich, as ever, was keen to be in the thick of the action, telling Giacomo that, 'something is happening, but it's impossible to find out what; as soon as anything significant occurs, you will hear the news from [me]'.[30]

Giacomo immediately began to worry that there might be a plot brewing against him, telling Minna that, 'it is even possible that the King will withhold his approval on religious grounds'.[31] He may have been thinking back to Moses Mendelssohn, whose unanimous nomination to the Academy was refused twice by Frederick the Great, who had not wanted to see a Jew, however famous he might be, elected to his Academy. Giacomo's nomination was eventually approved, however, and he became a member of the Prussian Academy in May 1833. Heinrich, as he had wished, had been the first with the news, which he had heard from one of his acquaintances, Eduard Gans, Professor of Law at Berlin University, and a member of the Academy committee.

Heinrich's position was not an easy one. It was, perhaps, his bad luck to be the only failure in an outstanding family. Heine criticised him for not achieving fame like his brothers: 'This poor man, who had no wish to be a great tragic poet, or a great astronomer, or a musical genius, crowned with laurel, a rival to Mozart and Rossini, preferred to spend his money on walking sticks.'[32]

Heinrich cannot have been unaware that he was the butt of jokes in Berlin. He had a penchant for pretty young actresses, and a story had circulated in the city that when he had overheard an actress remarking that she liked liverwurst, he had sent her a carriage loaded with a hundredweight of the sausages.[33] At the height of the Königstadt Theatre's 'Sontag fever', Lea Mendelssohn had commented to her sister-in-law that Heinrich and his cousin Paul Ebers were making fools of themselves over the singer, and that a joke was going the rounds that Sontag had hired guards to protect her from the attacks of a bear (Bär/Beer) and a boar (Eber).[34]

Another story claimed that a visitor to the city had remarked to Amalia that, as she had a composer, a writer and a scientist among her sons, it was a pity that she did not have one who was a painter to complete the set. 'Ah well,' Amalia is said to have replied, 'I may not have an artist yet, but I do have a *Pinsel*.' A *Pinsel* in German is both an artist's paintbrush, and a slang word for simpleton.[35] The story does not have the ring of truth – Amalia would never have spoken of any of her sons in such a disparaging way – but it does suggest that Heinrich's foibles and weaknesses were public knowledge, and provided lively entertainment for Berlin society.

Heinrich's genuine desire to support his brothers was mixed with a not unnatural longing to play a significant role in life himself. He wanted to be a successful businessman, but Wilhelm had side-lined him from the family concerns, and he was rapidly running through his own money. He may have found it easier to act the part of the great financier away from Berlin, where he was only too well known. During a stay in Vienna in 1834, it seems that he used his elder brother's fame and his family's good name to impress people. He was delighted with the flattering articles in the Viennese newspapers and journals about Giacomo, and the fact that everywhere he went, he heard extracts from *Robert le Diable* being played: 'Giacomo is idolised by everyone here, large and small, there is really no other word for it.'[36]

During his stay in Vienna, Heinrich was – or at least claimed to have been – drawn into delicate negotiations with the Austrian court over the offer of a very significant honour to his brother. He told Amalia that that he had been approached secretly – and at a very high level – on behalf of the Emperor, Franz I, to find out whether Meyerbeer would accept an honour, and, if so, whether he would prefer a title or an order. Heinrich assured his mother that he had already written to Giacomo on the subject, and had urged him to dedicate his next opera to the Emperor, to be sure of capitalising on his favour. However, nothing came of this scheme, most probably because Franz I died shortly afterwards, in March 1835. It was not until 1850 that Meyerbeer was honoured by the Austrian Emperor, when he was created a Knight of the Order of Franz Joseph.

Despite the ultimate failure of this scheme, Heinrich revelled in the fact that his relationship to the celebrated Meyerbeer made him such a high-profile figure in Vienna that the Emperor's emissaries made approaches to him. He took advantage of this reputation when he met Therese Peche, a promising young actress at the Burgtheater. Peche became friendly with Heinrich, to the extent that he persuaded her to give him her savings to invest on her behalf. Unfortunately, Heinrich's financial abilities did not match his ambitions, and the money was either lost or squandered. It was not too long before Peche realised that she was unlikely ever to see her earnings again.

The story might never have reached Berlin, but for the fact that Peche accepted an invitation to make a guest appearance there in the following spring. The Mendelssohn family were keen to entertain the up-and-coming young actress, and invited her to dinner. Lea, aware that Peche knew nobody in Berlin, and that Heinrich was interested in anything to do with the theatre, seated her next to him at the dinner table. She noticed that Heinrich, instead of being pleased, had seemed startled and embarrassed, and she had wondered why.

The next day, Peche visited Lea and told her the story of her dealings with Heinrich in Vienna – or at least, her version of them. Lea retailed the news to her Viennese cousin, Henriette von Pereira-Arnstein: 'my hair is still standing on end from the tale she has told me about Heinrich Beer! I have long thought him capable of any ineptitude, stupidity, dissipation, and profligacy, but not of the kind of recklessness that leads to the wickedest depravity.'[37]

Peche had no doubt been swayed by the Beer family's reputation as financiers in giving her money to Heinrich, but Lea hinted that there may have been something more between them. According to Lea, Betty had appeared unhappy at the fatal dinner party, and Lea wondered whether 'she might have noticed something in Vienna'. Lea had also heard a rumour that Therese Peche had accepted a valuable gift from Heinrich in Vienna, which, if it was true, threw a more dubious light on her relationship with him. The story was not unlikely, as Heinrich always enjoyed distributing largesse.

All the Beers were open-handed, and giving expensive presents to their friends was a family habit. This was sometimes embarrassing for the recipient, especially if there was a possibility that acceptance of these gifts might be misinterpreted by the public. Michael had once offered his friend Karl Immermann a gift of money, knowing that Immermann wanted to travel, but could not afford to do so. Immermann had refused, which had embarrassed Michael, who had feared that his intended generosity had offended his friend.[38]

In 1816, Jacob had pressed Carl Maria von Weber to accept a valuable gold box, with Giacomo's portrait on it, as a keepsake. Weber had recorded in his diary that he had been in some embarrassment, but had felt that he could not refuse the gift for fear of hurting Jacob's feelings. He had asked his wife not to mention this incident to anyone, 'as people in the world are small-minded enough to interpret it wrongly, and ascribe my genuine admiration of their son's works to other considerations'.[39]

Four years after this incident, in 1820, Weber's long friendship with the Beers had nearly foundered when he had felt obliged to return a gift that Jacob and Amalia had sent him – a pair of valuable silver candlesticks – around the time that he had staged *Emma* in Dresden. He had noted in his diary, 'God forbid that I should hurt these good people, but I owe it to my peace of mind.' Weber had to return the gift twice, however, as the Beers were insistent, and the incident had caused some bad feeling in the family. Heinrich, Wilhelm and Michael had complicated matters by withholding Weber's letters on the subject from their parents, presumably to spare them pain, and von Weber had been forced to write a letter to the brothers explaining that he could not risk putting himself in a position where he might be suspected of taking bribes.[40]

However, whether Therese Peche had accepted valuable gifts from Heinrich in Vienna or not, and whatever their personal relations may have been, it seems that he had mishandled her money to the extent that Lea Mendelssohn feared that prosecution was inevitable. The Mendelssohns were horrified to discover that the actor Karl Seydelmann, from Stuttgart, had also entrusted money to Heinrich for investment. Lea recognised that Heinrich did not have any deliberate intention of defrauding people, but he was so feckless that money simply slipped through his hands.

The Mendelssohns clearly felt some degree of responsibility, presumably because Heinrich was a part of their extended family. Heinrich and Wilhelm were by this time at odds with one another, and Lea's husband, Abraham, took on the task of mediating between them, so that some of Heinrich's dwindling capital could be taken out of the family business to repay Peche without having to resort to the courts.

Both the Beer and Mendelssohn families were anxious to conceal this scandal from Amalia and Betty, as well as from the wider public, and Abraham gave Heinrich a serious lecture about his behaviour, in an attempt to make him see the error of his ways.[41] Heinrich must have felt his disgrace; the next January, in a New Year's letter to Giacomo, he remarked that, 'May the Lord give you lasting health and as much joy this coming year as I have had pain and trouble in this one ... keep your old love and sympathy for me, as you are the only person who recognises that I exist in the world; but enough of me, this isn't a pleasant conversation.'

Giacomo was fond of Heinrich, and still sometimes referred to him by the affectionate childhood diminutive of 'Hänseken' – 'little Hans' – but the rest of the Beer family were not as tolerant, and their relations with their black sheep were, by now, less than cordial. Heinrich asked Giacomo to pass on his New Year greetings to Amalia, 'if she wants a greeting from me, and Wilhelm hasn't forbidden it'. [42]

Heinrich had never been a strong character – his weakness for women and his carelessness with money had been evident as far back as his teenage years in Darmstadt. Nonetheless, he had positive character traits that attracted people: Hegel and Carl Maria von Weber had been genuine friends, and the actor Karl Seydelmann also had a real affection for Heinrich. Seydelmann was eager to obtain engagements at the Berlin theatre in the mid-1830s, and he trusted Heinrich to act on his behalf. This arrangement does, in fact, appear to have been successful, as Seydelmann made a number of guest appearances in Berlin over the period that he was using Heinrich as his Berlin 'agent'.

Seydelmann valued Heinrich's loyalty and warm-heartedness, as well as his willingness to exert himself on behalf of his friends. His letters to Heinrich are deeply affectionate; in September 1837 he told him that, 'Wherever I might travel, I will never find so rich a source of love as I have in your house. I can't tell you how much I long to return there.'[43] This comment came two years after Lea Mendelssohn's report that Seydelmann had entrusted his money to Heinrich; whatever the outcome of the matter, it did not seem to have lessened Seydelmann's faith in Heinrich's good heart, or altered his affection for him.

The same could not be said for Heinrich's relations with his family, however. Wilhelm, in particular, had little patience with his elder brother's financial incompetence, and even Amalia, whose faith in her sons was, in general, unshakeable, despaired of him at times. It appears that Heinrich's life had begun to go downhill in earnest after the deaths of Ludwig and his friend Hegel in 1831. These tragedies had deepened the rift between Heinrich and Betty, instead of bringing them together, and by the mid-1830s, their marriage was over in all but name. By the end of the decade, with few friends, and family relations cooling, Heinrich was rapidly becoming an isolated figure.

## Notes

1. Unpublished letter, Michael Beer to Eduard von Schenk, 4 May 1827, Bavarian State Library Munich, Schenkiana II.12.Beer, Michael.

2. Unpublished letter, Michael Beer to Eduard von Schenk, 4 March 1833, Bavarian State Library Munich, Schenkiana II.12.Beer, Michael.
3. Michael Beer, *Sämmtliche Werke* (Leipzig: Brockhaus, 1835), p.xxviii.
4. Lea Mendelssohn Bartholdy, *Ewig die deine. Briefe an Henriette von Pereira-Arnstein*, Wolfgang Dinglinger and Rudolf Elvers (eds) (Hannover: Wehrhahn Verlag, 2010), vol. 1, p.289.
5. Giacomo Meyerbeer, *Briefwechsel und Tagebücher*, Heinz Becker, Gudrun Becker and Sabine Henze-Döhring (eds) (Berlin: Walter de Gruyter, 1960-2006), vol. 2, p.305.
6. Meyerbeer, *Briefwechsel und Tagebücher*, vol. 2, p.307.
7. Michael Beer, *Briefwechsel*, Eduard von Schenk (ed.) (Leipzig: Brockhaus, 1837), p.43.
8. Meyerbeer, *Briefwechsel und Tagebücher*, vol. 2, p.170.
9. Georg Heinrici (ed.), 'Briefe von Henriette Herz an August Twesten (1814-1827)', *Zeitschrift für Bücherfreunde*, Neue Folge 5 (1914), p.344.
10. Lea Mendelssohn Bartholdy, *Ewig die deine*, vol. 1, p.244.
11. Letter, Carl Maria von Weber to Caroline von Weber, 19 December 1825, Carl-Maria-von-Weber-Gesamtausgabe. Digitale Edition, http://weber-gesamtausgabe.de/A042536 (Version 3.4.2 vom 8. Februar 2019).
12. Abigail Mellen and Allaire Brisbane Stallsmith (eds), *The European Travel Diaries of Albert Brisbane 1830-32* (Lewiston, NY & Lampeter: Edwin Mellen Press, 2005), p.170.
13. Redelia Brisbane, *Albert Brisbane. A Mental Biography with a Character Study* (Boston, MA: Arena Publishing Company, 1893), p.83.
14. Lea Mendelssohn Bartholdy, *Ewig die deine*, vol. 1, p.244.
15. Eva Weissweiler (ed.), *Fanny and Felix Mendelssohn: "Die Musik will gar nicht rutschen ohne Dich"* (Berlin: Propyläen, 1997), p.79; Hans-Günter Klein and Rudolf Elvers (eds), *Tagebücher: Fanny Hensel* (Wiesbaden: Breitkopf and Härtel, 2002), p.16.
16. Thomas Kliche, *Camacho und das ängstliche Genie. Innenansichten der Familien Mendelssohn und Meyerbeer* (Hützel: Backe-Verlag, 2014), p.23.
17. Felix Mendelssohn Bartholdy, *Sämtliche Briefe*, Helmut Loos and Wilhelm Seidel (eds) (Kassel: Bärenreiter, 2008-17), vol. 3, pp.120-1.
18. Heinrich Heine, *Säkularausgabe. Werke, Briefwechsel, Lebenszeugnisse* (Berlin and Paris: Akademie Verlag and Editions de CNRS, 1970-), vol. 12, pp.63-4.
19. Klingemann, Karl, *Felix Mendelssohn-Bartholdys Briefwechsel mit Legionsrat Karl Klingemann* (Essen: G.D. Baedeker, 1909), p.44. The guests were: Friedrich von Stägemann, Prussian politician; Martin Lichtenstein, doctor and first director of the Berlin Zoological Gardens; Carl Ritter, geographer; Georg Hegel, philosopher; Alexander von Humboldt, explorer and naturalist.
20. Brisbane, *Albert Brisbane*, p.83.
21. Felix Mendelssohn Bartholdy, *Sämtliche Briefe*, vol. 1, p.235.
22. Heine, *Säkularausgabe*, vol. 12, pp.63-4.
23. Hegel, Georg Wilhelm Friedrich, *Briefe an und von Hegel*, Johannes Hoffmeister (ed.) (Hamburg: Felix Meiner Verlag, 1952-54), vol. 3, p.178.
24. Brisbane, *Albert Brisbane*, p.83.
25. Hoffmeister, *Briefe an und von Hegel*, vol. 3, p.349.
26. Ibid., p.340.
27. *Berliner Conversations-Blatt für Poesie, Literatur und Kritik*, 17 and 18 January 1828.
28. Meyerbeer, *Briefwechsel und Tagebücher*, vol. 2, pp.277-8.
29. Ibid., p.290.

30.  Ibid., p.285.
31.  Ibid., p.311.
32.  Heine, *Säkularausgabe* vol. 12, pp.63-4.
33.  Lea Mendelssohn Bartholdy, *Ewig die deine,* vol. 1, p.532.
34.  Ibid., p.150.
35.  Karl von Holtei, *Charpie. Eine Sammlung Vermischter Aufsätze* (Breslau: Verlag von Eduard Trewendt, 1866), p.174.
36.  Meyerbeer, *Briefwechsel und Tagebücher,* vol. 2, p.365.
37.  Lea Mendelssohn Bartholdy, *Ewig die deine,* p.335.
38.  Peter Hasubeck (ed.), *Karl Lebrecht Immermann: Briefe* (Munich and Vienna: Carl Hanser Verlag, 1978), vol. 1, pp.723 and 732.
39.  Letter from Carl Maria von Weber to Caroline Brandt, 29 June 1816, Carl-Maria-von-Weber-Gesamtausgabe. Digitale Edition, http://weber-gesamtausgabe.de/A040913 (Version 3.4.2 vom 8. Februar 2019).
40.  Carl Maria von Weber, diary entry 2 March 1820, and letter to Heinrich, Wilhelm and Michael Beer 09 March 1820, Carl-Maria-von-Weber-Gesamtausgabe. Digitale Edition, http://weber-gesamtausgabe.de/A061206 and A041599 (Version 3.4.2 vom 8. Februar 2019).
41.  Lea Mendelssohn Bartholdy, *Ewig die deine,* pp.335 and 340.
42.  Meyerbeer, *Briefwechsel und Tagebücher,* vol. 2, pp.500-1.
43.  Unpublished letter, Karl Seydelmann to Heinrich Beer, 11 September 1837, Theaterwissenschaftliche Sammlung, University of Cologne, Au9711.

# 18

## The Beer Observatory

Wilhelm's lack of tolerance towards Heinrich's failings stemmed, at least in part, from his position as *de facto* head of the family. After Michael's death, Wilhelm had become the youngest of the Beer brothers, but given Giacomo's absorption in his musical career in Paris, and Heinrich's irresponsibility, he had taken their father's place not only in the family businesses, but also in the Luisenstift boys' home, and in the Königstadt theatre. Although he consulted with Giacomo on major decisions affecting the family's finances, Wilhelm bore the sole responsibility for the day-to-day running of the business concerns. His dedication to furthering the family's interests went much further than just looking after their financial affairs, however. He was equally keen to promote the Beers' reputation by supporting his brothers' claims to fame in any way that he could.

After Michael's death, Wilhelm was determined to have an edition of his younger brother's complete works published, to ensure that his legacy was preserved. Eduard von Schenk agreed to take on the role of editor of this project, and to write a biographical introduction to the works, which were published in 1835. Wilhelm also collaborated with Karl Immermann to produce a volume of Michael's correspondence, which von Schenk also edited. This collection consisted mainly of literary exchanges between Michael and Immermann himself. Wilhelm had originally intended these letters to be included in the collected works, but they were eventually published as a stand-alone volume in 1837.

Wilhelm was equally eager to promote Giacomo's career, telling him that 'my soul is bound to your fame with indissoluble bonds'.[1] He not only oversaw productions of Giacomo's works in Berlin, but he also travelled to other cities to attend premieres. He kept an eye on the press, and was quick to correct any errors he spotted in newspaper reports and articles on his brother's operas. His personal interests took a back seat in his correspondence with Giacomo, which revolved around the latter's work as a composer, with occasional mention of business or family matters.

There are few hints in the letters between them that by the late 1820s, Wilhelm's early interest in mathematics was developing into a serious commitment to scientific research. From 1824 onwards, he had taken instruction in higher mathematics from Johann Mädler, a lecturer at Berlin's teachers' training institute. The two men shared an interest in the natural sciences, and they both became members of the Berlin Geographical Society. Over the winter of 1827, they had attended an important series of public lectures on geography and astronomy, given by Alexander von Humboldt in the hall of the Sing-Akademie.

Von Humboldt's eminence and fame attracted natural scientists from all over the country to these talks, which were reported widely in the German press. The lectures were also accessible enough to become hugely popular with Berlin society: the King and the entire court attended the series, and, unusually for the time, women were admitted. Fanny Mendelssohn told Felix's friend Karl Klingemann that, 'The crush is terrible, the audience imposing, and the lectures infinitely interesting. The gentlemen may mock as much as they like, but it's wonderful that nowadays we, too, have the opportunity to listen to intelligent discussion.'[2] Her brother, Felix, attended the lectures, and noted Heinrich Beer's presence, telling his cousin Georg that, 'what Humboldt and Ritter have left me unclear about, Heinrich Beer explains to me.'[3]

For the majority of the society audience, these lectures were an interesting and instructive way of passing some of the long winter evenings, but for Wilhelm and Mädler, the astronomy lectures in particular were revelatory. They were astonished by the power and accuracy of the latest refractor telescopes, which had been developed around fifteen years previously by the Bavarian inventor Joseph von Fraunhofer. With the introduction of these precision instruments, the surfaces of the nearest celestial objects – which in reality meant the moon and Mars, given that Venus had an impenetrably thick atmosphere – could be mapped to a previously unattainable degree of accuracy. Work on these projects was still at a rudimentary stage, however, and the field was open to newcomers. This was an age when amateurs could still make significant contributions to science, and Wilhelm and Mädler were inspired by the idea that, with the right equipment, they could improve on the current state of knowledge.

In 1828, Wilhelm bought a state-of-the-art Fraunhofer telescope, and early the next year he had it installed in a revolving turret on the roof of the Tiergarten house. The villa had become Wilhelm's home; after Jacob's death, he had moved there with his wife Doris and their family. By 1828 they had four children: two girls, Elise and Julie, and two boys, Georg and Julius. Wilhelm had made major alterations to the villa, adding on a second floor, which became Amalia's domain, while he and his family took over the original first-floor living rooms.

The villa was well-suited to housing an observatory, not just because of its size, but also because of its location in the Tiergarten, which was situated outside Berlin. The Royal Observatory, which was in the central Dorotheenstadt quarter, had to compete with the lights of the city. The Observatory's Director, Johann Encke, no doubt appreciating the potential of the project, assisted with the setting-up of the Fraunhofer telescope in the Beer villa.[4]

Wilhelm and Mädler initially began working together on observing the moon, but in September 1830, they switched their attention to Mars. At that point, Mars was nearer to the earth than usual, as it was in opposition, that is, the earth was passing directly between Mars and the sun, so that the three bodies formed a straight line, with the earth in the middle. Moreover, this was a particularly favourable opposition, as Mars was especially close to the earth in its orbit, and so at its largest and brightest, providing ideal conditions for observation.

Previous astronomers had noticed grey areas or flecks on the planet's surface, and had concluded that these were most probably transient, cloud-like effects produced by atmospheric conditions. The only observer so far who had speculated that these patches might, in fact, be permanent geographical features of the planet's surface, was Wilhelm's friend and fellow director at the Königstadt theatre, the lawyer Georg Kunowsky, who was also a keen amateur astronomer, and owned a Fraunhofer telescope.

In the favourable conditions of autumn 1830, Wilhelm and Mädler spent seventeen nights observing the visible, southern half of Mars, and drawing maps of what they saw. They were able to record enough data to conclude definitively that the surface patches were not weather phenomena, but, as Kunowsky had suspected, permanent geological features. This allowed them to plot the outlines of a map of the southern part of Mars, using a grid system that they had established. They also recorded the shrinking of the southern polar cap, which suggested that it was formed of ice, and reacted to seasonal weather changes, like the polar caps on earth. In November 1830, they gave a talk to the Geographical Society summarising their initial findings, using a globe to demonstrate the topography of the southern hemisphere of Mars.

On two further occasions, in 1832 and 1837, Mars was again in a favourable position for observation. In 1837, its northern half was visible, giving Wilhelm and Mädler the opportunity to observe the parts of the planet's surface that they had not been able to map previously. This time, they were permitted to use the Royal Observatory, which in 1835 had been moved from the Dorotheenstadt to the Kreuzberg, a small hill outside the city, and equipped with a large, new refractor telescope. They were now in a position to plot an outline of the topography of the whole planet. One of their initial aims had also been to work out the rotational period of Mars, which could only be done once a clear, fixed feature on the planet's surface had been identified as a reference point. They made several computations, one of which, at 24 hours, 37 minutes, 23.7 seconds, is extremely close to the currently accepted value of 24 hours, 37 minutes, 22.6 seconds.

Wilhelm and Mädler published the first ever map of the surface of Mars in Paris in 1840. A German edition followed the next year. Their work was superseded some decades later, but its importance in the history of the cartography of Mars is indisputable: the influential French astronomer and writer Camille Flammarion, while pointing out that a 'phalanx' of astronomers had contributed to the study of Mars, noted that, 'Beer and Mädler deserve to be remembered as the true pioneers.'[5]

William Sheehan, a modern historian of astronomy, has commented with respect to the mapping of Mars that, 'Beer and Mädler tower so far above their contemporaries that there is a distinct danger of forgetting the other observers who were active at the time.'[6] In the late nineteenth century, a Martian sea and a continent were both named after Wilhelm Beer, but this changed around the turn of the century, when it was decided to use more neutral designations for the larger features of the planet, although there is still a 'Beer crater' on Mars, and one on the moon.

Over the 1830s, while working on the mapping of Mars, Wilhelm and Mädler were also observing the moon. An accurate map of the surface of the moon had not yet been produced, despite its close proximity to the earth. The enormous number of tiny craters covering its surface had created insuperable difficulties for previous astronomers, who were using less powerful telescopes. Before he and Mädler began their work, Wilhelm carried out a survey of all the previous attempts at mapping the moon, and in 1833 he gave a talk to the Geographical Society on the subject.

Over the next few years, the partners spent over 600 nights observing the moon, resulting in 104 drawings of the visible part of its surface. These sketches were used to create a highly detailed map in four parts, or quadrants, which they called the *Mappa Selenographica*. The first two quadrants were published in 1834, the remaining two followed in 1835 and 1836. Wilhelm told the writer Wolfgang Menzel that Mädler, who produced the drawings, must have spent several thousand hours sketching at the telescope. Wilhelm was chiefly responsible for the mathematical work, which, as he told Menzel, was mostly finished by 1833: 'All the calculations, and the measurement of fixed points of the first and second orders, already lie behind us.'[7]

In 1837, Wilhelm and Mädler published a two-volume description of their work on the moon, *Der Mond, nach seinen kosmischen und individuellen Verhältnissen* [The Moon in its Cosmic and Individual Conditions]. The book gave the diameters of 148 major craters and the height of 830 mountains. Wilhelm was particularly keen that the book should contain an exposition of his mathematical input, saying, 'I cannot demand that people take my word for it, without any insight into how exactly or inexactly, how skilfully or otherwise we have proceeded; in a word, how much reliance they can place on the measurements.'[8]

Both the map and the accompanying book were internationally acclaimed at the time of their publication, and they remained the most accurate source of information on the moon for many decades. The map was not surpassed until the 1870s, when photography first became available to astronomers. Alexander von Humboldt wrote to Wilhelm on the publication of *Der Mond*, saying that, 'There has been no astronomical work of comparable significance published in Germany for a long time', adding, 'it is fortunate that there is no Nemesis for, or rather, against, *real* talent, or your family would be in serious trouble.'[9]

The publication of *Der Mond* attracted attention across Europe: in autumn 1838, a thirty-page summary of the work in English appeared in the *Edinburgh New Philosophical Review*. Wilhelm admitted himself that the reception of his work with Mädler had exceeded his wildest hopes. In 1836, following the appearance of the last quadrant map, Wilhelm and Mädler were jointly awarded two significant honours: the Lalande Prize, given by the French Academy of Sciences for scientific advances in astronomy, and the Prussian Gold Medal for Arts and Sciences. Both men were also honoured individually for their work: Mädler was appointed as an observer at the Prussian Royal Observatory, and in 1838 he was granted the title of 'Professor' by the King. Wilhelm was awarded the title of Kommerzienrat [Counsellor of Commerce], and in November 1836 he was created a Knight of the Order of the Dannebrog by the Danish King, Frederick VI, who was interested in astronomy.

This was one of the very few occasions on which Wilhelm mentioned his personal achievements in his correspondence with Giacomo. He wrote to his brother on 12 November 1836, asking him to publicise the award in the French press: 'Be so good as to have it published in as many French newspapers as possible that the King of Denmark has created me a Knight of the Order of the Dannebrog for my services to astronomy. Firstly, I would like it, and secondly, it will do away splendidly with any basis for scandal, if there is any dirty dealing.'[10] He also sent Giacomo reviews of the *Mappa Selenographica* to distribute to French journals. Wilhelm's mention of 'dirty dealing' is probably a reference to rumours that he had merely used his wealth to provide the observatory, and that Mädler had carried out all the scientific work.

The public recognition that Wilhelm received as a result of his scientific work meant a great deal to him. He admitted himself that he had a weakness for honours and awards, and he was clearly anxious to make a good impression on people who had the ability to confer them. This was not a particularly attractive trait, and it sometimes worked to his disadvantage: in his eagerness to forward not just his own interests, but also those of his friends, Wilhelm could appear vain and socially ambitious, which led to some of his colleagues distancing themselves from him.

The most damaging of these incidents occurred in 1841 when Wilhelm, with the best of intentions, devised a scheme to obtain a Prussian honour for the German-Danish astronomer Heinrich Schumacher, professor of Astronomy at Copenhagen and director of the Altona Observatory. Wilhelm had corresponded with Schumacher since the early 1830s, when he and Mädler had begun submitting articles to Schumacher's journal, the influential *Astronomische Nachrichten* [Astronomical Notes]. The two men had become friends. They had similar political views, as royalists who deeply admired the monarchs of their respective countries, and they also shared a decidedly snobbish interest in acquiring honours. We only have Wilhelm's side of the correspondence, but it is clear that they both enjoyed discussing the minutiae of the various levels of orders and their classes, and scheming to help one another obtain awards.

Wilhelm felt that he had found a kindred spirit in Schumacher, telling him, 'I believe that, apart from my mother, you are the only living being to whom I can reveal my weaknesses so openly.'[11] He was keen to impress Schumacher with his family's closeness to the Prussian royals, and sent him a copy of a letter from Frederick William IV to Amalia, congratulating her on the success of a fundraising event she had held in aid of blind war veterans.

Schumacher, who had influence at the Danish court, had been instrumental in obtaining Wilhelm's award of the Order of the Dannebrog in 1836. Three years later, he assisted Wilhelm in having this order upgraded from Knight to Commander level. When Wilhelm had received the Swedish Order of the Wasa 3rd Class, Schumacher had also advised him on the best way to set about getting this order upgraded.

Wilhelm wanted to reciprocate these favours. Schumacher already had the Prussian Order of the Red Eagle 3rd Class, and Wilhelm saw an opportunity in spring 1841, following the accession to the Prussian throne of a new King, Frederick William IV, to have this honour upgraded. He approached his friend Alexander von Humboldt, who had great influence at the Prussian court. Humboldt advised Wilhelm to obtain a copy of the current *Astronomical Notes* yearbook from Schumacher, which he (Humboldt), would then present to the King.

Wilhelm told Schumacher that Humboldt had asked for the yearbook and a covering letter to the King, which Schumacher duly sent. It seems, however, that Schumacher then began to worry that Wilhelm might be leading him into committing some sort of social solecism. He had, on previous occasions, expressed a fear that Wilhelm lacked the necessary finesse in arranging these matters. Instead of discussing the matter with Wilhelm, however, he wrote directly to von Humboldt to say that if, as he suspected, the initial suggestion had in fact come from Wilhelm Beer, and not Humboldt himself, he would prefer Humboldt not to present the yearbook and letter to the King.

He protested that he had never angled for honours, and was not prepared to compromise his principles 'to suit the wishes of a well-meaning friend who, with the best of intentions, is inviting me for a ride on his hobby horse'.[12] This is disingenuous, to say the least, given his correspondence with Wilhelm on the subject over a number of years. Schumacher could not, in any case, have been unaware of Wilhelm's intentions, as Wilhelm had previously told him that 'I wish I could bring you into contact with our present King. Do you have anything you can send him?'[13]

Schumacher's unease continued to grow, however, and he began to feel uncomfortable about the fact that he had accepted a number of generous gifts from Wilhelm, including a particularly valuable Louis XV diamond snuffbox. In an agony of anxiety that his acceptance of these presents might now appear in a dubious light, he confessed all to Humboldt.

Humboldt, no doubt annoyed at being put into an awkward position, reacted with extraordinary vehemence. He told Schumacher that he was 'appalled by all the complexities of diamond snuffboxes, dedications and Commander Crosses in which the uncomfortable and not quite unselfish activity of the man in the moon [Wilhelm] has sought to entangle you'.[14] He clearly assumed that the present of the snuffbox had been a bribe, intended to persuade Schumacher to use his influence at the Danish court to have Wilhelm's award of the Knighthood of the Dannebrog upgraded. In fact, the gift was given more than a year before Schumacher had approached the Danish King on Wilhelm's behalf.

Schumacher, horrified, rushed to assure von Humboldt that he would bow to his superior judgement and his knowledge of etiquette. Humboldt responded that it was perfectly acceptable for a man of Schumacher's status to approach the King in this way through him. Besides, he added, he had run into the King recently in the Palace, and had already handed the items over to him. Shortly after this, Humboldt wrote again to Schumacher to tell him that the King had been delighted with the gifts, and had awarded him the Order of the Red Eagle 1st Class.

None of the men involved comes entirely well out of this story. Schumacher's and Wilhelm's correspondence reveals a mutual obsession with status and social climbing, but Schumacher's scramble to disassociate himself from his friend rather than risk Humboldt's disapproval is unedifying. It is hard to avoid the conclusion that he was happy to be sponsored at the Prussian court by the aristocratic Humboldt, but not by the Jewish Wilhelm Beer.

In their letters to one another, both Schumacher and Humboldt refer to Wilhelm by names such as 'the moon man' and 'our friend in the moon'. Humboldt also alludes to Wilhelm's Jewishness, telling Schumacher that: 'This is, to be sure, an Oriental question, and will not divide us. The Oriental's game is easy to see through! There is self-interest when he hurries, unbidden, to help others; and he always goes to the assistance of the strongest, which is strategically not stupid ...'[15]

Wilhelm's relations with Schumacher cooled considerably after this incident. When he sent Schumacher another gift, it was sent back by return of post. He never knew of Humboldt's correspondence with Schumacher, and was puzzled by his friend's rejection, telling him, 'It hurts me deeply that you don't want to accept my small keepsake ... I am proud and honoured to have the friendship of such a man as you, but in weak moments I think that you need not be so severe with me.'[16]

Wilhelm was, of course, equally unaware that Humboldt was not discreet enough to keep the story to himself: in a letter to the Prussian astronomer Johann Encke, Humboldt told Encke that he had been involved in the most uncomfortable correspondence with Schumacher through the 'vain intrigues of the Oriental moonman ... Read the enclosed (which is to be kept secret), a truly frightful story of a diamond box sent in exchange for a Commander's Cross. How could the usually so wily Conferenzrat

[Schumacher] not have seen through it all, and how could he have kept the present even for a day?'[17]

The incident with Schumacher was not the first time that Humboldt had shown a degree of contempt for Wilhelm that was mixed with a genuine admiration for his achievements. In 1837, when Wilhelm had been awarded the honorific title of Geheimer Kommerzienrat [Privy Counsellor of Commerce], Humboldt had commented to the astronomer Friedrich Bessel, director of the Königsberg Observatory, that 'The King has made Wilhelm Beer a Privy Counsellor, because the Semite childishly wanted it, a fantasy that can be excused given so much real and fine work.'[18]

All great men have their weaknesses, and Humboldt occasionally had a sharp tongue. Wilhelm was not the only one of his acquaintances to suffer from this trait. In letters to colleagues, Humboldt referred to the astronomer Wilhelm Struve as 'the tyrant of Pulkovo'[19]. In 1845, several years after the incident with Schumacher, he told Johann Encke that he had received a letter from Schumacher containing 'yet more long, diplomatic explanations about the old moon snuffbox'.[20]

Most probably, Humboldt genuinely did not understand why titles and honours should hold such significance for Wilhelm. The two men came from very different worlds: Humboldt was a nobleman by birth, and whatever physical hardships he may have had to endure on his expeditions, in his own country he had never had to fight for respect or respectability; all doors had been automatically open to him.

Wilhelm had been born not just a commoner, but a complete outsider. He aspired to join the establishment, and the awards he undoubtedly schemed and manoeuvred to obtain were signs to him of acceptance into this exclusive and elite group. However, Humboldt's use of the word 'fantasy' to describe Wilhelm's desire for the title of Geheimer Kommerzienrat suggests that, whether consciously or unconsciously, he saw Wilhelm's aspirations to join his caste as futile.

Humboldt was, in fact, correct in this: it was not possible for Wilhelm to reach the highest levels of society in Prussia, where Jews were barred from the nobility. This was not the case everywhere in Europe; the Austrian Jewish banker Bernhard von Eskeles had been created a baron as early as 1822. When, in 1842, Wilhelm's daughter Julie married the Jewish banker Samuel von Haber, who also held an Austrian baronetcy, Wilhelm saw an opportunity to gain an Austrian title for himself, with his son-in-law as sponsor. Haber had links to Tuscany, which was ruled by a member of the Austrian Hapsburg family, and in 1844 he supported an application by Wilhelm for a Tuscan title.

Alexander von Humboldt, who was prepared to help Wilhelm, despite his scathing comments to others, wrote a letter of recommendation. The Duke of Tuscany approved the request, and Wilhelm was created 'Baron Guglielmo De Beer Prussiano' of the small town of Colle di Val d'Elsa. His coat of arms displayed the constellation of the Plough (also known as the Great Bear or Bär) and two crossed flaming torches. Wilhelm had achieved the pinnacle of his ambitions. There was only one fly in the ointment: as a foreign title, Wilhelm's Tuscan baronetcy could not be recognised or used in Prussia.

The only surviving portrait[21] of Wilhelm, probably painted in the early 1840s, is revealing: he is dressed formally, ostentatiously wearing all his orders to date: the Cross of the Commander of the Dannebrog hangs on its white and red ribbon around his neck, the green sash of the Swedish Commander of the Wasa Order lies across his left shoulder, and the military

Wilhelm Beer (Funke, lithograph after Franz Krüger, Berlin c. 1850). Stiftung Stadtmuseum Berlin. Reproduction: Michael Setzpfandt, Berlin

medal for participation in the Wars of Liberation is pinned to his collar. He is also, in contravention of the rules, wearing the large cross of the Wasa Order 3$^{rd}$ Class, which was replaced by the Commander's sash, but which Wilhelm found so impressive-looking that he decided to continue wearing it.

He had complained to Schumacher, who was at the time still his confidant in these matters, that, 'Now I have to put aside a croix en sautoir that looks really good, to wear a crazy great sash that, without the star, looks like a dog without a tail.' The sash had its uses as an imposing piece of costume, however; when Wilhelm wore it to the homage ceremony for the new King of Prussia, he noted with satisfaction that several people 'nearly burst with envy'.[22] In his portrait, Wilhelm has a look of pride, but he does not look like a man who is entirely comfortable in his own skin: he holds himself stiffly, and his gaze contains more than a hint of defiance and challenge.

Wilhelm's astronomical work, which had brought him international recognition and respect, came to an end in 1840 when Mädler, who had married that year, accepted the post of director of the Russian observatory in Dorpat [then part of the Russian Empire, now in Estonia]. Their last joint work, a compilation of various observations on the solar system, was published in the same year. Mädler's departure was a serious blow for Wilhelm. He was losing not just a collaborator, but the man who had been his closest friend for over sixteen years. Wilhelm was urged by his friends to find another working partner, but he could not contemplate replacing Mädler.

At the time that Mädler left, the partners had been planning further work, to investigate the small section of the far side of the moon that is occasionally visible through the moon's oscillation. Alexander von Humboldt remarked to Johann Encke that Wilhelm's complaints about Mädler's 'breach of contract in respect of their mutual ownership of the other side of the moon' in leaving Berlin before they could carry out the work, were both 'very amusing and psychologically revealing'.[23]

Wilhelm's career as an astronomer need not, in fact, have ended with Mädler's departure. His reputation was such that several respected institutions offered him a professional position after Mädler's move to Dorpat became public knowledge. Wilhelm Struve, the founder and director of the new Russian observatory at Pulkovo, near St Petersburg (Humboldt's 'tyrant of Pulkovo'), invited Wilhelm to join him there as a colleague. Wilhelm was also offered a position in the French Academy of Sciences – a rare opportunity that Humboldt advised him to accept, describing it as 'real, European-wide recognition for a great, monumental work'.[24] Schumacher had also made Wilhelm an offer of a job before the rift occurred in their friendship. The details are not known, but it must have been flattering, as Wilhelm told Schumacher that, on receiving the offer, 'I went around the whole day in a kind of happy intoxication'.[25]

These offers of posts at highly regarded scientific institutions were extremely flattering, but, in the end, Wilhelm turned down all opportunities to become a professional astronomer. It cannot have been an easy decision. He had a genuine passion for astronomy, and, while still an amateur, had achieved an international reputation. It was painful for him to accept that, from now on, he would be an onlooker, rather than an active participant in the progress of the science he had loved. In a letter to Schumacher, he described himself bitterly as 'a zero in the field of astronomy now'.[26]

Unfortunately for Wilhelm, his retirement from active involvement in astronomy after 1840 has also led some historians to underestimate his role in the projects with Mädler. Although he was clearly perceived as a serious scientist by his contemporaries – he was corresponding with both Schumacher and Bessel, two of the most important astronomers of the age, by 1835, and Alexander von Humboldt expressed frequent admiration for his work – he has been described by a number of later historians as a mere dilettante or patron, whose only function was to provide the cash for Mädler's work.

In 1996, William Sheehan remarked that, 'It has long been recognised that most of the actual mapping was done by Mädler; Beer's main contribution was in allowing him to use the observatory!'[27] Wilhelm's own description of their work confirms that Mädler was indeed responsible for the major and time-consuming task of drawing up the charts, and was almost certainly the 'senior partner' in scientific terms, but it also reveals that Wilhelm, who financed the project, was also an active contributor to the scientific work, providing the mathematical input.

There can be little doubt that if Mädler had not left Berlin, Wilhelm would have carried on with his astronomical work, but on his friend's departure, he felt unable to take the huge step of uprooting his family and moving to another country. There were just too many reasons against such a change, including a downturn in his health – he was suffering from increasingly severe and painful attacks of gout that left him temporarily disabled.

He was also an extremely busy man. He felt his responsibilities as head of the family businesses particularly keenly, partly because his brothers' money, as well as his own, was invested in them. The sugar refineries were a constant worry. From time to time, the profits were affected by circumstances outside his control, such as the cheap import of sugar from England, the rise of the cultivation of beet sugar as a local rival to imported cane sugar, and changes in taxation. In 1829, Wilhelm had even suggested to his brothers that they should all consider taking a substantial portion of their money out of the refineries, although this proved unnecessary, as the business recovered.

Heinrich was another ongoing source of concern. Unfortunately, it seems that the contretemps with Therese Peche had not taught him a lasting lesson, but had only temporarily dampened his spirits. In September 1837, Amalia, who had always urged the busy and often distracted Giacomo to keep in regular touch with 'Hans', wrote to him saying that: 'I must ask you, dear Giacomo, not to be too friendly towards Heinrich, you have to understand that the trick he has recently played on Wilhelm is shameful.'[28]

It is not clear exactly what form the 'trick' had taken, but it was certainly connected with finance, and must have been serious, as, six months later, Wilhelm told Giacomo that, 'Altogether we can hope for nothing better than to drag the band of thieves that surround him before the criminal courts.'[29] Wilhelm had also confided in Alexander von Humboldt, who had assured him that he would keep an eye on official proceedings, and help the Beers where he could.[30]

It appears that Giacomo's brother-in-law, Adolph Mosson, was a prominent member of the 'band of thieves' that Heinrich had fallen in with. Giacomo had already had a contretemps with Adolph, who was the black sheep of the Mosson family, earlier that year. He had been furious to discover that Adolph had persuaded both Minna's mother and her aunt Hanna to disinherit Minna and her children in his (Adolph's) own favour.

In August 1837, Giacomo was in Berlin in connection with family business. He told Minna that Adolph was also in Berlin, but had not visited either him or Amalia, adding, 'I can understand, however, that given the many bad, indeed despicable tricks he has been guilty of against our family in connection with Heinrich, he might be reluctant to show himself to us.'[31]

Whatever Adolph Mosson's sins were, some of them, at least, had caught up with him by July 1838, when Giacomo told Minna that he had been sentenced to six month's imprisonment in Stettin, although he did not know the reason why. As for Heinrich, although there is no suggestion that he was actually declared feeble-minded as Heinrich Heine claimed,[32] the family decided around this time that he could not be trusted to manage his own financial affairs, and placed him under guardianship.

Sad though it was for the Beers to have to take such a step, the removal of Heinrich from any position where he could affect the family's financial security must have come as a relief to Wilhelm. In the late 1830s, he was not only juggling the management of the family businesses with his scientific work with Mädler, demanding as that was, but he was also becoming a key figure in Berlin's financial circles.

Wilhelm had been an elder of the Berlin Corporation of Merchants since 1836. That same year, he had become one of the earliest investors in train travel in Prussia, when he had been elected to the boards of the Berlin-Potsdam and Potsdam-Leipzig Railway Companies. At the time, steam trains were not long past the experimental stage: Stephenson's 'Rocket' had proved the viability of the locomotive to a sceptical British public only seven years previously. A number of European countries had already begun developing plans for national railways, but in Prussia the government was reluctant to offer state support.

Frederick William III and his ministers had believed that the investment needed would be too great for the projects to be profitable, and that, in any case, the mechanical problems involved were likely to prove insuperable. Consequently, they preferred to continue to support the extension and improvement of the road and canal networks. Given this lack of interest, the development of rail transport was left entirely to entrepreneurs and private investment. The new rail companies were not slow to take advantage of this opportunity: the Potsdam-Berlin line was in operation by the end of 1838, and was followed quickly by the much more ambitious route that linked Berlin with Leipzig. Over the next few years, following the success of his first investments in the railways, Wilhelm joined the boards of the Potsdam-Magdeburg, and the Lower Silesian-Märkische Railway Companies.

In the early 1840s, Wilhelm's experience in railway management led him into a new sphere of activity. As it became clear that rail transport was here to stay, the question of whether the state should support the Prussian infrastructure, or whether it should be left to private entrepreneurs, became a major national debate. Wilhelm had strong opinions on the subject, believing that some form of national investment and direction was necessary to create a linked-up network, and to avoid the dangers of economic booms and crashes.

Wilhelm was keen to join the debate, and found a public forum for his views in the two major Berlin newspapers, the *Vossische Zeitung* and the *Spenersche Zeitung*. He began submitting articles to both papers in the mid-1840s, at first anonymously, but later under his own name. This new area of activity as an economic commentator and publicist would have important consequences. Wilhelm had already had enough occupations for several men – as a cavalryman, astronomer, businessman and railway director – but over the next five years he would take up a final and very public career, as a national politician.

# Notes

1. Giacomo Meyerbeer, *Briefwechsel und Tagebücher*, Heinz Becker, Gudrun Becker and Sabine Henze-Döhring (eds) (Berlin: Walter de Gruyter, 1960-2006), vol. 3, p.153.
2. Sebastian Hensel, *Die Familie Mendelssohn 1729-1847* (Berlin: B Behr's Verlag, 1903), vol. 1, p.173.
3. Felix Mendelssohn Bartholdy, *Sämtliche Briefe*, Helmut Loos and Wilhelm Seidel (eds) (Kassel: Bärenreiter, 2008-17), vol. 1, p.239.
4. My main source of information on Wilhelm's astronomical work is Jürgen Blunck (ed.), *Wilhelm Beer. Genius der Astronomie und Ökonomie 1797-1850* (Berlin: Staatsbibliothek zu Berlin, Preussischer Kulturbesitz, 1997).
5. As quoted in Sheehan, *The Planet Mars: A History of Observation and Discovery* (Tucson, AZ: University of Arizona Press, 1996), p.45.
6. Ibid., p.50.
7. Unpublished letter, Wilhelm Beer to Wolfgang Menzel, 10 February 1833, Berlin-Brandenburg Academy of Sciences and Humanities, NL Menzel, Nr. 71.
8. Unpublished letter, Wilhelm Beer to Heinrich Schumacher, 17 December 1836, Staatsbibliothek zu Berlin, Preussischer Kulturbesitz, Nachlass Heinrich Christian Schumacher.
9. Unpublished letter, Alexander von Humboldt to Wilhelm Beer, 25 August 1837, Universitätsbibliothek Johann Christian Senckenberg Frankfurt am Main, Autogr. A. von Humboldt.
10. Meyerbeer, *Briefwechsel und Tagebücher*, vol. 2, pp.561-2.
11. Unpublished letter, 11 March 1839, Staatsbibliothek zu Berlin, Preussischer Kulturbesitz, Nachlass Heinrich Christian Schumacher.
12. Kurt Biermann (ed.), *Briefwechsel zwischen Alexander von Humboldt und Heinrich Christian Schumacher*, (Berlin: Akademie Verlag, 1980), p.102.
13. Unpublished letter, Wilhelm Beer to Heinrich Schumacher, 29 October 1840, Staatsbibliothek zu Berlin, Preussischer Kulturbesitz, Nachlass Heinrich Christian Schumacher.
14. Biermann, *Briefwechsel*, p.103.
15. Ibid., p.103.
16. Unpublished letter, Wilhelm Beer to Heinrich Schumacher, 14 July 1841, Staatsbibliothek zu Berlin, Preussischer Kulturbesitz, Nachlass Heinrich Christian Schumacher.
17. Biermann, *Briefwechsel*, p.104 n. 6.
18. Hans-Joachim Felber (ed.), *Briefwechsel zwischen Alexander von Humboldt und Friedrich Wilhelm Bessell* (Berlin: Akademie Verlag, 1994), p.109.
19. Biermann, *Briefwechsel*, p.116.

20. Biermann, *Briefwechsel*, p.116.
21. The original oil painting, by F. Krüger, dating from the early 1840s, has vanished, but engravings have survived.
22. Unpublished letters, Wilhelm Beer to Heinrich Schumacher, 26 June 1840 and 30 December 1840, Staatsbibliothek zu Berlin, Preussischer Kulturbesitz, Nachlass Heinrich Christian Schumacher.
23. As quoted in Blunck, *Wilhelm Beer*, p.56.
24. Unpublished, undated letter, Alexander von Humboldt to Wilhelm Beer, Universitätsbibliothek Johann Christian Senckenberg Frankfurt am Main, Autogr. A. von Humboldt.
25. Unpublished letter, Wilhelm Beer to Heinrich Schumacher, 18 January 1841, Staatsbibliothek zu Berlin, Preussischer Kulturbesitz, Nachlass Heinrich Christian Schumacher.
26. Unpublished letter, Wilhelm Beer to Heinrich Schumacher, 17 November 1841, Staatsbibliothek zu Berlin, Preussischer Kulturbesitz, Nachlass Heinrich Christian Schumacher.
27. Sheehan, *The Planet Mars*, p.46.
28. Meyerbeer, *Briefwechsel und Tagebücher*, vol. 3, p.63.
29. Ibid., p.150.
30. Unpublished letter, Alexander von Humboldt to Wilhelm Beer, 25 August 1837, Universitätsbibliothek Johann Christian Senckenberg Frankfurt am Main, Autogr. A. von Humboldt.
31. Meyerbeer, *Briefwechsel und Tagebücher*, vol. 3, p.60.
32. Heinrich Heine, *Säkularausgabe. Werke, Briefwechsel, Lebenszeugnisse* (Berlin and Paris: Akademie Verlag and Editions de CNRS, 1970-), vol. 12, p.63.

# 19

## The 'Anxious Genius'

In Paris, after the huge success of *Robert le Diable*, Giacomo was under pressure to produce another opera that would make a similar impact. In October 1832, he had signed a contract with the director of the Paris Opéra, Louis-Désirée Véron, to deliver a new work by the end of the following year. He already had a subject in mind: by the time that the contract was signed, Giacomo and his librettist, Eugène Scribe, had begun work on the text of their next *grand opéra*, *Les Huguenots* [The Huguenots].

The opera was set in Paris, at the time of the massacre of French Protestants by Catholics on St Bartholomew's Day in August 1572. This dramatic event forms the background for a tragic love affair between a Protestant man, the Huguenot Raoul de Nangis, and a Catholic woman, Valentine de Saint-Bris. At the climax of the opera, as the lovers try to escape the slaughter on the night of the massacre, accompanied by Raoul's old servant Marcel, they are secretly married amid scenes of chaos. Shortly afterwards, Raoul is wounded by a mob. He, Marcel and Valentine are challenged by a group of Catholic fanatics led by Valentine's father, the Comte de Saint-Bris, who does not recognise his daughter until it is too late. The three declare themselves Huguenots, and are shot by Saint-Bris' men. The dying Valentine forgives her father.

Scribe had used Prosper Merimée's 1829 novel, *Chronique du règne de Charles IX*, which was set in the French court at the time of the massacre, as a basis for his text. The libretto of *Les Huguenots* is typical of *grand opéra* in its depiction of the helplessness of individuals in the face of overwhelming social and political upheaval – and so had strong relevance to the more recent revolutionary history of France – but it is also a powerful indictment of the subversion of religion for political ends.

In one of the opera's most famous scenes, the 'Blessing of the Daggers', Catholic monks bless the weapons to be used in the massacre, thus legitimising the bloodshed, and driving the conspirators into an ugly frenzy of aggression. But although fanatacism and hatred exist on both sides, the central characters embody the ideal of the transcendence of love over dogma. The Catholic Valentine is prepared to sacrifice her faith and ultimately her life for the Protestant Raoul. Marcel, Raoul's old Huguenot servant, is initially fanatical in his hatred of Catholics, but his intolerance is eventually overcome by his admiration for Valentine. Marcel comes to recognise that love and human life are more important than sectarian loyalties, and he blesses the couple's union in the face of death.

Giacomo's contract with Véron had allowed a period of one year for the completion of the opera, but this was to prove unrealistic, given both the scale of the work, and the composer's time-consuming involvement in the development of the text and the characters. Giacomo was not happy with Scribe's first attempt at a libretto for *Les Huguenots*, which he saw in September 1833, as he felt that Scribe had failed to capture any real sense of the historical setting. As he planned to leave France shortly afterwards, to take Minna, who was unwell, to Italy for the winter, there was no time for the problems to be resolved before the stipulated date, and he was forced to pay Véron a fine of 30,000 francs for breaking the contract.

The money was not important to Giacomo, but the incident did nothing to ameliorate his dislike of Véron: at the time that the contract was being negotiated, in 1832, he had remarked that: 'Véron is dreading the moment as much as I am, when two people like us, who neither trust nor like each other, but are necessary to one another, are forced to propose mutual security measures.'[1]

Giacomo used his time in Italy over the winter of 1833 to re-work parts of the opera with his old friend and librettist, Gaetano Rossi. Rossi wrote a number of additional passages, which Giacomo took back to Paris with him early the next year. Scribe then developed the ideas contained in the new text in collaboration with the poet Émile Deschamps. The main result of this re-working was to increase the importance of the role of Marcel, who became one of the opera's main characters. Giacomo negotiated a new contract with Véron in September 1834, and eventually regained the 30,000 francs when he completed the score in May of the next year.

Giacomo's problems did not end with the submission of the score, however. In August 1835, Véron retired from his post as director of the Opéra. In accordance with his contract as the first private manager of the institution, the government subsidies, which had been on a large scale at the beginning of the venture, had been diminishing each year, increasing the risk that a major failure could adversely affect Véron's personal finances. With his customary sharp business sense, Véron timed his departure to ensure that he retired with a huge fortune – much of it due to the success of *Robert le Diable*, the outstanding production of his tenure. Véron was replaced by the Opéra's stage designer Henri Duponchel, who was appointed director on 1 September 1835.

The rehearsals for *Les Huguenots* began in June 1835, a couple of months before the change in the Opéra's management. They were to last an astonishing eight months, and would take a toll on Giacomo's health and wellbeing. The schedule was punishing – by late December there were two rehearsals daily, each lasting three to four hours. The star tenor, Adolph Nourrit, who was singing the role of Raoul, and the soprano Cornélie Falcon, who was playing Valentine, added to the stress by insisting on making alterations to their parts, and refusing to sing pieces they did not like. The Parisian socialite and theatregoer Charles de Boigne commented that: 'Never will we know the true cost of rehearsals to Meyerbeer in terms of insomnia, anxiety, fear, work, and despair. He saw everything, he thought of everything, he supervised everything: libretto, music, staging, scenery, costumes, songs and dancing.'[2]

Fortunately for Giacomo, he had a few loyal friends and supporters he could rely on to help him through this difficult period. Chief among these allies was Louis Gouin, a high-ranking civil servant in the Parisian postal service, who had become Giacomo's business manager in Paris. Gouin is first mentioned in 1826, soon after Giacomo had arrived back in Paris after his marriage to Minna. How the two men first met is not known, but Giacomo very quickly came to trust Gouin implicitly. By the early 1830s, Gouin was combining his day job with keeping a sharp eye on Giacomo's affairs in Paris: dealing with Véron and with the press on the composer's behalf, looking after the receipts from the performances, and distributing free tickets to Giacomo's friends and supporters.

The task of distributing complimentary tickets, which Gouin took on for Giacomo, was an important one. In the French theatre of the nineteenth century, it was accepted practice for management to place people strategically in the audience, to start the applause at the right moment. There was, in fact, an official group of these 'applauders' at the Paris Opéra; their leader, Augustin Levasseur, was an important person, not least in his own eyes. He routinely met with the director of the Opéra before major premieres to discuss how he would deploy his 'troops', who were rewarded with free tickets for their participation. Louis Véron commented that Augustin always wore strangely garish clothes, 'like a general, one might say, who, if not through the richness, then at least through the oddity of his clothing, would always be visible to his troops, even in the midst of danger'.[3]

Along with Gouin, Giacomo also had support from some family members during the rehearsal period. Amalia and Wilhelm travelled to

Paris in September 1835, and both stayed there with him until the premiere had taken place at the end of the next February. Wilhelm was deeply involved in his astronomical work with Mädler at the time, and had intended to return to Berlin before the end of the year, but Giacomo persuaded him to stay on in Paris, telling Minna in December 1835 that 'Wilhelm's stay here is not only beneficial for my spirits, he has already done some good. He has greatly improved my relations with Duponchel and Nourrit.'[4]

It must have been a trying time for both Amalia and Wilhelm, given Giacomo's nervous irritability, and the perfectionism that so often led to clashes with the theatre management and performers. Giacomo was aware of his debt to both his brother and his mother, whom he referred to by her family nickname of 'the Nonne', from the Italian word for grandmother, *nonna*. He told Minna that, 'I must always be thankful that the Nonne and Wilhelm were able to give me some encouragement and comfort by their presence in this difficult time.'[5]

On 29 February 1836, after some last-minute delays, the premiere of *Les Huguenots* finally took place. All of the main roles were taken by singers who were among the greatest of their time: alongside Adolph Nourrit as Raoul and Cornélie Falcon as Valentine, the soprano Julie Dorus-Gras sang Queen Marguerite de Valois, and the bass Nicolas-Prosper Levasseur played Marcel. The premiere had been sold out two months in advance, and the lucky ticket-holders had to push their way to the doors through crowds desperate to obtain entry.

The audience was at first taken aback by the setting of the opera; they had expected *Les Huguenots* to be another *Robert le Diable*, with mythical and supernatural elements. By the end of the evening, however, they had warmed to the production, and over the next few weeks its popularity soared, with the critics fanning the flames of the rising frenzy that gripped the theatre-going public. The Paris correspondent for the *Allgemeine musikalische Zeitung* reported after the first performance that 'everyone was beside themselves, and I myself cannot recover from my musical inebriation'.

A second review in the same paper commented that the opera was 'one of the most admirable creations of the human spirit'.[6] Liszt called it 'an immense success' and thought it surpassed *Robert le Diable*. After a break in performances in June, the crowd demanding tickets was so great that gendarmes were called in to protect the box office, and the Opéra management had to fit two extra rows of seats into the auditorium.

Several thoughtful critics, including the composer Hector Berlioz, commented that the opera needed to be heard several times before it could be fully understood and appreciated. The reporter for the important *Revue des deux Mondes* had refused to give a verdict immediately after the premiere, feeling that he needed time to digest the complexity of the work, but, six weeks later, announced that any criticism must fall silent before such an overwhelming success. In September that year, the *Revue des deux Mondes* published an extremely long and gushing 'open letter' from the writer George Sand to Giacomo, who she addressed as 'Carissimo Maestro'.

Of course, the opera was not universally admired. The theme of religious strife, and the borrowing of church music, made the work controversial. Giacomo had woven traditional religious tunes into the score; most famously, Martin Luther's well-known hymn 'Ein fester Burg ist unser Gott' [A Mighty Fortress is Our God], which recurs throughout the opera. This robust Lutheran chorale and Marcel's Huguenot battle songs contrast with the ethereal choral hymns to the Virgin Mary that are sung by the Catholic crowds on their way to church.

Giacomo's ability to produce these powerful representations of Christian emotion reveals an ability to understand and empathise with adherents of other faiths. However, in some countries, including Prussia, the opera was banned for its religious content. In others, the action was moved from Paris to other places considered less controversial, such as England at the time of the Civil War. In Catholic Munich, it was produced in 1838 as *Die Anglikaner und die Puritaner* [Anglicans and Puritans], and in the Habsburg lands the setting was changed to the struggle between the Guelphs and the Ghibellines in twelfth-century Italy.

*Les Huguenots* was not the first opera to feature a religious conflict; Fromental Halévy's *grand opéra*, *La Juive* [The Jewess] had been premiered in Paris just a year before the first performance of *Les Huguenots*. *La Juive*, which also had a libretto by Scribe, was set in Constance in 1414, at the time of the Catholic Council of Constance. The main characters are a Jewish father and his adopted daughter. It is hard to imagine Giacomo addressing the question of prejudice against the Jews onstage as directly as Halévy.

Some of Giacomo's detractors were disturbed by his cosmopolitanism. He had created a unique style which could not be pigeonholed as belonging to any national school, and advocates of such schools disliked what they saw as his eclecticism. Although many such criticisms were purely a matter of musical taste and judgement, some had an anti-Semitic flavour. But no matter how good most of the reviews were, Giacomo was always upset by any negative comments, and he tended to ascribe them to personal spite. Heinrich Heine described Giacomo as an 'anxious genius' who feared public opinion, and was terrified by the slightest criticism: 'He is never satisfied, a single wrong note in the orchestra is a dagger blow to him, which he feels will almost kill him. This agitation continues to haunt him even when the opera has been performed and received with frenzied applause.'[7]

Even so, Giacomo was more amused than hurt by the indignation of the correspondent for the *Gazette de France*, who was offended that Meyerbeer, as a Jew who had personally experienced the intolerance of Protestants, should misuse his genius to present an opera that glorified Protestantism.[8] The reviewer had missed the point: the opera did not 'glorify' any religion, but rather criticised the pointlessness and tragedy of placing ideology and dogma above human life and love. Other reactions which alluded to Giacomo's Jewish heritage were more hurtful. The pianist and composer Robert Schumann, who heard *Les Huguenots* in April 1837 in Leipzig, was particularly scathing in his review of the opera.

Schumann was, of course, perfectly entitled to dislike Giacomo's music, and to say so as trenchantly as he chose. However, he was one of the first influential musicians to criticise Giacomo on the basis of his Jewishness. Schumann did occasionally express derogatory views on Jews in private. In the joint diary he kept with his wife, Clara, he had said with reference to the convert Felix Mendelssohn, that, 'Jews remain Jews ... The stones we have helped gather for their Temple of Glory they occasionally throw at us. Therefore, do not do too much [for them] is my opinion.'[9] Schumann's anti-Semitic views are implicit in his review of *Les Huguenots*:

> I can hardly express the way in which the whole thing filled us with such disgust that we could only try to defend ourselves against it; we were limp and exhausted from anger ... I am no moralist but it is shocking for a good Protestant to hear his most precious song bawled from the stage, shocking to see the bloodiest drama in his religion's history dragged down to the level of a fairground farce ... Debauchery, murder and praying, there is nothing else in the Huguenots: you will search in vain for a sustained pure thought, a truly Christian sentiment.[10]

Giacomo was aware of Schumann's aversion to him. In 1846, he was present at a soirée in Vienna where Clara Schumann gave a performance on the piano: 'I could not greet her, as the wife of a man who has treated me with such malicious hostility, but I applauded her playing enthusiastically and said "bravo" as she walked past me.'[11]

He did not meet Robert Schumann in person until 1850, when he attended a concert where Schumann was conducting his own work, *Das*

*Paradis und die Peri.* Giacomo noted in his diary that, 'on this occasion I saw, for the first time, the face of the man who, as a critic, has persecuted me for the last twelve years with deadly enmity.'[12]

Despite the voices of dissent, however, *Les Huguenots* was an undoubted triumph. Such was the importance of the work, that it could not be ignored: it had made Giacomo the leading operatic composer of the day. After the third performance, even he had admitted that, 'What pleases me most of all is that even the *opponents* of this opera talk of it as one of the most significant musical events of modern times.'[13]

The success of *Les Huguenots* was to be enduring: it became the first opera ever to reach 1,000 performances at the Paris Opéra – to this day, only Gounod's *Faust* has been staged there more often. It became hugely popular internationally, achieving 385 performances in Berlin by 1932, and 249 at London's Covent Garden by 1927. It was not only successful in Europe, but in places as far afield as Cairo, New York, Rio de Janeiro, Sydney and the Dutch East Indies.[14] There have been hundreds of arrangements and transcriptions of the music for piano and voice, by Liszt, Johann Strauss the Elder, Schubert and Vaughan Williams among others.

*Les Huguenots* had been an undisputed triumph for Giacomo, but the lengthy period of rehearsals leading up to the premiere had brought a troubling issue in his personal life to a head. His chief supporters during this stressful time, apart from Louis Gouin, had been his brother and his mother. His wife, Minna, had not been in evidence; she had remained in Baden-Baden, her favourite spa town in Germany, at a distance of three days' coach travel from Paris. Amalia had stayed on in Paris after the premiere until the end of May, and Giacomo had written to Minna to emphasise how devotedly his mother had dedicated herself to him:

> She has so generously sacrificed eight months of her life, and I must call it a great sacrifice to have lived through this anxious, stormy period of rehearsals before the premiere with me, without her having any sort of compensatory amusement, for she goes nowhere! ... You owe her a great deal, because I don't think I would have survived the six months from September to March if I had had to bear these agitations alone, without being able to pour them out daily to a friendly soul.[15]

This could not have made comfortable reading for Minna. She disliked Paris intensely, and was convinced that living there was bad for her health. She had created a life for herself that was centred on a round of stays in

German spa towns, and she was not willing to relinquish this comfortable existence. Giacomo joined her in the summer whenever he could, but the demands of his career meant that he needed to spend much of the year in a major city, with access to first-class opera houses. As he also felt strongly that he could not work as a composer in Germany, the couple were leading what amounted to separate lives:

> The fact that, as you say, you can only feel at home in Germany, is of course an unhappy circumstance for you, but no less so for me, as so far France and Italy are the only hospitable countries in which I have been able to practise my profession, my art, with success and recognition, while Germany has rejected me and heaped scorn on me.[16]

Giacomo had been willing to compromise, however, and had looked for a suitable house to buy in Baden, which could have been used as a family base, while he continued to spend periods in Paris. However, it transpired that, even as late as the mid-1830s, there were potential legal problems in his owning a property there as a Jew, and the plan had fallen through. Under the circumstances, Giacomo had insisted that Minna should not live entirely alone when they were apart, telling her that, 'the only possible decent way for a young woman to live separately from her husband is to be at the side of her mother'.[17]

Luckily, Johanna Mosson was both able and willing to spend most of her time living with her daughter. In December 1835, when the rehearsals for *Les Huguenots* were at a particularly demanding stage, Giacomo had acknowledged to Minna that he owed her mother a good deal, telling her that if Johanna had not been willing to act as chaperone, he would have been forced to give up his musical career.

It is not clear what Minna's medical problems were, but they seem to have been related to chest and throat weaknesses. Her pregnancies may have contributed to her frailty: the couple, who both wanted more children, consulted doctors before each pregnancy to check whether Minna was strong enough to go through with it. Minna certainly considered herself an invalid; she described herself to Giacomo as 'nothing but a broken plant that needs all its strength just to cling to the earth'. In response to his pleas for her to come to Paris just for a few months each winter, she told him that

> … when I think it all over, and test my strength and my crying need for peace and a regular life, I always come back to the conclusion that

my presence there would be a burden for you rather than being a source of encouragement and support. It is this conviction, in part, which has brought me to the terrible decision of this unforeseeable separation.[18]

Giacomo missed Minna's presence in his life as a wife and partner. He was worried that her affection for him might be diminishing, and he showed distinct signs of jealousy. He reminded her that her position, as a woman living without male protection, made her vulnerable to malicious speculation. He was alarmed to find that she had been receiving visits from young men alone in her rooms in Baden-Baden. He wrote to forbid this, telling her that, although he trusted her, it was vital that she remained above suspicion in the eyes of society.

Minna had replied that the men were interested in meeting their little girl, Blanca, rather than her, an explanation that Giacomo did not find convincing: 'Perhaps your maternal pride can allow you to believe that, but when young men take to visiting a beautiful young woman, only a parent could attribute it to their wish to get to know a four-year-old girl.'[19]

He was also unhappy to discover that she had become friendly with the writer Alfred de Musset, whose *Confession of a Child of the Century* chronicled his affair with George Sand. Giacomo told her that, 'someone who mocks decency in his works' was not fit to know her, adding wryly, 'Unfortunately, he is also much younger and better-looking than me.'[20] He ordered Minna to break off contact with de Musset. Giacomo was very aware that Minna was attractive to men, and worried that her behaviour might, however innocently, encourage their attentions. There is nothing to suggest that Minna was unfaithful to her husband, but she was certainly obstinate, and she may have been a little naive.

In August 1836, Minna was again pregnant. Giacomo was anxious for her to spend the winter in Paris with him, but she was unwilling to do this. He wrote to her in the strongest terms he had yet used, asking her how she could know whether she could live in Paris or not, if she refused to make the attempt:

If you want something, you can do it. In 1827, because you really *wanted to*, you *could* travel in the sixth month of pregnancy from Paris to Berlin, and in 1830, in the eighth month of pregnancy, from Paris to Baden. On the other hand, when you were pregnant with Alfred you *could not* travel from Berlin to Paris.[21]

He revealed his fear that her reluctance to come to Paris concealed a lack of interest in being with him: 'Have you withdrawn your heart from me so completely that the prospect of our being together weighs nothing in the decision to come to Paris? I hope to God not.' However, in the end, as he told her, he did not want to force her to do anything against her will: 'If you really want so much to finish your pregnancy in Baden, I don't feel I have the strength to oppose you.'

In the face of his pleas, Minna relented and spent the winter of 1836 in Paris, where their second surviving daughter, Caecilie, was born on 10 March 1837. This concession did not resolve the couple's problems, however. Minna remained adamant that the city was bad for her health, while Giacomo continued to be disturbed by her independent spirit. He was deeply shocked when, in April 1838, she told him that she was going to Frankfurt to visit the trade fair on her own, while her mother was in Berlin, and without waiting for him to join her, as they had previously agreed. He responded that,

> It is sad enough in itself, and does not look good in the eyes of the world, that we are so often separated, and I am always seen to be travelling alone ... But if people see me going one way and you the other, and apparently avoiding meeting one another in a place where you will be today, and I will be in a fortnight's time – what can people think, but that we detest one another, and keep out of one another's way?[22]

Later that year, he persuaded her to make one last attempt at spending the winter in Paris, telling her that, if she really could not live there, he would give up his career in music for the sake of her health. Minna agreed, with some reluctance, to this request, and arrived in Paris in the autumn of that year. While the couple were there, an old friend of Giacomo's from Munich, the clarinettist Heinrich Baermann, came to Paris on a concert tour with his son Carl, also a clarinettist. Carl Baermann kept a diary of their time in Paris, which, together with his letters to his wife, reveals a good deal about the Meyerbeers' life there. He found Giacomo friendly, approachable and modest, despite his great fame, and eager to assist his old friends in any way he could. Baermann was also impressed by the warmth of the family relations: 'It is such a happy family ... They all love each other so much.'

Baermann was convinced that Minna, who he thought an interesting and spirited woman, was very ill: 'We were with Meyerbeer's wife, who is very ill, and, I fear, practically incurable. It seems to me that she has a sort of tuberculosis of the larynx. I am terribly sorry for her, or rather for him, as it would be better for her if she were called into the next world.'[23] He felt that Minna had not long to live – although, as it turned out, despite her own pessimism about her health, she was to survive to the age of 82, outliving her husband by some twenty years.

Baermann says that Giacomo was the perfect host, introducing him and his father to useful contacts, holding dinner parties for them, and taking them around Paris. He had to find the time to do this in an already extremely busy life – Baermann describes how he and his father came back to their lodgings late one evening to find Meyerbeer there, just sitting, absolutely exhausted, on their sofa.

On top of the demands of rehearsals and the endless round of business meetings with librettists, theatre directors, conductors and singers, Giacomo attended the theatres as often as he could, while fitting in soirées at Countess Merlin's and the Princess Belgiojoso's salons, mixing with musically inclined diplomats such as Lord Burghersh and Prince Galitzine, and with writers and musicians such as Berlioz, Paganini, Balzac, Liszt, and George Sand. It is perhaps a measure of his status at the time that, when Hector Berlioz was nominated as a Chevalier of the Légion d'Honneur, he chose Giacomo as a sponsor.[24]

Giacomo's professional and social position in Paris had also made him an important contact for aspiring German musicians and writers who came to the city in the hope of making an international career. He had remained on friendly terms with Heinrich Heine, who was insistent in asking for loans, and for complimentary boxes at the Opéra for his friends. Heine apparently felt free to ask for money and favours from Giacomo as, in his own words, 'things cost me comparatively more than they do you, as one franc is worth more to me than 400 francs are to you'.[25]

Heine, a complex character at the best of times, had a tendency to cloak his demands for money in mysterious terms, hinting at difficulties and plots, and at his own ability to assist Giacomo in their 'common interests', in ways that he never defines clearly. He understood and played on Giacomo's weaknesses – his fear of bad publicity and of intrigues – and he represented himself as an ally against a hostile world. Giacomo may have believed these dark hints, or he may have felt that it was politic to keep Heine on his side, but he should perhaps have remembered Michael's comment that Heine's friendship was more dangerous than his enmity.

Theirs was not a one-way relationship, however, nor was it based entirely on money. Giacomo admired Heine's poetry, and set some of his verses to music. In between his operas, Giacomo composed songs to texts by various contemporary poets and writers – including his brother Michael as well as Heine, Goethe and Émile Deschamps. These small compositions, published as sheet music, were both accessible and popular. They were sung in salons and in people's homes as well as at public concerts, and kept the composer in the public eye during the long intervals between the appearances of his operas.

Heine, for his part, was prepared to lend Giacomo his professional support as a reviewer, and had written a friendly article on *Les Huguenots* for the Augsburg *Allgemeine Zeitung*, saying that '[Meyerbeer] is probably the greatest master of counterpoint now living, and the greatest artist in music … in the foyer of the Opéra yesterday, his artistic understanding was compared, quite rightly, with that of Goethe.'[26]

In an essay on the French stage, however, he described *Les Huguenots* in curious – and strangely ambiguous – terms as 'a Gothic cathedral, whose heaven-seeking spire and colossal cupolas seem to have been planted by the bold hand of a giant, while the innumerable, delicately fine festoons, rosaces and arabesques which cover it like a lace veil, testify to the tireless patience of a dwarf'.[27]

In 1838, Giacomo's friendship with Heine led him into an ill-advised involvement in the poet's private affairs. Heine had asked Giacomo to intercede on his behalf with his wealthy uncle Salomon, telling Giacomo that he was 'the only person I can speak openly to about the most private misfortunes'.[28] Heine had quarrelled with this uncle, who had promptly withdrawn an annual allowance that Heine had relied on to keep the wolf from the door. Heine hoped to persuade his uncle to change his mind, and hit on the idea of asking Giacomo to approach Salomon later that year, when he knew Giacomo would be visiting Hamburg.

Giacomo agreed to help, and arranged a meeting with Salomon. He may have been swayed by the fact that he was acquainted with Salomon Heine, who had been one of his father's business colleagues. He wrote to Heine after the visit to tell him that,

> I hope you will be pleased with your ambassador. I have just come from your excellent uncle and after lengthy discussion I have fixed it all up. The sum is that which you wished, that is, 4,000 francs a year, beginning from 1st January 1839, and I have stipulated that it should be paid quarterly in advance. You will therefore receive 1,000 francs on 1st January.[29]

Heine and Giacomo undoubtedly had some fellow-feeling as emigrant German artists working in a foreign land. Heine had even less choice than

Giacomo in living abroad: his works had been banned in Germany since 1835 due to his radical political views. The two men also shared the bond of their Jewishness – as Heine had with Michael. When Heine had suggested to Giacomo that anti-Semitism was becoming an 'outmoded' weapon, Giacomo had replied bitterly that,

> Ninety-nine percent of readers are Gentiles, and so always have and always will approve of *Richess*, if it is administered with a little skill – What is to be done? No Pomade de Lion or Graisse d'ours, no, not even the font of baptism can make the little piece of foreskin that we were robbed of on the eighth day of our life grow back again; and those who don't bleed to death from the operation on the ninth day will bleed from it their whole life long …[30]

Giacomo had little hope that the Jews' situation in Germany would improve. In 1836, Frederick William III had approved an edict that forbade the Jews to use Christian first names for their children, and ruled that they should be officially known as 'Jews' and not 'Israelites', a term that was considered more polite, and that had gained currency since the Emancipation Edict some twenty years previously. Giacomo had described the new rules as a return to the Middle Ages.[31]

It is hardly surprising that, under these circumstances, he felt that he could not contemplate working in Berlin as a composer. However, this left him, at the end of the 1830s, in a serious and apparently insoluble dilemma. He was at the top of his profession, enjoying unprecedented fame and popularity, yet, given his wife's continuing refusal to live in Paris, his home life was under tremendous strain. There seemed to be only two choices at this point: to allow his marriage to collapse, or to give up his career as a composer.

## Notes

1.  Giacomo Meyerbeer, *Briefwechsel und Tagebücher*, Heinz Becker, Gudrun Becker and Sabine Henze-Döhring (eds) (Berlin: Walter de Gruyter, 1960-2006), vol. 2, p.232.
2.  Thomas Forrest Kelly, *First Nights at the Opera* (New Haven, CT and London: Yale University Press, 2004), p.169.
3.  Louis Désiré Véron, *Mémoires d'un bourgeois de Paris* (Paris: Librairie Nouvelle, 1857), vol. 3, p.234.
4.  Meyerbeer, *Briefwechsel und Tagebücher*, vol. 2, p.492.
5.  Ibid., p.494.
6.  Ibid., p.681 n 512,1.

7.    Heinrich Heine, *Säkularausgabe. Werke, Briefwechsel, Lebenszeugnisse* (Berlin and Paris: Akademie Verlag and Editions de CNRS, 1970-), vol. 7, pp.278 and 280.

8.    Meyerbeer, *Briefwechsel und Tagebücher*, vol. 2, p.513.

9.    Gerd Nauhaus (ed.), *The Marriage Diaries of Robert and Clara Schumann: from their Wedding Day through the Russia Trip*, Peter Ostwald (trans.) (Boston, MA: Northeastern University Press, 1993), p.31.

10.    *Neue Zeitschrift für Musik*, No. 19, 5 September 1837, pp.73-4.

11.    Meyerbeer, *Briefwechsel und Tagebücher*, vol. 4, pp.169-70.

12.    Giacomo Meyerbeer, *The Diaries of Giacomo Meyerbeer*, Robert Letellier (ed. and trans.) (Madison, NJ: Fairleigh Dickinson University Press, 1999-2004), vol. 3, p.22.

13.    Meyerbeer, *Briefwechsel und Tagebücher*, vol. 2, pp.511-12.

14.    Robert Letellier, *The Operas of Giacomo Meyerbeer* (Madison, NJ: Fairleigh Dickinson University Press, 2006), pp.150-1.

15.    Meyerbeer, *Briefwechsel und Tagebücher*, vol. 2, p.522.

16.    Ibid., p.549.

17.    Ibid., p.488.

18.    Ibid., pp.496 and 498.

19.    Ibid., p.401.

20.    Ibid., p.401.

21.    Ibid., p.549.

22.    Meyerbeer, *Briefwechsel und Tagebücher*, vol. 3, p.115.

23.    Ibid., p.691 n 177,2.

24.    Meyerbeer, *Diaries*, vol. 1, p.529.

25.    Meyerbeer, *Briefwechsel und Tagebücher*, vol. 2, p.452.

26.    Heine, *Säkularausgabe*, vol. 7, p.230.

27.    Ibid., p.278.

28.    Meyerbeer, *Briefwechsel und Tagebücher*, vol. 3, p.105.

29.    Ibid., p.163.

30.    Ibid., p.196.

31.    Meyerbeer, *Briefwechsel und Tagebücher*, vol. 2, p.543.

# 20

## Return to Berlin

In June 1840, a new director was appointed to the Paris Opéra. Léon Pillet's tenure would mark an almost decade-long break in Giacomo's successful relationship with Europe's premier opera house. In 1841-42, Giacomo began negotiating with the Opéra for the production of a major new work, called *Le Prophète* [The Prophet]. However, tensions quickly appeared between Giacomo and Pillet over the question of the casting for the premiere. Giacomo was not happy with Pillet's choices, but the director was not prepared to compromise. In particular, he wanted to secure the leading female role for his mistress, an ambitious mezzo-soprano called Rosine Stoltz, who had begun her career in Brussels, and had been engaged by the Paris Opéra in 1837.

*Le Prophète* [The Prophet] was darker and more sombre than its predecessors. The libretto was based on the history of the radical Protestant Anabaptist sect whose leaders took over the city of Munster in February 1534, driving out the Prince Bishop and declaring the city the 'New Jerusalem'. One of the leaders of the movement was a tailor from the Low Countries known as Jan or Jean of Leyden, who announced himself to be the successor of the Biblical King David.

Jean was crowned 'King of Jerusalem' in Munster, where his regime promoted polygamy, and imposed a form of communism on the population, declaring all property to be held in common. Jean's reign soon descended into chaos and debauchery, and the city was retaken by the Bishop of Munster's troops in June 1535. The Anabaptist leaders, including Jean, were tortured and executed, and their bodies were put into cages that were hung from the steeple of St Lambert's church. To this day, the cages can still be seen, although the human remains have been removed.

Scribe's libretto focused on a fictionalised version of the role of Jean of Leyden in the rebellion. Most unusually, one of the major characters in the opera was that of an elderly woman, Jean's mother, called Fidès in the libretto. The mother's role eclipses that of the other female lead, Jean's fiancée, Berthe. Jean leaves both women behind in Leyden when he leads the Anabaptists to Munster, but, in the central scene of his coronation as divine King in Munster cathedral, Fidès appears and recognises this 'son of God' as her own son. Jean realises that, if he acknowledges this old peasant woman as his mother, he will lose all credibility as a divine ruler, and he forces her to recant her claim publicly. In the apocalyptic finale, as Munster collapses in flames, and with Berthe already dead, Fidès reappears to join her son in death.

Giacomo had described the part of Fidès, which was written for a singer with a mezzo/contralto voice, as perhaps the most interesting role in the opera. It was crucial that the part was allotted to a singer he could work with, and one he felt was absolutely right for the role. He had told his Parisian agent and confidante Louis Gouin that the character of the mother was filled with 'maternal, religious and resigned love, always gentle, and with only one moment of strong energy, in the finale of the 4th act'.[1]

Giacomo felt that Rosine Stoltz, who had a powerful character and a strong mezzo-soprano voice to match, was unsuited to the part of the self-sacrificial mother figure. Pillet's refusal to back down, and Giacomo's equally determined refusal to agree to his choice of Stoltz, created an impasse. Pillet, who was anxious to acquire a new Meyerbeer work for the Opéra, continued to negotiate with Giacomo, but was unable to break the deadlock. Their difficulties became public knowledge; a Parisian newspaper reported in February 1842 that Meyerbeer was withholding the work from the Opéra, and would wait for better times to stage it.

The 'better times' would not come until Pillet's departure from the Opéra in 1847. In the meantime, however, an event had occurred in Berlin that was to change the direction of Giacomo's life. In June 1840, shortly after Pillet's appointment as director of the Opéra, Frederick William III of Prussia had died, and was succeeded by his son, the 45-year-old Frederick William IV. The accession of the new King was greeted with enthusiasm in Prussia. Frederick William was widely believed to hold more liberal views than his father, whose solemn promise to create a constitution for Prussia, which he had made in 1815 at the end of the Wars of Liberation, had never been carried out.

However, in the long run, the new King would prove to be a disappointment to the liberals: he was a highly emotional and, in many ways, impractical man, whose views were heavily influenced by his religious faith. He had a Romantic ideal of Germany as the saviour of a reawakened Christendom in Europe, and a belief in the validity of medieval concepts of kingship, which he imagined he could reinvent for the modern day. The new King was drawn to the traditional Prussian concept of the exercise of paternalistic authority through the provincial 'estates' or corporate bodies, who owed personal loyalty to the monarch, and he made it clear on his accession that he had no intention of granting a constitution.

Frederick William's attitude to the Jews was influenced by these ideas. In a cabinet order of 1841, shortly after he had become King, Frederick William asserted that Jews should always be tolerated in Prussia. At the same time, however, he proposed a return to the idea of the Jews as a separate caste or national group, suggesting that this would demonstrate respect for the uniqueness of Jewish history. This plan, which included the reintroduction of a ban on Jews serving in the military, provoked strong protest not just from the Jewish population, but also from the government and from the provincial administrations. The proposals, which never became law, were widely seen as a return to the old days of segregation, and were a sign that the King was out of step with contemporary political and social thought.

Frederick William's Jewish proposals were a sign of his conservatism, and not neccessarily an expression of personal prejudice; he was on the friendliest of terms with the Beer family, probably because he had known them since the days when he and his younger brother, Prince William, had shared their piano tutor, Franz Lauska, with Giacomo. Both of the princes had maintained a positive attitude towards the Beers into their adult lives. Frederick William had retained a particular liking and respect for Amalia, describing her to Alexander von Humboldt as 'a wonderful woman, incomparable!'[2] Prince William, the future German Emperor, was also fond of Amalia, assuring Giacomo that 'we all value and love this worthy woman.'[3]

When Giacomo had visited Berlin in Frederick William III's reign, he had been routinely invited to dine both with the Crown Prince, and with Prince William. In 1837, while in Berlin, he had written to Minna in Baden-Baden, describing a particularly auspicious day, when he had dined at midday with the Crown Prince, his wife Princess Elisabeth, and Princess Augusta, Prince William's wife, all of whom had behaved in a very friendly manner towards him. Princess Augusta, who, as he told Minna, was an admirer of his music, had invited him to tea and supper that same evening, along with the Crown Prince, and Prince Carl. Despite this flattering attention from the younger royals, Giacomo was piqued that 'the *King*, however, has taken no notice of my stay here.'[4]

In autumn 1841, a little over a year after the accession of Frederick William IV, Giacomo was in Berlin on family business affairs. Minna was pregnant again, and Giacomo had decided that he would remain in Berlin with her until the birth, which was expected in the early summer of 1842.

There was no pressing reason for him to return to Paris, given the situation with the Opéra, and, in addition, Amalia was anxious to have him in Berlin, as Heinrich was again causing problems for the family. Giacomo had confided in Louis Gouin in July 1841 that,

> My second brother Henri (who you don't know), who has already caused my mother a good deal of grief, is now up to something that is likely to kill her. He wants to divorce his wife, who is a respectable and dignified woman, in order to marry a person who I don't know, but of whom my mother has said that it would be a misfortune if she were to come into our family.[5]

Given Heinrich's passion for the theatre, it is possible that the woman in question was an actress. Amalia, who, according to Giacomo, was crying all day and unable to sleep at night, had begged Giacomo not to leave Berlin before effecting a reconciliation between Heinrich and Betty.

Heinrich was closer to Giacomo than he was to Wilhelm. During the period of Heinrich's involvement in the dubious business proceedings that had led to his being put under guardianship, he had rather pathetically written to Giacomo to say that, 'I have never done you any harm; I am, and remain, your brother.'[6] Nonetheless, Giacomo felt that bringing Heinrich and Betty together again would be a difficult, if not an impossible, task, given that they had been living apart for some time, and there was a long history of bad feeling on both sides. In another letter to Gouin a week or so later, Giacomo repeated his belief that, if the projected divorce were to come about, it would kill his mother.

Giacomo was not as reluctant to remain in Berlin as he would have been a few years previously, however. In common with many Prussians, he felt at the time that the accession of the new King was ushering in a more tolerant and progressive era. His eager comments in a letter to Heinrich Heine, who was in Paris, on the new atmosphere in Berlin are in sharp contrast to his usually pessimistic and bitter views on Prussia: 'You would not believe what a complete turnaround there is here, what new vitality has appeared in social and intellectual life since the accession of this intelligent and truly humane King; and how many formerly harsh judgements about people and things have disappeared and are continuing to vanish.'[7]

Giacomo's extended visit to Berlin also coincided with a major change in Berlin's artistic life: the end of the twenty-year tenure of Gaspare Spontini as General Music Director to the Court. Spontini had been Frederick William III's favourite composer, and could do no wrong in the old King's eyes. Frederick William IV preferred German opera, and as Crown Prince, he had been disappointed when his father had appointed the Italian composer to the post. Spontini was not a conciliatory man by nature, and by the beginning of the 1840s, he was engaged in a bitter power struggle with Count von Redern, the Director of the Royal Theatres. In the course of this rivalry, Spontini was unwise enough to publish an article in the Leipzig papers in which he appeared to suggest that the late King had failed in some of his contractual obligations towards him.

Spontini was not popular with the Berlin public – there was an element of xenophobia in their dislike of him – and they strongly resented this article. Feelings ran so high that von Redern advised Spontini not to appear in the opera house to conduct a performance of Mozart's *Don Giovanni* in April 1841. Spontini ignored this advice, a decision which, predictably, resulted in disaster for him. The audience began heckling as soon as he appeared on the conductor's podium, and the uproar became so uncontrollable that the performance had to be halted. This was not the end of Spontini's humiliation, however, as he was charged with *lèse majesté* for insulting the late King, and sentenced to nine months imprisonment. Frederick William had no option but to suspend him from his post, and Spontini, having lodged an appeal against his sentence, left Berlin in a hurry.

Giacomo, although he did not get on with Spontini personally, was not impressed with the Berlin public's treatment of a fellow composer:

> This terrible outbreak of public rage en masse against a defenceless individual, and particularly as this individual is a great and rightly famous artist, and on top of that a foreigner, seems to me to overstep all authority of the theatre public, which only has a right to exercise its powers of judgement on art works and artistic trends, and never on the person and the private relationships of the artist.[8]

It is extremely unlikely that Spontini would have defended Giacomo in the same way if the positions had been reversed, and Giacomo knew it. In a letter to Louis Gouin later that year, after Spontini had gone to Paris, he referred to 'the rage and the hatred that he nourishes towards me', and warned Gouin that 'we must expect that he will spread all sorts of calumnies and lies about me.'[9]

The rest of the Beer family were equally well aware of Spontini's feelings towards Giacomo. Amalia had told Giacomo that it had infuriated Spontini that, whenever foreign royalty visited Berlin, there was a command performance of *Robert le Diable* at the Opera, and the house was always packed.[10] Years previously, Michael had warned his Bavarian friend Eduard von Schenk against becoming personally acquainted with Spontini, after Schenk had expressed interest in meeting the composer following a successful production of his *La Vestale* in Munich. Michael had told Schenk that 'anything Spontini says about my brother Meyerbeer can be trusted less than Christ could trust Judas, who betrayed the saviour for thirty pieces of silver, whereas Spontini would betray Meyerbeer for half of that, and probably just for the sheer pleasure of it'.[11]

Frederick William IV had been annoyed by the public disorder in the opera house, and was inclined to blame von Redern and the police department for not doing more to prevent it. He behaved generously towards Spontini, giving him a full pardon for the offence of *lèse majesté*, and offering him a farewell package that included a substantial pension. Spontini accepted, but then, having thought about it, demanded a further payment of nearly 50,000 thalers. The King's response was to refer the matter to the courts.

Spontini withdrew the demand, but his fate as General Music Director was, in any case, sealed. Frederick William, prompted by von Redern and Alexander von Humboldt, had already decided on Spontini's successor by autumn 1841. Giacomo recorded in his diary on 5 November that Count von Redern had suggested to him that the post might be offered to him, and had sounded him out as to whether he would accept. For Giacomo, the acceptance of this prominent position in Berlin would solve a number of problems. It would allow him to put some distance between himself and Paris, where relations with the opera house had become strained. It would also delight the two women closest to him – his wife and his mother. If he was able to work in Berlin rather than in Paris, even for a limited period of time, it would give him the chance to recover the closeness of his marriage.

Events moved swiftly in early summer 1842. Frederick William, when he had been Crown Prince, had expressed surprise to Giacomo that *Les Huguenots* had been banned in Berlin, and had told him that he had a strong desire to see the work staged there. He was as good as his word: once he was King, the ban on *Les Huguenots* was lifted, and the opera was produced in Berlin on 20 May to great acclaim. On 31 May, Giacomo was appointed a founding member of a new Order which Frederick William had instituted. A civilian version of the old military Prussian order of *Pour le mérite*, the order would be awarded to men who had distinguished themselves in the arts and sciences. It would be open to both Prussian and foreign candidates.

Alexander von Humboldt had been appointed as Chancellor of the Order, and was advising the King on the choice of founding members. The candidates included both Giacomo and Felix Mendelssohn. It appears that the King, despite his friendliness towards the Beer family, was hesitant about including Giacomo in the list, as he was worried that his late father, Frederick William III, might not have approved. Von Humboldt was insistent, telling the King that,

> you must not overlook Meyerbeer ... If you name only Felix Mendelssohn, the Christian, you will stir up a major controversy. You cannot be deterred by any feeling of piety towards your late father, who was universally respected. No one thought ill of him, as he was brought up in a different era, whereas you belong to the modern world ... [and besides] Meyerbeer's mother made the most noble sacrifices for Christians in our hour of need.[12]

The King listened to Humboldt's advice: Giacomo was among the first musicians to receive the honour, along with Mendelssohn, Lizst and Rossini. Other early members included the English scientist Michael Faraday and the French neo-classical artist Jean-Auguste-Dominique Ingres. The King did not, it appears, hold a grudge against Spontini, who was also awarded the *Pour le mérite*, but not until the next year – once he was safely out of Berlin for good.

On 11 June 1842 – a week after Minna had given birth to their third daughter, named Cornelie – Alexander von Humboldt sent a cryptic note to Giacomo saying that 'Your affair – ours – is now completed and signed! Today! Tell no one, as usual.'[13] Later that day, Frederick William issued a cabinet order appointing Giacomo as Spontini's successor in the post of General Music Director to the Berlin Court. This was both a singular honour for Giacomo as an individual, and a landmark in Prussian-Jewish relations. The contract was generous: the King stipulated that six months of the year were to be spent in Berlin, which would give Giacomo time away from his duties to concentrate on composition, and on the production of his works in other opera houses. During the first two years of his tenure, this six-month period would be shortened to four months, to allow for existing obligations.

Giacomo would be in charge of court music, and the production of operas and other musical entertainments. To his dismay, however, Felix Mendelssohn was appointed Director of Church Music to the Court, which was considered an inappropriate role for a Jew. Mendelssohn was, of course,

Giacomo Meyerbeer c. 1840

a convert, but although his parents had had him baptised for pragmatic reasons, he had grown up a devout Lutheran. However, personal relations between the two composers had by this time deteriorated to such a degree, that Giacomo described Mendelssohn as his worst enemy. The previous year, he had gone to the lengths of leaving Berlin to avoid attending a banquet at which Mendelssohn would also be present.

Mendelssohn disliked Giacomo's works. He had seen *Robert le Diable* in Paris in 1831, and had described the opera as cold and heartless, lacking any warmth or truth. He had added that if this was the kind of thing the public wanted, then he would rather dedicate himself to church music.[14] Felix's dislike of *Robert* was perhaps not surprising, as his taste in music was generally conservative. He was a great admirer of Bach, who had fallen out of fashion in Germany in the later eighteenth century, but whose legacy had been preserved by the Berlin Sing-Akademie. Mendelssohn's staging of the *St Matthew Passion* in Berlin in 1829 was a milestone, and had marked the beginning of a resurgence of interest in Bach's works.

Giacomo was not the only target of Felix Mendelssohn's criticism – he called Rossini a windbag, and described Liszt as having a lot of fingers but no brain – but his most bitter and most personal invective was aimed at Giacomo. There was really no need for rivalry, as the two men were composing in different fields. However, although Mendelssohn had enjoyed enormous success with his orchestral works and oratorios, he had ambitions to compose a successful opera. Not long after Giacomo's first real international triumph, with *Il Crociato*, Mendelssohn had staged his first opera, *Die Hochzeit des Camacho* [Camacho's Wedding], based on a story from Cervantes' *Don Quixote*, in Berlin in 1827.

It had been a failure, and Felix had left the theatre before the end of the opera. The planned second performance had been cancelled. It must have been a shattering blow to a young man used to hearing himself described as a musical genius, and having his every work praised to the skies. Felix had been a child prodigy, whom Goethe, among others, had compared to the young Mozart. Giacomo and Minna, with more than a tinge of malice, sometimes referred to Felix as 'Camacho' in their letters.

Giacomo certainly did not relish the prospect of Felix producing a successful opera; in January 1842, he noted in his diary that he had heard the news from Paris, in confidence, that Mendelssohn, 'the most dangerous and intriguing of my enemies, who hates me to death', had obtained a libretto from Scribe for a five-act opera, and had secured a contract with the Paris Opéra.[15] The proposed opera was never written, however, and the subjects that Scribe had offered Mendelssohn were eventually set to music by other composers. Given their mutual antipathy, it was fortunate that Giacomo and Felix did not need to work directly with one another in Berlin.

Following the announcement of his appointment, Giacomo returned to Paris for a few months, before moving to Berlin to take up his duties at the end of 1842. His departure from Paris was reported in all the French newspapers, and he was seen off by a group of friends and admirers, including Frédéric Chopin and Gaetano Donizetti, along with the inevitable Heinrich Heine. Giacomo's new duties in Berlin included organising and supervising concerts at court, many of which starred guest musicians such as Franz Liszt and Hector Berlioz.

Somewhat ironically, given the bad feeling that Wilhelm Beer had stirred up a few years earlier in his efforts to obtain a Prussian order for his friend Schumacher, Giacomo was instrumental in obtaining the Order of the Red Eagle for Berlioz, through Alexander von Humboldt's good offices. Giacomo noted in his diary in June 1847, when Berlioz was in Berlin for a court performance of his new work *La Damnation de Faust*, that he had passed on Berlioz's wish to be awarded the Order of the Red Eagle to von Humboldt, who had promised to speak to the King about it. The next day, Humboldt told Giacomo that the King had granted Berlioz the Order of the Red Eagle 3rd Class.

In his role as General Music Director, Giacomo was responsible for composing small works for special occasions at court, such as the 'torch dances' that were traditionally held to celebrate royal betrothals and marriages. His first torch dance was composed for the marriage of Princess Marie to the Crown Prince of Bavaria, Ludwig I's son Max, in autumn 1842. Marie was the daughter of Amalia's old friend Princess Marianne, and Amalia had written to congratulate Marianne on her daughter's engagement.[16]

Giacomo's major court composition in his first years as General Music Director was a masque, *Das Hoffest von Ferrara*, which was performed at a palace masked ball in February 1843. The King awarded Giacomo the Prussian Gold Medal for Arts and Sciences for this composition – the same medal that Wilhelm had received for his scientific achievements in 1836.

Giacomo was also responsible for the supervision of the Berlin Opera. He took his duties very seriously, and worked conscientiously to advance the interests of his fellow musicians during his period in office, using his position to improve their pay. The long letter he wrote to the Minister of the Royal Household, Prince Sayn-Wittgenstein, petitioning for a raise in the orchestra members' salaries, was detailed and well researched. He argued his case passionately, telling the minister that in his opinion there was both a moral and an artistic imperative to improve the musicians' pay.[17] He also made a personal contribution by distributing his own salary among them.

Giacomo also worked to improve the position of his fellow composers, arranging for the Royal Opera to pay composers ten percent of receipts from performances, and for three new compositions by living German composers to be produced each year. As soon as this latter had been agreed by the King, Giacomo invited his old friend Louis Spohr to Berlin to stage his latest opera, *Die Kreuzfahrer* [The Crusaders], and held a banquet for Spohr after the performance.

In August 1843, less than a year after Giacomo had taken up his post, the musical life of Berlin suffered a serious blow when the Opera House burnt down. Theatres were prone to catching fire: the Fenice in Venice had been destroyed in a blaze in 1836, and the Théâtre Italien in Paris had met the same fate in 1838 – the theatre's administrator, Carlo Severini, had died jumping from a window to escape the flames. Gas lighting was a major cause of fire. Ballerinas were especially vulnerable, as their gauze skirts could easily go up in flames if their dancing took them too near the footlights. The year after the Berlin Opera had burnt down, the English dancer Clara Webster died as a result of burns sustained when her dress caught fire from a gas jet on the stage of the Drury Lane Theatre. Safety did not seem to improve much over the century, as perhaps the worst fire in theatre history took place in 1877, when the Opéra-Comique in Paris burnt down, with the loss of over eighty lives.

Fortunately, no one died in the fire at the Berlin Opera, which began after the evening's performance on 18 August 1843. There had been a mock gunfight in the ballet that evening, and it is likely that a piece of smouldering material from this scene began the fire. By 11 o' clock, the whole building was ablaze. The fire, which could be seen for miles around, was eventually extinguished by the combined efforts of the army and the fire brigade, but the iconic building, created a century previously by Frederick the Great, had been reduced to a smouldering heap of rubble and ashes. Frederick William IV ordered the Opera to be reconstructed immediately by the architect Carl Ferdinand Langhans, to a design that restored the building's original appearance.

While the Opera was being rebuilt, performances continued in the Royal Playhouse on the Gendarmenmarkt square. One of the operas staged there, in January 1844, was a work by a young German composer who had become a protégé of Giacomo's. Richard Wagner's *Der fliegende Holländer* [The Flying Dutchman] was his fourth opera, but it would be the first to achieve a major success. Giacomo had known Wagner since 1837, when Wagner had written to him from the East Prussian capital of Königsberg, introducing himself as a struggling young composer, and asking for Giacomo's assistance. At the time, Wagner had already composed two operas, *Die Feen* [The Fairies] and *Das Liebesverbot* [The Love Ban], the latter based on Shakespeare's *Measure for Measure* – but with little success. He was unhappy in East Prussia, which he described as an inhospitable and insignificant place, and hoped that Giacomo would help him to stage his operas in Paris.[18]

Giacomo had replied to the letter, although by the time he did so, Wagner had left Königsberg. Giacomo had no further contact with Wagner until the summer of 1839, when Wagner and his wife Minna had appeared in Boulogne, where Giacomo spent part of the summer with Amalia every year. Wagner had brought two completed acts of his new opera *Rienzi* with him, which he played to Giacomo, who was favourably impressed. Wagner and his wife moved to Paris in October, where he began bombarding Giacomo with long and impassioned letters pleading for his assistance, both in staging his operas, and in lending him money.

Wagner's letters reached bizarre heights of flattery; he assured Giacomo that 'my head and my heart are no longer my own, they belong to you, my master, I have only my hands – will you use them? – I know I must become your slave in mind and body'. He signed one letter as 'your belonging' and another as 'your subject, forever bound to you with heart and blood'. These high-flown passages and protestations of humility and gratitude contrast rather oddly with an overweening confidence in his own future success: 'one day, when, as I have no doubt, I will have become amazingly famous …'[19]

Wagner was, of course, correct in predicting his future fame as a great composer, but at the time that Giacomo received the letters, his correspondent was not the demigod of Bayreuth, the creator of the great *Ring* cycle, but merely an unknown young man, whose letters might have seemed the ravings of a madman to their recipient. Giacomo might, understandably, have ignored them, but he saw something in Wagner and his music, telling his confidante Louis Gouin that, 'this young man interests me, he has talent and passion, but fortune is not smiling on him'.[20]

He did his best to assist Wagner, by introducing him to people who could help him, including both the director and the conductor of the Opéra, and by recommending his work to several Parisian theatres. He tried to interest the director of the Renaissance Theatre, Antenor Joly, in *Das Liebesverbot*, on several occasions taking Wagner to meet Joly, who at first appeared interested in staging the work, but the negotiations then faltered. Wagner appeared to believe that Giacomo could command Joly to accept the work, begging him to 'have pity on me, send the wicked Antenor a letter, a sort of ukase or papal bull'.[21] Giacomo, who was away from Paris, charged Gouin with furthering the discussions with Joly, but the Renaissance theatre went into bankruptcy, dashing Wagner's hopes.

In reality, as a complete unknown, Wagner had little chance of breaking into the operatic world in Paris, and his expectations at this time were unrealistically high. Giacomo had served an eight-year apprenticeship in Italy, and had been recognised as a major composer, before attempting to stage a work in Paris, and, even then, he had waited for an invitation to bring an opera to the French capital. Although he found Wagner's work interesting, and took pains to introduce him to the notice of useful people, it was hardly surprising that he was not successful in interesting Parisian theatres in staging the early operas of a young German composer who had no track record of success.

Giacomo did, however, play a part in launching Wagner's career in their homeland. In March 1841, he recommended Wagner's third opera, *Rienzi*, to the Dresden Court Opera, describing the work to the opera's director as 'rich in imagination and of great dramatic effect'.[22] *Rienzi* was premiered in Dresden on 20 October 1842. It was Wagner's first success, and marked a major change for the better in his life; he moved to Dresden that year, and was appointed Royal Saxon Court Conductor in 1843, giving him a measure of financial security.

Giacomo also recommended Wagner's fourth opera, *Der fliegende Holländer*, to Count von Redern in Berlin. Giacomo sent von Redern the libretto and score, telling him that, given Wagner's talent and his extremely difficult circumstances, he 'doubly deserves that the major court theatres, as official protectors of German art, do not close their doors to him'.[23] As the leading opera composer of the time, Meyerbeer's recommendations undoubtedly carried enormous weight. *Der fliegende Holländer*, which was premiered in Dresden in January 1843, was staged in Berlin on 7 January 1844. The day after the Berlin performance, Giacomo hosted a dinner for Wagner. At this stage in his life, Wagner still appeared to be grateful to Giacomo for his efforts, calling him 'my revered patron' and describing himself as 'your most sincere pupil and servant'.[24]

Giacomo had himself composed a new work that year for the Berlin stage. The Royal Opera house was due to re-open in December 1844, and the King had asked his music director to produce a festal opera for the occasion. This work, a patriotic German-language *Singspiel* called *Ein Feldlager in Schlesien* [An Army Camp in Silesia], would be the only new opera by Giacomo to appear between the premieres of *Les Huguenots* in 1836 and *Le Prophète* in 1849.

The libretto was based on an incident in the life of Frederick the Great during the Seven Years' War. The text was originally written in French by Scribe, but that fact was never made public, for fear of alienating the nationalistic German audiences, and the libretto was ascribed to the Berlin music journalist Ludwig Rellstab, who, in fact, only translated it into German. This was financially advantageous for Rellstab, who received the royalties for performances of the work in German-speaking countries, but Scribe did not lose out, as Giacomo compensated him for his losses.

The characters included a gypsy girl, Vielka, and King Frederick the Great, who could not be seen on stage, however – his presence was signalled by the sound of a flute being played off-stage. The soprano role of Vielka was shared between Leopoldine Tuczek, who had moved to Berlin from Vienna in 1841, and a new young star, Jenny Lind, who had enjoyed great success in the role of Alice in *Robert le Diable* in her native Sweden. Giacomo had invited Lind to Berlin to take up the role, feeling that she would be a great acquisition for the Berlin Opera. While acknowledging her talent, and exerting himself to work closely with her on her role, Giacomo did not appear to particularly like the singer. He described her to his mother as being as 'stiff and pretentious' in her behaviour as Henriette Sontag was 'loveable and natural'.[25]

The premiere took place on 7 December 1844. Tuczek sang the part of Vielka in the first three performances, then alternated with Lind, who sang the role six times. The King was delighted with the success of the opera, which became very popular in Berlin, where it was performed sixty-five times before the end of the century. The second act, which depicted scenes of military life at the Prussian army camp in Silesia, was frequently played on its own at royal gala occasions. The opera was still so popular in Prussia in 1850, six years after its premiere, that a special excursion train was laid on from Magdeburg to Berlin, to ferry people to the capital for a performance of *Ein Feldlager*. The work was never published, however, and it remained a local success with limited appeal.

## Notes

1.  Giacomo Meyerbeer, *Briefwechsel und Tagebücher*, Heinz Becker, Gudrun Becker and Sabine Henze-Döhring (eds) (Berlin: Walter de Gruyter, 1960-2006), vol. 3, p.311.
2.  Ibid., p.719 n 329,1.
3.  Meyerbeer, *Briefwechsel und Tagebücher* vol. 2, p.321.
4.  Meyerbeer, *Briefwechsel und Tagebücher*, vol. 3, p.59.
5.  Ibid., p.354.
6.  Ibid., p.39.
7.  Ibid., p.368.
8.  Ibid., p.345.
9.  Ibid., p.364.
10. Meyerbeer, *Briefwechsel und Tagebücher* vol. 2, p.462.
11. Unpublished letter, Michael Beer to Eduard von Schenk, 14 November 1827, Bavarian State Library Munich, Schenkiana II.12.Beer, Michael.
12. Ulrike Leitner (ed.), *Alexander von Humboldt / Friedrich Wilhelm IV. Briefwechsel* (Berlin: Walter de Gruyter, 2013), p.217.
13. Meyerbeer, *Briefwechsel und Tagebücher*, vol. 3, p.406.
14. Meyerbeer, *Briefwechsel und Tagebücher*, vol. 2, p. 622 n 160,2; Felix Mendelssohn Bartholdy, *Sämtliche Briefe*, Helmut Loos and Wilhelm Seidel (eds) (Kassel: Bärenreiter, 2008-17), vol. 2, p.458.

15. Meyerbeer, *Briefwechsel und Tagebücher*, vol. 3, p.392.

16. Unpublished letter, Amalia Beer to Princess Marianne of Prussia, 29 December 1821, Fischbacher Archive, D 22 Nr. 23/26, Hessische Staatsarchiv, Darmstadt.

17. Meyerbeer, *Briefwechsel und Tagebücher*, vol. 3, pp.438-41.

18. Ibid., pp.25-8.

19. Ibid., pp.261, 262, 241, 229.

20. Ibid., p.281.

21. Ibid., pp.230-1.

22. Ibid., p.341.

23. Ibid., pp.386-7.

24. Ibid., pp.382, 388.

25. Meyerbeer, *Briefwechsel und Tagebücher*, vol. 5, p.29.

# 21

## The 'Queen Mother'

Giacomo's return to Berlin as General Music Director had been a public honour, but as far as his private affairs were concerned, his attempts to reconcile Heinrich and Betty, as he had expected, proved fruitless. The couple had been at odds for too long to make up their differences and resume a life together. When Betty had married Heinrich in 1818, she had followed her head rather than her heart, making what she had thought to be a sensible choice that would guarantee her a carefree and materially comfortable life. She had been aware that much would depend on her ability to manage her volatile young husband, and had thought that she was capable of doing so. She could not have foreseen that Heinrich's instability would spiral out of control after the death of their only child.

This tragedy had ended any hopes Betty might still have harboured of making their marriage work. In an effort to alleviate her overwhelming grief, she had immersed herself in charitable work. In early 1833, just eighteen months after Ludwig's death, Betty had joined the management team of a new Jewish orphanage in Berlin, the Baruch Auerbach Institute. Auerbach was a teacher, and a member of the forward-looking Society of Friends. His brother, Isaac, had been one of the lay preachers at the Beer Temple back in 1817.

Baruch Auerbach believed that the existing institutions for orphaned children fell short of meeting all their needs. Unusually for the time, he took the children's emotional, as well as their physical, wellbeing into consideration: 'Orphans are not just poor children who need only to be given shelter and bread, but parentless children, who above all need parental love, a father's and mother's heart.'[1] The Institute's statutes included the statement that one of the main aims of the orphanage was to 'replace [the children's] lost parents, or to minimise that loss as far as is possible'.[2]

Auerbach was aware that this could not be achieved entirely successfully in an institution, but he felt that the orphanage could supply a degree of maternal care by including among its staff a group of volunteer 'honorary mothers'. Each of these women would take a small number of boys under her personal charge, supervising their welfare and providing them with clothing, linen, and bedding. Each 'mother' was expected to be present at the main midday meal for at least one day a week, to oversee the standards of the food, which, as specified in the statutes, was to be 'nourishing, tasty, and generously apportioned, in brief, as it would be in a decent middle-class family'.[3] The women were also expected to take an active part in the running of the orphanage, by holding their own regular conferences, and by attending board meetings every six months.

Auerbach's orphanage, which was a private establishment, encountered some resistance from the Berlin Jewish communal authorities, who saw it as a rival to a project of their own. They had been planning since 1829 to found an orphanage in memory of the philosopher Moses Mendelssohn, but they had not raised all the necessary funds by the time the Auerbach orphanage was opened on 3 April 1833. Wilhelm Beer had not thought the Mendelssohn orphanage worth supporting, advising Giacomo that, 'I'm of the opinion we shouldn't give a red cent to it, the whole idea is totally impractical.'[4]

The initial group of nine honorary mothers at the Auerbach Institute was headed by the elderly Sara Levy, Felix Mendelssohn's great-aunt, and included Betty Beer as a founding member. In addition to her duties as an honorary mother, Betty took on an administrative role: Auerbach described her as 'our excellent secretary' in the Institute's first annual report, published in 1834.[5] She also raised money to support the Institute from among her family and friends; one of the first gifts had been given by Amalia in memory of Michael. Every year on the anniversary of Michael's death, a special thanksgiving service was held at the orphanage. Heinrich had also agreed to support the Institute with an annual donation of thirty-six thalers.

Betty continued to work voluntarily for the orphanage for many years. Her commitment to it was clearly linked to Ludwig's memory, as she gave an annual party for the orphans on his birthday every March. Unusually for the Beer family, in this instance it was one of the daughters-in-law who led the way, and Amalia who followed. Early in the second year of the orphanage's existence, Sara Levy had suggested to Auerbach (perhaps prompted by Betty) that it would be advantageous to ask Amalia to join the group of honorary mothers, given her wide experience in charitable work. Amalia had hesitated at first, unwilling to take on a commitment that she felt she might not be able to fulfil, due to her bouts of ill health and frequent absences from Berlin.

Auerbach, keen to have the celebrated Madame Beer associated with his organisation, negotiated with her, offering her a position as an advisor, and assuring her that she would only be approached on important matters.

He added that this would not only be of great use to the Institute, it would be an honour. Amalia agreed to this, and by the end of the second year, the group of honorary mothers had been expanded to eleven women, including Amalia – who was annotated in the orphanage's list as 'Dame of the Order of Louise' – and both Betty and Doris Beer.[6]

The Auerbach Institute had a long and honourable history as a model orphanage. In 1844, a girls' section was founded. The boys' future was secured by giving them vocational training – many of them went on to work in science, the arts and business – and the girls were given decent dowries to enable them to marry respectably. The Institute survived until 1942, when the last orphans and their teachers were deported to the Riga ghetto.

Betty's interest in the orphanage may have provided her with some distraction from the unhappiness of her marriage. Up until the late 1830s, she and Heinrich had preserved a façade of unity. Presumably, however, Heinrich had left home when he had decided that he wanted to divorce Betty in 1841, as by the next year, the couple were living apart.

In late October 1842, Heinrich had a stroke while out walking in the street, and was carried unconscious to his lodgings. He had come down in the world by that time, as he was renting rooms in a tailor's house, and had little contact with his family. Nonetheless, when they heard the news, both Amalia and Betty hurried to his bedside. It is unclear whether Heinrich had been living in these lodgings with his mistress, but if so, it is highly unlikely that she would have been permitted to attend his sickbed while Amalia and Betty were there. They both remained with him day and night until he died a few days later, without regaining consciousness, at the age of 48.

Whatever their differences with Heinrich during his lifetime, the Beers were determined to observe the decencies with regard to his death. Amalia sent mourning cards to their friends announcing the family's 'inexpressible loss' – a phrase that annoyed Lea Mendelssohn, who thought it a bit rich in the circumstances. She commented that Heinrich's death had 'suddenly elevated him to an object of pity and regret'.[7] However, in death as well as in life, Heinrich was to prove a source of gossip for the Berlin public, and of embarrassment for his family: a rumour circulated in the city that in his will, he had left legacies to ten illegitimate children and a whole host of women.

This story was purely a figment of the popular imagination, although it seems that Heinrich may in fact have had an illegitimate child, presumably by the woman he had wanted to marry. There is a brief entry in Giacomo's diaries in the 1850s referring to 'maintenance' connected with Heinrich, but no further details are given.[8] Unfortunately, Heinrich's reputation did not fade from public memory as quickly as the Beer family would have liked: in 1846, four years after his death, an anonymous and scurrilous memoir of Heinrich's life went on sale in Berlin. The family consulted lawyers, but were told that there was nothing they could do to prevent the unknown author selling the booklet. Giacomo, who had retained an affection for his feckless younger brother, made a point of attending the annual memorial service for Heinrich that was held at the Auerbach Institute, and left a sum of money in his will to ensure that these services continued after his own death.

At the time of Heinrich's death, Lea Mendelssohn had commented caustically that the entire complement of Berlin's actors and actresses had turned out for his funeral, which she considered a fitting tribute, given that they had been the chief recipients both of his boundless admiration and his reckless spending. Lea had little sympathy for the Beers; she told her cousin in Vienna that Amalia was indeed shattered by grief, but that, in her opinion, Heinrich had been spoilt by an 'unwise' education and upbringing, and that Amalia's distress probably stemmed as much from feelings of guilt and self-reproach as from grief.[9]

One of the kindest condolence letters that Amalia received came from Heinrich Heine. Heine had despised Heinrich, and had, to say the least, mixed feelings towards Michael and Giacomo, but he had a genuine affection for Amalia, and understood that, whatever Heinrich's misdemeanours and deficiencies, he had been her son, and her grief for him was real:

> ... be assured, that no one shares every sorrow that afflicts you with deeper sympathy [than I do]. There can be no talk of comfort here – only fools offer comfort, and only people without hearts let themselves be comforted. I am not one of the former, and you are not one of the latter. Few people have such a rich and sensitive heart as you do ... I would like to be with you at this moment and silently kiss your hand.[10]

Heine calls Amalia by her family nickname of 'Nonne' in this letter, which suggests a close relationship between them.

In one of a series of essays he published in 1837, based on his letters to the writer August Lewald, Heine had remarked on Amalia's generosity, saying that he always sent anyone in need straight to her, knowing that she would help them.[11] Amalia was known throughout Berlin not just for her charitable work with institutions such as the women's associations and the Auerbach orphanage, but also for her inability to turn away anyone in real need. She was popularly nicknamed the 'Queen Mother' for her philanthropy, her unwavering devotion to her sons, and her lavish parties in the Tiergarten villa.

In the years since the Beers had acquired the villa in 1816, it had been developed into an appropriately magnificent setting for Amalia's salon. In 1824, during the 'golden summer' when both Giacomo and Michael had been at home, and Jacob had been happily occupied with the opening of the new Königstadt theatre, the Beers had built a grand concert hall in the villa's grounds. The pillared hall had been designed by Theodore Ottmer, who had been a pupil of the great architect and city planner, Karl Schinkel. Ottmer's first significant commission as a 21-year-old had been the Königstadt theatre.

He had designed the Beer's concert hall on similarly sumptuous lines: the interior was decorated in pink, white and gold, its mirrored walls reflecting back the candlelight from sparkling chandeliers. Lea thought the hall 'truly gorgeous' – noting that even the large stoves installed to heat it in winter were tastefully disguised as antique caryatids. The architect's designs had apparently been added to by Wilhelm, however, and the results of this did not please Lea: 'In short, everything designed by Ottmer is tasteful and beautiful; but as Wilhelm Beer adds his "I'm an architect too" contribution to all his parents' buildings, there is some patchwork and pastiche among it all.'[12]

Lea also admired the villa's gardens, where Amalia would entertain up to 250 people at grand *al fresco* dinners in the summer. Amalia's visits to Italy had inspired her to create a blaze of southern colour under the grey Berlin skies: groves of oak and cypress trees surrounded beds of exotic flowers and hothouses filled with orange and pomegranate trees. Lea thought the garden 'a real enchanted isle in the sandy Exerzierplatz!'[13]

Giacomo's Italian librettist, Gaetano Rossi, had sourced and sent Amalia many of the exotic plants she had sought for her garden: carnations, tuberoses, irises, and rare Egyptian arums. Rossi, who knew how to flatter, had assured Giacomo that he had sent a case of plants to Berlin addressed to 'Madame Amalia Beer, Dame of the Order of Louise of Prussia' – to make quite sure that it did not go astray.[14] There was a reminder of Amalia's special relationship with the royal family in the garden: she had placed the bust of Queen Louise, which Princess Marianne had presented to her, on a pedestal in a grove of cypress trees.

In 1845, the composer Louis Spohr's wife, Marianne, described a summer dinner party they attended in the 'magnificent park' of old

Madame Beer in the Tiergarten. The dinner, which consisted of 'over twenty courses of the finest and rarest food', was served in a garden pavilion. Marianne was seated between Giacomo and Alexander von Humboldt, and opposite Count von Redern and the British ambassador to Berlin, the Earl of Westmorland. The Earl and Countess of Westmorland, who were well known musicians and patrons of the arts, were close friends of Giacomo's. The conversation, according to Marianne Spohr, was lively 'in the Berlin style, full of jokes and wordplay'. After the sumptuous meal in the pavilion, coffee was served in the open air, where the guests could hear music floating across from the nearby Kroll's restaurant.[15]

This restaurant was part of a gigantic building complex that had been erected on the western edge of the Exerzierplatz, close to the Beers' villa, in 1844. Kroll's, as it was generally known after its owner, the restaurateur Joseph Kroll, could cater for up to 5,000 guests in its three main dining halls, while fourteen other rooms were available for smaller parties. The building also hosted exhibitions, balls and concerts: Giacomo and Wilhelm had attended a crowded masked ball at Kroll's in March 1844, shortly after its opening, and had watched the 'tumult' from the safety of a private box.[16] That same year, Count Atanazy Raczinsky, a Pole employed in the Prussian diplomatic service, had built a Renaissance-style palace on the eastern edge of the Exerzierplatz, opposite Kroll's. The once-deserted parade ground, which had been known to the Berliners as 'the Sahara' because of its dust and sand, had become a fashionable and attractive area for visitors and pleasure-seekers.

Prince Hermann von Pückler-Muskau – the man who had failed in his mission to find an English bride some decades earlier – was frequently in Berlin, and remarked that he preferred Amalia's entertainments to the more formal gatherings of the Prussian aristocracy, adding that, 'There is far more discernment, talent and knowledge to be found there, and also the food is better.'[17] The food would certainly have been of the highest standard – the Beers could afford the best of everything. However, Amalia's parties were distinguished not just by the wonderful food, the lovely setting and the well-known guests; other hostesses could provide those same ingredients, but Amalia's events were high points in the Berlin social round.

Lea Mendelssohn thought that wealth alone did not bestow the ability to become a really successful hostess; after all, Amalia's sisters came from the same privileged background that she did, but their parties never rose above the run-of-the-mill. Lea believed that the secret of Amalia's success lay in the simple fact that she enjoyed herself enormously at all her own social events, and genuinely wanted her guests to enjoy themselves too, and share her pleasure.[18]

Amalia's birthdays were especially festive, with carriages rumbling between the city and the villa all day, bringing friends and acquaintances to make congratulatory visits. There was always a private dinner for intimates of the family. The King himself took an interest in these occasions. On the day after Amalia's 74th birthday celebrations in 1841, Alexander von Humboldt wrote to Wilhelm Beer describing a conversation he had had with the King:

> I told him that evening that I (being almost a member, and half a fossil, of your family) had been invited ... He cried out: 'I should have known that earlier, then I could have tasked you with conveying my most sincere best wishes to Madame Beer. She is a wonderful woman, incomparable! ... Did the party go right up into the cupola, to the observatory?' [19]

Amalia's gatherings were not the only social events in the Tiergarten villa in the late 1830s and 1840s, however. Prior to Johann Mädler's leaving Berlin, Wilhelm had presided over astronomical conventions at the villa; the last of these was held in 1841.[20] Wilhelm also had his own salon, hosting gatherings on two evenings a week. According to the writer Adolph Streckfuss, 'An invitation to the Beer house was for many young scholars, artists and scientists a goal of the highest aspiration, for to be admitted into the intellectual circles that gathered there was as much an honour as a pleasure. The Beer house was thus hugely significant in the scientific development of the time.'[21]

An article in the *Zeitung für die elegante Welt* [Newspaper for the Elegant World] in September 1843[22] described Wilhelm's salon as 'one of the first in Berlin', where prominent people from the government, journalism, art, science and business gathered. The article went on, however, to criticize Wilhelm's events as being stiff and formal, lacking 'elasticity' and the artistic spirit: 'People eat well, drink well and aestheticise; the master of the house[23] opens his mouth wide – but no young lady asks, how so?' The implication seems to be that the salon is male-dominated, and that the women do not question the men's wisdom: 'The lady of the house is beautiful and the daughter charming, but the men are too occupied with their food, and when they have eaten, they make their bows and they go.'

The article emphasised the quiet modesty of the Meyerbeers' family life in comparison with Wilhelm's pretensions: 'At Meyerbeer's you forget he is rich, he is just a man and an artist ... there is nothing more comfortable than a family meal at Meyerbeer's...' It also commented on Minna Meyerbeer's dislike of Paris:

> Madame Meyerbeer undoubtedly possesses grace and modesty, but more than this, she has spirit, a very marked, independent spirit and character, and this character is so German ... that in Paris, where she had one of the first houses, and where ministers, poets, counts and dukes fought for a place, she was bored and had a continual homesickness for Germany.

The article's author was certainly right in surmising that the family's return to Berlin had been a welcome one for Minna, and that this had probably played a role in Giacomo's decision to accept the post of General Music Director. However, the move had not proved entirely beneficial for Giacomo in professional terms. Around the time of his appointment, the Beers' friend Count von Redern had been moved from his post of Director of the Royal Theatres, to become the superintendent of musical performances at court. Giacomo, with his twin responsibilities for court music and the Opera, would still be working for Redern in one capacity, but he would also be responsible to Redern's replacement as Director of the Royal Theatres, Theodor Küstner.

Giacomo had got on well with the courteous and diplomatic von Redern, who was familiar with procedures at the Prussian court, but he found Küstner, who had been a theatre director in Munich, a much more difficult man to deal with. There were faults on both sides. Küstner was keen to save money, and did not want to pay the high salaries demanded by the best singers, while Giacomo was not willing to compromise on the quality of the productions at the Opera.

These differences could perhaps have been managed if the two men had been able to collaborate, but their relationship deteriorated quickly to a point where neither trusted the other. Küstner was determined to show Giacomo who was in charge, and failed to treat him with the respect due to a world-famous composer. In response, Giacomo often went over Küstner's head to the King, using von Redern or Alexander von Humboldt, who both supported him, as intermediaries.

Küstner began to deliberately place obstacles in Giacomo's way, for example, deciding, at the last minute, to stage another opera shortly before the premiere of Giacomo's *Ein Feldlager in Schlesien*, thus upsetting Giacomo's rehearsal schedules, and not leaving him enough time for preparation. Giacomo found the situation so difficult that he tried to resign from his responsibilities towards the Opera several times, but the King would not release him. Frederick William understood his frustrations, however, telling Count Wittgenstein that, 'I have discovered that Meyerbeer, who is the gentlest, most conciliatory, mildest man in the world, has been driven to the limits of his forebearance and patience by the continual difficulties and complications created by Küstner ... Tell Küstner that I have investigated this matter thoroughly, and that his ill will [towards Meyerbeer] is obvious.'[24]

Despite his support for Giacomo, the King also wanted to retain Küstner, who was an able and experienced director. Various solutions were put forward, including that of separating the management of the spoken drama theatre from that of the Opera – as had been the situation prior to 1811, when the two institutions had been amalgamated under Iffland – and appointing a court employee as director of the Opera. Prince William became involved, telling Giacomo that it was 'a matter of national pride' to have him, with his well-deserved European fame, at the head of the Opera in Berlin.[25] Giacomo saw only too clearly, however, that these efforts to resolve his difficulties would merely serve to increase Küstner's determination to assert his authority, and to win what had, against Giacomo's will, become a personal power struggle.

In this situation, Giacomo's thoughts began turning to Paris. In his absence, the Opéra had gone into a state of decline; in 1845, the hugely influential music critic François-Joseph Fétis had told Giacomo that it was dead. A new Meyerbeer opera would revive its fortunes – and also raise Giacomo's profile in Paris. He had begun to worry that he would be forgotten by the fickle Parisian public unless he brought out another major work soon – the premiere of *Les Huguenots* was by this time nine years in the past.

Heinrich Heine had been assiduous in fanning the flames of Giacomo's habitual anxiety over the previous few years. Giacomo had noted in his diary in October 1841, 'A letter from Heine, who is again demanding money, and upset me about many other matters.'[26] Heine, who was well aware of Giacomo's fear of bad publicity, represented himself as a vigilant defender of Giacomo's reputation. He wrote to Giacomo in May 1842, claiming that he was protecting Giacomo's interests against the attacks of the Escudier brothers, the owners of the journal *La France musicale*.

One of Heine's long-term aims appeared to be to displace Louis Gouin as Giacomo's confidante in Paris. He commented that, 'Gouin, however much he might claim otherwise, has behaved without tact or delicacy. There really is something crudely offensive in his nature, and he even attacks me in a provocatively insolent manner that could annoy me if I didn't have your interests at heart.'[27] Heine did not appear to understand the depth of trust between the two men.

Heine also wrote to Giacomo in June 1844 to report on Spontini's activities. Giacomo had been right in suspecting that after Spontini had left Berlin under a cloud, he would attempt to spread lies about him in Paris. Spontini was, in fact, telling anyone who would listen to him that he had lost his position, and been driven out of Berlin, purely through the intrigues and malice of the Beer family. He was, according to Heine, gathering documents that would 'prove' this unfounded assertion, and was threatening to publish his story. Heine, as Paris correspondent for a number of German papers, told Giacomo that he had spiked the Italian's guns by reporting these ridiculous assertions in the press and making fun of them. His article had already appeared in the Augsburg daily papers in the previous month.

Although Heine represented this article as evidence of his loyal support of Giacomo, telling him that, 'this time, the press has reined in the press',[28] in reality, by publishing these stories he was giving them wider currency. In any case, the article did nothing to deter Spontini from his campaign to damage his successor. In early 1846, when he wrote to the Prussian King asking to come to Berlin to conduct a performance of his opera *La Vestale*, he finished his letter by arrogantly advising Frederick William to 'get rid of your wandering Jew'. According to Minna, the King was so incensed that he ordered a really rude letter to be drafted for him in response, and rejected the first two drafts as not being strong enough, before signing the third.[29]

The troubled relationship between Giacomo and Heinrich Heine began to turn irreversibly sour after the death of Heine's Uncle Salomon in 1844. Salomon had not specified in his will that the annuity he paid Heine should continue after his death, and his heir, Heine's cousin Carl, had consequently stopped the allowance. When Heine asked Giacomo to negotiate with Carl, Giacomo felt unable to involve himself any further in what was really a family affair, and declined.

Heine was insistent, however, and enlisted the help of his friend, the socialist and political activist Ferdinand Lassalle. He told Lassalle on 27 February 1846, 'Put the thumb screws on the bear [Bär = Beer]. Do whatever is necessary to make the bear dance to our tune. He must write a letter directly to Carl, in confidence, and not send it through me.'[30] Lassalle had already approached Giacomo, who had noted in his diary on 19 February:

Visit from Lassalle, who spoke to me in a flowery way, but under his very transparent allegory let me know that Heine is going to write articles against me. The real reason for this animosity is that before my departure from Paris I refused to loan him [Heine] the 1,000 francs he had demanded from me, after I have already lent him so many thousands in my life – and he has never, of course, repaid me a penny.[31]

In the end, Giacomo yielded to Lassalle's persuasion, and wrote a letter to Carl Heine in which he referred to Heinrich Heine as 'this great poetic genius ... of whom his German Fatherland is rightly so proud!'. Carl had replied angrily that 'I would rather Dr [Heinrich] Heine had less talent and a more honest character', adding that he had given Heine 4,000 francs at the beginning of that year, but was not prepared to restore the annuity, as Heine was threatening to smear Salomon's memory publicly.[32]

This outcome only served to stoke Heine's bitter feelings towards Giacomo, who took the precaution of asking Louis Gouin to keep a copy of his letter to Carl Heine, in case it was needed in the future to prove the truth of events. Giacomo told Gouin that, 'you have no idea what a dangerous enemy [Heinrich Heine] is, and what immense harm he can do'.[33]

Heine's desperation to regain his annuity may have been motivated in part by the onset of a serious illness. In his letter to Carl Heine, Giacomo had mentioned Heinrich's declining health. In August 1846, a false report of Heinrich Heine's death appeared in the newspapers, to which Giacomo responded in his diary: 'Peace be to his ashes! He was an old friend of mine, and only occasionally, when self-interest drove him to it, my enemy. But I think he had a fondness for me, as I had for him.'[34] Heine was not, in fact, dead yet, and would reappear in Giacomo's life.

Towards the end of 1846, Giacomo felt that he had to make a final decision as to his future in Berlin. The news, in June that year, that the King was considering founding a conservatoire, with Felix Mendelssohn at its head, had horrified him; he had commented that if that were to happen, he would have to leave. The situation with Küstner had still not been resolved, as it had been deemed too expensive and impractical to again split the spoken and musical theatres.

When Giacomo heard in mid-November that Küstner had been reconfirmed in his post, and that consequently the two men would have to continue working together, it was the last straw. He asked the King for an indefinite leave of absence, given that he felt that he could not, under the circumstances, guarantee an appropriately high standard of performance at the Opera. He was determined to resign his responsibilities for the Opera altogether, but he was willing to continue to compose and direct music for court occasions, as and when required. Frederick William finally, although reluctantly, agreed to this compromise solution.

Before Giacomo left Berlin, however, an opportunity arose for him to use his talents to fulfil an ambition of his mother's. Michael's 1827 drama *Struensee* had always been banned in Berlin, as it was forbidden to portray relatives of the royal family on the stage. In 1846, the censorship rules in this regard were relaxed. Coincidentally, the dramatist and editor of the *Zeitung für die elegante Welt*, Heinrich Laube, had recently written a play on the same subject, and with the same title, as Michael's, and, given the changed situation, Laube's *Struensee* was being considered for production in Berlin.

The Beer family were terrified that Laube's more recent drama would be preferred to Michael's older version, and Amalia lobbied von Humboldt to ensure that this did not happen. The King agreed that Michael's play should be staged ahead of Laube's, and asked Giacomo to write incidental music for it, which he composed over the summer of 1846. It consisted of an overture and eleven short pieces, which either accompanied the action, or served as entr'actes.

Frederick William could not be there himself for the premiere, which took place on 19 September 1846. Giacomo was nervous, as he had heard that Laube and his friends had been furious that his play had been rejected in favour of Michael's, and that they were planning some sort of noisy demonstration at the performance, but, to his great relief, this did not happen. The only inappropriate sounds were the chattering of the audience during the entr'actes, which irritated him.

Alexander von Humboldt was present, and visited Amalia – 'Madame mère', as he affectionately called her – in her box after the performance, where, deeply moved and tearful, she gave him a 'damp embrace'. Humboldt reported to the King that the play had been a brilliant success, and he commented almost ecstatically on Giacomo's music: 'At times it anticipates the action, at times accompanies it, gentle as a flower-scented breeze, then grim and harrowing, or gripping and suspenseful, heralding tragedy. Thoughts, speech and musical form coalesce organically, both brothers are one person.'[35]

Giacomo had produced a deeply moving score to accompany his brother's play. His incidental music for Michael's *Struensee* did not only delight their mother; it became his most popular piece of non-vocal music. The successful performance in Berlin also sparked a revival of the play, which, by the following summer, had been staged, with its accompanying music, in ten German cities, as well as in Prague and Budapest, and was being translated into Italian. Pleased though he was by these developments, Giacomo could not help being saddened by the fact that Michael had not lived to see 'all of Germany ... opening the doors of its theatres with such success to his wonderful *Struensee*'.[36]

The play found appreciation at the English court, where Prince Albert read it, and Queen Victoria requested to hear Giacomo's music to it in one of her court concerts. Victoria and Albert were admirers of Giacomo's music; when the Queen had visited Prussia in 1845, Giacomo had been responsible for organising the musical entertainments during her visit. She later chose him to compose the overture to the concert for the opening of the London International Exhibition in 1862.

Giacomo left Berlin in December 1846 for Vienna, where a revised version of *Ein Feldlager in Schlesien* was due to be staged, under the title of *Vielka*. He knew that, in its original, patriotic form, as a vehicle for the glorification of Frederick the Great and, through him, the Prussian Hohenzollern dynasty, the opera could never have succeeded in Austria, Prussia's rival in the German Federation, where any reminder of the Seven Years' War would not have been welcome.

In this revised version, Frederick was turned into an Austrian duke, and the character of Vielka took on far more importance. *Vielka* was performed at the Theater an der Wien in Vienna early the next year, with Jenny Lind in the title role. The opera was successful, but after fourteen performances in Vienna, Giacomo refused to give permission for any further productions, or to have the music published. *Ein Feldlager* had been commissioned by, and for, the Berlin court, and was too closely linked with Prussian patriotism to be suited to an international audience.

## Notes

1. *Monatsschrift für Geschichte und Wissenschaft des Judentums*, issue 8 (1856), p.318.
2. *Statuten des von Baruch Auerbach gegründeten jüdischen Waisen-Erziehungs-Institut zu Berlin* (Berlin, 1839), p.9.
3. Ibid., p.17.
4. Giacomo Meyerbeer, *Briefwechsel und Tagebücher*, Heinz Becker, Gudrun Becker and Sabine Henze-Döhring (eds) (Berlin: Walter de Gruyter, 1960-2006), vol. 2, p.95.
5. *Erster Jahresbericht über das Jüdische Waisen-Erziehungsinstitut zu Berlin* (Berlin: 1834), p.11.
6. *Zweiter Jahresbericht über das Jüdische Waisen-Erziehungsinstitut zu Berlin* (Berlin, 1835), pp.19, 22.

7. Lea Mendelssohn Bartholdy, *Ewig die deine. Briefe an Henriette von Pereira-Arnstein*, Wolfgang Dinglinger and Rudolf Elvers (eds) (Hannover: Wehrhahn Verlag, 2010), vol. 1, pp.531-2.
8. Meyerbeer, *Briefwechsel und Tagebücher*, vol. 6, p.55. The word used is *Alimente*, which means maintenance, usually in the case of an illegitimate child.
9. Lea Mendelssohn Bartholdy, *Ewig die deine*, vol. 1, p.531-2.
10. Heinrich Heine, *Säkularausgabe. Werke, Briefwechsel, Lebenszeugnisse* (Berlin and Paris: Akademie Verlag and Editions de CNRS, 1970-), vol. 22, p.35.
11. Heine, *Säkularausgabe*, vol. 7, p.276.
12. Lea Mendelssohn Bartholdy, *Ewig die deine*, vol. 1, pp.128-9.
13. Meyerbeer, *Briefwechsel und Tagebücher*, vol. 1, p.468.
14. Ibid., pp.462-5.
15. Walter Ederer, 'Louis Spohrs Besuche in Berlin' in Hartmut Becker and Reiner Krempien (eds), *Louis Spohr. Festschrift und Ausstellungskatalog zum 200. Geburtstag* (Kassel: Georg Wenderoth Verlag, 1984), p.84.
16. Meyerbeer, *Briefwechsel und Tagebücher*, vol. 3, p.495.
17. Emily Bilski and Emily Braun, *Jewish Women and Their Salons. The Power of Conversation* (New Haven, CT & London: Yale University Press, 2005), p.41; Werner Mosse, *The German-Jewish Economic Elite, 1820-1935: A Socio-cultural Profile* (Oxford: Oxford University Press, 1989), p.305.
18. Lea Mendelssohn Bartholdy, *Ewig die deine*, vol. 1, pp.103, 114.
19. Meyerbeer, *Briefwechsel und Tagebücher*, vol. 3, p.719 n. 329,1.
20. Unpublished, undated letter, Wilhelm Beer to Heinrich Schumacher, Staatsbibliothek zu Berlin, Preussischer Kulturbesitz, Nachlass Heinrich Christian Schumacher.
21. Heinz Becker, 'Die Beer'sche Villa im Tiergarten' in Hans J. Reichhardt (ed.), *Berlin in Geschichte und Gegenwart. Jahrbuch des Landesarchivs Berlin* (Berlin: Siedler Verlag, 1990), p.76.
22. *Zeitung für die elegante Welt*, No. 39, 27 September 1843, pp.949-50.
23. The writer uses the word 'Domherr' – Canon, literally 'Master of the Cathedral'. The words are a paraphrase of a verse from one of Heine's poems: The canon opens his mouth wide/Says love should not be too rough/or else it will damage the health/The young lady lisps 'How so?'.
24. Meyerbeer, *Briefwechsel und Tagebücher*, vol. 3, p.788 n. 548, 1.
25. Ibid., p.578.
26. Ibid., p.374.
27. Ibid., p.402.
28. Ibid., p.513.
29. Meyerbeer, *Briefwechsel und Tagebücher*, vol. 4, p.5.
30. Heine, *Säkularausgabe*, vol. 22, pp.207 ff.
31. Meyerbeer, *Briefwechsel und Tagebücher*, vol. 4, p.29.
32. Ibid., pp.74-5, 81-2.
33. Ibid., p.238.
34. Ibid., p.103.
35. Ibid., pp.535-6.
36. Meyerbeer, *Briefwechsel und Tagebücher*, vol. 5, p.127.

# 22

## Revolution and Reaction

In the early hours of 25 February 1848, the writer and politician Alphonse de Lamartine proclaimed France's Second Republic to cheering crowds from a balcony of the Hôtel de Ville, the old headquarters of the Paris Commune in the revolutionary days of 1792. The previous day, Louis-Philippe, the Citizen King, had abdicated and left Paris, bound for exile in Great Britain, where he would spend the rest of his life. The uprising that had ended his eighteen-year reign had been triggered by economic depression coupled with a widespread desire for a more democratic form of government. The cancellation of a political meeting in Paris in late February had sparked demonstrations that had spiralled rapidly into general disorder: the people flooded onto the streets in protest, and the regime fell within days.

Giacomo had been in Paris during the insurgency, and had been an eyewitness to these stirring events. He noted in his diary on 24 February:

> I spent nearly the whole day on the streets watching the progress of the uprising, which in the course of the day developed into a real revolution. At 2 o' clock, the King abdicated and the Tuileries was stormed by the people. I saw the most valuable furniture, books etc. being thrown out of the windows of the royal palace and then burned on a great bonfire in the palace courtyard. The royal carriage was set alight and pushed in flames through the street, and then also thrown onto the bonfire. It was the same in the Tuileries; I went into the rooms, where thousands of people were surging in and out.[1]

Giacomo commented that two of the ministers of the new provisional government, the lawyer Adolphe Crémieux, who had been appointed Minister of Justice, and Michel Goudchaux, the Minister of Finance, were Jews. Crémieux was a friend of Giacomo's, and a fellow freemason. Both belonged to the oldest of the French lodges, the 'Grand Orient de France'. Giacomo seldom expressed his political views, but as a freemason, he is unlikely to have been as deeply conservative as his brother Wilhelm, who had – as Wilhelm himself put it – an 'ultraloyalist heart'.[2]

The electrifying news of the successful February uprising in Paris spread rapidly throughout Europe, sparking demonstrations and rallies against the conservative order that had dominated the continent since the end of the Napoleonic Wars. In Austria, the unthinkable happened on 13 March, when the architect of post-war Europe, Chancellor Clemens von Metternich, was forced out of office, and, like the ex-King of France, fled to England. Left without the support of his powerful Chancellor, the epileptic and ineffective Habsburg Emperor, Ferdinand I, was forced to agree to the Austrian people's demand for a constitution.

In Bavaria, Michael Beer's patron, King Ludwig I, abdicated in favour of his more popular son, Max. Ludwig's middle-aged passion for the notorious dancer Lola Montez had contributed to his fall, although Lola had fled the country by the time the crowds had stormed the royal armoury in Munich on 4 March, forcing the King to accede to their demand for a national parliament.

In Berlin, restless crowds began gathering daily in the large, open-air spaces of the Zelten piazza in the Tiergarten, close to the Beers' villa. Over the first few weeks of March, these initially informal meetings turned into a type of unofficial 'parliament', where up to twenty thousand people listened to speeches, elected delegates to speak on their behalf, and voted on resolutions. They began liaising with the municipal authorities in Berlin's city hall, whose members were sympathetic to their demands. This display of popular autonomy was seen as deeply threatening by both the Prussian government and the King.

Frederick William IV was a dreamer and a conservative. He believed implicitly that he was King by the grace of God, and that, consequently, he was not answerable to any earthly power. The central experience of his youth – his family's flight to the remote east of Prussia after the humiliating defeat by Napoleon – had imbued him with a deep yearning for continuity and tradition, while his religious and Romantic preoccupations had led him to see the Wars of Liberation of 1813-15 in terms of a crusade, in which Germany had reversed the consequences of the atheistic French Revolution.

Frederick William was ill-equipped to understand the scale of the social and economic changes that were taking place. The emerging middle classes – property-owners, professionals, intellectuals and businessmen – were frustrated by the intransigence of a political system that denied them a voice. They were not calling for the abolition of the monarchy, but they wanted the right to participate in government through a democratic process, and an end to censorship.

At the lower end of society, the situation of the poor was steadily worsening. Overpopulation and a series of crop failures had led to unemployment and famine in the countryside, and the rural poor had crowded into the cities. In the first half of the nineteenth century Berlin's population had doubled from 200,000 to 400,000, with most of the new arrivals settling in deprived areas on the outskirts of the city, which quickly became slums.

The nature of poverty was changing: it was no longer something that affected individuals in specific circumstances, such as illness, old age or seasonal variation in work, but a permanent condition for whole groups of people. The workers in Prussia's important textile industry were particularly hard hit. A flood of cheaper imports from England, where the industrial revolution was more advanced, had lowered the demand for domestically produced cloth. The imposition of tariffs on English cloth might have offered some protection, but this was vehemently opposed by a powerful lobby of aristocratic Prussian landowners, who relied on exporting their agricultural produce to England.

The fall in demand for locally produced cloth, combined with rises in food prices following crop failures, caused riots in areas where unemployment was rife. The revolt of the poverty-stricken Silesian weavers in June 1844 was, in reality, a hunger riot rather than a political protest, but it was brutally suppressed by the Prussian army. Eleven people, including two women and two children, were killed.

The weavers' uprising became emblematic of the intractable social problems facing the state. The solution, for many politically-minded people – including the young Karl Marx, a member of the radical German emigré group in Paris – lay in a fundamental transformation of social structures. Failure to address the root of the problem could only lead to disaster: Heinrich Heine's famous poem, 'Die Schlesischen Weber' [The Silesian Weavers], which first appeared in Marx's journal *Vorwärts!* [Forward!] in July 1844, contains the repeated line, 'Germany, we're weaving your shroud'.[3]

In the turbulent years of the mid-1840s, Wilhelm Beer had become an important voice in any public debate on the Prussian economy. From 1844, he had begun publishing a series of articles in the major Berlin newspapers. These were focused on the development of the railways, and in particular the question of state or private ownership of the rail network. This question was to have an influence on developments in the banking system, and consequently on the wider political situation in Prussia. In 1842, the state had offered a small degree of support to the rail industry, with the establishment of a state 'railway fund', and guaranteed returns for investors on five stretches of line considered crucial to state interests.

Wilhelm did not believe, however, that these measures were sufficient to avert the financial crisis that he predicted would result from the unregulated growth of the railways. He was proved correct: the government's decision to leave the construction of the rail network solely in private hands had meant that there was a lack of planning and coordination at a national level. The subsequent proliferation of small privately-owned rail lines across the country resulted in an unprecedented demand for loans to finance these projects.

It rapidly became clear that the Prussian banking system would not be able to satisfy the huge demand for credit for the railways in the longer term, unless it was reformed. Unlike most other European countries, Prussia had no note-issuing banks, and still relied on an inflexible and old-fashioned system of government notes issued by the Treasury. Even the Royal Bank itself was forbidden to issue banknotes.

Inevitably, in this situation, the sudden growth in demand for credit in the rail sector affected other areas of the economy that were also dependent on credit, including the property market. Wilhelm described the financial crisis in Berlin in 1845 in a letter to Giacomo:

> You have no idea of the crisis that trade is in here. I am 49 years old, and have been in business since my 13th year, but I have never seen two days like the first two of this week ... I had sensed trouble ahead, and ... have already sold my Milanese, Amsterdam and Potsdam-Magdeburg [shares] at the highest prices.[4]

Wilhelm's proposals on how to overcome the problems in the banking sector included the establishment of a note-issuing bank, to increase the circulation of money and make more capital available to trade and industry. This bank would be funded by shareholders, but would function under state supervision. Wilhelm worked with the well-respected Berlin Merchants' Corporation to present these ideas to the ministers and to the King, and at the same time he orchestrated a vigorous press campaign, publishing pamphlets and articles in support of his proposals for banking reform.

The government eventually opted for a compromise solution. On 1 January 1847, the old Royal Bank was re-structured as the Prussian Bank, a half state-owned, half privately-funded institution that was authorised to issue paper money. Wilhelm's influential position in Berlin's financial world was affirmed when he became one of five bankers appointed to form the Central Committee of this new national bank, which, after German unification in 1871, would become the hugely important Reichsbank.

By 1847, the Prussian government had realised that its policy of leaving the development of the railway system in private hands had been a mistake. This change of mind had been sparked by the unsettling news that the French were constructing a national rail network that, in time of war, would be able to move troops and supplies extremely rapidly to the borders of Germany. The Prussian government could not rely on private investors, who were influenced solely by profitability, to consider the needs of the military.

It was clear that, in order to counter the threat posed by the French system, the Prussian state would have to take over the planning and construction of strategic rail lines. The financing of this project, however, was delayed by a law that had been enacted in 1820, which required the approval of a central gathering of all the provincial Diets for government loans above a certain level. The loan needed to finance the strategic railways was well above the specified limit.

The provincial Diets were not designed to be regional 'parliaments'; they had no powers to enact laws or raise taxes. Their function was limited to advising the government on local matters, and overseeing the administration of their respective regions. Frederick William IV, and his father before him, had both been anxious to keep the Diets within these limits, and both saw the convocation of a 'United Diet', as required by the 1820 law, as highly dangerous. It would be the first national assembly of deputies in Prussia, and as such, might be seen by the public, and by the Diet members themselves, as a step towards constitutionalism.

Successive governments had carefully avoided the need to call a United Diet by keeping loans to a minimum. The large amount of finance needed for the railways, however, meant that this policy of avoidance was no longer possible, and in February 1847, Frederick William reluctantly convened a meeting of the United Diet. In his opening speech, the King made it absolutely clear to the deputies that this assembly did not constitute a parliament of any description, and that it was to confine itself to the question of granting the required railway loan.

His worst fears were realised, however, when the more liberal delegates seized the opportunity to form themselves into an influential bloc. The conservatives were unable to do the same, as they tended to have more diverse perspectives and aims, and were less easily identifiable as a group. In June, the liberal-led Diet refused to grant the railway loan until and unless the King granted the assembly the right to meet at regular intervals. The King dissolved the Diet immediately, without any plans for its re-convention.

Although the United Diet of 1847 had not achieved any hard results, the organised resistance to the will of the King and government that it had demonstrated had been a sign of the inevitability, and the imminence, of political change. The unrest that followed spurred Wilhelm Beer into writing articles and pamphlets on wider political issues in Prussia. He had always been a robust character, and he found that he enjoyed the cut and thrust of newspaper campaigns, which gave him the opportunity not only to sway public opinion, but also to influence government policy. Wilhelm was politically conservative. He had supported the King's rejection of a constitution for Prussia when he had first come to the throne, telling his friend Schumacher, 'In my opinion, he was quite right to refuse a constitution, it wouldn't have suited us at all and would only have led to disaster.'[5]

Wilhelm's deepest concern was for the fate of small businessmen and property owners. He disliked and distrusted socialist ideas, believing that too much government control over the economy posed a threat to individual freedom. The major social question of poverty did concern him – he gave the profits from one of his booklets to assist the poor in Silesia – but he rejected any idea that a fundamental change in the social structure was necessary to redress the problem. Instead, he was a strong believer in workers' self-help, and, for example, supported an association for non-profit-making building companies.

In his articles on the credit crisis, Wilhelm had shown a particular concern to avert the collapse of the property sector, as this would affect the group of citizens he felt were the backbone of the state, the small property owners:

> When a citizen has been able to save a small amount of capital through life-long hard work and frugality, and wants to use it as a deposit for buying a piece of property, the state should look on this person as the most respected and the most welcome of all citizens, as small property ownership creates the genuinely conservative citizen, whose interests and existence are fundamentally bound up with the welfare and the continued existence of the state itself.[6]

Wilhelm was convinced that the existence of private property was central to the interests and wellbeing of the state. Although he took a liberal stance in defending free trade, he consistently opposed the introduction of property tax, which he saw as threatening property rights – which would, of course, affect him directly as co-owner of the Beer family home, the Tiergarten villa.

As a member of the Central Committee for the Prussian Bank, Wilhelm had a major share of the responsibility for steering the national finances through the crisis years. In mid-March 1848, the unrest in Berlin came to boiling point as the meetings in the Zelten spilled over into the streets, and the Chief of Police moved troops into the city. The appearance of armed soldiers on the streets increased the tension, and the protests looked set to develop into a full-scale insurgency. The atmosphere within the palace was equally tense: the King's advisors fundamentally disagreed on how to deal with this unprecedented situation. Prince William, a hard-liner, urged his brother to authorise a full-scale military attack on the crowds, while the Governor of Berlin, the thoughtful and intelligent General von Pfuel, counselled caution.

In private, Pfuel despaired of the King ever really grasping the salient points of the situation. He told Karl Varnhagen von Ense that Frederick William did not know or understand the first thing about constitutional government, and that, indeed, both his long habit of thought and his heredity had combined to make him practically incapable of understanding. Consequently, 'he wants his ministers to be blind followers of his will, he thinks he is cleverer than anyone else, he will tell you to your face that he sees more clearly than you can, and is better able to judge these matters'.[7]

However, when the shattering news of Metternich's fall broke in Berlin on 15 March, the King opted for granting concessions. He promised to abolish censorship, and to reconvene the United Diet to decide on a constitution for Prussia. The mood of the crowd changed from belligerence to joy as these concessions were announced, and they surged into the city centre to celebrate. The military found the rejoicing crowds difficult to control, and, as the situation threatened to spiral out of control, the King made the fateful decision to replace the conciliatory General von Pfuel with the more hardline General von Prittwitz. As the troops tried to disperse the crowds, the accidental discharge of weapons by two soldiers turned the celebrations to angry protest, as the rumour spread that the army had deliberately fired on civilians. Barricades went up on all the main streets within hours, and the army responded with infantry and artillery attacks. Over 300 civilians died in the fighting in Berlin over the night of 18-19 March.

General von Prittwitz requested permission to withdraw his troops from Berlin and bombard the city with heavy artillery, but Frederick William could not agree to this declaration of war on his own subjects – despite the urging of his brother, Prince William, who was fully in favour of bludgeoning the citizens into quiescence. Instead, Frederick William decided to appeal to his people. On 19 March, he issued a proclamation promising that if the barricades were taken down, the troops would leave Berlin. The next day, he gave the order for the army to begin pulling out of the city.

The gamble paid off, and the fighting ceased, but the mood of anger in the city did not die down. The King and Queen were forced to stand on the palace balcony that day, and pay homage to the bodies of the dead. A loud voice from the crowd roared 'hat off!' to the King, who meekly removed his hat. In private, Frederick William was reported to be a broken man. He retired to Potsdam, where he was surrounded by a conservative group who urged him towards counter-revolution. Prince William, who had quarrelled violently with his brother and had called him a coward, had left Prussia for a temporary exile in London.

Wilhelm Beer was horrified by this turn of events, and roundly condemned the King's granting of concessions to the democrats: 'What did the adoption of a monstrously liberal constitution do for Louis XVI? A few months later, his head was chopped off ... What did our own King's granting of all the so-called freedoms of the red republic do for him? Within an hour, the barricades had gone up in Berlin.'[8]

By summer 1848, the King's concessions had set a new political order in place. Elections for a Prussian National Assembly had been held in May, and had returned a large number of liberal deputies. The Assembly was tasked with drafting a constitution, but, by the autumn, relations between this fledgling democratic body and the government had begun to deteriorate. After a clash in Silesia between the army and a crowd of protestors, in which fourteen civilians had died, the Assembly's deputies demanded that measures be taken to ensure the army acted in accordance with constitutional values. This threatened to undermine one of the King's most cherished principles, his direct command of the army. In November, he responded by appointing his uncle, the ultraconservative Count von Brandenburg, as Minister President, and asking him to form a government.

Wilhelm Beer, although a conservative, was dubious about the appointment, describing it to Giacomo as a huge mistake to hand over the government to a man 'whose name is a byword for reaction'.[9] His own preference would have been for Wilhelm Grabow, the President of the Assembly from June to October 1848, a centre-right conservative, and a less controversial figure. Nonetheless, once Brandenburg had been appointed, Wilhelm supported him publicly, even commenting in a later pamphlet that a public monument should be erected to Brandenburg and his colleagues in government, in recognition of all that they had done to halt the progress of what Wilhelm consistently referred to as 'the red republic'.

The National Assembly, however, was not happy with Brandenburg's appointment, and sent a deputation to the King in protest. One of the delegates was a radical Jewish doctor from Königsberg, Johann Jacoby, who had become a figurehead of the opposition movement. When the King made it clear that he would not rescind the appointment, Jacoby remarked in his hearing that kings seldom wanted to hear the truth. Wilhelm was outraged at this disgraceful behaviour by a fellow Jew. He told Giacomo that, 'Things looked very dangerous in Berlin the day before yesterday. The manner in which the Chamber took up this matter, the appointment of a deputation, the insult which the King had to endure from the cursed Jew Jacoby ...'[10]

Once Brandenburg was appointed, however, events moved swiftly. Martial law was declared on 11 November, and, less than a month later, on 5 December, the King took the drastic step of dissolving the National Assembly. On the same day, he promulgated a new constitution for Prussia. It was a clever move: in granting a constitution, the King was seen to be fulfilling his promise to meet the people's demands for representation, but, in reality, he was also ensuring that this was a constitution on his terms. The most important point, at least for Frederick William, was that he retained sole command of army. However, the cabinet would now be responsible to a government composed of an upper house, or First Chamber, and a lower house, or Second Chamber.

The First Chamber was to be elected by voters above a certain tax level, that is, wealthy individuals. This was an outcome that pleased Wilhelm, who had wanted to see an upper house along the lines of the old corporate bodies, which he had felt would be necessary to act as a balance to a more democratic lower house. The electorate for the Second Chamber was, in fact, very wide for the time, as it included virtually all males. This was a triumph for the democrats; however, when the first elections to this lower house, in May 1849, returned too many liberals, the King demonstrated who was in charge by simply changing the suffrage system to a three-class structure which gave wealthier voters more weight.

Wilhelm, who was already a member of the Berlin City Council, was elected to the First Chamber of the new Prussian Parliament on 13 February 1849, as member for Angemunde, Upper and Lower Barnim, Prenzlau and Templin. One of the major issues he would face as a member of this parliament was the question of the unification of Germany. In May 1848, following the collapse of the German Confederation in the uprisings, a German national assembly, composed of delegates from the governments of the various states, had met at Frankfurt am Main, to draft a constitution for a united Germany.

During the days of the Berlin revolution, Frederick William had declared support for the national cause. He had made an extraordinary tour of Berlin on horseback, carrying the German tricolour, and announcing to the cheering crowds that Prussia would become part of a unified Germany. His understanding of the concept was not necessarily the same as that of the delegates at Frankfurt, however: he had his own unique view of a united Germany as a revival of the old Holy Roman Empire, perhaps with a Prussian King at its head, elected by other heads of state, and responsible to a Hapsburg Emperor.

Wilhelm Beer also supported the concept of a unified Germany, but with strong reservations. In particular, he felt that any unification should not be at the expense of Prussia's ability to decide its own future, and to protect its own political interests: 'Prussia alone is everything; Germany without Prussia is nothing. If there is talk of a central power in Germany, then it must reside in Berlin.'[11] Wilhelm despised the Frankfurt assembly, privately referring to its members as 'scoundrels' and 'rabble'. He was the most 'Prussian' of the Beer brothers, and he had been deeply affected by his service in the army in the Wars of Liberation: he was adamant that Prussia should never give up command of its army to any outside body.

Despite his hard-headedness in economic affairs, Wilhelm's attachment to king, country and army was deeply emotional; he went so far as to identify Prussia with Israel, calling the Prussians the new 'chosen people of God', and he poured out a panegyric to the army in his 1849 pamphlet, *Die Drei-Königs-Verfassung*:

> Prussian army! Oh, divine music of the word, as Schiller puts it …
> Where is there, or has there ever been, an army of greater courage,
> morale, discipline and loyalty … Where is there, or has there ever
> been, an officer corps in every respect so highly educated, and so
> honourable. Your 200-year history of marvellous feats, from the
> Battle of Fehrbellin to the … liberation of Europe from the

ignominious yoke of Napoleon, which was achieved by you alone, your recent deliverance of Germany, which, without you, would by now be a scene of blood and fire, will ensure you for all eternity the grateful respect of every friend of the Fatherland.[12]

The mention of 'blood and fire' refers to Wilhelm's belief that the outcome of the Frankfurt parliament's proposal for a united, democratic Germany would be an apocalyptic civil war that would combine the horrors of the French Revolutionary Terror and the Thirty Years' War.

One of the major issues faced by the Frankfurt parliament was whether a united Germany should, or should not, include Austria. This was a complex question, given that the Austrian Empire contained a number of non-German states, such as Hungary, and it was difficult to see how these could be accommodated in any German union. Consequently, on 27 March 1849, the Frankfurt assembly voted for a German state without Austria.

The assembly also elected Frederick William of Prussia as German Emperor, and a deputation travelled to Berlin to offer him the imperial crown. Frederick William refused it without hesitation. In his view, a crown offered by a democratic body was worthless. Wilhelm Beer was fully in agreement with the King's refusal, believing that if he accepted the crown, he would 'descend from the rank of a King of Prussia to that of a shoe shiner, as he will be subjecting himself to this mob that I hate so passionately'.[13]

Wilhelm's fierce loyalty to the Prussian Crown and his hatred of 'the mob' was untypical of many Jews across Europe at the time, who tended to be supporters of the revolutionary movement, and were frequently to be found among its leaders. His conservatism seems to have been rooted in his early experiences in the army, and in his desire to join the upper classes – reflected in his eagerness to obtain honours and awards – rather than to disempower them.

Wilhelm's outspokenness was appreciated by the royal family – Prince William wrote to him in December 1849 to thank him for his efforts – but it made him unpopular in other quarters. He was frequently lampooned in the satirical papers that had sprung up in Berlin during the revolution, including the *Berliner Grossmaul*, the 'Berlin Loudmouth', and the *Kladderadatsch*, a word with several meanings, including 'shambles', 'unholy mess', or 'scandal'.

Wilhelm was not unduly perturbed by these attacks. He was not averse to deliberately stirring up trouble in the newspapers: in 1848, he had published an article under the fictional name of 'Dr Kitow' in the popular

Berlin newspaper, the *Vossische Zeitung*, attacking Theodor von Küstner's management of the court theatres. Giacomo, who did not share Wilhelm's relish for controversy, was not amused, telling his brother that the article was not helpful, particularly since he and von Küstner were no longer at loggerheads, now that Giacomo had resigned from his theatre duties in Berlin.

Giacomo was much more thin-skinned than Wilhelm, and he was – understandably – both furious and deeply upset when, in June 1849, the *Kladderadatsch* printed an article suggesting that he was having affair with Princess Augusta, Prince William's wife. The paper did not dare name the Princess directly, but its meaning was clear. Princess Augusta was a highly intelligent woman, politically liberal, and very interested in music. It was well known that her marriage with Prince William had been dynastic, and that they were not warmly attached to one another. She was friendly towards Giacomo, and had most probably taken music lessons from him – she describes herself in a letter to him as his pupil.[14] This friendship was perfectly explicable in terms of their mutual love of music, and his position at the court of her brother-in-law, but the more scurrilous Berlin newspapers did not hesitate to impugn her reputation in attacking the Beers.

Giacomo was particularly distressed by this scandalous report, as his relations with the Prussian royal family had continued to be warm after his departure from Berlin; on his periodic returns to organise court concerts, he was always invited to dine privately with the King and with the princes. However, it seems that even this close degree of friendship with the royals did not make him acceptable to all Prussians. While at the Bohemian spa of Franzensbad in August 1847, he had noted in his diary that, 'General von Hannecken organised a commemorative dinner today, on the birthday of the late King, to which he invited all the Prussians except me. Always the same story …'[15]

Giacomo was nothing if not pragmatic, however, and had also quickly developed good relations with the new Republican regime in France, noting, in his diary for 1848, dinners with the Minister of the Interior, and with the President of the Republic, Napoleon Bonaparte's nephew, Louis Napoleon. Happily for Giacomo, the change in political regime had also coincided with a change in the management of the Paris Opéra: in autumn 1847 Léon Pillet's tenure had come to an end. He had been replaced by the scenery designer Henri Duponchel (who had held the post previously, from 1835 to 1841), and the theatre director Nestor Roqueplan, who had been appointed as joint directors.

The *Revue & Gazette musicale* had immediately assumed that Meyerbeer would return to Paris, commenting that 'Did not M. Meyerbeer inaugurate M. Véron's tenure with *Robert le Diable* and M. Duponchel's with *Les Huguenots*? Here are two precedents that augur well.'[16] The *Revue* was right, as it turned out; with Pillet's departure, Rosine Stoltz had lost her power base, and she resigned her position in the Opéra that year. Giacomo could begin negotiations with the new directors for the casting of *Le Prophète*, and by the end of 1847, it had been agreed that the tenor Gustave-Hippolyte Roger would take the role of Jean, and Pauline Viardot-Garcia that of Fidès. Rehearsals began in September 1848, and *Le Prophète* finally appeared on 16 April 1849, thirteen years after a work by Giacomo Meyerbeer had last been premiered on the stage of the Paris Opéra.

Giacomo's habitual anxiety at first nights had been increased by the expectation generated by the long wait, and he had reminded his mother to send a note of blessing for the premiere: 'The "Prophet" will be given next Monday 16th April. Don't forget, dear Nonne, to bless it on that day. You know what inexpressible value I place on your blessing.' As he always did, he carried his mother's note with him during the performance: 'I read the motherly blessing that you sent me in your letter at the prescribed time, with reverence and emotion, fervently kissed your dear name, and carried your letter close to my heart until the end of the performance.'[17]

Amalia's support for this particular opera may have held a special significance for Giacomo, as the central figure of Fidès has been seen as a tribute to her: the mother faithful to her son unto death. Many of the reviews commented at length on the importance of Fidès's role; the *Revue des deux mondes* said of her encounter with her son at his coronation, that, 'There is a profound and genuinely biblical feel in this scene, which reveals the admirable character of this woman, in whom the whole of the interest of the drama is summed up, and who is certainly one of the most impressive creations of M. Meyerbeer's genius.'[18]

The opera's hero – or anti-hero – Fidès's son, Jean of Leyden, who leads the Anabaptists into Munster and is crowned as prophet, priest and king in its cathedral, is a complex and ambiguous character. He is, it seems, a true visionary, but it is not clear whether he is also an imposter, or whether he is really so caught up in his mystical dreams of divine power that he genuinely comes to believe that he is the Son of God. It is similarly unclear whether Jean is using the deeply sinister Anabaptists for his own ends, or whether they are manipulating him.

The opera, with its themes of religious fanaticism, revolution, political power and suffering, could not fail to fascinate a world which had been so recently convulsed by real revolution. *Le Prophète*'s success was reflected in its record-breaking finances: in its first ten nights, it earned between 9,000 and 10,000 francs for every performance. Giacomo recorded in his diary that, 'The publishing fees that I have received for the score are the highest that have ever been paid up to now.'[19] They totalled 44,000 francs for the rights in France, England and Germany.

Reviews were for the most part dazzlingly affirmative. Berlioz, who had some reservations, nonetheless commented that, 'the success of *Le Prophète* was immediate, magnificent, and without comparison. The music alone assured it …', while Théophile Gautier rated Giacomo as 'the most essentially dramatic composer to be heard at the Opéra since Gluck'.[20] Many commentators were struck by Giacomo's use of new instruments such as the bass clarinet, and his highly innovative and original musical language. They felt that the work was modern and progressive, and that it needed to be heard several times before it could be properly understood – a comment that had also been made about *Les Huguenots*.

Giacomo was delighted with the reaction, telling his mother that the premiere had been 'a great and brilliant success', adding that the audience reaction to the coronation scene had exceeded his expectations: 'People cried at this scene, as if they were at a tragedy.' Viardot's performance had justified Giacomo's determination that only she should sing the role of Fidès: 'As singer and as actress she raised herself to tragic heights that I have never before seen in the theatre.'[21] Giacomo's willingness to use new inventions in the stagings of his works was also in evidence; the novel use of electric light to represent the rising sun at the end of act 3 amazed the audience.

The dark story of the libretto and the highly dramatic and original music combined with the lavish staging to thrill contemporary audiences. *Le Prophète* was as successful in other cities as in Paris; when it was first performed in Vienna, tickets changed hands for enormous prices, and the military were called in to control the crowds storming the theatre. In Berlin, however, as was always the case, the reviews were mixed, with some showing hostility towards Giacomo.

Heinrich Heine had already prepared his own response to the opera: a viciously mocking poem, which he sent to the Augsburg *Allgemeine Zeitung* shortly after the premiere. In his letter to the editor, Gustav Kolb, he commented that '[Meyerbeer's] new opera was given yesterday evening, after all that the most assiduous intrigue and immense wealth could do to ensure that this pitiful work is trumpeted as a wonder of art.' He suggested that it would be amusing if Kolb appended the satirical verse to one of the gushing reviews he would doubtless receive.[22] Kolb declined to accept the poem, but it was eventually printed, later that year, in a Hamburg paper.

By this time, Heine was very ill, and bedbound. His illness was not understood at the time, and has since been the subject of much speculation, with suggestions ranging from multiple sclerosis to lead poisoning. Giacomo visited him in late 1848 and spring 1849, giving him 500 francs each time. He reported to Amalia that

> The poet Heine is in a terrible state. His whole body is so crippled that he can't move at all, and yet has to endure the most terrible cramps. When I left Paris six months ago he extorted 500 francs from me, and another 500 now, on my return. In these times, that is a lot of money, especially for him, given that he has proved so ungrateful. But I could not withhold my sympathy from his awful situation.[23]

Giacomo's own position was now too secure for Heine to be able to damage him: after his long absence from the international stage, *Le Prophète* had confirmed him as indisputably the leading operatic composer of the time. In May 1849, he was honoured by the new French regime by being appointed a Commander of the Légion d'honneur.

Several pieces from *Le Prophète* became popular in their own right, and some have remained so up to the present day. The coronation march from act 5 has been used on state occasions. In 1851, Louis Napoleon, like his uncle before him, seized power from the Republic, and in 1852 became the Emperor Napoleon III. In the January of the following year, when he married a Spanish countess, Eugenie de Montijo, in Notre Dame Cathedral in Paris, the bride entered the cathedral to the march from *Le Prophète*.

The 'skaters' ballet' from act 3 is equally well-known. The act opens in the Anabaptists' camp outside Munster, in the depths of winter. In the premiere, the dancers, representing people bringing supplies across the frozen lake to the camp, used roller skates to simulate ice-skating. The music from the ballet became known as *Les Patineurs* [The Skaters]. In February 1937, the choreographer Frederick Ashton produced a ballet to an arrangement of the music by Constance Lambert which became hugely successful. It has been performed more than 350 times at the Royal Opera House, and was one of the first ballets to be televised, in a broadcast from Alexandra Palace in May 1937.

# Notes

1. Giacomo Meyerbeer, *Briefwechsel und Tagebücher*, Heinz Becker, Gudrun Becker and Sabine Henze-Döhring (eds) (Berlin: Walter de Gruyter, 1960-2006), vol. 4, pp.368-9.
2. Ibid., p.461.
3. Heinrich Heine, *Säkularausgabe. Werke, Briefwechsel, Lebenszeugnisse* (Berlin and Paris: Akademie Verlag and Editions de CNRS, 1970-), vol. 2, pp.137-8.
4. Meyerbeer, *Briefwechsel und Tagebücher*, vol. 3, pp.632-3.
5. Unpublished letter, Wilhelm Beer to Heinrich Schumacher, 29 October 1840, Staatsbibliothek zu Berlin, Preussischer Kulturbesitz, Nachlass Heinrich Christian Schumacher.
6. Article in *Spenersche Zeitung* 2 June 1847, as quoted in Jürgen Blunck (Ed.), *Wilhelm Beer. Genius der Astronomie und Ökonomie 1797-1850* (Berlin: Staatsbibliothek zu Berlin, Preussischer Kulturbesitz, 1997), p.86.
7. Konrad Feilchenfeldt (ed.), *Karl Varnhagen von Ense. Tageblätter* (Frankfurt am Main: Deutscher Klassiker Verlag, 1994), p.482.
8. Wilhelm Beer, *Die Drei-Königs Verfassung in ihrer Gefahr für Preussen* (Berlin: F. Schneider, 1849), p.4.
9. Meyerbeer, *Briefwechsel und Tagebücher*, vol. 4, p.454.
10. Ibid.
11. Wilhelm Beer, *Die Drei-Königs-Verfassung*, p.25.
12. Ibid., pp.7-8.
13. Meyerbeer, *Briefwechsel und Tagebücher*, vol. 4, p.456.
14. Meyerbeer, *Briefwechsel und Tagebücher*, vol. 3, p. 710 n 264, 1.
15. Meyerbeer, *Briefwechsel und Tagebücher*, vol. 4, p.285.
16. Ibid., p. 579 n 268, 1.
17. Ibid., pp.484 and 486.
18. Ibid., p.627 n 488, 3.
19. Ibid., p.488.
20. Ibid., p.622 n 488, 3.
21. Ibid., pp.486-7.
22. Ibid., pp.615-16 n 475, 1.
23. Ibid., p.448.

# 23

## Finale

In June 1849 Wilhelm experienced a particularly severe attack of the painful gout that he had been suffering from for more than a decade. He took a six-week cure in Marienbad, but, shortly after his return to Berlin, he developed permanently swollen glands. Giacomo, who saw his brother while on a brief visit home, noted in his diary that, 'I am extremely worried despite the fact that he appears brisk and cheerful; this persistent glandular swelling is a bad business.'[1] Wilhelm may have appeared cheerful but, in fact, he was both physically ill and emotionally troubled. In September that year, he made a rare comment on his private life when he told Giacomo that he wished that their mother was ten years younger, as, 'If you knew more about my domestic circumstances, and what a joyless existence threatens me if we were to lose her, you would pity me.'[2]

Wilhelm did not explain any further, but the remark suggests that by this time, his relationship with his wife, Doris, was no longer happy. The atmosphere in the Tiergarten villa was certainly uncomfortable, as there was tension between Amalia and Doris. Minna, who was based in Berlin and kept her husband informed about family affairs, told Giacomo that Amalia referred to Doris, who lived below Amalia, in the first-floor rooms of the villa, as 'her down there', and talked of her as someone who 'thinks only of her own pleasure'.[3]

By February 1850, Minna had become alarmed by the decline in Wilhelm's health. She told Giacomo that she thought that Wilhelm did not realise quite how serious his illness was, and that she found it disturbing to watch him and his family 'pursuing distractions'.[4] It is possible that Wilhelm did not want to face the reality of his situation: Giacomo had been concerned to hear that he was consulting one doctor after another, seeking different opinions.

Minna had been worried enough to discuss Wilhelm's prognosis with Dr Schönlein, the Beers' trusted family doctor, who had not been optimistic. She told Giacomo that when Doris had asked her what Schönlein had said, she had taken the decision to be completely frank with her, but had not divulged the truth to Amalia. She added that Schönlein was avoiding Amalia, as he did not want to have to give her his professional opinion on Wilhelm.

By the time Giacomo arrived in Berlin in early March 1850, to oversee rehearsals for the premiere there of *Le Prophète*, Wilhelm was confined to bed. He drifted in and out of delirium over the next few weeks, but on 27 March his condition suddenly deteriorated, and Giacomo was called away from a rehearsal to his bedside. Wilhelm died at 5.30 that afternoon, at the age of 53, from what appears to have been a form of lymphatic cancer. Giacomo was deeply distressed at the loss of this dearly loved brother, who had been his faithful supporter and friend, but he was also extremely concerned for Amalia, noting in his diary: 'God help my 83-year-old mother, who is now burying her third son, to bear this dreadful blow.'[5] Giacomo told his aunt Henriette that Amalia had not left Wilhelm's bedside for a moment during the four weeks of his final illness.

Wilhelm's burial took place on 31 March 1850. The newspapers reported that it was one of the largest funerals that had taken place in Berlin in recent years. Over 100 carriages followed the coffin in the cortege, which started at the Beer villa, then moved through the Brandenburg Gate and down the long avenue of Unter den Linden to the Jewish cemetery in the Schönhauser Allee. The King had sent one of his mourning carriages as a mark of respect; he also sent Amalia a handwritten note of condolence. The funeral was attended by the Prussian President, Count Brandenburg, and several government ministers, along with representatives of the arts and sciences, including Alexander von Humboldt and the astronomer Johann Encke.

Wilhelm, like his father and grandfather before him, had held positions of responsibility in the Berlin Jewish community – the only one of Jacob's children to do so. He had become a member of the Poor Commission in 1836, and a senior member of the board of the Moses Mendelssohn Orphanage in 1838 – despite his original distrust of the latter project. The funeral sermon was given by the teacher Baruch Auerbach, whose own private orphanage had been supported by the women of the Beer family for many years.

A week after the funeral, on 7 April, a prayer service was held for Wilhelm at the new Jewish Reform Temple in Berlin, which had been founded a few years previously under the leadership of the liberal rabbi Samuel Holdheim. There does not appear to have been any public commemoration at the old community synagogue, whose rabbi, Michael Sachs, was deeply traditional. Sachs would not have had close links to the Beers. Although Amalia was devout, she was not strictly observant – she and Jacob had abandoned the dietary laws decades previously – and her sons, while remaining steadfastly Jewish, only attended the synagogue on special occasions. Giacomo represented the family at the prayer service held at Holdheim's Reform Temple.

After Wilhelm's death, since neither of his sons had any leanings towards commerce or science, the remaining family businesses and his astronomical instruments were sold off. Doris did not remain in the Tiergarten villa with her mother-in-law for long. Giacomo's secretary in Berlin, Georges-Frédéric Burguis, wrote to him in October, commenting cautiously, 'I can report that up to now everything is going well between Madame Beer and Madame Doris Beer, and I hope that this will continue up to the 15th, when she [Doris] will be able to move into her lodgings.'[6] Doris moved initially to Französiche Strasse, but she seemed to find it hard to settle, as she had several addresses in Berlin over the next few years, before moving to her final home in Kasernenstrasse in 1855.[7] She died in 1859.

Three of Wilhelm's and Doris's four children – both their daughters, and their younger son, Julius – eventually settled in Paris. The two daughters, Julie and Elise, were married to successful bankers from the von Haber and Oppenheim families, and Julius, who was musical and had ambitions as a composer, had married the daughter of the wealthy Amsterdam-based banker Ludwig Bischoffsheim. A number of Wilhelm's grandchildren married into the French aristocracy.

Wilhelm's elder son, Georg, had proved less satisfactory than his siblings, however. He appeared to be following the course previously taken by his uncle Heinrich, and had already, in Wilhelm's lifetime, been put under legal restraint to stop him squandering his money. When Georg came into his inheritance, he went to Paris to join his sisters and brother. He led an unsettled life there, and Amalia and Giacomo, who were both fond of him, were concerned about his future.

In the autumn of 1850, as Georg was now the head of his family, but still unmarried, they decided to find him a wealthy bride. In a scenario reminiscent of the Beers' attempt to marry Giacomo off to Marianne von Eskeles in 1821, they tried to interest Georg in the daughter of the Parisian banker and art collector, Louis Fould. Georg, however, proved as reluctant as Giacomo himself had been some thirty years previously, and the plan fell through.

Giacomo was worried that Georg was getting into bad habits and bad company. He told Amalia that he thought it would be a good thing if Georg were to leave Paris: 'I am afraid he lives a dissipated life here. I saw him yesterday backstage in the Opéra – by chance he did not see me – talking in the most intimate way, in front of everyone, to two dancers from the corps de ballet. These creatures have such a bad reputation here that they are considered in the same light as common prostitutes …'[8] Giacomo was also afraid that Georg was frittering his inheritance away – he had arrived to call on his uncle in a very stylish and expensive new carriage, attended by an equally smart servant in livery.

Giacomo's fears were well-founded; within two years of Wilhelm's death, Georg had run through most of his inheritance. His ruinous career in Paris came to a halt and he handed over the money that remained to his brother-in-law, Samuel von Haber, in return for an annuity. Georg returned to Berlin and joined the Prussian army, which appeared to suit him – as it had suited his father. Amalia tried to obtain officer rank for her favourite grandson, but since George was Jewish this proved impossible, even with Alexander von Humboldt's help. Nonetheless, he had an honourable career, and took part as a Brandenburg Cuirassier in the wars with France in 1866 and 1870-71. He married Alexandrine Rosen, the daughter of a Warsaw banker, in 1860.[9]

The years following Wilhelm's death were a time of intense personal grief for Giacomo. His sister-in-law Betty, Heinrich's widow, died on 5 September 1850, on the day of Giacomo's 59th birthday and just six months after Wilhelm's death. She was 57. The contents of Betty's will astounded the Beer family and caused a minor public sensation, which embarrassed Amalia. Burguis reported to Giacomo three weeks after Betty's death, that 'The story of the late Mme BB's will has appeared in this morning's papers. This is greatly upsetting for Mme Beer.'[10]

The reason for this agitation was that Betty had added a codicil to her original will, without telling any of the family, in which she had left everything she possessed to Prince William of Prussia, later Emperor William I of Germany. If he died before her the money would go to his wife and children. Her intention, it seems, had been to show her loyal sympathy for the Prince's position during the March 1848 revolution, when he had become deeply unpopular and had been forced to flee Prussia for a period. The newspaper article which had so upset Amalia had speculated gleefully as to whether a codicil could overturn a previous will, and whether the Prince would be able to inherit the money.[11]

It is not known whether the future Emperor ever claimed his inheritance, but the royal family, including Prince William, continued to demonstrate their friendship towards the Beers, and in particular, their respect for Amalia. On one occasion, both Prince William and his younger brother Prince Carl visited Amalia at the Tiergarten villa to enquire after her wellbeing, after she had undergone a frightening experience. On 1 February 1851, Kroll's restaurant and winter gardens, which were situated very close to the villa, caught fire and were burnt to ashes. Giacomo noted in his diary that, 'Today at 1 pm the colossal Kroll establishment in the Tiergarten burnt down. By God's grace the wind was not blowing in the direction of my mother's house, which would otherwise inevitably have become a victim of the flames.'[12]

Giacomo had been concerned about Amalia for some time. She had become frail and the repeated blows of her children's deaths had affected her deeply. Her old friend, the former librettist and secretary of the Königstadt theatre in the 1820s, Karl von Holtei, had visited Berlin shortly after Wilhelm's death. He had hesitated to call on Amalia, fearing that an unannounced and unexpected visit by a friend from a happier time might upset the old lady.

However, on returning to his lodgings one evening he had found the Beer carriage at his door, with Amalia sitting inside it, waiting for him. She had invited him to go for a ride in her carriage with her. She was a dignified but lonely figure: all of her sisters, her husband, and three of her sons had died before her. She sat silently for a while, and then asked him if he would write an epitaph for Wilhelm's tombstone: 'I never thought that I would bury him too. All dead! All dead! And I am still living ...'[13]

Amalia celebrated her 86th birthday in February 1853. Giacomo wrote in his diary, 'How thankful I must be to almighty God that he has spared this dear, beloved woman to me for so long. May he keep her on earth for many more years in the fullness of health and clarity of mind, and grant her joy to the very end of her life. Amen.'[14] Despite her great age, Amalia was still entertaining at the villa; in April that year, while in Berlin, Giacomo had recorded attending a 'big dinner' given by his mother, with twenty-one guests.

The next year, however, in the first week of February 1854, shortly before Amalia's 87th birthday, Giacomo's worst fears were realised when he received a telegram with the news that his mother had suffered a stroke. On 7 February, he recorded in his diary that he was 'in mortal fear' as he had heard nothing further about her condition, but the next day brought a reassuring telegram, and letters confirming that she was on the mend.[15] Her recovery lasted until June that year. During the night of 11 June, Giacomo, who was in Berlin for the summer, was woken up to be told that Amalia had suffered another stroke.

She lingered for another two weeks, and died on 27 June. Her death was a hard blow for her only surviving son. Giacomo noted in his diary: 'Sad,

Amalia Beer in old age

disastrous day. At 12 midday my beloved mother's terrible agony began, that ended with her death at two hours past midnight. What a dreadful 14 hours! What a mother I have lost!'[16]

Alexander von Humboldt wrote to Giacomo expressing his own sympathy and that of the King. He described the King's feelings as 'genuine and unfeigned; the greatness of your mother's character (I can't think of a word that expresses it more appropriately) made a strong impression on the monarch in his youth'. Von Humboldt was away from Berlin, but told Giacomo that he would return there as soon as possible, 'where I am drawn by grief and an inextinguishable feeling of gratitude'.[17]

Amalia was buried on 30 June. The newspapers reported that from the early morning onwards an unusually large crowd of people from all classes of society gathered outside the villa in the Tiergarten. At 10 o' clock, the funeral procession set off for the Jewish cemetery in the Schönhauser Allee. The mourners walking behind the coffin were led by groups of orphans representing the Auerbach Institute and the Luisenstift. Behind the children came the mourning carriages of the King and the Crown Prince. Alexander von Humboldt and the Mayor of Berlin were among the chief mourners.

The Tiergarten villa was now owned jointly by Giacomo and Wilhelm's children. None of the Beer family ever lived in it again. From 1855-57, it was rented by the Prussian navy, who were moving their cadet training establishment from Danzig to Berlin, and used the villa as a temporary location while they found a more suitable establishment. The villa's glory days had passed. It was bought by a speculator, but was allowed to fall into neglect, and was eventually pulled down.

In 1854, Giacomo, now the only remaining member of his family following his mother's death, was entering the last decade of his own life. Professionally he was at the apex of his career, with the success of *Le Prophète* confirming his pre-eminence in the operatic world. In 1851, the work had achieved its 100th performance at the Paris Opéra, and it was frequently performed on state occasions in both France and Prussia. Giacomo continued to move in the highest social circles. In France, he was frequently invited by Napoleon III to attend court functions and to stay at Fontainebleau. He also continued to receive numerous honours and awards: in the first half of the decade, he was given an honorary doctorate of music by the University of Jena, elected to the Senate of the Berlin Academy, and decorated by the monarchs of Saxony and Austria.

Giacomo was also awarded the Commander's Cross of the Order of the Württemberg Crown, which conferred noble status on its holders, although he never used the form 'von Meyerbeer', which he was entitled to do. His ambitions were always focused on his professional status, rather than on social rank, although he could be very sensitive to what he felt were slurs on his position as a leading composer. He did not hesitate to return valuable gifts to royal patrons if he felt that these 'keepsakes' were an inappropriate gesture to a man of his standing.

Despite his fame, Giacomo was not content to rest on his laurels and was working on a fourth grand opera, *L'Africaine* [The African Woman], which he and Scribe had begun as far back as 1837. The leading female role, the 'African Queen' Sélika, had initially been conceived with the soprano Cornélie Falcon, who had created the role of Valentine in *Les Huguenots*, in mind. Giacomo preferred to write his major roles for a particular singer, and when Falcon had lost her voice irretrievably later that same year, at the age of only 23, he had relegated *L'Africaine* to the background in favour of *Le Prophète*. Over the next few years, his difficulties with the Paris Opéra direction and his responsibilities as General Music Director in Berlin had combined to delay both projects.

*L'Africaine* was not entirely side-lined, as he and Scribe worked on the libretto over the next two decades, with Scribe producing a major revision in 1853. It was a slow process, however, and Giacomo wrote two works for the Opéra-Comique in the 1850s before completing *L'Africaine* in the early 1860s. The Opéra-Comique was the second opera house in Paris; it did not, however – despite what its name implies – stage only comic works. The genre of *opéra-comique* was defined primarily by its mix of the spoken word and song. Bizet's *Carmen* was originally designated an *opéra-comique*, and only became an opera when its spoken passages were turned into semi-sung recitative. *Opéras-comiques* were, however, generally lighter (and shorter) than the grand operas staged at the Opéra. The genre's greatest exponent was the composer Daniel-François-Esprit Auber, whose works included *Fra Diavolo*, *Le domino noir* and *Le cheval de bronze*.

Giacomo's two works for the Opéra-Comique, *L'Étoile du Nord* and *Le Pardon de Ploërmel*, premiered in 1854 and 1859 respectively, proved his mastery of the genre. *L'Étoile du Nord* had its roots in his Prussian work, *Ein Feldlager in Schlesien*. *L'Étoile* is based on an episode from the life of the Russian tsar Peter the Great, when he had worked incognito as a carpenter in Karelia in order to learn about shipbuilding. The French Emperor and Empress, Napoleon III and Eugénie, attended the opening night and called Giacomo to their box to receive their congratulations personally, after seemingly endless curtain calls. The work went on to be performed 100 times in Paris in its first year.

Giacomo's second *opéra-comique*, *Le Pardon de Ploërmel*, was the last of his operas that he lived to see staged. Later known as *Dinorah*, after the name of its heroine, and set in Brittany among simple country people, the work was premiered on 4 April 1859. Unusually, Scribe did not provide the libretto, which was written by Jules Barbier and Michel Carré, who had produced texts for Gounod and Halévy. The work was admired for its technical musical perfection; Meyerbeer wrote the part of the heroine for the Belgian singer Marie Cabel, and the aria from the famous 'mad scene', in which Dinorah sings to her own shadow, became a test piece for coloratura sopranos.

Despite the continuing success of his operas, both old and new, Giacomo's habitual pessimism was still in evidence during the last decade of his life, and he was deeply sensitive to any signs that his works might be falling out of favour. In 1857, he wrote: 'The attitude of the press and even of individuals against me makes me fear that I am losing sympathy, that my star is sinking on the musical horizon.' A year and a half later, he commented that, 'Everywhere I look I see enemies, never friends.'[18] This last perception might have been influenced by the growing hostility that Giacomo experienced in the 1850s from two men whose enmity would prove to have a long-lasting and disastrous effect on his reputation.

In 1854, Heinrich Heine resurfaced in Giacomo's life. Heine, who was extremely ill by this time, wanted Giacomo's help in resolving a financial disagreement. Heine had convinced himself that a new ballet by the choreographer Paul Taglioni, which had recently been premiered in Berlin, was based on a poem of his, and that he was therefore entitled to royalties. He had been advised by a number of people that this was not the case, but he was determined to pursue the matter and wanted Giacomo to act as his agent. He gave Giacomo three days to reply, and hinted that if he received a satisfactory response, he would remove some material about Giacomo from a forthcoming book.

Giacomo thought Heine's letter 'impudent', and did not intervene in the matter. A few months later, in October 1854, Heine published a collection called *Vermischte Schriften* [Miscellaneous Writings]. The first volume included his contemptuous description of Heinrich Beer as a near-idiot, while the third volume contained an expanded version of an article he had written for an Augsburg newspaper in the 1840s, publicising Spontini's complaints that Meyerbeer had ousted him from Berlin.

In the revised article, Heine mischievously claimed that Spontini had told him that Giacomo had not actually written any of his operas himself: he had bought all his Italian works cheaply from impoverished Italian composers, while – of all people – Louis Gouin was the real author of the French operas. According to Spontini, Gouin did not want to be acknowledged as the composer in case it affected his position as a civil servant, and so allowed Meyerbeer to take the false credit. Gouin was, in any case, far too afraid to reveal the truth as he knew that Meyerbeer was capable of having him declared insane and locked up.

Heine's ostensible aim in publishing this essay was to caricature Spontini, whose arrogance, and his tendency to make offensive and absurd claims about his rivals, was well known. However, Heine certainly knew that the publication of these passages would annoy Giacomo, and he had also included an insulting description of Gouin:

> As Spontini expounded his hypothesis, I admitted that it was not completely improbable, and that, although the aforementioned Gouin's beefy appearance, his brick-red face, his low forehead, and his greasy black hair gave him more of the look of a cowherd or an ox-farmer than a composer, there was something in his manner that could give rise to the suspicion that he was the author of Meyerbeer's operas.[19]

Heine died on 17 February 1856. When Giacomo heard the news of his demise, he noted in his diary, 'I forgive him from my heart for his ingratitude and many wickednesses against me in his later writings.'[20] There was to be one last unpleasant shock, however. The year after Heine's death, his widow, Mathilde, informed Giacomo that she had found four poems satirising him among her late husband's effects, and that she intended to publish them unless he paid her a substantial amount of money.

Giacomo recorded a meeting with his publisher, Louis Brandus, to discuss the matter: 'Heine's widow has demanded 3,000 fr. to suppress the publication of the attacks on me, apparently contained in her husband's *oeuvres posthumes*. I have been weak enough to agree.'[21] In the end, he paid Mathilde Heine the enormous sum of 4,500 francs, but despite this legal agreement, a few years after Giacomo's death she went ahead with the publication of the three poems that attacked him most directly.

Giacomo was also troubled by a change of attitude on the part of Richard Wagner towards him in the 1850s. Wagner's growing dislike of Meyerbeer had been evident in his private letters for some years previously. In October 1847, Giacomo had noted in his diary that he had taken Wagner to dinner at his mother's villa in the Tiergarten. Wagner's comment on this in a letter to his wife was, 'I am dining with Meyerbeer today! He is leaving [Berlin] soon; so much the better!'[22] This change in attitude may have been partly due to the fact that, by this time, Meyerbeer had stopped lending Wagner money – he had refused a request for a loan of 1,200 thalers in November 1846.

Giacomo was aware that Wagner had criticised his operas – which was fair enough, given that Wagner's views on music had changed from the days when he had written his own grand opera, *Rienzi*, in imitation of Giacomo's style. However, Wagner's treatment of Meyerbeer in his writings was becoming so intemperate that it suggested a personal loathing; the German music critic Eduard Hanslick went so far as to remark in 1875 that Wagner 'passes judgement on Meyerbeer, not as on an artist, but as on a criminal'.[23]

Wagner was not in a good position in the early 1850s. More than a decade after his first approaches to Giacomo, he had not yet attained the overwhelming success that he felt he deserved. His personal life had also taken a turn for the worse; he had allied himself to the revolutionary cause in Dresden in the heady days of the 1849 uprising, and had been forced to flee to Zürich as a political refugee. There are certainly worse places than Switzerland to sit out an exile, but his situation made it difficult for him to stage operas in Germany, and his feelings of resentment towards Giacomo grew. Always the egotist, Wagner felt that Giacomo had not done enough for him, and the idea gradually began to take hold of him that he was being excluded from the theatres by the intrigues of the all-powerful Meyerbeer.

The huge success of *Le Prophète* in 1849 was a turning point for Wagner; it had placed Meyerbeer in a seemingly unassailable position, as the dominant force in European opera. Any composer who wanted to succeed on a large scale would first have to topple this idol of the public. Wagner's frustration turned into a determination to remove Meyerbeer from his path by destroying his reputation.

Around this time, Wagner began to use Giacomo's Jewishness as a weapon against him. Wagner had to come to feel that the pains Giacomo undoubtedly took to entertain, and appeal to, his audiences were evidence of a tawdry commercialism that desecrated real art. Wagner saw himself as a true German, devoted to his art for its own sake, in contrast to Meyerbeer, the cosmopolitan, international Jew who had turned music into a saleable commodity. In taking this stance, Wagner was most probably influenced by his friend, the violinist Theodor Uhlig, who had already published several anti-Jewish diatribes in the Leipzig music journal founded by Robert Schumann, the *Neue Zeitschrift für Musik*.

In 1850, Wagner submitted an article to the same newspaper under the pseudonym of K. Freigedank [K. Freethought]. It was called *Das Judenthum in der Musik* [Jewry in Music] and it was to become infamous. This first edition did not identify Giacomo by name, although it was perfectly clear from Wagner's comments that he was the main target of the rhetoric – along with Felix Mendelssohn, who had died three years previously. Both composers were named when the article was re-issued as a pamphlet in 1869, five years after Giacomo's death. The inclusion of the convert Mendelssohn in the essay indicates the racial tone of Wagner's argument, which seeks to identify Jews as aliens whose 'Hebrew art taste' debarred them from writing western music.

Wagner began by stating, as a fact, that all people are instinctively repelled by Jews. He asserted that Jews have no mother tongue, and claimed that their 'offensive' speech patterns were automatically incorporated into their music – that is, synagogue music – which he characterised as consisting of 'gurgling, yodelling and babbling' noises. The basic theme of his essay is that Jews are naturally and eternally 'other' and alien, and have no art forms of their own. Consequently, no Jew, no matter how talented or educated, can produce real art of any depth, but can only superficially mimic others, and so produce unnatural and distorted imitations of art.

The article was not, however, a mere effusion of anti-Jewish prejudice, although Wagner did admit to Franz Liszt in a revealing letter that 'I felt a long-repressed hatred for this Jewry, and this hatred is as necessary to my nature as gall is to the blood.'[24] *Das Judenthum* had a more specific aim, alongside the promotion of Wagner's views on art. The contention that Jews were unable to produce 'authentic' music was integral to Wagner's portrayal of Meyerbeer as a charlatan. Wagner was always hot-tempered, but the venom in his references to Giacomo suggests a visceral hatred that is not explicable, or justifiable, in terms of their musical differences.

Wagner told Liszt that he did not hate Meyerbeer, but that 'he disgusts me beyond measure', and referred to 'the period of my life, when he pretended to be my protector'. No doubt, the knowledge that he had needed Meyerbeer's assistance early on in his career had only served to increase Wagner's resentment. His comments in this letter on his view of the relations between a patron and the recipient of his benevolence throw an interesting light on his obsequious behaviour towards Giacomo in the early years of their relationship: 'This is a relation of the most perfect dishonesty, neither party is sincere towards the other; one and the other assume the appearance of affection, and both make use of each other as long as their mutual interest requires it.' Wagner went on to tell Liszt that he felt a pressing need to 'separate' himself entirely from Meyerbeer, to disassociate himself from his former patron.

In his 1851 work, *Opera and Drama*, Wagner attacked Meyerbeer openly. He reiterated his claim that, as a Jew, Meyerbeer had no mother tongue and was therefore insensitive to all language. Consequently, he had forced Scribe – who was otherwise a good dramatist – to produce 'the most incoherent nonsense, comprising motion without motive, situations which were a jumble of stupidity and characters too crazy to excite anything but laughter'.

Wagner let himself go in describing the kind of text Meyerbeer wanted from his librettists: 'a huge, parti-coloured, historico-romantic, satanico-pious, dogmatico-lewd, sancto-nonsensical, mystico-daring, sentimentally roguish, stagy conglomeration of all sorts, in order to provide him with the occasion for inventing fearfully curious music'.

Musically, he claimed, Meyerbeer was just an imitator who picked up on other peoples' ideas – like a starling hopping along behind a plough picking up worms. As soon as Rossini's early works had become popular, Meyerbeer had gone to Italy to learn to imitate him; when French grand opera took the musical world by storm, he had rushed to Paris to copy the style of Auber's *Muette* and Rossini's *William Tell*. The music that he produced in this way, 'with a huge ostentation', had 'such a frightful lack of substance, depth and artistic value, that we are tempted to rate his capacity at nothing'. It was in *Opera and Drama* that Wagner coined the phrase 'effects without cause' to characterise Meyerbeer's music, a catchy slogan which is still used today to denigrate Meyerbeer.[25]

In his autobiography, published in the 1870s after Giacomo's death, Wagner suggested that the failure of his opera *Tannhäuser* in Paris in 1861 was at least partially due to Meyerbeer's intriguing against him. Giacomo was in Berlin at the time of the premiere, but Wagner believed, or claimed to believe, that he had orchestrated a long-range press campaign to ensure Wagner failed in Paris: 'an urgent correspondence had been carried on from there [Berlin] with the editors of the principal Paris journals'. Wagner accused Meyerbeer of bribing critics to attack his music. As the date of the performance of *Tannhäuser* approached, he claimed that, 'From the press, which was entirely in the hands of Meyerbeer, I knew long ago what I had to expect.'[26]

Even Wagner's early biographer Ernest Newman – who does not have a good word to say for Giacomo as a composer – cites Wagner's comments on the Paris premiere as one of those matters that 'it would be unwise ... to believe without further evidence', along with Wagner's claims that Meyerbeer had bribed the influential critic Fétis to write articles against him, and that he had persuaded Berlioz to oppose Wagner by presenting Berlioz's wife with a valuable bracelet.[27]

Giacomo was certainly keenly aware of the power of publicity – something we take for granted nowadays, but that was a new phenomenon at the time – and his deep-seated fear of adverse publicity and anti-

Semitism led him to cultivate journalists and critics assiduously. He had learnt – at his mother's knee – the importance of getting on with influential people, and he undoubtedly courted critics and journalists, inviting them to his dinners and soirées, giving them gifts, and feeding them information about his activities.

Giacomo did himself no favours by this behaviour, which can, and has, been used to suggest that, if his operas had been left to depend on their own merits, they would not have been staged, or would not have been successful. However, although his excessive fear of criticism and his consequent attempts to manipulate the press reveal a character weakness, this is a very different matter from the wholesale bribery he has been accused of. No amount of bribery could have bought the world-wide and enduring success his operas enjoyed during his lifetime, and for decades after his death. His works were appreciated by, and influenced, other musicians, and were enormously popular with audiences across the world, from the Americas to Australia.

There is no evidence for the stories that Giacomo attempted – or wanted – to undermine other composers. He was well aware, however, that unpleasant rumours were being circulated about him. He had told Louis Gouin in 1855, well before the *Tannhäuser* debâcle, that he did not want to come to Paris during the period of rehearsals for Verdi's new opera, *Les vêpres siciliennes*, as he knew that he would be accused of intriguing against it: 'I know that this is perfectly contemptible of me, but that does not stop me having a distaste for coming to Paris in these circumstances.'[28]

Ernest Newman, writing about Wagner in 1912, remarked that, 'We need not take up any brief for Meyerbeer as a whole; but will anyone contend that if we could get *his* account of his dealings with Wagner, the current story would not have to be modified at many points?'[29] Newman was right in pointing out that Meyerbeer's side of the story was not available. Giacomo chose never to defend himself publicly in his lifetime, and he intended to keep the same silence in death: he had specified that his diaries and letters were not to be published, but should be kept in the private possession of his family.

The subsequent history of the Meyerbeer papers, including their dispersal to various locations during the Second World War, is a long one, but the net result has been that publication of his letters and diaries did not begin until 1960, and continued up to 2006. This century-long delay in making his personal papers available to the public has had a disastrous effect on his reputation, by allowing other people's versions of their relationship with him to have undisputed possession of the field. Meyerbeer's early biographers, who did not have access to his papers, tend to be unreliable: Jean Schucht's book, published in 1869, contains quotes from letters, purportedly written by Meyerbeer to Schucht, that are now recognised as inventions of the author, who only knew Meyerbeer slightly.

The publication, however belated, of Giacomo's personal papers has nevertheless thrown a new light on his relations with his contemporaries, in particular both Wagner and Heine. In the case of the 1861 Paris premiere of *Tannhäuser*, there is not a shred of evidence to support Wagner's contention that Giacomo had organised a cabal to ensure that the opera failed.

There are no letters to, or from, Giacomo on the subject, and what mention there is of the opera in his diary is far from hostile. Giacomo made special efforts to hear productions of his erstwhile protégé's operas, and travelled to Hamburg in April 1855 specifically to attend *Tannhäuser*. If he did not immediately understand the new direction that Wagner was moving in – he described *Tannhäuser* as formless and lacking in melody and clarity – he nonetheless recognised its greatness: 'The opera itself is indisputably a highly interesting musical work of art … [with] very great flashes of genius in the conceptualisation, orchestral colour, and at times even in a purely musical regard …'[30]

The disastrous Paris premiere of *Tannhäuser* is mentioned only once, in a diary entry of 15 March, when Giacomo, having heard the news of the fiasco, commented – ironically enough, in agreement with Wagner – that, 'Such an unusual demonstration of dissatisfaction with a work that, in any case, is so admirable and talented would appear to be the result of a cabal, and not a genuine popular verdict. In my opinion, it will only stand the work in good stead at later performances.'[31]

Giacomo was undoubtedly hurt when he realised that Wagner had turned against him, given the younger composer's earlier fulsome behaviour towards him. On the rare occasions when they met, he now treated Wagner with cool courtesy. When they ran into each other unexpectedly at a soirée in London in 1855, Giacomo noted briefly that, 'We acknowledged each other coldly, without speaking.'[32] Wagner, in his autobiography, describes the incident rather differently, saying that 'Meyerbeer was absolutely paralysed when he saw me … we found it impossible to exchange a word.'[33]

After the successful premieres of his two opéras-comiques, *L'Étoile du Nord* and *Le Pardon de Ploërmel*, Giacomo returned to work on *L'Africaine*. This last grand opera was set in Lisbon and Madagascar in the late fifteenth century, at the time of the explorer Vasco da Gama's voyage around the

Cape of Good Hope. In the libretto, da Gama is loved by two women, the Portuguese noblewoman Ines, and his African slave Sélika, who had been a queen in her own land. The action moves from Lisbon via a shipwreck to Sélika's home in Madagascar, where the Portuguese are taken prisoner. In the finale, Sélika sacrifices herself, by lying under the poisonous manicheel, or upas, tree and breathing in the deadly fumes, to allow da Gama and Ines to be together. The opera's themes of race, slavery and imperialism in the sixteenth century would have found echoes in the nineteenth-century world of empire-building.

The opera-going public of Europe had been waiting for *L'Africaine* for a quarter of a century: the French government minister Achille Fould had told Giacomo in 1853 that 'The Opéra needs you, dear maestro … we need to have a *grand coup* with a brilliant new work. You can do it, and you will do it, I have no doubt.'[34] Scribe's death in 1861 was a serious personal and professional blow, but Giacomo was determined to finish the opera and to see it staged.

In late April 1864, he fell ill. He rapidly became so weak that his two younger daughters travelled to Paris to be with him, although, as Minna and Blanca remained in Berlin, it seems that there was no serious anxiety. He continued to work on *L'Africaine*, and had just completed the score – some twenty-seven years after his original agreement with Scribe – when he died unexpectedly in the early hours of 2 May 1864. His last words to his family and friends on the previous evening had been, 'Thank you, my friends; go now, I wish you a good night and will see you in the morning.'[35]

His death came as a major shock to family, friends and the public. It was the only subject of news in Paris: hoardings across the city blazoned the headline 'Meyerbeer is no more'. Rossini composed a funeral dirge, 'Weep, weep, sublime Muse' for his old friend. In England, Queen Victoria wrote to her eldest daughter, Vicky, now Crown Princess of Prussia, 'Meyerbeer's death grieved me much; I do so admire his music, and so did darling Papa!'[36]

Giacomo had specified in his will that he wanted to be buried in Berlin, and it was decided that his body would be taken back to Prussia on a specially commissioned train. On 6 May, a solemn public ceremony was held at the Gare du Nord, before the funeral train left for Berlin. Giacomo was accompanied on this last journey by members of his family, along with his publisher, Louis Brandus, and the Director of the Paris Opéra, Emile Perrin.

The train was met at the Potsdam station on 7 May by a large crowd, headed by Prince George of Prussia. The funeral service was held at the

Meyerbeers' home at 6a Pariser Platz on 9 May, in the presence of the Prince and Emile Perrin, and with a sermon by the preacher and philosopher, Rabbi Manuel Joël. The cortege, accompanied by crowds of mourners, was led by three cavalry bands with muffled instruments. The coffin was followed by Prince George, Count von Redern and members of the diplomatic corps, and was accompanied by the royal equipages of the King, the Queen, and the Crown Prince and Princess.[37] As the cortege passed the Opera House, which was flying a mourning flag at half mast, the Opera's chorus sang a chorale. After a short ceremony at the Jewish cemetery in the Schönhauser Allee, Giacomo's body was finally laid to rest, alongside those of his family.

Rehearsals for *L'Africaine* had begun shortly before Giacomo's death, but, given his habit of producing the final version as rehearsals progressed, there was still a good deal of work to be done on the score. Minna Meyerbeer, in consultation with the Opéra's director, took the decision to ask the Belgian critic and musicologist François-Joseph Fétis, who had known Giacomo well, to produce a performing edition of the score.

The long-awaited premiere of *L'Africaine* took place on 28 April 1865, in the presence of the French Emperor and Empress. It was a posthumous triumph. Crowds of people who had not been able to obtain tickets waited outside the theatre, accosting audience members during the intervals to demand information. After the final curtain, a solemn funeral march was played, and a bust of Meyerbeer was brought onstage and crowned with a laurel wreath, as journalists rushed from the auditorium to local cafes, to telegraph their reports to newspapers.

The opera was well reviewed, and remained popular for several decades. It opened in London in the summer of 1865, and was premiered at the Metropolitan Opera in New York later that year, where it was subsequently performed fifty-eight times across the next twenty-three seasons.[38] In the 1860s alone, *L'Africaine* was staged in some fifteen countries, including Cuba, Uruguay, Russia, Turkey, Algeria and Egypt.

## Notes

1.   Giacomo Meyerbeer, *Briefwechsel und Tagebücher*, Heinz Becker, Gudrun Becker and Sabine Henze-Döhring (eds) (Berlin: Walter de Gruyter, 1960-2006), vol. 5, p.84.
2.   Ibid., p.82.
3.   Meyerbeer, *Briefwechsel und Tagebücher*, vol. 4, p.493.
4.   Meyerbeer, *Briefwechsel und Tagebücher*, vol. 5, p.157.
5.   Ibid., p.190.
6.   Ibid., p.299.

7. Berlin address books 1850-1855, Zentral- und Landesbibliothek, Berlin, https://digital.zlb.de/viewer/cms/82/.
8. Meyerbeer, *Briefwechsel und Tagebücher*, vol. 5, p.302.
9. Jürgen Blunck (ed.), *Wilhelm Beer. Genius der Astronomie und Ökonomie 1797-1850* (Berlin: Staatsbibliothek zu Berlin, Preussischer Kulturbesitz, 1997), p.134.
10. Meyerbeer, *Briefwechsel und Tagebücher*, vol. 5, p.280.
11. Ibid., pp.280 and 873 n 280.
12. Ibid., pp.336-7.
13. Karl von Holtei, *Charpie. Eine Sammlung Vermischter Aufsätze* (Breslau: Verlag von Eduard Trewendt, 1866), pp.184-5.
14. Meyerbeer, *Briefwechsel und Tagebücher*, vol. 6, p.36.
15. Ibid., pp.246, 247.
16. Ibid., p.331
17. Ibid., pp.333-4.
18. Giacomo Meyerbeer, *The Diaries of Giacomo Meyerbeer*, Robert Letellier (ed. and trans.) (Madison, NJ: Fairleigh Dickinson University Press, 1999-2004), vol. 4, pp.41 and 113.
19. Heinrich Heine, *Säkularausgabe. Werke, Briefwechsel, Lebenszeugnisse* (Berlin and Paris: Akademie Verlag and Editions de CNRS, 1970-), vol. 11, pp.55-6.
20. Meyerbeer, *Diaries*, vol. 3, pp.365-6.
21. Meyerbeer, *Diaries*, vol. 4, p.37.
22. Meyerbeer, *Briefwechsel und Tagebücher*, vol. 4, pp. 322 and 585 n 322, 1.
23. Eduard Hanslick, 'Meyerbeer – with special consideration of his last three operas', in Robert Letellier (ed.), *Giacomo Meyerbeer. A Reader* (Newcastle-upon-Tyne: Cambridge Scholars Publishing, 2007).
24. Francis Hueffer (ed.), *Correspondence of Wagner and Liszt* (New York: Scribner & Welford, 1889), vol. 1, p.145.
25. Richard Wagner, *Opera and Drama*, Edwin Evans (trans.) (London: WM Reeves, 1913), vol. 1, pp.146-69.
26. Richard Wagner, *My Life* (New York: Dodd, Mead and Company, 1911), pp.721-2 and 757-8.
27. Ernest Newman, *Wagner as Man and Artist* (London: Jonathan Cape, 1969), p.8 n 6.
28. Meyerbeer, *Briefwechsel und Tagebücher*, vol. 6, p.523.
29. Newman, *Wagner as Man and Artist*, p.29.
30. Meyerbeer, *Briefwechsel und Tagebücher*, vol. 6, p.533.
31. Meyerbeer, *Diaries*, vol. 4, p.202.
32. Meyerbeer, *Diaries*, vol. 3, p.323.
33. Wagner, *My Life*, p.631.
34. Meyerbeer, *Briefwechsel und Tagebücher*, vol. 6, pp.68-9.
35. Sabine Henze-Döhring and Sieghart Döhring, *Giacomo Meyerbeer. Der Meister der Grand Opéra* (Munich: CH Beck, 2014), p.192.
36. Meyerbeer, *Diaries*, vol. 4, p.343 n 17.
37. Ibid., pp.340-1.
38. Jennifer Jackson, *Giacomo Meyerbeer Reputation without Cause? A Composer and his Critics* (Newcastle upon Tyne: Cambridge Scholars Publishing), p.179.

# Epilogue

Minna Meyerbeer survived to the age of 82. She and the couple's three children had become a source of comfort and stability for Giacomo after the rocky years of their marriage in the 1830s. Giacomo and Minna had, in time, adapted to their 'semi-detached' lives. He was constantly on the move in connection with his work, and she continued to patronise spas throughout Europe. When the family came together, however, in Berlin or in a spa town such as Bad Ischl in Austria, where they spent the summer of 1848, it was a time of happiness and peace. As he left Bad Ischl in August that year, Giacomo commented, 'Early today at 10 o' clock I left Ischl, where I had spent six weeks in the bosom of my family, with my beloved wife Minna and my three delightful children, in quiet tranquillity and cheerful happiness.'[1]

All three of their daughters converted to Christianity and married non-Jewish men. Giacomo accepted his children's choices equably; he had endured a good deal of pain in adhering to his own vow to remain within Judaism, and had decided earlier in his marriage that, if he had a son, he would have him neither circumcised nor baptised.[2] His eldest daughter, Blanca, had been drawn to Catholicism as a teenager and had converted in 1851, well before she met her future husband Baron Emanuel von Korff, a lieutenant of Dragoons, who she married in 1857. Blanca was devoted to her husband, who had a very successful career in the Prussian army and eventually retired with the rank of General. However, von Korff turned out to be an inveterate gambler, and Giacomo was forced to pay out large sums over the years to keep this son-in-law from bankruptcy. The von Korffs had one child, their son Friedrich or Fritz, who died before the end of the century leaving no children.

The Meyerbeers' second daughter, Caecilie, developed a serious disorder, seemingly a type of anorexia, in her teens, which caused her parents great anxiety. A tall girl, at one point she weighed only five and a half stone. However, she recovered from this distressing condition in her twenties and married the Austrian geologist and anthropologist Baron Ferdinand von Andrian zu Werburg in 1869. Caecilie died in 1931, at the age of 94. She had settled in Salzburg, and in her extreme old age she retained a lively spirit and an interest in the world around her.

Caecilie's son, Leopold, a friend of the Viennese writer Hugo von Hoffmannsthal, was himself a minor poet and dramatist. After the First World War, Leopold became the director of Vienna's Burgtheater. Caecilie's daughter, Countess Gabriele von Wartensleben, was a pioneer of women's education. Gabriele studied in Zürich, Leipzig and Heidelberg, and in 1900 became the first woman to receive a doctor of philosophy degree from the University of Vienna. In the early years of the twentieth century she worked as a director of educational courses for women in Frankfurt am Main, where she also participated in work at the Frankfurt Psychological Institute. Gabriele published two studies and a book, all of which were contributions to the early development of Gestalt psychology.

The Meyerbeers' youngest daughter, Cornelie, married the Berlin painter Gustav Richter, whose best-known portraits include those of the Emperor William I and the Empress Augusta. Cornelie had inherited her grandmother's talent for hospitality and she became a successful social hostess in Berlin in the later years of the century. One of their sons, Gustav, also became a painter; another, Raoul, was a Nietzschean philosopher. Cornelie's youngest son, Hans, was a lawyer; it was his decision to open the Meyerbeer archive to scholarship in 1955. None of Giacomo's family inherited his musical talent. Wilhelm's son Julius came closest, as an amateur composer whose operettas were performed in the salons of Paris.

Giacomo's operas continued to be popular for several decades after his death, but as tastes changed over time, they began to sound old-fashioned. This was a natural process, and as composers such as Gounod, Verdi and Wagner came to the fore with new styles, Meyerbeer's works inevitably appeared less often in the repertoire. However, as the most popular and the most frequently performed opera composer of his time, and as an innovator who represents an entire epoch in music drama, Giacomo Meyerbeer continued and continues to occupy a significant place in the history of opera.

Meyerbeer remained an admired figure into the early years of the new century. In 1891, on the centenary of his birth, the critic Eduard Hanslick remarked – with clear allusion to Wagnerian empire-building – that: 'He had no need to found Meyerbeer Societies or to build a special Meyerbeer-Theatre; the entire public was his Society, and Europe was his Bayreuth.'[3] In 1912, a 'Meyerbeer Festival' was held in the Belgian town of Spa, where he had spent many summers, to celebrate the dedication of a monument to the composer's memory. The committee for the festival, which was under the patronage of the King of Belgium, included the Directors of the Paris Opéra and the Brussels Conservatoire, and the composers Engelbert Humperdinck and Richard Strauss.

Given his enormous popularity and influence in his lifetime and the succeeding decades, it is surprising to find that, in many twentieth-century textbooks and opera guides, Meyerbeer has often either been ignored, or given a brief, sometimes openly hostile, entry. It is particularly striking that many of these articles take Wagner's attitude towards Meyerbeer as an incontrovertible starting point. His opinions on Meyerbeer are still reproduced, divested of their background of personal enmity and anti-Semitism, as authoritative and objective judgements.

Meyerbeer himself was well aware that the opinions of famous men can have undue influence: in 1857 he commented to his publisher, Louis Brandus, that 'when [lies and slander of every kind] are uttered by so beloved and popular an author as Heine, they achieve an unfortunate significance'.[4] The weight given to Wagner's views – along with those of Heine, and also of Schumann, who famously said that he rated Meyerbeer with 'Franconi's circus people' – has resulted in a widespread image of Meyerbeer as a wealthy and untalented dilettante who intrigued ceaselessly against other, more talented composers; who pandered to the lowest common denominator; and who bribed theatres and critics to have his operas staged.

Wagner's denunciation of Meyerbeer, with its strong overtones of Jew-hatred, caught the mood of the times across Europe in the later nineteenth and the early twentieth centuries. This period saw the birth of modern anti-Semitism based on racial purity theories, developed initially by the British-born philosopher Houston Stewart Chamberlain, whose writings influenced Adolph Hitler. A zealous Wagnerite, Chamberlain married Wagner's illegitimate daughter with Cosima von Bülow, Eva, some twenty-five years after the composer's death.

Economic and political factors also contributed to the rise of anti-Semitism in the later decades of the nineteenth century. In 1869, the Law concerning the Equality of Confessions, which had removed all of the remaining restrictions on the Jews in Prussia and which was adopted by the new German Empire, had guaranteed legal equality to all regardless of religious affiliation. However, public opinion, as always, proved intransigent and discrimination continued in practice. After the financial crash of 1873 and the subsequent depression across Europe, German investors blamed Jewish bankers and stockbrokers for the crisis, accusing them of exploitation.

In France, the depression was exacerbated by the humiliation of France's military defeat by Germany in 1871, which produced a nationalism that had strong anti-Semitic overtones; the 'Dreyfus affair' has come to symbolise this mood change. This could not have happened in Prussia; not because of any greater acceptance of Jews in the military, but because by this time there were no Jewish officers in the Prussian army.

Successful people, like the Jewish economic and artistic elite of the late nineteenth century, are often envied by others. If they are also perceived as outsiders, that envy can easily turn to resentment and hatred. As early as 1863, the German musicologist Josef Schlüter called Meyerbeer 'an international Jew profiteer, the Jew who knows how to give the public what it wants in every respect'[5] – incidentally appearing to suggest that the works of an opera composer who aims to entertain the theatre-going public are intrinsically worthless.

In the 1930s Meyerbeer was on the list of composers banned by the Nazis, and his operas vanished from the European stage for more than a decade. After the Second World War, his works were seldom performed. Although this can be attributed to changing tastes in music drama, the perception of Meyerbeer that survived and become dominant was to some degree the image propagated by Wagner. In 1998, the Bloomsbury *Dictionary of Opera* commented that: 'Few composers have ever enjoyed a more inflated reputation … His vast and spectacular works … – described by Wagner as "effects without causes" – are now perceived to have cloaked a strictly limited musical talent … His influence on other composers has been overestimated.'[6]

Heine's opinions were also occasionally quoted. An English textbook on French nineteenth-century culture, published in the 1980s, dismissed Meyerbeer's operas as 'gaudy, meretricious and inauthentic', and described the romanticism of *Robert le Diable* as 'shop-soiled, or, as Heine put it with his customary deadly wit: "Meyerbeer has brought the fantastic down to the level of the tradesmen of the rue St Denis"'. The author remarks that Meyerbeer was, at the time of the premiere of *Robert*, 'a composer then almost unknown in France', who 'happened to be the son of a rich Berlin banker', and who paid the Opéra 30,000 francs to produce this work.[7]

These assertions – apart from the fact that Jacob Beer was a wealthy Berliner – are factually incorrect: Meyerbeer had already had an overwhelming success in Paris, and indeed across Europe, with *Il Crociato in Egitto* in 1825. The premiére of *Robert* was awaited by the public with excitement and anticipation, and Véron was prepared to invest large sums of money in the production, in the expectation of equally large profits. The mention of 30,000 francs is inexplicable, unless the author is mistakenly referring to the sum which Véron fined Meyerbeer several years after the appearance of *Robert*, for being late in producing the libretto for his next work, *Les Huguenots*.

Some assessments of Meyerbeer were more even-handed. *The New Kobbé's Opera Book* 1997 edition had detailed critiques of all of Meyerbeer's grand operas, and of *Le Pardon de Plöermel* (*Dinorah*), and commented that: 'He exploited his talent with consummate skill, wrote as effectively for grand voices as he did for the boulevardier audience, and influenced even composers far more gifted, like Verdi and Wagner. Monumental set pieces … still stir the blood of audiences …'[8]

Meyerbeer's works have continued to be attractive to singers: it is notable that the occasional revivals of his operas have often featured major operatic stars: Placido Domingo, Juan Diego Flores, Marilyn Horne, Jessye Norman, Shirley Verrett, and Joan Sutherland have all sung in Meyerbeer operas. There have been recent signs of a more sustained interest. Since the turn of the millennium, there have been performances in numerous cities across Europe, including London, Paris, Brussels, Liège, Venice, Sofia, Erfurt, Karlsruhe, Strasbourg and Metz. The Deutsche Oper in Berlin produced a cycle of Meyerbeer's operas between 2014 and 2017.

Whether or not his operas enjoy a major revival at some future date, Meyerbeer has spent long decades in the outer darkness of the operatic world. Musicological discussion is beyond the scope of this book, but criticism of his work has often had roots in non-musical factors, such as his cosmopolitanism, his wealth, and his Jewish descent.

Wealth was, indeed, both a blessing and a curse not just for Giacomo Meyerbeer, but for all of his family. Jacob and Amalia Beer's great wealth was a blessing, primarily because it allowed them to further their own social ambitions and their sons' artistic careers. It also gave them the wherewithal to become philanthropists. The Beers were known for their generosity: even Heine admitted that charity was a particular virtue of the Beer family,[9] while Karl von Holtei noted that Amalia was positively hounded by people begging for help, and that she never refused anyone in real trouble.

Giacomo was also pursued by people asking for loans – composers, journalists and writers prominent among them – and he was as generous as his mother towards those in need. When his Italian librettist, Gaetano Rossi, became impoverished in later life Giacomo sent him money, and he continued to support Rossi up until the librettist's death in 1855. He also asked his mother to help Rossi, telling Amalia that, 'It would be a great mitzvah [holy deed, fulfilment of Jewish law].'[10] The Beers looked on charitable giving as a religious duty: after one of Giacomo's daughters recovered from an illness he made a vow to perform an act of charity in thankfulness, and, in fulfilment of the vow, he paid for the education of a ragged 8-year-old boy he had seen begging outside his hotel in Paris.

However, the Beers' wealth and their generosity also exposed them to charges of bribery and of 'buying' success. This charge has been levelled at both Wilhelm and Michael, as well as at Giacomo. Wilhelm, whose success as an astronomer was entirely self-created, has been characterised as a dilettante who simply paid another man to do the work – his years of study of higher mathematics and his reputation among his contemporaries as a serious scientist either ignored or unknown.

Michael's early death has ensured that he remains a minor author, and it is certainly true that his parents' influence, as much as their money, secured the initial staging of his first work, *Klytemnestra*. However, the popularity of Michael's best plays – *Der Paria* and *Struensee* – over the following decades, and the admiration of major literary figures such as Goethe and August Schlegel, suggest that his work had intrinsic merit. When, in 1829, Michael had expressed concern about the future longevity of his works to his friend Karl Immermann, fearing that they might be destined, as he put it, for a 'quick death', Immermann wisely advised him not to think about the long term: 'the fate of your works is, of course, something of a lottery; but nothing that a man has put his soul into, has ever been completely lost'.[11]

Immermann's insight is perhaps applicable to the Beer family as a whole: whatever their reputation or lasting fame, the way that they lived their lives had value in altering the public perception of the Jews in a time of great change and upheaval. Jacob and Amalia Beer had been born into the Prussia of Frederick the Great, a time and place where they were seen as untrustworthy aliens and deemed unworthy of citizenship. Even after the high points of legal emancipation and the Wars of Liberation, as Jews in German society they faced innumerable visible and invisible barriers. Their decision to remain within Judaism and to try to reform it from the inside was a brave one, and drew a hostile response from Jewish converts to Christianity, as well as from Christians and orthodox Jews.

It was incomprehensible to many people that these intelligent, cultured people should choose to remain Jews. A story that Giacomo had remained Jewish solely because this was a condition of his inheriting his grandfather's fortune was particularly persistent in his lifetime, and is still repeated today. The story is an indication of the puzzlement that many people felt about his refusal to convert, as it explains Giacomo's resistance to conversion in terms that made it explicable – the age-old belief in the venality of the Jews.

Giacomo had, of course, voluntarily promised his mother that he would remain Jewish in honour of his grandfather. There were no conditions attached to Liepmann Meyer Wulff's will, beyond the stipulation that Giacomo would only inherit the house in Königsstrasse if he maintained the synagogue there. Liepmann's vast fortune would have passed to his grandchildren whether they converted or not. That all of the Beer children remained Jews must be credited, to a great degree, to the influence of their parents and the importance of the reform movement in their family.

Amalia, in particular, played a central role in her children's lives: she was a strong woman with a genuine warmth of personality that endeared her not just to her own family, who adored her, but to men such as Alexander von Humboldt, and to members of the Prussian royal family. Both Frederick William IV and the Emperor William I, who had known her from their childhood days, felt affection as well as respect for her.

The Beers' decision to remain Jewish was not without its cost, however, and it required stoicism and determination on their part to persist in their aspirations, despite public and private rebuffs and insults. Michael and Giacomo were both highly sensitive to anti-Jewish feeling, and Giacomo's extreme anxiety about negative publicity is a symptom of his deep insecurity. Wilhelm was outwardly more buoyant than his brothers, but his pursuit of honours and awards betrays his longing to be accepted into the establishment. Orders and titles were, for Wilhelm, visible symbols of social acceptance.

Despite the pain and frustration they undoubtedly felt, the Beers' high-profile achievements influenced their contemporaries' views on who the Jews were, and what they could achieve. The Beers provided living proof that it was possible to remain Jewish, yet move in the highest social, artistic and scientific circles. In the way that they lived their lives, they attempted to embody a positive answer to the question 'Can Jews be Germans?' Karl Immermann may have been right in his belief that fame is a lottery, but whatever posterity's judgement of their works, the Beers can surely be said to have poured their souls into everything that they did, and to have lived their lives well.

# Notes

1.  Giacomo Meyerbeer, *Briefwechsel und Tagebücher*, Heinz Becker, Gudrun Becker and Sabine Henze-Döhring (eds) (Berlin: Walter de Gruyter, 1960-2006), vol. 4, p.436.

2. Meyerbeer, *Briefwechsel und Tagebücher*, vol. 3, p.375.
3. Heinz Becker and Gudrun Becker (eds), *Giacomo Meyerbeer – Weltbürger der Musik* (Wiesbaden: Dr Ludwig Reichert Verlag, 1991), p.9.
4. Meyerbeer, *Briefwechsel und Tagebücher*, vol. 7, p. 180.
5. Robert Letellier (ed.), *Giacomo Meyerbeer. A Reader* (Newcastle upon Tyne: Cambridge Scholars Publishing, 2007), p.175 n 2.
6. James Anderson, *Dictionary of Opera* (London: Bloomsbury, 1998), pp. 364-5.
7. Frederick William John Hemmings, *Culture and Society in France 1789-1848* (Leicester: Leicester University Press, 1987), pp.278, 285.
8. The Earl of Harewood and Antony Peattie (eds), *The New Kobbé's Opera Book* (London: Ebury Press, 1997), pp.465-73.
9. Heinrich Heine, *Säkularausgabe. Werke, Briefwechsel, Lebenszeugnisse* (Berlin and Paris: Akademie Verlag and Editions de CNRS, 1970-), vol. 7, p.276.
10. Meyerbeer, *Briefwechsel und Tagebücher*, vol. 4, p.451.
11. Michael Beer, *Briefwechsel*, Eduard von Schenk (ed.) (Leipzig: Brockhaus, 1837), pp.114 and 118.

# List of Illustrations

1. Amalia Beer (Johann Karl Kretschmar c. 1803). Courtesy Stiftung Stadtmuseum Berlin – Hans-und-Luise Richter Stiftung. Reproduction: Oliver Ziebe, Berlin.
2. Jacob Herz Beer (Johann Heinrich Schröder, c. 1797). Courtesy Stiftung Stadtmuseum Berlin – Hans-und-Luise Richter Stiftung. Reproduction: Hans-Joachim Bartsch, Berlin.
3. Berlin c. 1808. In Bernard Lepsius, *Lili Parthey* (Berlin-Leipzig, 1926). Author's collection.
4. Giacomo Meyerbeer as a Young Man/J. Meyerbeer (lithograph). Courtesy Stiftung Stadtmuseum Berlin.
5. The Königstadt Theatre. In Felix Eberty, *Jugenderinnerungen eines alten Berliners* (Berlin, 1925). Author's collection.
6. Minna Meyerbeer. In Adolph Kohut, *Geschichte der deutschen Juden. Ein Hausbuch für die jüdische Familie* (Berlin, 1898-9). Author's collection.
7. Michael Beer. In Michael Beer, *Sämmtliche Werke* (Leipzig, 1835). Author's collection.
8. Wilhelm Beer (Funke, lithograph, after Franz Krüger c. 1850). Courtesy Stiftung Stadtmuseum Berlin. Reproduction: Michael Setzpfandt, Berlin.
9. Giacomo Meyerbeer c. 1840. In Felix Eberty, *Jugenderinnerungen eines alten Berliners* (Berlin, 1925). Author's collection.
10. Amalia Beer in old age. In Adolph Kohut, *Geschichte der deutschen Juden. Ein Hausbuch für die jüdische Familie* (Berlin, 1898-9) Author's collection.

# Bibliography

## Archives

Bavarian State Library, Munich
Berlin-Brandenburg Academy of Sciences and Humanities
Berlin State Library – Prussian Cultural Heritage
German Literature Archive, Marbach
Goethe and Schiller Archive, Weimar
Hessian State Archives, Darmstadt
Jagiellonian Library, Crakow
Klau Library, Hebrew Union College, Cincinnati
Leo Baeck Institute Archives
Saxon State and University Library, Dresden
Schleswig-Holstein State Library
Theatre Collection of the University of Cologne
University Library Johann Christian Senckenberg, Frankfurt am Main
University of Virginia Special Collections

## Published Sources

Adam, Jacob, *Zeit zur Abreise. Lebensbericht eines jüdischen Handlers aus der Emanzipationszeit*, Jörg H. Fehrs and Margret Heitmann (eds) (Hildesheim, Zürich, New York: Georg Olms Verlag, 1993)

Akademie der Künste, *Berlin zwischen 1789 und 1848. Facetten einer Epoche* (Berlin: Fröhlich & Kaufmann GmbH, 1981)

*Allgemeine musikalische Zeitung*

Aly, Götz, *Why the Germans? Why the Jews? Envy, Race Hatred, and the Prehistory of the Holocaust*, Jefferson Chase (trans.) (New York: Metropolitan Books, 2011)

Atterbom, Per Daniel, *Reisebilder aus dem Romantischen Deutschland* (Stuttgart: Steingrüben Verlag, 1970)

Aust, Cornelia, *The Jewish Economic Elite. Making Modern Europe* (Bloomington, IN: Indiana University Press, 2018)

Baader, Benjamin Maria, *Gender, Judaism, and Bourgeois Culture in Germany, 1800-1870* (Bloomington, IN: Indiana University Press, 2006)

Bach, Hans Israel, *The German Jew. A Synthesis of Judaism and Western Civilization 1730-1930* (Oxford: The Littman Library, 1984)

Balhar, Susanne, *Das Schicksalsdrama im 19. Jahrhundert: Variationen eines romantischen Modells* (Munich: Martin Meidenbauer Verlagsbuchhandlung, 2004)

Barbier, Patrick, *Opera in Paris 1800-1850. A Lively History*, Robert Luoma (trans.) (Portland, OR: Amadeus Press, 1995)

Barclay, David E., *Frederick William IV and the Prussian Monarchy* (Oxford: Oxford University Press, 1995)

Bauer, Frank, *Napoleon in Berlin. Preussens Hauptstadt unter Französischer Besatzung 1806-1808* (Berlin: Berlin Story Verlag, 2006)

Bauer, Karoline, *Aus meinem Buhnenleben*, Arnold Wellmer (ed.), vol. 1 (Berlin: Verlag der Königlichem Geheimen Ober-Hofbuchdruckerei, 1876)

Bauer, Karoline, *Aus meinem Buhnenleben*, Arnold Wellmer (ed.), vol. 2 (Berlin: R. v. Decker's Verlag, Marquardt & Schenk, 1877)

Bauer, Karoline, *The Memoirs of Karoline Bauer* (2 vols) (London: Remington & Co., 1885)

Baur, Wilhelm, *Prinzessin Wilhelm von Preussen* (Hamburg: Agentur des Rauhen Hauses, 1886)

Beci, Veronica, *Musikalische Salons. Blütezeit einer Frauenkultur* (Düsseldorf & Zürich: Artemis & Winkler, 2000)

Becker, Heinz, *Der Fall Heine-Meyerbeer. Neue Dokumente revidieren ein Geschichtsurteil* (Berlin: Walter de Gruyter, 1958)

Becker, Heinz, 'Die Beer'sche Villa im Tiergarten' in Hans J. Reichhardt (ed.), *Berlin im Geschichte und Gegenwart. Jahrbuch des Landesarchivs Berlin* (Berlin: Siedler Verlag, 1990), pp. 61-86.

Becker, Heinz, and Becker, Gudrun (eds), *Giacomo Meyerbeer. A Life in Letters*, Mark Violette (trans.) (Bromley: Christopher Helm, 1989)

Becker, Heinz and Becker, Gudrun (eds), *Giacomo Meyerbeer – Weltbürger der Musik* (Wiesbaden: Dr Ludwig Reichert Verlag, 1991)

Beer, Michael, *Sämmtliche Werke*, Eduard von Schenk (ed.) (Leipzig: Brockhaus, 1835)

Beer, Michael, *Briefwechsel*, Eduard von Schenk (ed.) (Leipzig: Brockhaus, 1837)

Beer, Wilhelm, *Die Gefahren der Differential-Zölle und der Revision des Zoll-Tarifs* (Berlin: Alexander Duncker, 1848)

Beer, Wilhelm, *Die Drei-Königs-Verfassung in ihrer Gefahr für Preussen* (Berlin: F. Schneider, 1849)

Beer, Wilhelm, *Patriotische Betrachtungen* (Berlin: F. Schneider, 1849)

Berg, Urte von, *Patriotischer Salons in Berlin 1806–1813* (Göttingen: Wallstein Verlag, 2012)

Bienert, Michael (ed.), *Berlin 1806. Das Lexicon von Johann Christian Gädicke* (Berlin: Berlin Story Verlag, 2006)

Biermann, Kurt (ed.), *Briefwechsel zwischen Alexander von Humboldt und Heinrich Christian Schumacher* (Berlin: Akademie Verlag, 1980)

Bilski, Emily D. and Braun, Emily, *Jewish Women and Their Salons. The Power of Conversation* (New Haven, CT & London: Yale University Press, 2005)

Blanning, Tim, *The Pursuit of Glory. Europe 1648-1815* (London: Penguin Books, 2007)

Blanning, Tim, *Frederick the Great, King of Prussia* (London: Allen Lane, 2015)

Blaze de Bury, Henri, *Meyerbeer et son temps* (Paris: Michel Lévy Frères, 1865)

Blumenthal, W. Michael, *The Invisible Wall. Germans and Jews. A personal exploration* (Washington DC: Counterpoint, 1998)

Blunck, Jürgen (ed.), *Wilhelm Beer. Genius der Astronomie und Ökonomie 1797–1850* (Berlin: Staatsbibliothek zu Berlin Preussischer Kulturbesitz, 1997)

Body, Albin, *Meyerbeer aux Eaux de Spa*, Brussels, 1885.

Bosold, Birgit Anna, *Friederike Liman. Briefwechsel mit Rahel Levin Varnhagen und Karl Gustav von Brinckmann sowie Aufzeichnungen von Rahel Levin Varnhagen und Karl*

*August Varnhagen. Eine historisch-kritische Edition mit Nachwort*, Ph.D. diss., (University of Hamburg, 1996)

Brophy, James, *Capitalism, Politics and Railroads in Prussia 1830-1870* (Columbus, OH: Ohio State University Press, 1998)

Brose, Eric Dorn, *The Politics of Technological Change in Prussia: Out of the Shadow of Antiquity, 1809-1848* (Princeton, NJ: Princeton University Press, 1993)

Bruford, Walter Horace, *Germany in the Eighteenth Century. The Social Background of the Literary Revival* (Cambridge: Cambridge University Press, 1935, re-issued 2011)

Bruford, Walter Horace, *Theatre, Drama and Audience in Goethe's Germany* (London: Routledge and Kegan Paul Ltd, 1950)

Brunschweig, Henri, *Enlightenment and Romanticism in Eighteenth-Century Prussia*, Frank Jellinek (trans.) (Chicago, IL and London: The University of Chicago Press, 1974)

Büsching, Anton Friedrich, *Beschreibung seiner Reise von Berlin nach Kyritz in der Prignitz* (Leipzig: Breitkopf, 1780)

Cavan, George, *Erinnerungen eines Preussen aus der Napoleonischen Zeit 1805-1815* (Grimma: Druck und Verlag des Verlags-Comptoirs, 1840)

Charlton, David (ed.), *The Cambridge Companion to Grand Opera* (Cambridge: Cambridge University Press, 2003)

Clark, Christopher, *Iron Kingdom. The Rise and Downfall of Prussia 1600-1917* (London: Penguin Books, 2007)

Conway, David, *Jewry in Music. Entry to the Profession from the Enlightenment to Richard Wagner* (Cambridge: Cambridge University Press, 2012)

Cowgill, Rachel, and Poriss, Hilary, *The Arts of the Prima Donna in the Long Nineteenth Century* (Oxford: Oxford University Press, 2012)

*Central-Verein-Zeitung*

Delbrück, Friedrich, *Die Jugend des Königs Friedrich Wilhelm IV von Preussen and des Kaisers und Königs Wilhelm I* (Berlin: A. Hofmann & Comp., 1907)

Diekmann, Irene A. (ed.), *Juden in Berlin. Bilder, Dokumente, Selbstzeugnisse* (Leipzig: Henschel Verlag, 2009)

Diemel, Christa, *Adelige Frauen im bürgerlichem Jahrhundert. Hofdamen, Stiftsdamen, Salondamen 1800-1870* (Frankfurt am Main: S. Fischer Verlag GmbH, 2014)

Dubin, Lois C., 'The Rise and Fall of the Italian Jewish Model in Germany: From Haskalah to Reform, 1780-1820' in Elisheva Carlebach, John Efron, and David N. Myers (eds), *Jewish History and Jewish Memory. Essays in Honor of Yosef Hayim Yerushalmi* (Hanover NH: Brandeis University Press, 1998)

Dwyer, Philip (ed.), *The Rise of Prussia 1700-1830* (Harlow: Pearson Education Limited, 2000)

Eberty, Felix, *Jugenderinnerungen eines alten Berliners* (Berlin: Verlag für Kulturpolitik, 1925)

Ederer, Walter, 'Louis Spohrs Besuche in Berlin' in Hartmut Becker and Reiner Krempien (eds), *Louis Spohr. Festschrift und Ausstellungskatalog zum 200. Geburtstag* (Kassel: Georg Wenderoth Verlag, 1984)

Efron, John, *German Jewry and the Allure of the Sephardic* (Princeton, NJ and Oxford: Princeton University Press, 2016)

Elon, Amos, *The Pity of It All. A Portrait of the Jews in Germany 1743-1933* (London: Penguin Books, 2004)

*Erster Jahresbericht über das Jüdische Waisen-Erziehungsinstitut zu Berlin* (Berlin: 1834)

Feilchenfeldt, Konrad (ed.), *Karl Varnhagen von Ense. Tageblätter* (Frankfurt am Main: Deutscher Klassiker Verlag, 1994)

Feiner, Shmuel, *The Jewish Enlightenment*, Chaya Naor (trans.) (Philadelphia: University of Pennsylvania Press, 2002)

Feiner, Shmuel, *Moses Mendelssohn. Sage of Modernity*, Anthony Berris (trans.) (New Haven, CT and London: Yale University Press, 2010)

Feiner, Shmuel, and Naimark-Goldberg, Natalie, *Cultural Revolution in Berlin. Jews in the age of Enlightenment* (Oxford: Bodleian Library in association with The Journal of Jewish Studies, 2011)

Feiner, Shmuel, *The Origins of Jewish Secularization in Eighteenth-Century Europe*, Chaya Naor (trans.) (Philadelphia, PA and Oxford: Pennsylvania University Press, 2011)

Frey, Linda and Frey, Marsha, *Frederick I: the Man and his Times* (Boulder, CO: East European Monographs, 1984)

Freydank, Ruth, *Theater in Berlin von den Anfangen bis 1945* (Berlin: Henschelverlag Kunst und Gesellschaft, 1988)

Gay, Ruth, *The Jews of Germany. A Historical Portrait* (New Haven, CT and London: Yale University Press, 1992)

*Genealogie. Deutsche Zeitschrift für Familienkunde* (June 1966)

Gerhard, Anselm, *The Urbanization of Opera. Music Theater in Paris in the Nineteenth Century*, Mary Whittall (trans.) (Chicago, IL: University of Chicago Press, 1998)

*Geschichte des Bürger-Rettungs Institute in Berlin während der ersten 50 Jahren seines Bestehens* (Berlin: Ernst Siegfried Mittler, 1846)

Giebel, Wieland (ed.), *Die Franzosen in Berlin 1806 – 1808* (Berlin: Berlin Story Verlag, 2006)

Gilbert, Felix (ed.), *Bankiers, Künstler und Gelehrte.Unveröffentlichte Briefe der Familie Mendelssohn aus dem 19. Jahrhundert* (Tübingen: J.C.B. Mohr, 1975)

Glatzer, Nahum N., 'On an Unpublished Letter of Isaak Markus Jost', in *Leo Baeck Institute Yearbook* 22 (Oxford: Oxford University Press, 1977) pp. 129-137.

Glatzer, Ruth (ed.), *Berliner Leben 1648-1805* (Berlin: Rütten & Loening, 1956)

Glatzer, Ruth (ed.), *Berliner Leben 1806-1848* (Berlin: Rütten & Loening, 1956)

Glückel of Hameln, *The Memoirs of Glückel of Hameln*, Marvin Lowenthal (trans.) (New York: Schocken Books, 1977)

Goldfarb, Michael, *Emancipation. How Liberating Europe's Jews from the Ghetto Led to Revolution and Renaissance* (New York: Simon & Schuster Paperbacks, 2009)

Gottschalck, Friedrich, *Almanach der Ritter-Orden* (Leipzig: Georg Joachim Goeschen, 1819)

Grattenauer, Carl, *Erklärung an das Publikum über meine Schrift Wider die Juden* (Berlin: Johann Wilhelm Schmidt, 1803)

Grattenauer, Carl, *Erster Nachtrag zu seiner Erklärung über seine Schrift Wider die Juden* (Berlin: Johann Wilhelm Schmidt, 1803)

Grattenauer, Carl, *Wider die Juden. Ein Wort der Warnung an alle unsere christliche Mitbürger* (Berlin: Johann Wilhelm Schmidt, 1803)

Gubitz, Friedrich Wilhelm, *Erlebnisse, nach Erinnerungen und Aufzeichnungen* (3 vols) (Berlin, 1868)

Guest, Ivor, *The Romantic Ballet in Paris* (London: Dance Books Ltd., 1980)

Guest, Ivor, *The Paris Opéra Ballet* (Alton: Dance Books Ltd., 2006)

Gurlt, Ernst, *Zur Geschichte der Internationalen und Freiwilligen Krankenpflege im Kriege* (Leipzig: F.C.W. Vogel, 1873)

Hagemann, Karen, *Revisiting Prussia's Wars against Napoleon. History, Culture and Memory* (Cambridge: Cambridge University Press, 2015)

Hahn, Barbara, *The Jewess Pallas Athena. This Too a Theory of Modernity,* James McFarland (trans.) (Princeton, NJ and Oxford: Princeton University Press, 2005)

*The Harmonicon*

Hegel, Georg Wilhelm Friedrich, *Briefe an und von Hegel* (3 vols), Johannes Hoffmeister (ed.) (Hamburg: Felix Meiner Verlag, 1952-54)

Heine, Heinrich, *Säkularausgabe. Werke, Briefwechsel, Lebenszeugnisse* (Berlin and Paris: Akademie Verlag and Editions de CNRS, 1970-)

Heinrici, Georg (ed.), 'Briefe von Henriette Herz an August Twesten (1814-1827)', *Zeitschrift für Bücherfreunde,* Neue Folge 5 (1914)

Heinsius, Theodor, *Geschichte des Luisenstifts bis zum Schlusse des Jahres 1808* (Berlin: 1809; reprinted Berlin: Archiv für Kunst und Geschichte, 1982)

Hemmings, Frederick William John, *Culture and Society in France 1789-1848* (Leicester: Leicester University Press, 1987)

Hensel, Sebastian (ed.), *Die Familie Mendelssohn 1729-1847* (2 vols) (Berlin: B. Behr's Verlag, 1903)

Henze-Döhring, Sabine and Döhring, Sieghart, *Giacomo Meyerbeer. Der Meister der Grand Opéra* (Munich: CH Beck, 2014)

Henze-Döhring, Sabine and Moeller, Hans, 'Sieben unveröffentliche Briefe Michael Beers an seine Familie' in Sieghart Döhring and Jürgen Schläder (eds), *Giacomo Meyerbeer. Musik als Welterfahrung* (Munich: Ricordi, 1995)

Hertz, Deborah, 'Amalia Beer als Schirmherrin Bürgerlicher Kultur und Religiöser Reform' in Christiane Müller und Andrea Schatz (eds), *Der Differenz auf der Spur. Frauen und Gender in Aschkenaz* (Berlin: Metropol Verlag 2004)

Hertz, Deborah, *Jewish High Society in Old Regime Berlin* (New York: Syracuse University Press, 2005)

Hertz, Deborah, *How Jews Became Germans. The History of Conversion and Assimilation in Berlin* (New Haven, CT and London: Yale University Press, 2007)

Herz, Henriette, *Berliner Salons. Erinnerungen und Porträts,* Ulrich Janetzki (ed.) (Frankfurt am Main, Berlin and Vienna: Verlag Ullstein GmbH, 1984)

Hofschröder, Peter and Fosten, Bryan, *Prussian Cavalry of the Napoleonic Wars (2): 1807-15* (London: Osprey Publishing, 1986)

Holmsten, Georg, *Die Berlin-Chronik. Daten, Personen, Dokumente* (Düsseldorf: Droste Verlag, 1984)

Holtei, Karl von, *Charpie. Eine Sammlung Vermischter Aufsätze* (Breslau: Verlag von Eduard Trewendt, 1866)

Israel, Jonathan I., *European Jewry in the Age of Mercantilism, 1550-1750* (Portland, OR: The Littman Library of Jewish Civilisation, 2003)

Jackson, Jennifer, *Giacamo Meyerbeer. Reputation without Cause? A Composer and his Critics* (Newcastle upon Tyne: Cambridge Scholars Publishing, 2011)

Jacobson, Egon & Hirsch, Leo, *Jüdische Mütter* (Berlin: Vortrupp-Verlag, 1936)

Jacobson, Jacob (ed.), *Die Judenbürgerbücher der Stadt Berlin 1809-1851* (Berlin: Walter de Gruyter, 1962)

Jacobson, Jacob (ed.), *Jüdische Trauungen in Berlin 1759-1813* (Berlin: Walter de Gruyter, 1968)

James, Leighton S., *Witnessing the Revolutionary and Napoleonic Wars in German Central Europe* (Basingstoke and New York: Palgrave MacMillan, 2013)

*Jenaische allgemeine Literatur-Zeitung*

*Journal für Literatur, Kunst, Luxus und Mode*

Kahn, Lothar, 'Michael Beer (1800-1833)', in *Leo Baeck Institute Yearbook* 12 (Oxford: Oxford University Press, 1967)

Katz, Jacob, *Out of the Ghetto, the Social Background of Jewish Emancipation 1770-1870* (New York: Schocken Books, 1978)

Kelly, Thomas Forrest, *First Nights at the Opera* (New Haven, CT and London: Yale University Press, 2004)

Kley, Eduard and Günsberg, Carl, *Zuruf an die Jünglinge, welche die Fahnen des Vaterlands folgen* (Berlin, 1813)

Kliche, Thomas, *Camacho und das ängstliche Genie. Innenansichten der Familien Mendelssohn und Meyerbeer* (Hützel: Backe-Verlag, 2014)

Kobbé, Gustav, *The Complete Opera Book* (London and New York: Putnam, 1919)

Koch, Hansjoachim Wolfgang, *A History of Prussia* (London: Longman Group Limited, 1978)

Kochan, Lionel, *The Making of Western Jewry, 1600-1819* (Basingstoke and New York: Palgrave Macmillan, 2004)

Kohut, Adolph, *Meyerbeer* (Leipzig: Verlag von Philipp Reklam jun., 1890)

Kohut, Adolph, 'Die Mutter Giacomo Meyerbeers', *Illustrierte Frauen-Zeitung*, Year XVIII, issue 17, 1 September 1891

*Königlich privilegirte Berlinische Zeitung von Staats- und gelehrten Sachen*

Kuhrau, Sven and Winkler, Kurt (eds), *Juden, Bürger, Berliner, Das Gedächtnis der Familie Beer–Meyerbeer–Richter* (Berlin: Henschel-Verlag, 2004)

Lackmann, Thomas, *Das Glück der Mendelssohns* (Berlin: Aufbau Taschenbuch, 2007)

Lassally, Oswald, 'Israel Aaron, Hoffaktor des Grossen Kurfürsten und Begründer der Berlin Gemeinde' in *Monatsschrift für Geschichte und Wissenschaft des Judentums*, 1935, vol 2, pp. 20-31.

Lehnert, Erik, and Piethe, Marcel (eds), *"Lasset uns Gutes thun und nicht müde werden ... "200 Jahre Luisenstift Berlin* (Berlin: Lukas Verlag, 2007)

Leitner, Ulrike (ed.), *Alexander von Humboldt / Friedrich Wilhelm IV. Briefwechsel* (Berlin: Walter de Gruyter, 2013)

Letellier, Robert Ignatius, *Meyerbeer Studies* (Madison, NJ: Fairleigh Dickinson University Press, 2005)

Letellier, Robert Ignatius, *The Operas of Giacomo Meyerbeer* (Madison, NJ: Fairleigh Dickinson University Press, 2006)

Letellier, Robert Ignatius (ed.), *Giacomo Meyerbeer. A Reader* (Newcastle upon Tyne: Cambridge Scholars Publishing, 2007)

Letellier, Robert Ignatius, *Robert le Diable. The Premier Opéra Romantique* (Newcastle upon Tyne: Cambridge Scholars Publishing, 2012)

Letellier, Robert Ignatius, *Les Huguenots. An Evangel of Religion and Love* (Newcastle upon Tyne: Cambridge Scholars Publishing, 2014)

Letellier, Robert Ignatius, *Giacomo Meyerbeer. A Critical Life and Iconography* (Newcastle upon Tyne: Cambridge Scholars Publishing, 2018).

Lowenstein, Steven M., *The Berlin Jewish Community. Enlightenment, Family and Crisis, 1770-1830* (Oxford: Oxford University Press, 1994)

Lund, Hannah Lotte, *Der Berliner "Jüdische Salon" um 1800. Emanzipation in der Debatte* (Berlin: Walter de Gruyter, 2012)

MacDonagh, Giles, *Frederick the Great* (London: Phoenix Press, 1999)

McKay, Derek, *The Great Elector* (Harlow: Pearson Education Limited, 2001)

Maimon, Salomon, *An Autobiography*, L. Clark Murray (trans.) (Urbana, IL and Chicago, IL: University of Illinois Press: 2001)

Mann, Vivian B. and Cohen, Richard I. (eds), *From Court Jews to the Rothschilds. Art, Patronage, Power 1600-1800* (Munich and New York: Prestel-Verlag, and The Jewish Museum, New York, under the auspices of the Jewish Theological Seminary of America, 1996)

Mansel, Philip, *Paris Between Empires 1814-1852. Monarchy and Revolution* (London: Phoenix Press, 2003)

Manz, Gustav, *Michael Beer's Jugend und dichterische Entwicklung bis zum "Paria" erster Teil einer Biographie des Dichters*, unpublished dissertation, University of Freiburg, 1891

Marcus, Jacob Rader, *Israel Jacobson, the Founder of the Reform Movement in Judaism* (Cincinnati, OH: Hebrew Union College Press, 1972)

Marcus, Jacob Rader, *The Jew in the Medieval World. A Source Book: 315-1791* (Cincinnati, OH: Hebrew Union College Press, revised edition, 1999)

Mendel, Hermann, *Giacomo Meyerbeer: Eine Biographie* (Berlin: Verlag L. Heimann, 1868)

Mendelssohn Bartholdy, Felix, *Sämtliche Briefe* (12 vols), Helmut Loos and Wilhelm Seidel (eds) (Kassel: Bärenreiter, 2008-17)

Mendelssohn Bartholdy, Lea, *Ewig die deine. Briefe an Henriette von Pereira-Arnstein* (2 vols), Wolfgang Dinglinger & Rudolf Elvers (eds) (Hannover: Wehrhahn Verlag, 2010)

Mendes-Flohr, Paul R. and Reinharz, Jehuda (eds), *The Jew in the Modern World. A Documentary History* (Oxford: Oxford University Press, 1980)

Meyer, Michael A., *The Origins of the Modern Jew. Jewish Identity and European Culture in Germany 1749-1824* (Detroit, MI: Wayne State University Press, 1967)

Meyer, Michael A., 'The Religious Reform Controversy in the Berlin Jewish Community', in *Leo Baeck Institute Yearbook* (Oxford: Oxford University Press, 1979), pp. 139-55.

Meyer, Michael A., *Response to Modernity. A History of the Reform Movement in Judaism* (Detroit, MI: Wayne State University Press, 1995)

Meyer, Michael A. (ed.), *German-Jewish History in Modern Times* (4 vols) (New York: Columbia University Press, 1996-98)

Meyerbeer, Giacomo, *Briefwechsel und Tagebücher* (8 vols), Heinz Becker, Gudrun Becker and Sabine Henze-Döhring (eds) (Berlin: Walter de Gruyter, 1960-2006)

Meyerbeer, Giacomo, *The Diaries of Giacomo Meyerbeer* (4 vols), Robert Letellier (ed. and trans.) (Madison, NJ: Fairleigh Dickinson University Press, 1999-2004)

*Monattsschrift für Geschichte und Wissenschaft des Judentums*

Mosse, Werner, *The German-Jewish Economic Elite 1820-1935. A Socio-cultural Profile* (Oxford: Oxford University Press, 1989)

Mitford, Nancy, *Frederick the Great* (London: Hamish Hamilton Ltd., 1970)

Moscheles, Charlotte, *Life of Moscheles* (2 vols) (London: Hurst and Blackett, 1873)

Müller, Ulrike, *Salonfrauen. Leidenschaft, Mut, geistige Freiheit* (Munich: Elisabeth Sandmann Verlag, 2013)

Newman, Ernest, *Wagner as Man and Artist* (London: Jonathan Cape, 1969)

Owen, John, *Travels into different parts of Europe, in the years 1791 and 1792* (2 vols) (London: Caddell & Davies, 1796)

Panwitz, Sebastian, *Die Gesellschaft der Freunde 1792-1935. Berliner Juden zwischen Aufklärung und Hochfinanz* (Hildesheim: Georg Olms Verlag, 2007)

Philipson, David, *The Reform Movement in Judaism* (New York: Ktav Publishing House Inc., 1967)

Philippson, Martin, "Der Anteil der jüdischen Freiwilligen an dem Befreiungskriege 1813 und 1814", *Monatsschrift für Geschichte und Wissenschaft des Judentums*, 1906, vol 50 issue.1 pp.1-21; issue 2 pp.220-246

Pottle, Frederick A., (ed.), *Boswell on the Grand Tour: Germany and Switzerland, 1764* (London: William Heinemann Ltd., 1953)

Probst, Friedrich Paul von, *Geschichte des Königlich-Preussischen Zweiter Dragoner-Regiments* (Schwedt, 1829)

Rachel, Hugo, Papritz, Johann and Wallich, Paul, *Berliner Grosskaufleute und Kapitalisten* (3 vols) (Berlin: Walter de Gruyter, 1967)

Rapport, Mike, *1848: Year of Revolution* (London: Little, Brown, 2008)

Reder, Dirk Alexander, *Frauenbewegung und Nation: Patriotische Frauenvereine in Deutschland im frühen 19. Jahrhundert (1813-1830)* (Cologne: SH-Verlag, 1998)

Redern, Friedrich Wilhelm von, and Horn, Georg *Unter drei Königen. Lebenserinnerungen eines preussischen Oberkämmerers und Generalintendanten*, Sabine Giesbrecht (ed.) (Cologne,Weimar and Vienna: Böhlau Verlag, 2003)

Rellstab, Ludwig, *Henriette, oder die schöne Sängerin* (Bielefeld: Aisthesis Verlag, 2008)

Richter, Kurt, 'Amalia Beer und ihre Söhne', *Central-Verein-Zeitung*, Year 13, issue 11, 15 March 1934

Romberg, Amalie von (ed.), *Vor Hundert Jahren. Erinnerungen der Gräfin Sophie Schwerin* (Berlin: Stargardt, 1909)

Salomon, Gotthold, *Selima's Stunden der Weihe, eine moralisch-reliogioses Schrift für Gebildetes weiblichen Geschlechts* (Leipzig: Carl Gottlob Schmidt, 1816)

Sheehan, William, *The Planet Mars: A History of Observation and* Discovery (Tucson, AZ: University of Arizona Press, 1996)

Schneider, Louis, *Die Preussichen Orden, Ehrenzeichen und Auszeichnungen. Geschichtlich, bildlich, statistich* (Berlin: Hayn, 1867)

Schneider, Wolfgang, *Berlin. Eine Kulturgeschichte in Bildern und Dokumenten* (Leipzig und Weimar: Gustav Kiepenheuer Verlag, 1983)

Schuster, Georg, 'Aus dem Briefwechsel der Prinzessin Marianne von Preussen', in Paul Clauswitz and Georg Voss (eds), *Erforschtes und Erlebtes aus dem alten Berlin. Festschrift zum 50jährigen Jubiläum des Vereins für die Geschichte Berlins* (Berlin: Verlag des Vereins für die Geschichte Berlins, 1917)

Singermann, Rabbi Felix, *Die Lippmann-Tauss-Synagoge* (Berlin: self-published, 1920)

Smart, Sir George, *Leaves from the Journals of Sir George Smart*, Hugh Bertram Cox and Clara L.E. Cox (eds) (Cambridge: Cambridge University Press, 1907; digitally printed version, 2014)

Sorkin, David, *Moses Mendelssohn and the Religious Enlightenment* (London: Peter Halban, 1996)

Sorkin, David, *The Berlin Haskalah and German Religious Thought* (London: Vallentine Mitchell, 2000)

Spiel, Hilda, *Fanny von Arnstein, Daughter of the Enlightenment 1758-1818* (New York and Oxford: Berg Publishers Ltd, 1991)

Spindler, Max (ed.), *Briefwechsel zwischen Ludwig I von Bayern und Eduard von Schenk*, (Munich: Parcus & Co., 1930)

Spohr, Louis, *Louis Spohr's Autobiography* (London: 1865)

*Stammbaum. The Journal of German-Jewish Genealogical Research*

*Statuten des von Baruch Auerbach gegründeten jüdischen Waisen-Erziehungs-Institut zu Berlin* (Berlin, 1839)

Stern, Carola, *"Ich möchte mir Flügel wünschen". Das leben der Dorothea Schlegel* (Hamburg: Rowohlt Verlag GmbH, 1990)

Stern, Carola, *Der Text meines Herzens. Das Leben der Rahel Varnhagen* (Hamburg: Rowohlt Verlag GmbH, 2004)

Stern, Selma, *The Court Jew. A Contribution to the History of the Period of Absolutism in Central Europe* (Philadelphia, PA: The Jewish Publication Society of America, 1950)

Stiftung Preussischer Schlösser und Gärten, *Luise, Kleider für die Königin. Mode, Schmuck und Accessoires am Preussischen Hof um 1800* (Munich: Hirmer Verlag, 2010)

*Sulamith. Zeitschrift für Beförderung der Kultur und Humanität unter der jüdischen Nation*

Taylor, Ronald, *Berlin and Its Culture* (New Haven, CT and London: Yale University Press, 1997)

Tewarson, Heidi Thomann, *Rahel Levin Varnhagen. The Life and Work of a German Jewish Intellectual* (Lincoln, NE and London: University of Nebraska Press, 1998)

Thomson, Joan L., 'Giacomo Meyerbeer: The Jew and his relationship with Richard Wagner', *Musica Judaica*, vol. 1, no. 1 (1975-76), pp.54-86

Tillard, Françoise, *Fanny Mendelssohn*, Camille Naish (trans.) (Portland, OR: Amadeus Press, 1996)

Todd, R. Larry, *Mendelssohn. A Life in Music* (Oxford: Oxford University Press, 2003)

Todd, R. Larry, *Fanny Hensel. The Other Mendelssohn* (Oxford: Oxford University Press, 2010)

Varnhagen, Rahel Levin, *Rahel Varnhagen im Umgang mit ihren Freunden (Briefe 1793-1833)*, Friedhelm Kemp (ed.) (Munich: Kösel-Verlag, 1967)

Varnhagen, Rahel Levin, *Familienbriefe*, Renata Barovero (ed.) (Munich: C. H. Beck, 2009

Verhaus, Rudolf, *Germany in the Age of Absolutism*, Jonathan B. Knudsen (trans.) (Cambridge: Cambridge University Press, 1988)

Véron, Louis Désiré, *Mémoires d'un bourgeois de Paris*, vol. 3 (Paris: Librairie Nouvelle, 1857)

Voss, Sophie Marie Gräfin von, *Neunundsechzig Jahre am Preussischen Hofe* (Leipzig: Duncker und Humblot, 1887)

Wagner, Richard, *Das Judenthum in der Musik* (Leipzig: J.J. Weber, 1869)

Wagner, Richard, *Opera and Drama*, Edwin Evans (trans.) (London: WM Reeves, 1913)

Wagner, Richard, *My Life* (New York: Dodd, Mead and Company, 1911)

Weber, Carl Maria von, *Mein vielgeliebter Muks. Briefe an Caroline Brandt aus den Jahren 1814-1817* (Munich: Verlag C.H. Beck, 1986)

Wendland, Folkwin, *Der grosse Tiergarten in Berlin. Seine Geschichte und Entwicklung in fünf Jahrhunderten* (Berlin: Gebr. Mann Verlag, 1993)

Weyl, Rabbi Meyer Simon, *Hoffnung und Vertrauen. Predigt wegen des Ausmarsches des vaterländisches Heeres gehalten am 28sten März 1813 in Gegenwart mehrere freiwilligen Jäger jüdischen Glaubens in der grossen Synagoge zu Berlin*, Isaac Levin Auerbach (trans.) (Berlin: August Wilhelm Schade, 1813)

Wilhelmy-Dollinger, Petra, *Die Berliner Salons* (Berlin: Walter de Gruyter, 1999)

Zamoyski, Adam, *Rites of Peace: The Fall of Napoleon and the Congress of Vienna* (London, New York, Toronto and Sydney: Harper Perennial, 2007)

Zamoyski, Adam, *Chopin. Prince of the Romantics* (London: HarperPress, 2010)

Zamoyski, Adam, *Phantom Terror. The Threat of Revolution and the Repression of Liberty 1789-1848* (London: William Collins, 2014)
*Zeitschrift für die Geschichte der Juden in Deutschland*
*Zeitung für die elegante Welt*
Zimmermann, Reiner, *Giacomo Meyerbeer. Eine Biographie nach Dokumenten* (Berlin: Henschel Verlag, 1991)
*Zweiter Jahresbericht über das Jüdische Waisen-Erziehungsinstitut zu Berlin* (Berlin: 1835)

## Websites

www.haskala.net                              Haskala Net, Potsdam University
www.weber-gesamtausgabe.de                   Carl Maria von Weber Complete Works
https://digital.zlb.de                       Zentral- und Landesbibliothek, Berlin
http://sammlungen.ub.uni-frankfurt.de/cm     Compact Memory, Goethe University

# Index

*Bold figures denote an illustration*

Aaron, Israel, financier, 6
Académie Royale de Musique, *see* Opéra, Paris
Achard, Franz, chemist, 32
Adam, Adolphe, composer, 178
Albert, Prince Consort of Great Britain, 284
Alexander I, Tsar of Russia, 45, 48, 57, 73, 74
Alexis, Willibald [Georg Wilhelm Häring], writer, 170
Alfieri, Vittorio, dramatist
    *Orestes*, 153
*Allgemeine musikalische Zeitung*, ix, 35, 75, 117, 119,
    120, 141, 142, 168, 206, 246
Andrian zu Werburg, Ferdinand von, geologist and
    anthropologist, 320
Andrian zu Werburg, Leopold von, theatre director, 321
Apponyi, Countess Therese, 186
Ariga [singer in Venice?], 145
Armansperg, Count Josef von, statesman, 207
Arnim, Achim von, writer, 137
Arnim, Countess Antoinette von, 95, 96
Arnstein, Fanny von, salonnière, 86
Arnstein, Freiherr Nathan von, banker, 163
Artaria, Johann, art dealer, 113
Ashton, Frederick, choreographer, 300
    *Les Patineurs*, 300
Assing, Dr., physician, 90
*Astronomische Nachrichten* (*see* Schumacher, Heinrich
    Christian)
Atterbom, Per Daniel Amadeus, writer, 170
Auber, Daniel-François-Esprit, composer, 171, 178, 309
    *Le cheval de bronze*, 309
    *Le domino noir*, 309
    *Fra Diavolo*, 309
    *La Muette de Portici*, 188-9, 190, 191, 314
Auerbach, Baruch, educator and orphanage director,
    272-4, 303
Auerbach Institute, 272-4, 275, 276, 308
Auerbach, Isaac, educator, preacher and writer, 109,
    110, 133
Augereau, Charles-Pierre-François, French Marshal, 74
*Augsburger allgemeine Zeitung*, 254, 299
August, Prince of Prussia, 91, 113
Augusta of Saxe-Weimar-Eisenach, Princess of Prussia,
    later Queen of Prussia and Empress of Germany,
    259, 297, 321
Austen, Jane, writer, 18, 132
Austen, Henry, brother of Jane, 132

Baader, Benjamin Maria, historian, 128
Bach, Johann Sebastian, composer, 34, 264-5
    *St Matthew Passion*, 265
Bach, Wilhelm Friedemann, composer, 34
Baermann, Carl, son of Heinrich, clarinettist, 252-3
Baermann, Heinrich Joseph, clarinettist, 252
Balzac, Honoré de, writer, 191, 253
Bamberger, Esther, wife of Liepmann Meyer Wulff *see*
    Wulff, Esther
Bamberger, Michael, father of Esther Wulff, 14

Barbier, Jules, librettist, 310
Bassi, Carolina, singer, 145
Bauer, Karoline, actress, 66, 168, 169, 170
Bäuerle, Adolf, dramatist, 170
Bavarian War of Succession, 20
Bayer, Franz, 115
Beaumont, Francis, dramatist
    *The Merchant of Bruges*, 88
Becker, Heinz, scholar, 176
Beer, Amalia [Malka; née Wulff] ix, 12, **19**, 27-8, 33,
    34-5, 38, 57, 58, 60-1, 62, 63-4, 64-5, 67, 68, 70,
    86, 118, 119, 121-2, 123, 132, 140, 142, 143, 144-
    5, 146, 147, 148, 153, 154, 163, 165, 167, 172, 173,
    175, 176-7, 184-5, 185-7, 196, 206, 212, 213-4,
    219, 221, 223, 224, 229, 239, 245-6, 249, 260, 261,
    268, 274, 275, 283, 298, 300, 302-3, 304, 305-6,
    **307**, 325, 326; ancestors, 2, 3-6, 7, 8, 14; and anti-
    Semitism, 36, 40, 91-2, 98-100, 117-18, 138-9;
    birth, 14; death, 306-8; marriage, x, 8, 16, 24,
    26-7, 29; and Order of Louise, 94-101, 112, 276;
    as philanthropist, 33, 51, 79-81, 83, 84, 90, 96, 97,
    100, 232, 273-4, 275-6, 324-5; and Prussian
    court, 38-41, 100-101, 259, 266, 278, 305-6, 308; and
    religion, xii, 15-16, 103,107, 108, 109, 128-9,
    303-4; salon, x-xi, 51-3, 64-6, 113-15, 116-17,
    119, 120, 152, 183, 276-8; youth, 15-20
Beer, Bela, wife of Juda Herz Beer, *see* Samuel, Bela
Beer, Doris, wife of Wilhelm Beer, 132, 177, 183, 228,
    274, 302-3, 304
Beer, Elise, daughter of Wilhelm Beer, *see* Oppenheim,
    Elise
Beer, Georg Friedrich Amadeus, son of Wilhelm Beer,
    91-2, 228, 304-5
Beer, Heinrich [Henoch]  xi, 87, 122, 123, 126, 143, 144,
    147, 167, 176, 177, 206, 208, 213, 218-221, 224,
    227, 228, 273, 304, 305, 310; birth, 29; as
    collector, 216; death, 274-5; death of son (Anton)
    Ludwig, 214-15, 218; and Hegel, 216-8; marriage,
    130-2, 215, 224, 260, 272, 274; and Mendelssohn
    family, 215-16, 217, 220-1, 222, 223; money
    problems, 58, 221-222, 223-4, 239-40; youth, 33,
    53, 57-8, 58-9, 60, 62, 83
Beer, Herz Aron, ancestor of Jacob Beer, 7
Beer, Jacob Herz [Juda Herz], ix, 12, 27, **28**, 29, 33, 34-
    5, 58, 59, 61, 65-6, 67-8, 72, 77, 84, 85, 86, 87, 90,
    113, 115, 119, 120, 121, 122, 132, 140, 143, 144,
    146, 147-8, 148-9, 163-4, 167, 182, 222-3, 276,
    303-4, 323, 325; ancestors, 1, 6-8, 26, 27; and
    anti-Semitism, 117-18, 202-3; birth, 26; as
    businessman, 31-2, 48-9, 62-3, 112, 122, 164-6;
    death, 175-8, 180, 196, 218, 228; marriage, x, 26-
    7, 29; as philanthropist, 50-1, 96, 97, 177, 324; as
    synagogue reformer, xii, 103, 106, 107-111, 112,
    125-8, 129-30, 133-4; as theatre director, 167-173,
    177-8; youth, 27
Beer, Juda Herz, grandfather of Jacob Beer, 7-8, 26, 27,
    32
Beer, Julie, daughter of Wilhelm Beer, *see* Haber, Julie
    von

Lightning Source UK Ltd.
Milton Keynes UK
UKHW022006230621
386037UK00006B/122